Center of the Heart

By

Marilyn Collier

Copyright © 2025 by – *Marilyn Collier* – All Rights Reserved.

It is not legal to reproduce, duplicate, or transmit any part of this document in either electronic means or printed format. Recording of this publication is strictly prohibited.

Table of Contents

Dedication i
Acknowledgments ii
About the Author iii
Introduction 1
January 1 ~ New Beginnings 3
February 1 ~ Passion 61
March 1 ~ A New Disposition 111
April 1 ~ April Fools 169
May 1 ~ First Born 225
June 1 ~ Identity 283
July 1 ~ God's Love Endures 337
August 1 ~ Female 401
September 1 ~ Wrath vs. Love 475
October 1 ~ Seasons of Change 541
November 1 ~ Niche 611
December 1 ~ Rabbi 683
Resourses 754
Additional Sources 759
Bibliography 760

Dedication

There are many people I want to thank. My heart is full of gratitude to them. But dedication is a stronger word and is set aside to acknowledge those who are forever on your side. Therefore, I dedicate this book to my earthly king, which is my husband, Bill, who is my greatest supporter and Jesus Christ, my eternal King. May this book bring glory to His name.

Acknowledgments

I would like to acknowledge my Sunday School class in Lagrange, Georgia, who was my inspiration to begin writing devotions. I also want to acknowledge my friend Sandi Herron, who has spent hours pouring over this book. She is a one-of-a-kind lady and a dear friend.

In everything, God is good, and, in His goodness, He has provided the Books Publishing Company for me; they have been patient, encouraging, and have spent hours of work to produce this finished manuscript. I am so thankful for their hard work and kindness. The person who leads this gracious team is Max Solace. I just cannot thank him enough. Not only has he been there every step of the way, providing everything I needed, but he has also become a friend.

My husband and family are the dearest to my heart and support me every day. I love them, and they make life worth living. They would walk through fire for me, and that is a wonderful gift from above. Thank you all.

About the Author

I live in Alabama with my husband. Who is my best buddy. I have three grown children and six grandchildren. We have two family businesses that keep us very close.

This is my first book, but I have had stories published in A Merry Southern Christmas by the Southern Christian Writers Conference and a story in the book published by Christian Writers for Life, Mother, What My Mother Taught Me About Life, Love and Faith.

I have a long history of teaching Bible Studies in BFS, Explorers Bible Studies, and have taught small groups. I became a Christian at 16. I love my husband, my family, the Bible, and Jesus.

Introduction

This devotional book is a life journey, one that I have been on for a long time. My hope is that you will come alongside me and walk with me one day at a time.

You see, I am not a superstar by any means. I am an ordinary person, just like you, with stories to tell from my heart. These stories come from a woman who has been blessed by Jesus. He is the real Hero of the whole book. In fact, He is the Hero of my life.

My prayer is that you will be able to relate to many of my analogies and gain some spiritual truths to encourage you as you journey through life.

I have reminded my grandchildren not to read looking for their names but to read searching for truth, growth, and wonder of our God. That is my hope for them and for you. If I have failed to do this, then this devotional book has failed you.

These devotionals all began when I was on staff at First Baptist in Lagrange, Georgia. I began to write them for our newsletter and then for the ladies in my Sunday school class. Decades later, I have refreshed and rewritten them over and over, with new ones along the way. Life keeps going, and so have these thoughts from the Lord.

I give praise, awe, and wonder to Jesus, who has spoken to my heart over and over. I hope and pray that He will speak to you also.

Each day, there will be **Ponders of the Heart** and **Prayer of the Heart.** Take time to ponder and pray.

Thank you, and God bless you, dear one!

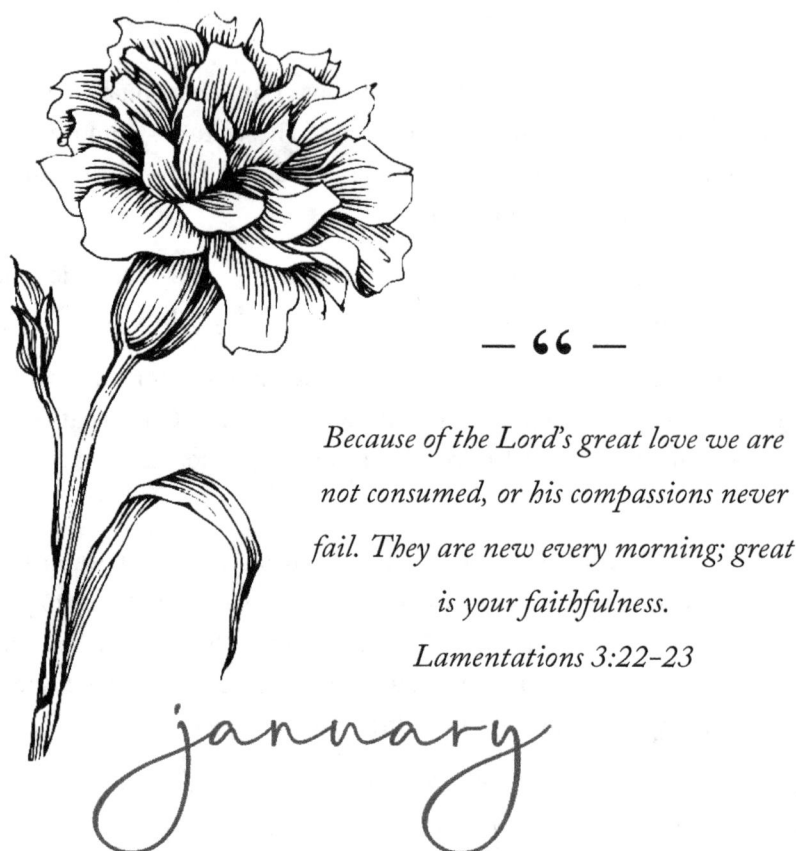

— " —

Because of the Lord's great love we are not consumed, or his compassions never fail. They are new every morning; great is your faithfulness.
Lamentations 3:22–23

january

January 1 ~ New Beginnings

In the summer of 2001, my precious daughter was excited about a new adventure. Julie was preparing to start a new career as a fourth-grade teacher. I, on the other hand, was full of worries. She was caught in the excitement, and I was caught in the change.

I told a friend, who was a teacher, of Julie's excitement. My friend said she was also excited because her job offered her a new beginning every year, and if she lost that excitement, it would be time to quit teaching.

Isn't it funny how we all deal with life differently? One person's excitement is another person's fear.

As I reflect on this new year, I want to be excited. I have no way of knowing what circumstances will come my way. Some will be good, and others will be difficult. What relationships will I have? Will they be strong? Will I lose friends and gain others? With all the uncertainty, do I dare to be excited, or should I be afraid?

"Blessed be the God and Father of our Lord Jesus Christ, who has blessed us with every spiritual blessing in the heavenly placed in Christ" (Ephesians 1:3 NKJV).

Paul seemed excited about life—not his natural life but his spiritual one. He was not worried about circumstances or relationships. He was too busy praising the God and Father of his Lord Jesus Christ. His focus was not earth-bound existence but heaven-bound life.

We live in this world but are not of this world. Our heavenly home waits for us, but until then, we place our hope in our spiritual blessings.

As we begin this New Year and this new month, I want to know and focus on my blessings in Christ. I am sure you do, too.

Ponders of the Heart

Read Ephesians chapter one, which lists our spiritual blessings.

What are you praying for as this new year begins?

What spiritual promises encourage you in this Scripture?

Prayers of the Heart

Dear Father,

As we begin this New Year, we want to be excited about Your blessings to us. We want to trust You with our bodies, souls, and spirits. Lord, show us the plans You have for us and how we can live focused on You. In Jesus' name, amen.

January 2 ~ Adoption

My daddy was my stepfather. Before my mom and dad said, "I do," my dad loved me. He chose to love me as his daughter, which made loving him quite easy.

Our heavenly Father chose us to be in Christ before the foundation of the world. In Ephesians 1:4-7, we read that He predestined us to be adopted as sons and daughters. He predestined that through the work of Christ, our redemption would be bought, and we would receive forgiveness of sins.

Are those truths more than you can understand? They are more than I can grasp, but the grace of God toward me makes loving Him easy.

Children bond with moms between zero and one and with dads between the ages of one and three. When my biological father left, I was three. He left me unconnected and insecure; that made me feel I must work to belong and to be loved and not left. I take this mentality into the relationships of my life. This creates pressure and fear, not at all what God intended for His children.

Ephesians is taking the time to reveal to us the wonder of God's predestined love, His heavenly redemption plan that was in place long before we were born. God knows in our fallen state, we try to earn His love. In fact, in our sinful nature, He knows we cannot come into His presence. Long before we were and behaved good or bad, He made a way for us to become His children. By faith in Jesus, we can receive a new nature. A redeemed, eternal nature. This is His work of love for us.

We are now sealed with the Holy Spirit of promise. God has made it easy for us to love Him by making us secure in the beloved. Oh, the wonder of His grace that loves and forgives.

"In Him you also trusted, after you heard the word of truth, the gospel of your salvation; in whom also, having believed, you were sealed with the Holy Spirit of promise, who is the guarantee of our inheritance until the redemption"
(Ephesians 1:13-14 NKJV).

Ponders of the Heart

Do you struggle with God choosing you?

Do you realize it is God's job and promise to conform us to the image of His Son?

Why not, in prayer, ask God to reveal to you insight into these deep spiritual truths?

Read 1 Peter 1:3 and Romans 8:28-29.

Prayers of the Heart

Dear Father,

Oh Lord, do we dare call You our Father? What a joy to call You Dad. What a wonder it is to know You choose us and You love us. You have made a provision for us to receive Your love, forgiveness, and Your nature. Father, Your grace amazes me. In Jesus' name, amen.

January 3 ~ Prayer

One day, I lost something important and needed prayer. While talking to a little boy in the church daycare center, I said, "Jonathan, would you please pray for me? I have lost something and need to find it." Jonathan bowed his head, closed his eyes, and began to pray. He said, "Dear God, thank you for my mommy and daddy. Thank you for this day, and take care of my mommy and daddy while they are at work. Amen."

In Jonathan's mind, he had prayed, and I agreed. I love the prayers of children. One of my favorite childhood memories of my youngest daughter is her praying for Annie Armstrong. She said, "Dear God, I don't know what Annie Armstrong needs, but will you please give it to her?" She had heard so much about Annie Armstrong's Easter offering she knew this lady needed prayer.

In Ephesians chapter one, Paul prays for those who have faith in the Lord Jesus:

"that the God of our Lord Jesus Christ, the Father of glory, may give to you the spirit of wisdom and revelation in the knowledge of Him, the eyes of your understanding being enlightened that you may know what is the hope of His calling, what are the riches of the glory of His inheritance in the saints, and what the exceeding greatness of His power toward us who believe, according to the working of His mighty power which He worked in Christ when He raised Him from the dead and seated Him at His right hand in the heavenly places, far above all principality and power and might and dominion, and every name that is named, not only in this age but also in that which is to come" (Ephesians 1:17-21 NKJV).

This prayer is for wisdom and revelation so we might know our God. Knowing God is a gift from our heavenly Father. It comes from revelation, not intellect. I'm thankful for this since I am not the brightest star in the sky. Paul prays that the eyes of our hearts or understanding be enlightened so we will know the purpose and hope of God's calling. The focus is not on us but on Jesus.

This enlightenment is a gift, not an earned privilege. It is a power beyond death, for it brought Jesus out of the grave. I want to pray this for myself and for all who want to know Him. Even for those who don't know, they do.

Come to us, Holy Spirit. Please give us revelation.

Ponders of the Heart

What are His promises?

How do these promises affect how you feel?

Ephesians 2:12-13 are great passages to remind us of our calling in Christ.

Prayers of the Heart

Dear Father,

We do pray that You will open the eyes of our hearts. Lord, we want to know You. We want to see the wonder of Your power and grace. Draw our hearts to You by Your Spirit. In Jesus' name, amen.

January 4 ~ Showers

As I crawled into bed last night, I said to my husband, "Wouldn't it be awful if you couldn't take a hot shower at night?" He agreed completely.

My Bill is a two-a-day shower guy. He takes a shower in the morning and at night. I take a bath at night, and when I wash my hair, I take a shower.

A lot of bathing goes on in our house. In our opinion, they are very important. Don't you love how hot water can wake you or prepare you for a good night's sleep?

When I took a bath this morning, I thought about the streams of living water, the water of life that flows within the heart of every Christian. As I enjoyed the warm water, I thought about my greater desire for God's living water to shower my life.

Even though physical showers are wonderful, in the depths of my soul, I long to be washed in the Spirit of God in such a way that He bathes my life with His life.

Does this sound like a pipe dream to you, or do you feel the Spirit in you quicken? Can't you just feel His refreshing life covering you with new hope and new zeal to live for Him?

"For my people have committed two evils: They have forsaken Me, the fountain of living water, and hewn themselves cisterns, broken cisterns that can hold no water" (Jer. 2:13 NKJV).

My quest for this living water is found in Him, and when I seek life from any other source, I lose my way. If you are like me, you do that too often. It breaks my heart. What in the world can we do to keep close, seeking our Lord? Our answer, our promise, comes from His Word.

"Ho! Everyone who thirsts, come to the water: and you who have no money, come and buy and eat. Yes, come, buy wine and milk without money and without price. Why do you spend money for what is not bread and your wages for what does not satisfy?" (Isa. 55:1-2 NKJV).

Ponders of the Heart

What is one thing you have bought that proved to be a waste of money?

Who is our Living water?

Have you asked Him to refresh your soul today?

Read Revelation 7:17.

Prayers of the Heart

Dear Father,

We can't find our way to the living water without Jesus. Lord, we come to surrender to Your sweet presence, to seek Your life. We come to You to experience the flow of Your life in our souls. Oh Lord, we love You. In Jesus' name, amen.

January 5 ~ Unconditional Love

I would like to share this entry in one of my journals with you. It goes like this:

Dear Precious Lord,

Show me how far I am from knowing You. Father, here I am; please open the interior of my soul and show me where I am today. Do I wish to worship You and know You, or do I wish to use You for a better life? Father, how sad. Here, You are holy and full of majesty, and I would choose Your blessings over You.

Lord, in the flesh, this is all I know, all I am taught, all that I see, but Lord, the gift of the cross delivers me from such bondage. Oh, Lord, You have planted Your mercy and grace over me.

You, Father, have given me a new heart, nature, and desire. A desire to know You. Father, if all were gone, my husband, my children, my grandchildren, my friends, my home, Lord, would I seek You? Would I seek Your face? Not to fix my life, but because You are my life.

My husband is my love. He provides for me, protects me, and comforts me. He has loved me in so many ways as if I were his precious treasure. When I am sick, sad, or afraid, he is there for me. I love and treasure the way he loves me, but if Bill could not do those things, I would still love him. He is still my sweetheart, and I would just want to be near him. That is how the Lord loves us. We can't protect him, comfort him, provide for him, but he still loves us. He doesn't need us. He created us to be in fellowship with him.

This is hard to believe. We know we cannot live up to His standards. Isn't that why He sent Jesus? He lived up to all God's standards, every one of them. When Jesus gives us His righteousness, we can accept God's unconditional love. Free to be in fellowship with Him and to live a new life.

Ponders of the Heart

What is one thing you could do to draw closer to God today?

Who needs unconditional love from you?

Read Hebrews 10:14-18.

God has made a way for us to be in fellowship with Him. It is the only way to live a life of love and freedom.

Prayers of the Heart

Dear Lord,

Thank You for Your unconditional love. Help us understand Your acceptance of us because of our faith in Jesus. We want to sit at Your feet, free from guilt and shame. We want to love our husbands, our children, our grandchildren, and the people in our lives with the same love You have given to us. Change us, Lord, by the power of Your Spirit, we pray. In Jesus' name, amen.

January 6 ~ Changes

Julie, my youngest, was born six years after Tracie and eight years after Chris. I was a young mother looking forward to a bit of relief from little children, and here I was having another baby. I wondered if I would ever have all my children in school. Then, as the years passed, changes continued, and each season had its own challenges.

There was the season I wondered if all my children would be out of school. Would they ever be out of college? Before I knew it, there was the day my last child moved into her own apartment and started a new career. Where did the days go? Wasn't it yesterday she was a curly-headed little girl learning to swim and getting ready to go to school? Oh, the flowing ebbs of change.

I now find myself longing more for yesterday than tomorrow. What is that all about? Then my heart draws me to the deepest longing of my soul, which is the Lord, and there I find my peace.

"I will love You, O Lord, my strength. The Lord is my rock and my fortress and my deliverer; My God, my strength, in whom I will trust; My shield and the horn of my salvation, my stronghold" (Psalm 18:1-2 NKJV).

God is our rock in a changing world and our strength in the middle of uncertainties. He is our fortress and our deliverer. When changes come and rock our boat, He is the One we can trust.

I struggle with change; at times, it goes too slow, and other times too fast. I am reminded that God is not subject to time, and a day is like a thousand years, and a thousand years like a day. We will one day step out of time, and we will then share in His eternal clock. Until then, the ebbs of change will always be upon us, but we have hope because we can stand firm on the Rock.

Ponders of the Heart

Read 1 John 4:4 and 1 John 4:18-19.

What do the Scriptures say about God's power?

What do we learn about His love and our security?

Prayers of the Heart

Dear Father,

In the changes of life, we struggle, but in Your goodness and greatness, we rejoice. Thank You, Father, that You are our strength and solid rock. Lord, You are the same yesterday, today and tomorrow. We can rest in You. Oh, Lord, how we praise You. In Jesus' name, amen.

January 7 ~ Daddy's Girl

In My Utmost for His Highest, Oswald Chambers asks the question, "Has our Lord exchanged your life with His vital life?" What a great question. How does our Lord work His life into us?

The Lord gives us His life at the moment of salvation, but His life working out in us is a journey, a process. How does this look? One way is through trials, tribulation, and sometimes broken hearts. Believe me when I say I don't like this answer. It is true God uses everything in our lives. He wastes nothing.

I had a dear lady in my Sunday school class who was an honest-to-goodness "daddy's girl." She lost her dad unexpectedly, and it threw her life into a tailspin. Her first reaction was to escape, not to the Caribbeans, the mountains, or the ocean. She went back to school.

She went back to school to become a nurse. This was a huge feat for a middle-aged woman. It was hard for her, but she worked and did well. She even escaped, in a way. Not completely, but somewhat. Later, she realized it was time to grieve the loss of her dad, but she now felt more prepared.

Her long-range plan was to become a hospice nurse. This was her journey of healing. Healing by helping others. So often, that is God's plan. He often uses the hard things in our lives to help others who are dealing with the same issues in life.

God will continue to be with her as she grieves and heals from the loss of her dad. Even though being a hospice nurse did not last long, God still had her on the right path. Later, her husband had a stroke, and he had a built-in nurse. His loving wife took on the role of his nurse. Last I heard, they are both doing well.

In hindsight, it is easy to see how God knew the future and prepared her. His life in her gave her the tools and the compassion to care for others and her husband. God is amazing and faithful to His children.

Ponders of the Heart

Can you remember a time when all you could do was hold on?

Did you have a verse that sustained you?

Read Romans 8:28, Ephesians 2:10, and Psalm 30:5.

We can rest in Christ's sufficiency even when we are in a dark place because joy comes in the morning.

Prayers of the Heart

Dear Father,

Trials are hard, and we fear tribulation, but Lord, help us trust You. Lord, work Your life in us. Help us want Your heart and life more than we want comfort. Oh, Father, be our comfort in the middle of every trial. Be our peace in the middle of every storm. Lord, we need You. In Jesus' name, amen.

January 8 ~ Riley

How does God exchange our old ordinary life with His vital life? As I thought about this question I started thinking about my niece's son, Riley, when he was a young boy. He was the happiest little boy I have ever seen. Perfect? No. Happy? Yes!

From day one, Riley's family has adored him and loved him well. But he never thought the world revolved around him. He was born the month my dad died, and his birth was a reminder of God's love and grace to a hurting family.

As a young boy, Riley's family showered him with love but taught him the importance of others without diminishing their delight in him. Riley's mom encouraged him to laugh, play, and show love and respect to others.

Riley would amaze me with his wit, charm, warmth, joy, spunk, and freedom. His little rebellious spirit flared up now and again, but the security he felt, which was rooted in love, caused him to listen. He gave a little more attention to his mom and dad's instructions than you usually see in a young child. Riley grew up in a home filled with grace.

God is the Father of grace. When we realize His great love and delight in us, we live in freedom. Secure in His care, we experience joyful living. Joy comes in knowing that God covers our backs, our future is secure, and all our days are in His safe care.

He is a Father who corrects. How we treat others is important, but He always corrects us with merciful love. God insists that we listen. He does not speak to us in a gruff voice or with an iron-hard grip. God comes to us with grace and love in His eyes.

We often need to check ourselves and the concept we have of God.

"The Lord, the Lord God, merciful and gracious, longsuffering, and abounding in goodness and truth" (Exodus 34:6 NKJV).

We have such a wonderful God. He is full of goodness. Do you ever wonder how He sees you? I must admit that I do.

"For you are a holy people to the Lord your God; the Lord your God has chosen you to be a people for Himself, a special treasure above all the peoples on the face of the earth" (Deut. 7:6 NKJV).

"The Lord your God is in your midst, The Mighty One, will save; He will rejoice over you with gladness, He will quiet you with His love, He will rejoice over you with singing" (Zeph. 3:17 NKJV).

How I love those verses and what joy it is to ponder over who He is and how He loves us. My heart is full of humble worship and praise as I see the heart of our mighty, heavenly Father.

Ponders of the Heart

What do you feel when the Word of God says that you are holy and chosen?

Can you picture God singing over you?

What a humbling thought that our Creator delights in us.

Prayers of the Heart

Dear Father,

Your goodness of character and grace makes You so worthy of our praises. The thought of You treasuring us and rejoicing over us, even to the point of singing about us, is more than we can take in.

Lord, the only thing we can say is thank You for loving us, redeeming us, and making us Your very own. Teach us to love and delight in others without making them our world. Father, help us to come close to You. In Jesus' name, amen.

January 9 ~ Worth

Not long ago, I was looking at the bright, beautiful faces of young ladies who will be presented as debutantes. I must confess that part of me says "pooh" to such stuff, but the little Cinderella inside of most women says, "Aha." There is a desire in all of us to be special and to have worth.

God has placed that inside of us.

I often feel worthless to those I love and to God. When my thoughts turn in this direction, it is because I am trying to find worth in my looks, performance, or service, not in my being.

These are times when I need the Holy Spirit to quicken my spirit and remind me what God says about me.

Our identity is who we are to God. In Romans 8:18, Paul says,

"I consider that our present sufferings are not worth comparing with the glory that will be revealed in us."

What is this glory that will be revealed in us? Romans 8:29 gives us insight:

"For whom He foreknew, He also predestined to be conformed to the image of his Son."

One day, we will walk before the Father, and the glory of His Son will be formed in us. We will be the debutantes of heaven, completely clothed in Christ's glory and conformed to His image. No wonder Paul was able to say this present suffering was nothing, for he kept his hope in his heavenly home.

We, like Paul, are confined to this world for a time. We will never find fullness and completeness on this side of heaven. But someday, His children will live in completeness, and we will shine, not in self-centeredness or prideful vanity, but in the presence of His glory.

Oh, what a wonderful future we have.

Ponders of the Heart

What are you dealing with right now that has you frustrated?

How do you picture heaven?

Read Romans 8:20-25 and Psalm 42:5.

God understands how frustrating this life can be, but we have hope because He has given us a future. Praise the Lord.

Prayers of the Heart

Dear Father,

Help us rest as we hope in You. Lord, You have given us a new nature and a new name. You are our God, and we are Your children. Lord, help us focus and rest on the hope that is ours in Jesus. In Jesus' name, amen.

January 10 ~ Seasons of Life

The statement that life is full of change is true. Are you in a season of change right now? If you are not, get ready; it is coming. If you are in one of those seasons, you might describe your situation as that of a lost child. You might feel you have lost your identity or the direction of your life has been turned upside down.

When my middle child became a mother, that is how she felt. She felt like she was on a raft in the middle of the ocean with no land in sight. Her mind told her to fight back to the shore of familiarity.

She wanted to sleep all night again, have her shape back, and return to her activities. She wanted her old life back. Embracing the changes was hard for her, yet she couldn't resist this beautiful baby boy in her arms.

I can relate to a similar time. Chris, my oldest, was in school, and Tracie was beginning kindergarten. We had just moved to a new town. I was working with Bill, my husband, and lo and behold, I found myself expecting a baby. Life was throwing me a curve ball, and I was not sure how to manage this new season.

If I had known then what I know now, I would have embraced the change. I would have enjoyed the raft ride and trusted God.

He was taking me on a new adventure, a great adventure of self-discovery. This adventure would prove to be more fulfilling and wonderful than anything I could have planned on my own.

I sound so wise, don't I? So very mature. I think they call this hindsight.

Will I ever reach a point in a season of change when I can relax and stop fighting to get back to the shore of familiarity?

Can I take the advice I gave Tracie and trust the Lord? Will I learn to let go of what was and embrace what is and what is yet to come?

"Trust in the Lord with all your heart and lean not on your own understanding; in all your ways acknowledge him, and he will make your path straight"

(Proverbs 3:5-6).

Ponders of the Heart

Do you believe that God wants to give you the desires of your heart?

What causes you to fret and worry?

What gives you peace?

Read Psalm 37:4-8.

Prayers of the Heart

Dear Father,

Help us trust You and love You. If we really know You, we will love You, and if we love You, we will trust You. Father, help us embrace life with confidence that You are with us, and You will never forsake Your children or shame us. Help us remember that You are on our side. In Jesus' name, amen.

January 11 ~ Center of the Heart

When a person has open-heart surgery, you have two incisions that need to heal. One incision is made into the heart, and the other is made into the skin. Sometimes, the exterior wound will heal, and the interior wound does not. This is a serious matter. I'm thankful there are ways that a doctor can know this, for to be healed on the outside and not the inside is a dangerous thing.

So many of us appear to be okay on the outside. A young woman who is dressed well, has a good education, and a good job appears as if she has recovered from rejection and abuse as a child. By might and determination, she made the outside look good, but in the interior of her soul, she is the same little girl.

The wound of her heart is oozing with the infection of rejection, hurt, and shame.

Healing is possible if we allow God to heal our hurt and pour His love into our broken souls. Maybe you wrestle with deep hurt. A pain of rejection or shame. We all have those unhealed places.

We all have masks that hide our injured souls. Romans 5: 3-5 reads:

"And not only that, but we also glory in tribulations knowing that tribulations produce perseverance; and perseverance, character; and character, hope. Now hope does not disappoint because the love of God has been poured out in our hearts by the Holy Spirit who was given to us."

These hurts, tribulations, and human afflictions can produce perseverance in us, which produces character and hope. How does that work? It only works as God pours His love into us. The presence of the Holy Spirit produces hope.

His life can heal our interior wounds. We can learn to live with victory over the pain that haunts us. This is what Christ meant when He said He could set us free. His healing can be ours by the power of the Holy Spirit.

Ponders of the Heart

Do you have an old wound that won't heal?

Do you know someone who has a wound that is oozing with the infection of hopelessness?

Read Romans 8:38. Ask God to pour His healing love on those wounds.

We all need His love, which produces hope. We are told that Paul is persuaded that nothing can separate us from the love of God. We are secure in God's love because of Jesus, and His love will not disappoint us.

Prayers of the Heart

Dear Father, God,

Your Spirit in us confirms Your love for us. Father, heal every hurt and mend every wound with Your tender love. Thank You for the promise that nothing can separate us from Your love. This great truth will produce hope that does not disappoint. All praise, honor, and glory we give to You. In Jesus' name, amen.

January 12 ~ Granny, the Influencer

Collier, my oldest grandson, requested one more of his favorite breakfasts before returning to college. It is rare for me to stay at home with a business to run, but for him, my answer was yes. As his favorite omelet of ham, eggs, and cheese sizzled on the stove, my thoughts went back to my grandmother, Bessie Crawford.

My grandfather passed away, leaving Granny to raise ten children. I had cousins galore. Family gatherings were a madhouse with grandchildren of all ages running around. There were twenty-four of us, maybe more. I could never remember how many children Aunt Mary had, much less remember their names.

Granny was an influencer over our lives even though she could not drive a car, never had a career, nor owned her own home. When I was three until I turned six, Granny lived with us. After that, she lived with my Aunt Pauline but often visited our home on the weekends.

I picture Granny in her cotton housedress, her gray hair pinned back, with her rocking chair squeaking away as she read the Bible. Her Bible was so big it barely fit her lap. In her room, you sensed peace.

Because she could not drive, she had to depend on someone to take her to church. My mom was not a believer until she was in her seventies, but she always made sure Granny had a ride to church when she was with our family. If Granny went, I was sure to go with her.

I promised her that I would take her to church every Sunday when I had a car. Granny would smile and hug me not because of the promise I gave her but because she knew I had a heart for God long before I knew I was His.

My mom worked outside the home, and Granny was my caregiver. I enjoyed her complete attention as she sang hymns and scratched my back.

Her ability to make each grandchild feel special made her grandchildren debate who was her favorite. We all felt like her only grandchild. One of the things she would do was draw one of us aside and sneak a dollar in our hand. I have yet to find out where she got one dime of money, much less a dollar, but that dollar made each of us believe we were her favorite.

This Christian woman loved God, treasured children, and lived a life that portrayed peace. Her life shows that peace and satisfaction do not come from power, money, position, or fame. She had none of those things. What she did have was a walk with God.

Her influence was a gentle spirit that made time for me, a little girl whose home life was rocky. God used her influence to draw me to Himself.

Granny was strong, gracious, and loving. Her influence spilled over to my mother when it came to being a grandmother. My children received the same kind of loving spirit from my mom. Granny set the standard that I, as a grandmother, strive to be.

I want to influence my grandchildren to seek God and live for Him. This will only happen if I follow Granny's example and God's amazing grace.

Ponders of the Heart

Who are the women who influence your life?

What are the character qualities of women seen in the Scriptures you would like to resemble?

Read Ruth 1:15-17, Esther 4:16, and Luke 10:40-41.

God made us for fellowship with Him and with others.

Prayers of the Heart

Dear Father,

I have such a long way to go before I can be who You made me to be. I long to be more like Ruth, Esther, and Mary. Especially Mary. I can become so distracted in life. Help me, Holy Spirit, be more like Jesus. In Jesus' name, amen.

January 13 ~ Walk in the Spirit

Ah. Winter nights. I love to have the heat turned down and snuggle into bed with warm covers. With the air around me cool, almost cold, I can sleep ever so comfy.

At my age, there are nights when I am assaulted from the inside with an explosion of heat. I become a heating element that can put a glow in the room from the fire I feel inside. No warning, just boom, and heat is my middle name.

This fire comes from within and penetrates to the end of my fingernails. I think the modern term is a hot flash. Thankfully, in my case, it has been controlled by hormone replacement. I'm thankful for modern medicine.

When I was sixteen years old, I had another happening; this was the year I became a Christian. This is also your experience if you are a child of God.

He came to dwell within each of His children. He recreated our spirit. He replaced our old nature and gave us a new nature. Instead of hormone replacement, you and I received Holy Spirit replacement. After He recreated us, He placed His Holy Spirit in us. We are told to "walk in the Spirit, and you shall not fulfill the lust of the flesh" Galatians 5:16.

How do we walk in the Spirit?

Walking in the Spirit requires a couple of things. First, we must have the Spirit of God living in us. Second, we must be appropriate in faith and in how we live our lives. Agreeing with God by surrendering to the Holy Spirit.

When we surrender daily to His power, wisdom, and guidance, we learn to depend on Him. That is what walking in the Spirit means. It is much more about exercising faith than our "doing" the Christian life. Only Christ can live this life through us. How thankful I am that He has given us this gift by faith.

Ponders of the Heart

How can God's Word help you see the fullness of your salvation?

Have we been given the power to defeat the longings of the old flesh?

Read Galatians 5:16-18 and Romans 6:10-14.

Prayers of the Heart

Dear Father,

What a great salvation You have given us. We have redemption, forgiveness, and new life. Father, help us live from the inside out. We thank You for the gift of the Holy Spirit, who lives within our souls. Lord, help us not take this wonderful gift for granted. Holy Spirit be strong in us. Oh, how we love and need You, Lord. In Jesus' name, amen.

January 14 ~ Jesus, our High Priest

"Seeing then that we have a High Priest who has passed through the heavens, Jesus the Son of God, let us hold fast our confession. For we do not have a High Priest who cannot sympathize with our weaknesses, but was in all points tempted as we are, yet without sin. Let us therefore come boldly to the throne of grace that we may obtain mercy and find grace to help in our time of need" (Hebrews 4:14-16 NKJV).

Jesus, our great High Priest, understands earthly living. He experienced the temptations and trials we face but without sin. He suffered rejection, was misunderstood by family members and was falsely accused of wrong. He knew the pain of being deserted by friends and the agony of facing death and feeling alone. He understood the shortcomings of earthly living. Why was it important for Him to go through all of this? Was it so He could completely identify with us?

In a children's book titled Puppies for Sale by Dan Clark, a little boy sees a sign in the window that reads, "Puppies for Sale." He asks the store owner, "How much for a puppy?" The store owner tells him $50.00. The little boy only has $2.34. He pulls his money out and asks if he could just see the puppies.

The owner calls the mama dog, and out comes the little puppies. The little boy notices that one puppy is limping. He asks, "What is wrong with that puppy?"

"It's missing a hip socket."

The little boy says, "I want that puppy." The man tells the little boy that he doesn't want that puppy because the puppy will never be able to run and play. The boy informs the owner that he is exactly the puppy he wants.

"Fine," the man says. "You can have this one for free." The little boy gets terribly angry at this comment and informs the owner that he will pay the full price for the puppy. He is worth the full price.

The owner tries one more time to talk the boy out of the puppy. At that, the little boy pulled up his pant leg to reveal a badly twisted right leg, supported by two steel braces. "Well, sir, "he said, "I don't run so well myself, and the puppy will need someone who understands."

Jesus understands the trials and issues of our lives. He paid the full price for you and me. We were worth it to the Father and to the Son. Not based on our performance but based on His love. Jesus our great High Priest, came to earth and to identify with us completely, so when He purchased us, we would know He understands.

> *"For we do not have a high priest who is unable to empathize with our weaknesses, but we have one who has been tempted in every way, just as we are—yet he did not sin. Let us then approach God's throne of grace with confidence, so that we may receive mercy and find grace to help us in our time of need"* (Heb. 4: 15-16).

Ponders of the Heart

Are you in a tough time right now?

How does the scripture in Hebrews help you you can run to Jesus?

What is holding you back?

Read Romans 5:3-5.

Prayers of the Heart

Dear Heavenly Father,

Thank You for purchasing us with Your blood. You paid a high price for us. It was what You did that makes us valuable.

Let us come boldly to You because we are Yours. You tell us to come and receive Your grace in our time of need. What more could we ask for? Father, we praise You for Your goodness and Your grace. In Jesus' name, amen.

January 15 ~ Standing in Freedom

> *"It is for freedom that Christ has set us free. Stand firm, then, and do not let yourselves be burdened again by a yoke of slavery"* (Galatians 5:1).

We are told that we live in the land of liberty, but are we free?

I will have to admit that I do not feel very free. Culture can have us bound. There are prisons where we can very easily find ourselves enslaved to looking good, being right, and having control. These prisons are driven by our sinful nature.

Think of the millions of dollars people spend to look good. From dyed hair to the newest diet plan. Facelifts, tummy tucks, and Botox. We will do almost anything and pay outrageous amounts of money just to look good. If you could see the clothes in my closet and the creams and lotions in my bathroom, you would know I also want to look good.

Wanting to take care of ourselves is fine, but it should not be our identity or our main purpose in life. It is a trap because no matter how hard we try, our looks will fade. These bodies age.

What about being right? There are families that would still be speaking if someone had given up the right to be right. There are churches that would still be together if someone had given up the right to choose what color the carpet needed to be or the type of songs to sing.

Our culture is bombarded with everyone's opinions on social media. The pull to be right and to be heard is an epidemic. Being right is another prison that keeps us from having intimacy with our heavenly Father and one another.

I have a strong pull to be in control. It is an illusion to think I can control life; I can't, but I know the One who can. There is a stopping place, and if I let go and trust God, I can walk with hope and freedom. I fight and struggle until God gets me there. He never lets me go, no matter how hard I fight Him.

This struggle reminds me of when, as a young mother, I would try to change one of my children's diapers. What a fight it was. If they were still, it wouldn't have taken a minute to get the job done, but convincing them of this was impossible. If only they were still, freedom was right around the corner.

God's Word has powerful promises. He wants to set us free from the prisons of this world, and He wants to heal our broken souls with healing from above. He sent His Son for that very reason.

"The Spirit of the Sovereign Lord is on me because the Lord has anointed me to proclaim good news to the poor. He has sent me to bind up the brokenhearted, to proclaim freedom for the captives and release from darkness for the prisoners, to proclaim the year of the Lord's favor and the day of vengeance of our God, to comfort all who mourn, and provide for those who grieve in Zion—to bestow on them a crown of beauty instead of ashes, the oil of joy instead of mourning, and a garment of praise instead of a spirit of despair. They will be called oaks of righteousness, a planting of the Lord for the display of his splendor" (Isaiah 61:1-3).

Christ came to set us free. He can break the yoke of bondage over our lives, so freedom is not found in a 10-step program or fighting our way to the top to get our way. Freedom is found in surrendering to a person, and that person is Jesus.

Ponders of the Heart

How does God's Word encourage you?

What are the freedoms we enjoy because of Christ?

Have you taken time to thank Jesus today?

Read John 8:36, Romans 6:18-23, and Romans 8:32.

Prayers of the Heart

Dear Heavenly Father,

You have set us free in Jesus, Your Son. Show us those things that keep us enslaved. Father, help us give those things up so we might walk in the freedom we have been given in Jesus. Thank You, Lord, for Your love, grace, and mercy. In Jesus' name, amen.

January 16 ~ The Struggles of Attitudes

In the devotional book My Utmost for His Highest, Oswald Chambers says, "To have a master and teacher is not the same as being mastered and taught."

These are two different attitudes. One is an attitude of complete trust, while the other is being controlled with resistance. Oswald Chambers goes on to say,

"Having a master and teacher means that there is someone who knows me better than I know myself, who is closer than a friend, and who understands the remotest depths of my heart and is able to satisfy them fully. It means having someone who has made me secure in the knowledge that he has met and solved all the doubts, uncertainties, and problems in my mind."

In the Old Testament, God chose a prophet by the name of Hosea to speak to His people about their departure from Him. For Hosea to understand God's heart for His people, God had Hosea marry Gomer. She was an unfaithful wife whose heart was full of desires for adultery.

Gomer had zero commitment to her husband. Her heart was full of dissatisfaction. She leaves the love of her husband to go after lustful desires and finds herself in a mess.

Hosea is compelled by love to pursue his wife and bring her home. When Gomer gets to the end of herself, and she is on the bottom rung of sin's filth, Hosea buys her off the slave block. He becomes her master, but his desire is not to master her but to forgive, cleanse, and restore her.

In Romans, Paul uses Abraham as an example of a man who has entered a relationship with God that is based on faith in God and His promises.

Yet he did not waver through unbelief regarding the promise of God, but was strengthened in his faith and gave glory to God, being fully persuaded that God had power to do what he had promised"
(Rom. 4:20-21).

The amplified Bible includes the words unbelief and distrust. That really hit me hard. Sometimes, it is hard to trust God in my circumstances, but it grieves me to realize not trusting Him means I distrust Him. I want to live convinced He is able and willing to do everything He promises.

The amplified Bible adds to the word persuaded, fully convinced, fully satisfied, and assured. This is the attitude of faith. This attitude can only be ours when we realize our needs and begin to want Jesus as our teacher and master who understands the deepest depths of our hearts and who is able to satisfy them completely.

God's promises written by Hosea were not just for Gomer but for us.

"In that day," declares the Lord, "you will call me 'my husband,' and you will no longer call me 'my master.'" "I will betroth you to me forever; I will betroth you in righteousness and justice, in love and compassion. I will betroth you in faithfulness, and you will acknowledge the Lord" (Hosea 2:16, 19-20).

As God's children, we can rest in His faithfulness.

Ponders of the Heart

Do you know Christ has covered all your sins, past, present, and future?

What does the word reconciliation mean to you?

Read Hebrews 9:27-28 and Romans 5:9-11.

Prayers of the Heart

Dear Lord,

How we love You, need You, and long to know You. We want You to be our Teacher and Lord. Teach us Your wonderful promise and the depth of Your love. Give us the courage to stand firm in our faith in You. In Jesus' name, amen.

January 17 ~ Who Are We?

My daughter, Tracie, was the first girl in my husband's family for over 45 years. Bill's dad was an only child, and so was his mother. They had three boys, so the girls were somewhat of a mystery. Dick, Bill's dad, had his own ideas about little girls.

One of his favorite stories about Tracie was their trip to the store, where he bought her two skirts. He said when he saw the skirts, he was sure Tracie would love them. Not so. Tracie told her granddaddy she didn't want a skirt. He was sure she was going against her girl-ness.

He went ahead to the check-out, where she made her protest a little louder. She yelled, "I don't want no skirt." He continued the task of buying them as Tracie continued to protest. He carried her out of the store with her yelling at the top of her lungs, "Granddaddy, I told you. I don't want no skirt." Dick was convinced that either he didn't know about little girls or Tracie wasn't acting like one. He felt she was going against her basic identity.

In Genesis, God said: "So God created man in His own image; in the image of God He created him; male and female He created them. Then God blessed them, and God said to them, 'Be fruitful and increase in numbers; fill the earth and subdue it" (Gen.1:27-28 NKJV).

Even though Dick was wrong in determining Tracie's girl-ness by what she wanted to wear, he was not wrong in knowing that she was a girl. This gender identity is so basic that we all respond to it. When a baby is born, we ask if the child is a girl or a boy.

There is darkness in our thinking if we think we can change who God has made us. When we do, we exchange the truth for a lie. That is very sad to me. If we change the truth for a lie, we are headed down the road of bad thinking and wrong actions. The proof of this is everywhere in our culture today.

It is easy to be affected by what the world thinks. But as Christians, we want to be careful that we are influenced by God's Word. The Lord wants what is best for us, and that is why He gave us His Word so we will know the truth. The Creator of the Universe formed us in our mother's womb, and His work is perfect and always right.

There are good people who are confused and deceived on the issue of gender. How this must grieve God to see how the enemy has cheated us. I treasure my unique role as a woman, and I do not want the world to rob me of this joy.

I am also aware and thankful that God has chosen us for a purpose: to conform us to the image of His Son. One day in the by and by, I don't know exactly what we will be, but we will be like Jesus. That is God's promise, and we cannot mess Him up.

Ponders of the Heart

Have we listened to the world and not to God's desire for us?

How have we exchanged His truth for a lie?

Read Romans 1.

Ask God to reveal how we have exchanged truth about ourselves for lies. He will open our eyes to His truth if we ask Him.

Prayers of the Heart

Dear Father,

Thank You for making Yourself known to us by the glory of creation. Your greatness is everywhere. Creation shouts Your power. Father, You give us hope, salvation, and peace through Jesus Christ our Lord. Teach us to celebrate who You made us to be, Your dearly loved children. In Jesus' name, amen.

January 18 ~ Death and Life

Death and life, what a mystery. Special people are always leaving this world as others are arriving. Julie, my youngest daughter, reminded me of this when she was a teenager working for our daycare center.

She is natural with children. There she was with 10 or 11 three-year-olds running around asking her questions, handing her things, telling her this and that, and she was calm. As I watched her, I thought about my grandmother.

Granny was the mother of ten children and the grandmother of more than I can count. She was so comfortable with children.

We could all be in the room running around, making noise, but she was completely calm. We felt her love as she enjoyed the chaos.

As I watched Julie that day, I remembered that Granny died three weeks before Julie was born. I pictured them passing each other in the spiritual realm and God giving Julie the gift of loving children as He welcomed Granny to her eternal home.

If I died tomorrow, life would go on, but who would love my husband and my children? Who would clean my house, wash my husband's clothes and fix his dinner? These are things I get to do and I feel responsible for doing. Could this be a sign of self-importance?

"I have been crucified with Christ; it is no longer I who live, but Christ lives in me, and the life I now live in the flesh I live by faith in the Son of God who loves me and gave Himself for me" (Gal.2:20 NKJV).

The Lord has a purpose for each of our lives, and we are responsible for doing them with all the strength He will provide. We can die to self-importance and live out of the life Christ gave us. When this life is over, God will provide for those who remain. He is our provider.

The important things we do each day can be done through the perfect love and power of the Lord. Not only could He do them through us, but He would receive the glory. For the first time, I began to realize what the words of Paul meant when he said, "To live is Christ and to die is gain" (Philippians 1:21).

Ponders of the Heart

Who do you depend on? You or God?

What things keep you from trusting in God?

Read Isaiah 53:12, Galatians 6:1, and 2 Corinthians 5:15.

Prayers of the Heart

Dear Father,

Jesus died and rose again so we could live for Him and not for ourselves. So, Father, we turn away from our boasting in the self-life, and we boast only in the cross of our Lord Jesus Christ. Sweet freedom and rest are ours because we can allow the life of Jesus to live through us. In the words of Paul, we rejoice, "to live is Christ and to die is gain." In Jesus' name, amen.

January 19 ~ Is God Enough?

My playhouse as a child was my dad's old black Mercury. Of course, it was not a car in my mind; it was my make-believe elephant. Daddy allowed me to enjoy his old car, but there were two items in the car that I was not allowed to play with. One of these was a piece of gum, and the other was a coat hanger. Both were kept in the glove compartment.

You see, Dad's car had a slight problem. The gearshift was attached to the steering column with a coat hanger and a piece of gum. I'm not sure how it worked, but I know that occasionally the coat hanger would break, and Dad would coast to the side of the road, then quickly he would take the extra coat hanger, the stick of gum, and repair the car on the spot.

You can see how important it was that I did not touch the coat hanger or chew the gum, no matter how badly I thought I needed it.

My dad was a resourceful man. He used his ingenuity to "make do" with the things we could not afford to fix or replace. Even though I lack his resourcefulness, we have things at our house that I would consider "make-do" items.

One would be the door to our dishwasher. The spring on the bottom of the door is broken, and when you open the door, you better be ready because it falls open with gale force.

I have other "make-do" shoes, clothes, pots, towels, and all kinds of items. I'm sure you know what I mean.

As I think about the "make-do" things in my life, I wonder if I do the same with my family. We are called to listen, support, and love our families.

What about our hearts? Have we given them to God, or have we become "make-do" Christians? Our worship is to honor Him and not be superficial. Our lives are to yield to Him and not resist Him in selfish pursuits.

Matthew 22:37 tells us to love the Lord with all our heart and soul and to keep our minds focused on Him.

The Lord has been asking me this question, "Am I enough?" My reply has been, "Oh yes, God, You are enough." But is He?

I can't help but think about the ocean shore at the end of fun in the sun.

People have built sandcastles and walked, ridden, and made tracts all over the beach. When the tide comes in, all the castles and tracks are washed away. I have tracks of living all over my life. God has a way of coming in, and with the tide of His power, He wipes away the castles I have built and the tracks that have filled my life.

That is where I find myself at times. Not knowing what form His power will take. Not knowing what He would wipe away to clear my path. This can scare me, but in my heart of hearts, I know He is enough.

"The word of the Lord came to Abram in a vision: Do not be afraid, Abram I am your shield, your very great reward" (Genesis 15:1).

In a world filled with empty pursuits trying to remove God in every nook and cranny, we can live and proclaim another "e" word, and that is the word enough. He is enough for me. He is enough for you.

He fills the emptiness of life with Himself and takes "make do" sinful people and given us Christ's righteousness, and that is more than enough.

Ponders of the Heart

What does the word hope mean to you?

What or Who is our true hope?

Read Romans 8:24-25 and Ephesians 4:4.

Prayers of the Heart

Dear Father,

You are enough. You fill our emptiness with Yourself. You are our righteousness, You are our hope, and You are our very great reward. In Your grace and mercy we have more than enough and it is in Jesus' name we pray, amen.

January 20 ~ Proud

Animals are hilarious. They all have their own unique personalities. Our Tex was so sweet, yet she was jealous of my children's dogs. Our youngest daughter had a cat who chose to be an inside cat. Not my idea. He had his own personality, which was unpredictable.

I wish you could have seen this cat's walk. You would have thought he ruled the universe. He walked or, should I say, strutted around our house like he was king of the jungle or at least king of our home. You got the impression that he was in charge, he was fearless, and you were there to serve.

All was well with Mr. Kitty unless there was a sudden noise or sudden movement, and then Mr. Kitty would run like a mouse. He didn't like surprises.

I'm a little like Mr. Kitty, acting as if I have it all together. I wonder if others see me and think I strut. All they would need to do is make a sudden move, and they would see my façade crumble. Walking around in my strength is one step away from falling. I need the Lord's strength, not mine.

I do not have control over things in my life. Oh, I guess I have days where I strut. Days when I can fool others, even myself, but deep inside, I know I am dependent and desperate for Jesus. On days when I live out of this truth, He can use me and fill my heart with joy and courage.

It is a paradox, but I am the strongest when I realize my weakness. Paul said that he took pleasure in his infirmities, for Christ's sake. According to 2 Corinthians 12:10, when he was weak, he was strong. He is our strength and our wisdom. Apart from Him, we are doomed, but with Him, we are more than conquerors.

Why we try to fool each other or fool ourselves is a mystery. What we need and long for is a deep relationship with Jesus. We can waste time strutting and pretending. Life is much too short. I just hope the next time I try to strut, someone will come up and say, "boo." That should bring me back to my senses.

The best way to be brought back to our senses is by the Word of God.

"I am the vine, and you are the branches, he who abides in Me and I in him, bears much fruit; apart from Me you can do nothing" (John 15:5)

Ponders of the Heart

When was a time when you walked around pretending to be someone you were not?

Why do you think we live so much of our lives pretending?

Read Romans 7:21-25, Psalm 101:5, and Proverbs 6:16-19.

God's Word helps us see the struggle we have in living the Christian life. There are also verses to see how God feels about things we fall into. Thank goodness He doesn't leave us there without help.

Prayers of the Heart

Dear Father,

Keep our hearts far from things You hate, our mouths free from slander, our eyes tender, and our hearts full of humility and grace. You have saved us from the wretched people we are apart from You. You have saved us through Jesus Christ our Lord. We thank You, and we give You praise. In Jesus' name, amen.

January 21 ~ The Worst of All Sin

Pride is the worst sin of all. This is my sin, the sin of self-righteousness. This was Satan's downfall. His pride caused a rebellion in heaven and robbed humanity until this very day. Pride blames circumstances on others and pushes the love of God away. It leaves us cold and makes us miserable.

I believe if we are not careful, it is the sin of the church today. We Christians can walk around thinking we are something. Judging the world and thinking we come up smelling like roses instead of realizing that we stink apart from the Rose of Sharon, Christ.

I'm reminded of the story in Scripture where Jesus goes to eat at the house of Simon the Pharisee. There, He meets a person driven by pride and one by love.

During the meal, a woman bows down and anoints Jesus's feet and dries His feet with her hair. Her heart was broken over her sin, and she realized her need for a Savior. Her faith led her to Jesus for forgiveness. In humility and sorrow, she worshipped and gave her heart to Him.

Simon's goodness came through as outward actions, keeping the rules and living the law. He judged everyone, and no one measured up, not even Jesus.

I pray we will not find ourselves walking in Simon's shoes. I have had them on and don't want to wear them anymore.

The Lord woos us home to remind us that He forgives our sins and gives us His peace and acceptance.

In Luke 7:50, Jesus told the woman who washed and anointed His feet with valuable perfume, "Your faith has saved you; go in peace."

Ponders of the Heart

What consequences have you experienced because of pride?

How have you experienced living with the power of the Holy Spirit?

Read Prov. 11:2, Prov. 16:18, Phil. 2:3-5, and 1 Peter 5:5-6.

With pride comes disgrace, and with a humble spirit, wisdom.

Prayers of the Heart

Dear Father,

How can we thank You enough for all You have done for us? Father, we have failed so often, but You gave us Your Son and the Holy Spirit. Help us live the life that releases us from the bondage of the flesh and empowers us to live a new life we find in You. We need You, Lord. In Jesus' name, amen.

January 22 ~ God Our Provider

2 Kings 4:1-7 is the story about a widow who comes to Elisha for help because her husband has died, and she has no way to pay his creditor. The creditor will come and enslave her two children if the debt is not paid.

I don't know if you remember this story, but I sometimes get Elijah and Elisha mixed up. I have read this story before, but it struck me this time.

Elisha asks her what she has, and she tells Elisha she has a little oil in a jar. This means she is in deep trouble.

He tells her to ask her neighbors for empty jars. This might be the first case of recycling. She obeys Elisha and knocks on her neighbors' doors, asking for empty jars. She takes her children in, shuts the door, and fills the jars with oil. The oil pours out, filling every jar until she has no more. Then Elisha tells her to sell the oil jars to pay off her debt, and she and her children can live on the rest.

Can you imagine the faces of the widow and her children as they filled jar after jar with the oil, and it kept flowing? The Scripture says she tells her son to bring her another jar, and he tells her there are no more. Then, at once, the oil stopped flowing. I wonder if she thought, "I wished I had asked that old grumpy Mr. Smith for his empty jars."

God is generous to His people. He is not a stingy Father. He is our provider and will provide for those who ask and obey. He can take the little things we have and cause them to increase to meet our needs. Do we believe this? Have you experienced it in your own life? I have, and yet I still forget to believe He will. Elisha told her to pay off her debt first, and then she and her children could live on the rest. There is a life message there for all of us.

This chapter has remarkable stories about God's power through His prophets and tells us things we need to know about our God. I'm thankful for some of my Bible classes that have brought me back to read about the great prophets and our great God, His power, and His provision for His people.

Ponders of the Heart

How has God provided for you?

Are you in need of rescue?

Read 2 Kings 4:42-44 and Mark 6:30-44.

God can use our limited resources and provide all we will ever need.

Prayers of the Heart

Dear Father,

How often we forget to give You all we are and all we have and watch what You can do with them. Help us listen to You as You guide us so we can see how You provide for us. Father, if we did, I am sure we would be amazed. Lord, take what we have and use it for Your glory. You are our Bread of Life. In Jesus' name, amen.

January 23 ~ Righteousness from God

"God made him who had no sin to be sin for us so that in him we might become the righteousness of God" (2 Corinthians 5:21).

Why was Christ baptized, and what was the meaning? This symbolic picture helps me understand the purpose of His baptism.

Picture the spotless Lamb of God, who is pure, perfect, and righteous, being baptized. Don't forget this meek man is fully God. Now, picture a polluted lake, one where raw sewage has been pumped for years. Trash is everywhere, floating all over the water along with dead fish. No life could co-exist with such pollution. The water has become so foul that you can only stand beside it by covering your nose; the stench is unbearable. At that moment, you see a hearse back up to the edge of the water and throw a dead body into the lake. You wonder How many dead bodies are in there?

As you stand there with your nose covered, Jesus walks into the water, and He immerses Himself into the lake. You watch in horror as He lowers His head below the water's surface. Then, at once, the smell is gone, the garbage disappears, the fish return to life, and the dead bodies begin to rise.

Jesus is so pure, powerful, and penetrating that His precious purity removes all pollution, death, and stench.

From then on, anyone who immerses himself in the lake rises to new life, pure life, and they are regenerated. The impurities of this world and our own sinfulness are no match for Jesus.

He plunged Himself into our sinful world so it could be purified. We plunged ourselves into Him so we can be pure.

Jesus came to identify with us so we could identify with Him. He came to walk human life with perfection so we could walk with Him into eternity.

What a glorious Christ we serve.

Ponders of the Heart

How clean are we because of the work of Jesus on the cross?

How many of our sins did He die and cleanse us from?

Read 1 John 1:7 and Hebrews 10:14.

Prayers of the Heart

Dear Father,

How can we thank You enough for Your provision for our purification? You have given us new life in Your Son. Lord, help us understand and believe all that Jesus has done for us. Open our hearts to You and help us love and fellowship with one another. In Jesus' name, amen.

January 24 ~ The Price of the Kingdom

"The Kingdom of heaven is like a treasure hidden in a field. When a man found it, he hid it again and then in his joy went and sold all he had and bought that field" (Matthew 13:44).

Imagine a man working on a leased field. Hard labor, toiling day after day for the necessities of life. No advancement in sight, laboring, the essentials, nothing for tomorrow, just enough for the day. There is little hope or purpose in a life like that.

One day, he hits what he thinks is a rock. He had removed thousands of rocks from the rocky soil. He bends over to dig his fingers in the dirt and discovers this is not a rock. He works hard at getting the chest out of the ground. Could it be? Yes, it is a hidden treasure. He begins to realize this treasure would be his if he owned the land. He goes and sells all he has and buys the land.

We are left pondering Jesus' words. What is He trying to say to us? Would we be willing to sell all we have for the Kingdom? Does the Kingdom of God mean that much to us?

There is an old Christian song titled "He is Everything to Me." Whenever I sing that song, it captures the longing I have for God to be everything to me. My spirit sings that song with all I am, but my flesh patterns are still strong.

I believe the secret of this life is found when we realize we are everything to Him. He liquidated heaven to purchase us. God gave the riches of heaven when Christ came to earth and lived as a man and to pay for our sins on the cross. It was His blood that God took in our place.

We are a treasured possession to God, and the price was the death of His Son.

Once we realize what we mean to God, we recognize He is everything to us. He is the author of our faith. He pursued us and paid the price for our redemption. We were bought with the riches of heaven, Jesus.

Ponders of the Heart

Do you realize the wonder of God's love for you?

Have you been trying to earn His love?

Read 1 John 4:10, Hebrews 12:2, and Deuteronomy 7:6.

Spend time thinking about the gift of eternal life and the price Jesus was willing to pay for you. We were the hidden treasure. He gave all for us so we might belong to Him and live with Him forever. That is something worth thinking about.

Prayers of the Heart

Dear Father,

Help us realize that we do not deserve Your grace, but You call us worthy by faith in Your Holy Son. You have given us new life in Christ, and we now belong to Your family. Help us see ourselves as dearly loved children. You pursued us first. Thank You, Father, for loving us so much. In Jesus' name, amen.

January 25 ~ Imprint of Jesus

When a baby picks up their head from a nap, the room is filled with life. The rest the little one enjoyed is seen all over his face. The imprint of the sheet is across that tender cheek, leaving a wrinkle. You don't mind the imprint because it tells you the nap was good. Then, before that wrinkle completely disappears, the little one is rubbing those eyes, and the need for rest is claiming him once more.

Now for those of us who are no longer babies, we have acquired another kind of wrinkle. Not one from sleep but one from age. Those creases are permanently imprinted on our faces. We might say they are ugly and unsightly, and we wish with all our hearts that they could be removed.

Premature wrinkles can reveal the lack of rest, hardships, and stresses of life, while lines from years of life can reveal and enhance the character, kindness, and realness of the person. The latter has an inward glow of life that overflows.

Before you disagree, think for a moment. My mind goes back to my grandmother and dear saints whom I have had the privilege to know. Some have gone on to be with the Lord, while others still bless my life. Aging has a way of helping us let go of some things that didn't really matter anyway. Freeing us to give our lives into the hands of the Lord, which is indeed rest, or does Scripture call that faith?

What kind of imprints are you carrying? Wrinkles from sheets, hardships, stresses, age, or could you be one who carries the imprint of Jesus? You will carry either the imprint of this age or the age to come.

"Now when they saw the boldness of Peter and John, and perceived that they were uneducated and untrained men, they marveled. And they realized that they had been with Jesus" (Acts 4:13 NKJV).

Oh, how wonderful that we can have the imprint of Jesus on our lives. He will be in us and flow through us. The Scripture tells us that Jesus is the hope of glory, and He is the light that shines out of the darkness. He can show His glory through us. Stephen died, showing the imprint of Jesus, and people marveled. Stephen left this life resting in the arms of Jesus.

"And gazing at him, all who sat in the council saw that his face was like the face of an angel" (Acts 6:15 NKJV).

When we look to Jesus, our lives can reflect His light to the world around us even if they choose not to believe.

Ponders of the Heart

Do you realize that the Spirit of God lives in you?

Do you find peace and rest in this wonderful truth?

Read Romans 8:6-9.

Prayers of the Heart

Dear Father,

How our hearts turn to You in praise. We can live free of condemnation as we cling to hope in Jesus. Hope is not wishful thinking but depends on the promises of Your Word. Jesus, You have provided for us a righteous standing with God, and we are alive in the Spirit because of You. Thank You, Father, In Jesus' name, amen.

January 26 ~ Focus and Peace

"You will keep him in perfect peace, whose mind is stayed on You because he trusts in You" (Isaiah 26:3 NKJV).

What came first, the chicken or the egg? Without a doubt, I believe the chicken. Why? Because God created the chicken, and the chicken then laid the egg. That seems so reasonable to me. What comes first, God's perfect peace or trust in God?

The Lord is such a mystery to us, yet our deepest desire. He is the One who has placed this desire in us and keeps it alive and burning. Our focus and trust in Him are more of a process, a journey. Sometimes, it seems I trust God because I have no other choices. That is when I have come to the end of myself. Trust frees me from fear, and I wonder what took me so long.

My peace is gone when I lose focus on Him because peace is a person, not just a state of mind. How true this statement is and yet how profound. I will only understand this for a while, and then the world rushes in to steal my focus and peace.

The clouds of this world can steal our view of God. There are so many deceptions to distract us from the focus we need. We are easily distracted, and the world knows how to dangle the glitter of diversion before us. Before we know it, we are off chasing ourselves like a dog chasing his tail. God knows the more we experience Him, truly experience Him, nothing else will do. His grace is irresistible.

Trusting and focusing on God are the most fundamental needs we have for life. We have no idea what will come today or what life will demand from us today, but God does.

Only He is completely trustworthy and worthy of our worship and praise.Lord, help us keep our hearts and minds focused on You.

Ponders of the Heart

Do you sometimes lose your focus on God's promises?

What promise of God is most precious to you?

Read Proverbs 3:5-6 and Psalm 34:8.

Prayers of the Heart

Dear Father,

Forgive us when we think we can walk through life in our self-sufficiency. Forgive us when we fall for the distractions of this world. The Holy Spirit stirs our desires back to You. Help us keep our focus and our trust in You, our peace. We pray for Your mercy. Oh Lord, how we need You. In Jesus' name, amen.

January 27 ~ Sprinkle Me Clean.

"Then I will sprinkle clean water on you, and you shall be clean; I will cleanse you from all your filthiness and from all your idols. I will give you a new heart and put a new spirit within you; I will take the heart of stone out of your flesh and give you a heart of flesh. I will put My Spirit within you and cause you to walk in My statutes, and you will keep My judgments and do them" (Eze. 36:25-27 NKJV).

What great verses full of promises. These are some of my favorites. The Lord promises to give us a clean life, a new heart, and a new spirit. But sometimes I notice that my heart has turned cold. I'm not one who likes being cold. Not even for one minute. How can it be that my heart can turn cold without me even noticing? I am amazed at how quickly this can happen.

As I examine my life, I wonder, "How did I wander so far from the Lord?" Sometimes, I have allowed my walk with God to become routine. My time with Him is an activity instead of my lifeline. I have become self-consumed, self-centered, and my own god.

My heavenly Father helps me realize that I have covered my new heart with the things of this world, which is why my heart feels cold.

When I am cold and dirty, nothing fixes me like a good hot bath. Baths do wonders for my body, but what can fix my soul? Ephesians 5: 25-27 tells us that Jesus washes His church with His Word.

Maybe you, like me, sense what we need is a good spiritual bath. Why don't we take advantage of washing in His word, and maybe by spring, we will discover a new thawing and growth for our weary souls?

Ponders of the Heart

Do you or do you know someone who could use a fresh touch of God?

Are you longing for a new beginning in the Lord?

Read John 1:1-4 and 1 John 1:1-4.

Prayers of the Heart

Dear Father,

We praise You and thank You for Jesus, the living Word. All things were made by Him and for Him. He is more than we could ever ask for. I am so thankful for those who walk with Him and touch Him and have written about their time with Him. Oh, Lord, take our cold hearts and warm them as we focus on Your promises found in Your Holy Word. In Jesus' name, amen.

January 28 ~ Give Me Serenity.

F. LaGard Smith, a professor in California, would escape in the summers to the hillsides of Cotswold in England. There, he would live in a small cottage and walk along the hills and valleys of this quaint English village. He loved to have his friends come from the States, where they would discover the wonder, beauty, and peace of his Cotswold.

Smith loved to see how the tranquility of nature transformed these busy people. As I read about him, I remember my visit to Galilee. I pictured Jesus walking along the Sea of Galilee and watching the sunrise over the mountains just as I did when I was there. It was easy picturing Him walking along the shoreline, talking with the fishermen, and holding little children in His lap. I didn't like picturing Him in Jerusalem and on the cross, but Paul has a verse in Corinthians that reminds me that Jesus came for the main purpose of the cross.

"For I determined not to know anything among you except Jesus Christ and Him crucified" (1 Corinthians 2:2 NKJV).

Jesus was a teacher, prophet, healer, and lover of children, but He fulfilled His purpose on the cross for us.

I had dreamed of owning a piece of land with water. A place called Camp Serenity. I dreamed this for others and myself. This camp would be a place for people to come and rest. They would leave their laptops and cell phones at the door. No telephones, televisions, or Wi-Fi in their rooms.

Instead, guests would find soft blankets, large windows overlooking the lake, and the quiet peace of God's nature all around. My husband would take them fishing, and we would have cups of coffee on the swing as we studied God's Word. There would be laughter and deep conversations as we talk about children, love, and God.

Jesus walked along the Sea of Galilee, prayed on the hills, and sought the serenity of the wilderness. Why, to prepare Him for the cross.

When I think about the agony Jesus endured, I wonder which was harder: the garden of Gethsemane or the cross? Some of my hardest battles are the battles of my will.

My Camp Serenity is in my study, where I go each morning to meet with the Lord. I love the solitude and my time with Jesus, and this is where I want to stay. But He said I must pick up my cross, which means I must be about my day and follow Him.

"Then Jesus said to His disciples, 'If anyone desires to come after me, let him deny himself and take up his cross and follow me. For whoever desires to save his life will lose it, but whoever loses his life for my sake will find it" (Matthew 16: 24-25 NKJV).

He is not saying we don't need our time of serenity. We need daily periods of time to reflect and be alone with the Lord. We need time to refresh and rest. But Jesus has called us to walk the path of sacrifice. He has said we must follow Him, and it is there we find our true life. The way of the cross leads home.

I still like the idea of Camp Serenity, but for now, I just pray for the strength to follow Jesus. Yes, I need to meet with Him each day and drink up the wonderful pleasure of being with Him, but when He gently pushes me and says, "Let's roll,"

I pray I will go where He takes me and allow Him to do His work through me. I want to roll up my sleeves, take up my cross, and follow Him all the way home.

Ponders of the Heart

What is God's desire for His children?

What do you read in Scripture that helps us live for Him?

Read Psalm 23:1-3 and Acts 4:29-30.

Prayers of the Heart

Dear Lord,

You are our Shepherd. You lead, and we will follow. You know how weak we are, but You can keep us and lead us. You restore our souls.

Father, we need You to keep us far away from evil. Grant us the boldness to speak Your word even when we feel threatened or afraid. Use us, to do signs of wonder in Your name. We are Your children, and we love You. In Jesus' name, amen.

January 29 ~ To Much of a Good Thing

Julie is six years younger than Tracie and eight years younger than Chris. She always felt we had her "too late." We felt we had her at just the right time.

In Julie's junior year of college, she had the opportunity to take a trip to Italy for 13 days. I wonder if that was the time Chris and Tracie thought they were born too early.

Have you ever thought that way about something? If only I were taller or shorter, had this job or that job, had more money or more time off, then I would be complete, happy, and finally at rest. We are good at looking at circumstances and thinking the grass is greener on the other side.

I read a book once that talked about bondage we can experience in life because we place too much hope in things, circumstances, and people instead of placing our hope in Christ.

Here is a list titled "Too Much of a Good Thing."

Physical rest becomes laziness.

Quietness becomes non-communication.

Self-care becomes selfishness.

Self-respect becomes conceit.

Anger becomes raging and a bad temper.

Judgment becomes criticism.

Generosity becomes wastefulness.

Self-protection becomes dishonesty.

Carefulness becomes fear.

Cautiousness becomes unbelief.

It is easy to see that without the Spirit of Christ ruling in our hearts, even a good thing can trip us up.

If I am not careful, after a week of vacation, I find myself wanting to rest more. Rest is necessary, but my old flesh wants to take a good thing and try to get life out of it.

Fear can also be an excuse for being overly careful. I can become so cautious that I lose my ability to relax and enjoy the moment. This ends up making everyone around me miserable, especially me. There is a balance between being careful and being controlled by fear.

I often put expectations on my husband, children, and friends to be for me what only Christ can be. Christ is where I find my rest, joy, strength, and contentment. Knowing this truth is good, but there are times I still wander from it.

He truly is our Life. God wants to bless His children, and He wants us to enjoy the good gifts and blessings He gives us. I also want to take the time to thank Him and enjoy the beautiful blessings in my life. But I also want to remember that my greatest blessing, your greatest blessing, is Jesus Christ our Savior.

"For in Christ all the fullness of the Deity lives in bodily form, and you have been given fullness in Christ, who is the head over every power and authority"
(Colossians 2: 9-10 NKJV).

Ponders of the Heart

What are the idols we have in our day?

Why is Christ more worthy of our worship?

Read Colossians 2:11-15 and Jeremiah 2:5.

I do not want the idols of this age to rob me of fellowship with Jesus, my Savior.

Prayers of the Heart

Dear Father,

Thank You that we belong to You. We praise You, Father, and we only ask for mercy. Quicken in us Your truth, especially when we try to get life from anything else but You. In Jesus' name, amen.

January 30 ~ What We Need Most

"Hezekiah turned his face to the wall and prayed to the Lord, 'Remember, O Lord, how I have walked before you faithfully and with wholehearted devotion and have done what is good in your eyes,' And Hezekiah wept bitterly" (Isaiah 38:2-3 NKJV).

Isaiah had just told Hezekiah that he would not recover from his illness but would die. Hezekiah, in deep anguish, turns to God in prayer. God hears his prayer, sees his tears, and gives Hezekiah 15 more years to live. How wonderful.

Hezekiah responds, "But what can I say? He has spoken to me, and he himself has done this. I will walk humbly all my years because of this anguish of my soul. Lord, by such things, men live, and my spirit finds life in them, too. You restored me to health and let me live."
(Isaiah 38:15-16 NKJV)).

Is he glad he is going to live? You bet. But the wonder to him is that God had spoken. He receives more than physical life; he experiences God in the depth of his soul.

I was the coordinator of a weekend event at the church. We spent money and time to make this weekend special. Members opened their homes to people who flew into town to help.

The Friday night of the event, all went well. As we left the church, snowflakes began to fall. It was beautiful. By the next morning, the whole city was under a white blanket of snow. The roads were icy, and travel was impossible.

All the people on the committee were in a panic. I was getting call after call with all kinds of ideas of what to do. Since there was nothing we could do, I took a walk. The weekend was called "Experiencing God."

My walk on the snow-covered roads took my breath away and filled me with peace. I was experiencing God's world. I felt Him telling me to stop fretting and look at the wonder of His creation. It was not what we had planned. It was what He planned.

Can you remember a distressful time when God touched your soul with His presence? In the depth of who we are in Christ, there is nothing we want more than His presence. Nothing satisfies us like being with Him. Nothing. He is our need and our treasure.

Ponders of the Heart

When things take a wrong turn, who do you turn to?

Have you ever had a wrong turn be God's perfect plan?

Do you ask God in prayer for His will over yours?

Read John 17:3, John 15:5, and Philippians 3:9-11.

Prayers of the Heart

Dear Father,

We confess that what we need most in life is You. Sometimes, our prayer might be for relief, but our real need is to see You. As Your children, we are thankful for Your tender care and mighty presence. In Jesus' name, amen.

January 31 ~ Prayers of the Heart

"Be very careful, then, how you live—not as unwise but as wise, making the most of every opportunity, because the days are evil. Therefore do not be foolish, but understand what the Lord's will is" (Ephesians 5:15-17).

Dear Father,

How thankful I am that You are the One who saved me, and the One who will keep me. I want to accept and receive the gift of Your salvation. Walk in the light and enjoy fellowship with You.Lord, You know this is my heart, for You have given me these desires by Your grace. Thank You.

Lord, I do not want to waste the life You have given me. Grant me a spirit of wisdom so I will understand Your will and live a life for You.

Holy Spirit, pour Your Spirit out on Your people! Our nation needs a revival. Begin with Your church and Father, please do not pass me by.

I want to stand firm in faith and be ready to stand the test of time. Remind me that You have given me divine power to stand if only I will agree with You and receive Your power.

"Finally, be strong in the Lord and in his mighty power. Put on the full armor of God so that you can stand against the rulers, against the authorities, against the

power of this dark world and against the spiritual forces of evil in the heavenly realms. Therefore put on the full armor of God, so that when the day of evil comes, you may be able to stand your ground, and after you have done everything, to stand" (Eph. 6:10-13).

Lord, help us, your people, put on Your armor. Then, we will have the belt of truth, the breastplate of righteousness, the shoes of peace, and the helmet of salvation. Lord, we want to put on the sword of the Spirit and the shield of faith so we can stand in this broken world. Our prayer is that we can help those who don't know You find their way to You. In Jesus' name, amen.

february

— 66 —

Now to him who is able to do immeasurably more than all we ask or imagine, according to his power that is at work within us, to him be glory in the church and in Christ Jesus throughout all generations, for ever and ever! Amen.
Ephesians 3:20-21

February 1 ~ Passion

"They said to each other, "Didn't our hearts burn within us as he talked with us on the road and explained the Scriptures to us?" (Luke 24:32 NLT).

Passion in today's world is real but rarely mentioned in the church. Unfortunately, our culture has taken this word and placed sexual connotations on it.

When you hear the word passion, what are your thoughts?

Consider the scene in *Top Gun* when Tom Cruise has Kelly McGillis against the wall in her bungalow. She is on fire with passion. What about the scene in *Days of Thunder* when Nicole Kidman throws Tom Cruise against the wall after she accuses him of ignoring her? Whew!

The thoughts of these two scenes can heat the passion of the flesh. These are human emotions.

I have known such desire for my husband. Maybe not as flamboyantly as these movie scenes, but my passion for Bill is there all the same. I'm thankful for our relationship as best friends and lovers. The older I get, the best friends' relationship wins out, but that is another story altogether.

Desire can be physical between a man and a woman, but there is also spiritual passion. What is your passion? I know mine is God's Word. The spirit within me burns for the deep truths of God's Word.

wrong. When I go to His Word, passion ignites in my soul, and I say, "That is what I'm longing for." Nothing satisfies me like God speaking to me through His Word. I hunger for the richness of the Scripture, and there is seldom a day I go without it. But there are days when I travel; it is difficult to spend the moments I usually do.

When I return home, my soul is starving—not physically, but spiritually. I know I'm out of sorts, but it's hard to recognize what is

You may be agreeing and saying, "Yes! I know exactly what she is talking about."

It's because of the Holy Spirit I have a desire for the Lord. He is the one who pours passion into me. That is true for you also, my dear sister in Christ. Feel your passion and let your heart soar with love for God. Praise the Lamb, for He gives us a desire for the things of God.

Our walk with the Lord is much more than rules and duties; it comes from a hunger deep within our souls, for we are children of the King.

Ponders of the Heart

Do you struggle with direction and purpose for your life?

Have you asked God to light a fire in your soul?

Read Romans 12:1-7.

This is a great passage to read. It helps us find that desire for the deep truths of God. Ask Him to ignite the flame of His Holy Spirit in you.

Prayers of the Heart

Dear Father,

We praise You for the flame of passion in our souls. A desire deeper and stronger than the flesh. Thank You, Father, for the hunger and the thirst You placed in our souls that water or food cannot satisfy. You are the strength of our hearts and our portion forever (Psalm 73:26). In Jesus' name, amen.

February 2 ~ Busyness, Our Enemy

In the movie, *Coal Miner's Daughter*, Loretta Lynn is at the point of a nervous breakdown. She stands on stage and tells her fans Patsy Cline used to tell her, "Little girl, you need to run your own life." Loretta Lynn says, "But I can tell you it feels like my life is a running me."

Have you ever felt your life was "a running" you? I think we all find ourselves in those places. Each day is a challenge. There seems to be so much to do and little time to do them. Our busyness puts us in a frenzy with little time to stop and seek the Lord. No wonder we feel like we are running a marathon with no finish line in sight.

Richard Foster says our biggest enemies are busyness, crowds, and noise. I can certainly relate. I am amazed at the people who need someone, something to do or noise to drown out the silence. No wonder we have such a tough time hearing a word from the Lord.

When you think of the saints of old, you picture them hearing God in silent places. Moses was on the back side of the desert, Samuel was asleep on his cot, and Elijah could not hear the Lord in the wind, fire, or rain but in a gentle whisper. Jonah was in the belly of a fish, Saul on the road to Damascus, and John the Revelator on the island of Patmos.

God has never been about activity; He has always been about relationships.

I worked on a book for children, and one session dealt with the characteristics of God, and a question was asked, "Who's in charge?" The answer is, "God is!" We say that, but do we know, believe, and live that?

Busyness and noise make us think we are in control or God needs our help. The devil doesn't care what we spend our time doing if it keeps our minds off God.

The morning is my favorite time to meet with God. In the quiet hours of the morning, before activities overtake me, I seek Him.

"Hear my cry for help, my King and my God, for to you I pray. In the morning, Lord, you hear my voice; in the morning I lay my requests before you and wait expectantly" (Psalm 5:2-3).

Ponders of the Heart

Do you or do you know someone who could use a fresh touch of God?

Are you longing for a new beginning in the Lord?

Do you have a favorite time and place to meet the Lord?

Read Psalm 46:10 and Psalm 119:97-99.

I love how Psalm 46 reminds us to be still. Oh, how we need to take the time to be still and know God.

Prayers of the Heart

Precious Father,

How we thank You for being the God of rest and peace. Thank You, Lord, that we can have a deep relationship with You. Help us make You the priority of our lives. Teach us to hear Your voice and teach us to love those in our lives. In Jesus' name, amen.

February 3 ~ Clean

I love a clean house, and for a clean freak like me, seeing the finished results is significant.

Even though I can't relax if things are out of place, my dresser drawers and closets are not that organized. Some people worry more about their yards than the inside of their houses. Like me, they don't fret over what others can't see.

Jesus said to the Pharisees in Matthew 23:25-26, "Woe to you, teachers of the law and Pharisees, you hypocrites! You clean the outside of the cup and dish, but inside, they are full of greed and self-indulgence. Blind Pharisee! First clean the inside of the cup and dish, and then the outside also will be clean."

I don't often clean my dresser drawers and closets, but things feel especially nice when I do. Jesus was trying to tell the Pharisees that until the inside of their lives were clean, the outside would never measure up. The problem with our lives is that we can present a good front on the outside, but God looks at the condition of our hearts.

We can fool ourselves and others, but we never fool God. Our lives might appear good and righteous, but God is interested in our inner souls. He is the only One who can make us clean and pure from the inside out. That is grace that is greater than our fallen nature.

What would God say to us today if we would listen? He would say, "Child, let me help you. Let me do what you can't do for yourself. I have sent My Son, and He will take all your sins and give you His goodness, cleanliness, and righteousness. You will have a new heart and a new nature. Then, my child, you will be clean."

Jesus wasn't telling the Pharisees to clean the inside of their hearts. He showed them their need for Him. How aware are we of our need for Jesus? The Christian life is not about being moral; it is about knowing Jesus. He makes us moral by giving us His righteousness, which changes our desires.

Ponders of the Heart

What does a dead man need? Life!

Who are you depending on today for your goodness?

Read Matthew 23: 27-32 and John 14:6.

Prayers of the Heart

Dear Father,

We praise You. Lord, You see our need, and You are powerful enough to provide that need. Your love is sweeter than anything we can believe and more precious than gold.

Thank You for giving us a new, clean heart. Help us to live out of the new nature that You have provided. There is none like You. In Jesus' name, amen.

February 4 ~ Lonely Times

"But seek first the kingdom of God and His righteousness, and all these things will be given to you as well" (Matthew 6:33).

Families are different, and so are the children in families. We are all complex, and yet, in some ways, we are very much alike. We all need community and authentic connection. God made us with this need, but there are times when the community we need, the real connection, is with the Father, the Son, and the Holy Spirit.

Have you ever been in a circumstance where God was all you have? I experienced that when we moved.

The first move was away from our families. I was so lonesome. We were in a small town, and people were not very accepting. I was pregnant and sick. We were also trying to start a new business. God became my best friend; He was my only friend, and this lonely time became a precious work of the Lord in my life.

The second time we moved, it was more difficult for my family than for me. The fact that it was hard on them made it tough on me. This was when I began to pour out my soul to God by journaling. This discipline is still a part of my Christian life. It was there the Lord taught me to express myself in writing.

I don't mean He taught me proper English or how to spell. I wish He had. He taught me how to open my soul and pour it out to Him. There is nothing I do not tell my Lord, and He still loves me.

What a precious friend we have in the Lord. He is with us every day of our lives. He knows us better than we know ourselves. We are never alone, so don't try to run away from lonely times. Seek God and ask Him what He is up to. He might not tell you, but you will grow closer to Him. One day, you will look back and say, "Oh! This was what You were doing."

Ponders of the Heart

Do you remember a time when you were so lonely you didn't know what to do?

What did you do? Would you handle this differently now?

Read Proverbs 3:5-6, Matthew 6:33, and Psalm 37:3-4. These verses tell us how close He is and how much He knows our hearts and needs.

Prayers of the Heart

Precious Lord,

Thank You that You know what we need is You. Lord, direct our paths and our circumstances so we will come to know Your ways. Father, open our eyes so we can see that You are our very great reward and You love us. In Jesus' name, amen.

February 5 ~ The Guardian

The television series called *The Guardian* was about a young attorney whose father owned a successful law firm. This young man, Nick, was caught with drugs and sentenced to community service, where the poor came for legal advice.

His clients were mostly from the Department of Family and Children Services. Nick had to deal with children who had been mistreated and abused. He also works with his father, where he watches greed and the exploitation of people daily.

The whole show was a glowing look at the depravity of man, and Nick was no exception. He was constantly in trouble and lost more court cases than he won. He and his father had a terrible relationship. The show was depressing.

I asked my husband, "Why do we watch this show?" He said we were just hoping that something good would happen to someone. I think he was right.

The world we live in is full of people like Nick and his father. The heart of man is evil to the core. Our only hope is Jesus. How do I know? The Word of God is clear:

"As it is written: "There is no one righteous, not even one; there is no one who understands; there is no one who seeks God. All have turned away; they have together become worthless; there is no one who does good, not even one" (Romans 3:10-12).

"For the wages of sin is death, but the free gift of God is eternal life through Christ Jesus our Lord" (Romans 6:23 NKJV).

I wish I could have gotten the writers of *The Guardian* to let Jesus come and live in Nick. What a difference that would have made, a show that showed how Jesus brings light into the darkest situations.

God transforms lives. He gives us purpose and new attitudes. The Lord rebuilds marriages and gives hope where there is nothing but despair.

He can change a self-centered person into a prayer warrior. He can fill a person so full of joy that when they face death, they walk into eternity with peace.

Ponders of the Heart

What are the bleakest situations you know of right now?

Is God calling you to help? How?

Read Matthew 19:26 and 2 Samuel 7:18-19.

We can pray and ask God to use situations to draw that person to Him. What a joy to know that nothing is too hard for God.

Prayers of the Heart

Dear Father,

Your ways are not our ways. They are always better. Open our hearts to know Your ways and Your thoughts. Shine Your light in us and through us so others will see You. Father, You are powerful and mighty. Nothing can stand against You. In Jesus' name, amen.

February 6 ~ Walking in the Spirit

"So I say, walk by the Spirit, and you will not gratify the desires of the flesh. For the flesh desires what is contrary to the Spirit, and the Spirit what is contrary to the flesh. They are in conflict with each other so that you are not to do whatever you want. But if you are led by the Spirit, you are not under the law" (Galatians 5:16-18).

We are commanded to walk in the Spirit and not to fulfill the lust of the flesh. Exactly is the lust of the flesh?

Galatians has a pretty good list of those in chapter 5:19-21. They are things like adultery, hatred, jealousy, outbursts of anger, selfish ambitions, envy, murder, drunkenness, and more compile this list.

Sometimes, it is hard to believe we have such desires in us, and then, at other times, it is easy to see that we do.

I wish the lust of the flesh in Galatians 5 had never shown up in my life, but that would not be true. My goal is for them to show up less.

In the world of competition, we often see these sins acted out. There is healthy competition, but our culture too often defines a person by his or her performance.

One area where competition has gone amuck is in the world of sports. Instead of sports figures being good role models of discipline and effort for the good of the whole, we have arrogant, self-centered thugs honored as heroes. Pulling together to win has gone out the window for self-promotion and the pursuit of the almighty dollar.

In Waverly, Ohio, there is a story that *The Herald-Dispatch* says is destined to become legendary.

Jake Porter, a Northwest football team senior, had never touched the football in a game. He has a disorder called "Chromosomal Fragile-X," the most common cause of genetic mental retardation. Jake showed up on time for every practice and dressed in full uniform for every game. Yet, playing a contact sport like football was out of the question for him.

The coach of the Northwest football team, Dave Frantz, wanted Jake to have the opportunity to be in a real game before he graduated. He called Coach Derek Dewitt of Waverly High School, and a plan was devised that on the last play of the game, if the game was not close, Jake should take the snap and knee the ball. All agreed.

The game was not close. In fact, the score was Waverly High School 42 and Northwest 0. The coach of the defending team called Jake's coach over and said, "Let him score." Northwest's coach initially said, "Nah. You have a shut-out game." But after some discussion, he finally agreed.

At Waverly's 49-yard line, Jake entered the game at tailback, had his play, called in the huddle, and when the ball was snapped, all 21 players parted ways.

Jake was surprised when he slowly walked through the huge hole. He initially turned around to the original line of scrimmage and saw the offense and defense players pointing and guiding him toward the end zone.

This was not the way they had practiced the play, but when Jake figured it out, he took off. He ran 49 yards to his glory. It took around 10-12 seconds in all, and he was accompanied by the players on both teams. You can imagine the tears and shouts from the bleachers and the impact on Jake Porter.

That day, the game of football became a game, and a person with worth and purpose was validated as valuable.

The game ended with class, decency, and respect. We have some football heroes today who should take notice. In fact, we should all take notice. We were all made in God's image.

"Do nothing out of selfish ambition or vain conceit. Rather, in humility, value others above yourselves, not looking to your own interests but each of you to the interests of the others (Phil.2:3-4).

Ponders of the Heart

Do you wrestle with selfishness, or do you live with someone who wrestles with selfishness?

How can we have spirit-filled attitudes?

Read Philippians 2:1-18.

Prayers of the Heart

Dear Father,

Be our very life and help us with our stubborn wills. Help us walk by Your Spirit, so we will not satisfy the lust of our flesh. Lord, so fill our lives with Your life that our attitudes and actions are transformed by Your power. You are our hope and our treasure. Pour Your life in and through us in such a way that You receive glory and honor. In Jesus' name, amen.

February 7 ~ Costume Jewelry or Tarnished Silver

How is it possible for Christians to live miserable lives? The problem is many Christians see themselves as pieces of costume jewelry instead of tarnished silver. Costume jewelry is essentially worthless metal covered with an attractive coating. Many believers see themselves as sinners through and through, yet covered by the blood of Christ.

Tarnished silver is a truer image of what we are after conversion. While the infinite righteousness of Christ covers us, we're also new creations. Our silver is our new birth in Christ, but we are still bound in a sin-saturated world. Our new nature lives in old earthbound bodies tarnished in sin. The new you is not a sinner. You are a saint who struggles with the presence and effect of sin.

"Therefore, if anyone is in Christ, he is a new creation; old things have passed away; behold, all things have become new" (2 Corinthians 5:17 NKJV).

I'm not sure how God does His works, but faith in God's truths gives us the power to overcome the old ways of living. We accept what God has done for us and who we are by faith. Then, we can walk in the Spirit instead of walking in the ways of this world.

Once we understand and believe who we are, God will give us the power to walk accordingly.

Bob George says, "We have approached the Christian life as a subject to be learned rather than as a life to be lived. "

Christ is our life, and apart from Him, we will end up depending on ourselves to live the Christian life, and that will make us miserable. Only one lived the Christian life, and that was Jesus. The good news is He is willing to do that through us. Praise the Lord!

Ponders of the Heart

Read Romans 8:1-4 and 9-11.

Do these verses enlighten you about who you are in Christ?

How can these truths help you walk in joy?

What a joy to walk not in condemnation but as dearly loved children of God.

Prayers of the Heart

Dear Father,

The depth of Your gospel is beyond words of thanks. Lord, we love You. Thank You for the gift of salvation, justification, and sanctification. Help us appropriate by faith that which You have done for us. Help us believe Your Word regardless of how we feel. In Jesus' name, amen.

February 8 ~ Grandparents

Why is being a grandparent so wonderful? I've heard some say it is because you can love your grandchildren, but you are not responsible for how they turn out. I've also heard it is because they are your second chance to love unconditionally. I don't know why being a grandparent is so wonderful, but it is.

This reminds me of the story of Naomi, the mother-in-law of Ruth. She came home to Bethlehem after the death of her husband and two sons, full of bitterness about her circumstances and bitter toward the Lord.

"But she said to them, 'Do not call me Naomi; call me Mara, for the Almighty has dealt very bitterly with me'" (Ruth 1:20 NKJV).

Naomi's name meant pleasant, but she was not feeling very pleasant. She wanted her name to reflect what she was feeling, so she wanted people to call her Mara, which means bitter. This was a description of how she felt. Naomi had not been comforted by the devotion and the love of Ruth. She was stuck in feeling that God had dealt her an unfair and cruel hand. Naomi could not picture herself as being hopeful or pleasant again.

"The women said to Naomi: 'Praise be to the Lord, who this day has not left you without a kinsman-redeemer. May he become famous throughout Israel! He will renew your life and sustain you in your old age. For your daughter-in-law, who loves you and who is better to you than seven sons, has given him birth.' Then Naomi took the child, laid him in her lap and cared for him" (Ruth 4:14-16 NKJV).

She did hope again. Maybe the lesson of Naomi's life is a lesson for us. As grandparents, we become aware that life is bigger than we are. Life continues despite us, not because of us. Humbling, but really, it is freeing.

God is the provider and sustainer of life. God is bigger than we are, and He has a plan. Knowing God is in control frees us to love differently. There are no strings attached to the one loved or the one doing the loving.

Being a parent is overwhelming, and we take this responsibility and think we must do it on our own. I should have spent more time asking God to raise my children through me and less time trying to do it by myself. Life would have been more pleasant for us all.

There is another message we need to remember, and that is not to critique our children's parenting skills. We need to pray for them, encourage them, and remember that love covers a multitude of sins.

Ponders of the Heart

As a parent or grandparent, what is the best thing you can do for your children or grandchildren?

What changes would be helpful as you parent your children?

Read Philippians 4:4-9.

Prayers of the Heart

Dear Father,

How I praise You for the gift of family and the blessings of loving and caring for others. You take us to the end of ourselves and show us our selfishness. Father, we need Your love to pour through us. Thank You for the love You give and the power of Your Holy Spirit. In Jesus' name, amen.

February 9 ~ Birthmark

Julie, my youngest daughter, had a vascular birthmark when she was born called a hemangioma. It grew from the time she was born until she was about 18 months old. Our doctor told us it would begin to disappear and not to worry. He was right.

By the time she was three, it was completely gone. My little grandson also had a birthmark. In fact, he had three. He had a birthmark on his toe, neck, and his nose.

In one of the *Left Behind* books, Christians are given a spiritual birthmark. This mark is only visible to other Christians. It is the mark of the cross on their foreheads.

Do you think it would be good if, at our conversion, we were given a birthmark? The mark could be a cross on our foreheads or the name Jesus on our hand, saying we are His.

We are marked at the time of our new birth, not with an outward birthmark, but with the Holy Spirit. We can't see Him, but we often experience Him. More importantly, God is the one who can see those who are His. We are sealed and guaranteed a home in heaven because we have the Holy Spirit.

"And you also were included in Christ when you heard the message of truth, the gospel of your salvation. When you believed, you were marked in him with a seal, the promised Holy Spirit, who is a deposit guaranteeing our inheritance until the redemption of those who are God's possession—to the praise of his glory" (Eph.1:13-14).

We are born into this world with a sinful nature. This nature separates us from God. Jesus has made a way for us to be reborn, made new. Our response to His provision will decide our eternal destination. We will either accept His provision for new birth or reject it and remain in our sinfulness.

Which family mark are you wearing today? Remember, the mark of the sinful man can be removed where the mark of Jesus will never fade, rust, or be destroyed.

Ponders of the Heart

Do you struggle to be a person who lives in the power, wisdom, and love of the Spirit?

When people are around you, do they encounter the living Lord?

Read Romans 8:12-17 and Romans 12:1-2.

Prayers of the Heart

Dear Father,

Thank You for our spiritual birthmark, the Holy Spirit. Your seal on us guarantees we will always be Yours. Nothing can ever change that. Teach us to release ourselves to Your power, wisdom, and love. In Jesus' name, amen.

February 10 ~ Bath Time

"Tis so sweet to trust in Jesus, Just to take Him at His word; Just to rest upon His promise, Just to know " Thus saith the Lord." Jesus, Jesus, how I trust Him! How I've proved him o'er and o'er! Jesus, Jesus, precious Jesus! 0 for grace to trust Him more!"

What a great song of faith. Are we experiencing sweet trust in Jesus? Have we fully abandoned ourselves to the goodness of the Lord?"

Our grandson, Collier, loved his bath as a baby. When he was around ten weeks old, I was giving him a bath. I had my hand under his head, and he was having fun. His little eyes were focused on me while he kicked his feet and swung his little arms. He was cooing and jumping all over.

He wasn't afraid I was going to drop him. That thought was far from his mind. He was just enjoying his bath. I thought later about how freeing it is to be so trusting.

In this world, there would come a time when he would develop fears and mistrust, but for now, Collier could just trust the one holding his head above the water.

I asked the Lord to remind me of Collier and his bath the next time I was faced with a major decision.

A picture of me being held by God as I rest in the promise that He has me and I am safe in His care. I often overanalyze life instead of trusting and resting in the Lord. I don't think I am alone in this. Even as Christians, we can trust in things other than the Lord. We will trust in our wealth, power, or something else instead of focusing our eyes on Him.

The Lord has graciously given me a picture of what trust looks like. My hope for us is that we will focus on Jesus the way Collier focused on me. Trusting Him so completely that we are free to kick our feet and lift our arms in overjoying praise.

People will one day fail my grandson in one way or another, but Jesus never will. The song is true, "Tis so sweet to trust in Jesus!"

"But now, this is what the Lord says- he who created you, O Jacob, he who formed you, O Israel: 'Fear not, for I have redeemed you; I have summoned you by name; you are mine. When you pass through the rivers, they will not sweep over you. When you walk through the fire, you will not be burned; the flames will not set you ablaze, For I am the Lord, your God, the Holy One of Israel, your Savior" (Isaiah 43: 1-3 NKJV).

Ponders of the Heart

Read Deut. 31:8, Ps. 27:1-3, Is. 35:4, 2 Tim. 1:7, and 1 John 4:18.

What theme does each of these scriptures have in common?

Are you one who struggles with fear? Trust God's promises.

Prayers of the Heart

Dear Father,

You are so worthy of our love and trust. Open our eyes to Your goodness and our hearts to trust You. Father, the world cannot be trusted. Even our closest relationships disappoint us, but You, Oh Lord, are worthy of trust. Give us the ability to release ourselves completely into Your care. In Jesus' name, amen.

February 11 ~ We Matter to God.

One morning, I received a call from my son, Chris. He said, "Mom, say a prayer for Bud. He had a seizure last night." Bud was Chris' dog that he loved, and we all knew why. My son had years of living by himself, and Bud was his companion. His dog never cared that Chris was not a particularly good housekeeper. He did not worry about what Chris ate or how he spent his time. He was always happy to see his owner. Bud ate what Chris gave him and was never too busy to play. A dog's love is unconditional.

For us, Bud was not such a treasure. He was messy, hairy, smelly, and big. His tail knocked over a few glasses of coke, his paws tracked in plenty of mud, and his barks were loud enough to wake the dead. Bud is not such a prize for others, but we all appreciated the company he was for Chris. They were buddies—a man and his dog.

Wives can learn a little about how to treat their men by seeing a man with his dog. Maybe we need to require less of them and just love them. In requiring less, we might get more. If we were glad to see them when they came home, they might be more anxious to come home. I don't think we need to wag our tails or run around in circles, but you get my drift.

We would be more of a prize if we viewed our husbands as a gift. Our advantage over our husband's pets is we don't have to be messy, hairy, smelly, or "barky." A good scripture to think about is 1 Peter 3:1-4.

"Wives, in the same way, submit yourselves to your own husbands so that, if any of them do not believe the word, they may be won over without words by the behavior of their wives when they see the purity and reverence of your lives. Your beauty should not come from outward adornment, such as elaborate hairstyles and the wearing of gold jewelry or fine clothes. Rather, it should be that of your inner self, the unfading beauty of a gentle and quiet spirit, which is of great worth in God's sight."

Ponders of the Heart

What damaging attitudes have we developed toward our husbands or others in our families?

Are we expecting things from them only God can provide?

Do we honor our husbands and others God has placed in our lives?

Read Ephesians 5:15-21.

Prayers of the Heart

Dear Father,

Thank You for the gift of family. Help us treasure our husbands, children, grandchildren and our friends. Lord, we need people in our lives. Help us to treat them well. We want to glorify You in our marriages, families, and friendships. You are gracious to us, and we praise You for Your mercy. In Jesus' name, amen.

February 12 ~ The Feeling of Freedom

Little babies love to take off their clothes, kick up their heels, and enjoy the feeling of freedom. I have long lost that in my life. Give me sweat clothes, tennis shoes, flannel pajamas, and bedroom slippers. A form of freedom but covered, loose but protected, and hidden, not transparent. I'm okay with that.

Clothes are one thing, but what about our spiritual lives? The Lord has stripped me, leaving me feeling spiritually naked. He has a way of taking us, like one of those plastic writing boards, where He lifts the sheet and zips! We start a new season of life.

I remember being in a counseling school studying the exchanged life. The exchanged life is where Christ gave us His righteousness, took our sins and nailed them to the cross.

During this time, God wanted me to feel naked. He did not want me to go on with past knowledge. The Lord had new revelations for me to discover. I felt like a grown-up who had been stripped, and I wanted someone to give me back my sweat clothes. I had issues He wanted me to face and understand. So, God took me on a journey of discovery and revelation of His Word.

God is always right, and there are times we must be stripped of things that hinder us from freely receiving His best. If we depend on what we already know and stop reaching to know and discover more about Him, He will shake us up for our sake. He wants us to grow, soar, and love.

In this setting, He had me put away my old Bible, and I used a new one. It was a different translation with none of my verses underlined. God wanted me to learn new things about Him and have new insight into the Word. My old brain was learning, and it was so refreshing.

"Now to him who is able to do immeasurably more than all we ask or imagine, according to his power that is at work within us, to him be glory in the church and in Christ Jesus throughout all generations, for ever and ever! Amen" (Ephesians 3:20-21).

Ponders of the Heart

Can you think of a time when God stripped you?

Has there been a time when God made you look at what you believed about Him?

Read Joshua 1:9, Acts 9:10-16, and Acts 11:15-18.

The Lord wants us to grow in our relationship with Him, and sometimes that means that we need to let go of familiar things so we can experience fresh new thing about Him.

Prayers of the Heart

Dear Father,

We will be strong and courageous. We will not be terrified or discouraged, for You are our God, and You promise You will be with us wherever we go. Take us, Lord, and teach us great and mighty things we do not know. In Jesus' name, amen.

February 13 ~ Twister of Life

Years ago, a movie with Helen Hunt was about people who spent their time chasing weather conditions that could produce tornadoes. In this movie, Helen Hunt and her co-star found themselves living their dream. They were chasing a class five tornado.

It was destroying everything in its path, and they were running for dear life. They ran into a small building for safety, where they found thick pipes that ran deep into the ground. They quickly tied themselves to the pipes, and they wrapped the ropes again and again around their waist.

When the tornado hits, they are secure. The building is destroyed around them as the wind takes their bodies; they fly up into the sky. The ropes hold them tight, and they let go and watch the powerful fury of the twister. They find themselves awestruck and enjoying the awesomeness of a tornado firsthand.

I want to place myself in this movie. First, I doubt I would ever be in a car chasing a tornado, but if I happened to be in a place where there was one, I would not be happy. I would probably fall to the ground and say," I give up. That's it!" Now, if my co-star, my husband, picked me up and carried me to the building, he would still have to tie the ropes around my waist and tie me to the pipes. I would be screaming and whimpering and being of no use whatsoever.

Let's suppose my dear Bill did all that for me, and the tornado came and ripped the building away. I would be holding on to those pipes for dear life. If the wind was strong enough to peel my legs and arms free, I assure you I would have my eyes closed so tight that I would miss the whole thing. Fear would keep me from ever experiencing this phenomenon.

This has happened to me in my life with Christ. He has been trying to get me to let go of control since He tied me ever so tightly to Himself. You see, I am secure. He has me and will never let me go. I am firmly planted deeply in heaven with Him.

But when the wind of life chases me, and the fear of life overtakes me, I too often close my eyes and miss the awesome power of God in my life.

He has plans that were designed for me, but if I close my eyes, I miss what He wants to show me: His beauty and power. I sometimes let go just to grab hold again. Opening my eyes just to close them again.

I know God is spending my life teaching me to trust the One I am tied to. He is teaching me He is faithful, and I can trust Him.

Ponders of the Heart

What fears keep you from enjoying and trusting God?

Ask God to help you understand the truths in these verses.

Read Romans 5:3-5, Romans 8:37-39, and John 10:10.

Thank God that He wants to give you more out of life. He wants to give you an abundant life.

Prayers of the Heart

Dear Father,

Teach us to trust You. Help us open our eyes and see and experience the wonder of You as we experience all You have for us. Lord, help us not miss the plan You have for each of our lives. In Jesus' name, amen.

February 14 ~ Transforming Hearts

In 2 Kings 4, we read the story of Elisha and the Shunammite woman. This woman serves Elisha with food and shelter, and he tells her that she is going to have a son. This was a dream she had long put aside.

The son is born, but one day, he gets sick and dies. The Shunammite woman summons Elisha, and when he comes into the house, the son is lying dead on his bed; the prophet goes in and shuts the door. He lies down on the boy, and the Bible says he put his mouth to the boy's mouth, his eyes to the boy's eyes, and his hands on the boy's hands.

The boy grew warm. Elisha walked around the room and again lay down on the boy; the boy sneezed seven times and opened his eyes. What a remarkable story. Death became life as life touched death.

That's what happens when Christ gives life to our dead spirits. He is the source of all life and purifies us from our sins. Psalm 37:4 promises a change in the desires of our hearts if we delight ourselves in the Lord.

God works with the desires of our hearts, like how Elisha brought life to the boy in 2 Kings. He places His good heart over our sinful ones and gives us new hearts with new desires. He takes compassion, mercy, true things, and pure things and transfers them into our souls.

At the time of salvation, we are given eternal life, and from that day forward, He begins to transform us into the image of His Son. We now have hope where there was hopelessness and truth where there were lies. Our responsibility is to open our lives up to this great exchange.

Ponders of the Heart

Do you know that Christ has given you a new heart?

Are you trying to earn His gift of salvation, or have you received His salvation?

Read Isaiah 53:6, Ezekiel 36:25-27, and 2 Corinthians 5:21.

Prayers of the Heart

Precious Lord,

There is nothing You need, and yet You chose to love us. We cannot earn Your favor, but You give it. Lord, how precious is the knowledge of You? How wonderful is the goodness and compassion of Your love? Help us walk in the power and light of Your Spirit. In Jesus' name, amen.

February 15 ~ Routines and Freedom

Even though holidays are a break from our normal routine, they can be very demanding and trying. One task or activity leads to another, and this is how we live our lives.

When all my children were home, I never stopped. I was constantly on the go, and it was difficult for me to stop in the middle of a task. This made me miss opportunities to listen to my children.

Children come to us on their timetable, not ours.

I once heard a definition of freedom which said freedom is the ability to start and stop. If this is true, I was not free but enslaved by things a mom had to do. I wish this was all different now, but it is not. I still can be enslaved to activities. How about you?

"Then Jesus said to those Jews who believed Him, 'If you abide in My Word, you are my disciples indeed. And you shall know the truth, and the truth shall set you free. Therefore if the Son makes you free you shall be free indeed" (John 8:31-32,36 NKJV).

In this passage, Christ is talking about the freedom from sin. He is the one who has freed us from the penalty and the power of sin. The penalty is our justification, and the power over sin is ours as we depend on the power of the Holy Spirit inside of us.

These truths can set us free from the things that enslave us.

Our drive for activities over relationships, our desire for more over what we have, and the drive for power over peace have a root cause. The root cause is our shame-based identity. Christ came to take that away from us.

We are acceptable because of what Christ did on the cross. We are free from God's wrath, and we are children because of our union with Christ.

Read the lyrics to the song by Catesby Paget written in 1890, "Mind in Perfect Peace With God".

So nigh, so very nigh to God,

I cannot nearer be;

For in the person of His Son,

I am as near as He.

So dear, so very dear to God,

More dear I cannot be;

The love wherewith He loves the Son,

Such is His love to me.

Let your soul drink in these lyrics until your life soars.

Ponders of the Heart

What are some things that enslave you?

Read Ephesians 1:3-6, Colossians 1:12, Colossians 1:21- 22, Romans 8:38-39, Psalm 139:1-6, and 1 John 3:1.

When you read these verses, do they give you hope? Why?

Prayers of the Heart

Dear Father,

You have set us free by the gift of Your Son and the truths of Your Word. Give us the power and the will to walk in Your freedom. Break the chains of activities, worry, and shame. Let us, Your children, walk in confidence of Your acceptance and Your love. In Jesus' name, amen.

February 16 ~ Forgiveness so Necessary

Years ago, I was hanging wallpaper in the hall of our house. My youngest daughter, Julie, was a toddler at the time, and she made a special game out of this job. She thought it would be fun to run down our "L" shaped hall and jump on my back.

I hung sheets of wallpaper up and down the hall for hours, carrying Julie on my back. My exhaustion was overwhelming. The things a mom with small children can do. You and I both know this job would have been much easier if Julie had stayed off my back and on the floor.

That is the picture of what unforgiveness does in the heart of a Christian. You might as well tie the person on your back and carry them around with you wherever you go.

Unforgiveness weighs us down and robs us of joy, freedom, and peace. The posture of unforgiveness bends our backs, lowers our eyes, and the face of our Savior is lost from view.

There have been times when I was weighed down with unforgiveness. Holding on tight to a grudge that kept me from living a joyful life. I have found life is too short and important to waste with unforgiveness.

Forgiveness can be hard, but unforgiveness is much worse. We can lay our hurt down at His feet and be done with it. We are commanded to forgive, but if we think about how we have been forgiven, our hearts will let go of the bitterness that has taken root.

Keeping our eyes on Jesus is the motivation to let go and forgive. We do not have to do this alone. He will help us. As we fix our eyes on things above we can rest because God is on His throne and is worthy of our praise.

"I lift up my eyes to the mountains—where does my help come from? My help comes from the Lord, the Maker of heaven and earth. He will not let your foot slip—he who watches over you will not slumber; indeed, he who watches over Israel will neither slumber nor sleep" (Psalm 104:5).

Ponders of the Heart

Is there unforgiveness in your heart?

Are you ready to take it to the Lord and let it go?

Read Matthew 6:12, Colossians 3:13, and Ephesians 4:32.

Prayers of the Heart

Dear Father,

Show us any unforgiveness that is weighing us down. Fill our souls with the desire and the power to forgive. Father, we thank You for forgiving us and giving us freedom and peace. In Jesus' name, amen.

February 17 ~ Moments

"Why, you do not even know what will happen tomorrow. What is your life? You are a mist that appears for a little while and then vanishes" (James 4:14).

Even children seem to know how short life is. "Don't go to work, Daddy," they beg. "Stay home with me today." But adults, thinking they know what is important, go away for another day in business. The child grows, and childhood vanishes.

Life is made up of moments, and each one might not seem like much, but they make up our lives. There was the moment we entered this world and one when we will leave.

There are defining moments in my life. There was one when I was born. Which I don't remember, but I remember the moment I fell in love with my husband. We had dated before, and I had broken it off for some crazy reason. There had been months of not seeing each other, and then he called. He wanted to come to see me because he had heard I had been in the hospital.

When he arrived at my house that afternoon, I opened the door and fell in love. I still see him standing there in a navy blue Tee shirt with a Fellowship of Christian Athletes emblem on the front. He was so handsome; he took my breath away, and I have loved him ever since. That was a defining moment.

Then, there was the first time I held my firstborn son. That moment has changed every minute of my life since then.

I can still recall the first time I saw the deep blue sea. The ocean from the water's edge is one color, but the color of the water in the middle of the ocean is so rich and blue that I could not get over it. Living in Florida for most of my childhood, I was overwhelmed the first time I saw the mountains and experienced fall.

What about seeing snow and puppies? Our lives are made up of many "firsts," and we hold them in our memories.

One of my most treasured moments was the birth of my first grandchild. I had been with Tracie all through the labor. We pushed and panted and did everything except stand on our heads, but she had to have a c-section. I had to leave and wait in the waiting room with all the others.

Ryan brought his son, who was wrapped in a blanket, and showed us Collier. My son-in-law held his baby boy up to the window beside his face. Collier looked like a miniature Ryan. There was no way to hold back the tears. That was a "grand" moment.

Minutes that define us are not easy, but they are all necessary. We don't always understand why, but if our God is in control, He will use even the hard moments.

Like the moment I heard my dad had cancer and when he took his last breath, I was there for both. There were defining times between the news of cancer and his last breath. Some will be in my mind forever. They are both bitter and sweet.

Galatians 4:4-5 tells us of a moment that defines history.

"But when the set time had fully come, God sent his Son, born of a woman, born under the law, to redeem those under the law, that we might receive adoption to sonship."

That is one to show us why we exist.

For me, it was not the moment I became a wife, a mother, or a grandmother. No. Although those are important and wonderful, the one that defines me is the day I became a child of God.

Jesus, God's Son, made it possible for us to join His family because He came to earth and experienced time and space just like we do. His moments were planned so we could be redeemed. His perfect life offers us adoption, and this is ours because of the moments Christ lived, died, and was resurrected. The fullness of our adoption was complete in a moment, but the full benefit of our adoption is yet to come.

Ponders of the Heart

What are some defining moments in your life?

When was the moment you became a child of God?

Read 2 Corinthians 4:17 and 1 Corinthians 15:52.

God is putting the moments of our lives together for us so we might receive an eternal weight of glory.

Prayers of the Heart

Dear Father,

You are our guide and redeemer. You are our very great reward and the lover of our souls. Father, we love You, and we long to love You more. You are worthy of our Praise. Lord, we wait expectantly for the moment, the twinkling of an eye, when we will see You face to face. In Jesus' name, amen.

February 18 ~ Predestined

Are we predestined for salvation? What a loaded question. Being predestined for salvation has caused division many times in the body of Christ.

I have an opinion about that, and it has changed over the years. Not all my brothers and sisters in Christ agree with my opinion. The truth is that God's Word teaches that if we belong to Christ, we are predestined to conform to His image.

The Lord promises that He will complete His work in us. Read Romans 8:29. What wonderful encouragement to know He is and will conform us to the image of His Son.

God's mysteries are best handled with grace. We just can't understand the free will of man and the sovereignty of God and how they work together. That is just too much for us. I don't even understand how electricity or telephones work.

We can only go to our heavenly Father and ask Him to reveal what we need to understand. It will probably take all of eternity to understand and then some. The Bible teaches both. Am I chosen? Yes. Do I have free will? Yes. How do those two things work together? I don't know, but I know the One who knows.

We understand God is good, gracious, and merciful. Whatever and however He does things, they are perfect.

God can use our different views to challenge us to go back to Him and His Word. We won't always get the right answer, but we can experience the comfort of His presence and His peace. He gently reminds us He is the great "I am," not me or anyone else. That is a great relief and comfort for our souls.

"For now we see in a mirror, dimly, but then face to face. Now I know in part, but then I shall know just as I am known" (1 Cor.13:12 NKJV).

Ponders of the Heart

Have you disagreed with someone about their teaching of God's Word?

Are you judging or being self-righteous over the disagreement?

Read 1 Peter 3:15, 1 Peter 1:22, and 1 Peter 2:1-3.

God wants us to express our faith but with the right heart and spirit.

Prayers of the Heart

Dear Father,

Walking in spiritual pride instead of humble dependency on You is so easy. Forgive us when we are puffed up with spiritual pride. When we have the privilege of talking to someone about You and what we believe, please fill us with Your Spirit so our words are Your words, and our hearts reflect Your heart. Precious Lord, forgive us for boasting unless we boast of You. In Jesus' name, amen.

February 19 ~ The Emotion Fear

We all have fears. When I was a young girl, we lived near railroad tracks, and it was not unusual for hobos to get off the trains. We were told to be careful and never let a hobo in the house.

One day, I was alone in the house when a badly beaten man was at the door. My immediate thought was he was a hobo, and I was terrified. Fear clutched my heart as I ran to the bathroom and locked the door. After a moment, I heard my name, and the man ended up being my uncle, but it scared me just the same.

There is another fear I experienced as a young girl, and it was the fear of death. I can remember getting up in the middle of the night, convinced I was at death's door. I knew if I did, I was not ready to meet God.

I would promise to act better, and the next day, I would try so hard to be kind, sweet, and helpful. I always failed as I worked to keep my promise. Fear again would grip my heart. Do you know who gave me this fear? God did. He wanted me to begin to understand that I need a provision for my sin. The song "Amazing Grace" has a line that addresses this very thing:

"T'was Grace that taught my heart to fear."

This was what I was feeling. God, in His mercy, brought someone into my life to share that Jesus was the provision for my sin. He was the one who paid the price and would forgive, cleanse, and give me eternal life.

Jesus would robe me in righteousness so I could stand before a righteous judge. I knelt in my living room and accepted God's provision for my sin and His for new life. The first thing the Lord did was fill the void in my heart, and He took away my fear. The song "Amazing Grace" also says:

"And Grace, my fears relieved."

That is what grace can do. It relieves fear. God promises in His Word that He is not a spirit of fear (2 Timothy 1:7), and we don't receive a spirit of fear, but a spirit of sonship (Romans 8:15). He also says perfect love casts out fear, and God is love (1 John). His grace is wonderful.

Ponders of the Heart

What are you fearing today?

Do you need courage?

Read 2 Tim. 1:7, Romans 8:15 for courage, and Eph. 2:8-10 to drink in the wonder of His grace.

Ask God to provide the strength and the courage you need today.

Prayers of the Heart:

Dear Father,

Thank you for the provision of Jesus. Thank You, Lord, that by His blood we are cleansed. Thank You that by Jesus' righteousness, we are made righteous. Fill us with Your Spirit so we can walk free of fear and full of life. In Jesus' name, amen.

February 20 ~ Let's Dance.

I often think of and miss my dad. He has golden skin and high cheekbones, and when he smiled, his eyes would disappear. One thing he loved that made him smile was music and dancing. He was a fantastic dancer. My dad taught me the foxtrot, tango, cha-cha-cha, and the bunny hop.

In dancing, the man is the leader. He puts his hand on the small of the woman's back, and with pressure from his hand, he leads. There are principles in dancing that are important. Only one can lead, and the other must follow. If you both try to lead, then toe stomping occurs.

When Dad taught me a new dance, his hand was very commanding, but as I yielded and began to understand where he was leading, his hand would relax and become gentle. Then we could relax and enjoy the music and the dancing.

When Christ comes into our lives, we must learn to follow. There can only be one leader, or again, there will be toe-stomping. Christ's position is that of the Lord, and He knows the steps you and I need to take.

We need to let Him lead, and we need to yield to His control. Life will become more joyful that way. I did not say easy.

If I could dance with anyone, it would not be Gene Kelly or Fred Astaire; it would be my dad. I would love to dance with my dad one more time. He was a great dancer, teacher, and leader who enjoyed teaching and dancing with me.

Christ, even more, has chosen us to be His. He wants to lead us and guide our lives with His wisdom and power.

He is the great I Am and the source of true life. When we submit to the King of kings, we will move through life with His hand on our backs. I thank my dad for teaching me the principles of dancing so I can dance through life with my Jesus.

Ponders of the Heart

Have you accepted God's gift of salvation?

If so, are you now trying to live the Christian life on your own?

Read John 5:15, John 14:26-27, and John 16:12-15.

The Holy Spirit empowers us to live the Christian life. He is with us. We are not alone.

Prayers of the Heart

Dear Father,

Teach us to yield and not to lead. Teach us to feel and respond to the leadership of the Holy Spirit. Father, thank You that we don't have to live this life apart from You. Thank You for providing the Holy Spirit for this dance called life. In Jesus' name, amen.

February 21 ~ Seeking Position

My husband, Bill, isn't crazy about family reunions. I teased him about drawing a circle around himself and deciding, "I'm not moving from this spot." Of course, it doesn't matter; before long, everyone moves to his circle. He is a likable person, and others feel comfortable when they are with him.

My youngest daughter is a person little children are attracted to. She can walk into a store and have them wave at her. She doesn't seek their attention; it just happens. The best explanation I have is that is how God has gifted her and her dad.

We all know people who seek position, power, and recognition. It is true in our day, and it was true in Jesus' day.

In Matthew 20:20-28, a story is told about a mother coming to Jesus seeking a position for her sons. She wanted her boys to sit on the right and left of Jesus' throne when His kingdom came. The sons, James and John, would indeed be very important to His kingdom, but she didn't understand the Kingdom of God.

She is thinking as we might think. We want God to use us in His kingdom, but that must mean we will be rich, comfortable, popular, and blessed with earthly blessings.

Worldly blessings don't always look the same as God's.

Jesus said in Matthew 23:11-12, "The greatest among you will be your servant. For whoever exalts himself will be humbled, and whoever humbles himself will be exalted."

James would be killed for his faith, and John would be imprisoned for his. Jesus knew the price they would pay, and He would equip them for it.

Would the cost be worth it? Yes, it would. They would be kingdom builders. They would live with Him forever, but the road would be hard. They would need to give up superficial living for the supernatural.

There are lessons to learn from this and much to consider. Some people worship Jesus because they know who He is, and they just want His blessings. Others want their children blessed for a superficial life, while others want their children to bring glory to God, knowing it could mean hardships and sacrifice.

We might say we want to follow our Lord, but it is another thing to be ready. Finding our purpose and calling is what we need to seek.

Ponders of the Heart

Have you had to pay a cost to follow Jesus?

What have been the rewards and blessings of following Him?

Read 2 Corinthians 11:24-28, Ephesians 1:3-5, and Phil.1:6.

Prayers of the Heart

Dear Father,

Give us kingdom hearts and kingdom eyes. We want to live supernatural lives, but we do not know how; show us Yourself in the middle of this crazy, busy world. Use us and cover us with Your mercy and grace. In Jesus' name, amen.

February 22 ~ If

"Whoever finds their life will lose it, and whoever loses their life for my sake will find it" (Matthew 10:39).

The poem "If" by Rudyard Kipling has a line that reads, "If you can choose to lose when you could win." I have thought about that line. That is kingdom thinking over worldly thinking. In this world, everyone wants to win, be first, and be the best. This hits me because my family is extremely competitive. We play to win.

Julie, my youngest daughter, used to get so mad when she played the game Uno. My dad would lose to her on purpose, and he enjoyed every minute of it. He would choose to lose when he could win.

What a witness that was for me. Winning is not more important than people. It is a lesson I still need to work on. One thing that helps me is to remember when I win someone loses.

There were so many episodes of *The Andy Griffin Show* in which Andy would choose to make Barney look good when everyone else wanted to make fun of Barney. Why do we naturally do that? Maybe by seeing someone lose, we feel more like winners.

Jesus, the King of kings, came to earth as a man. He made Himself subject to time and space. He chose to die on a cross so we could win. Because the Spirit of Christ lives in us, we can choose to love when we want to hate. Choose to praise when we could complain. We can choose to submit when we want to rule. Christ has made us winners, so we don't have to try so hard to be one.

Losing ourselves to Jesus is what makes us winners in life. We find our victory in Him.

Ponders of the Heart

Do you know you are chosen and dearly loved?

We are called to be thankful. What are you the most thankful for today?

Read Colossians 3:12-17 and Galatians 5:16.

Prayers of the Heart

Dear Father,

Take our shame-based identity and replace it with the gift of belonging. Take away any need or wish to feel superior. Lord, to be first in Your kingdom is to serve. Father, we praise You for the gift of acceptance. Teach us to treasure others and honor them above ourselves. In Jesus' name, amen.

February 23 ~ Jars of Clay

"For we do not preach ourselves, but Jesus Christ as Lord, and ourselves as your servants for Jesus' sake. For God, who said, 'Let light shine out of darkness.' Made his light shine in our hearts to give us the light of the knowledge of the glory of God in the face of Christ. But we have this treasure in jars of clay to show that this all-surpassing power is from God and not from us" (2 Corinthians 4:5-7 NKJV).

2 Corinthians reminds us that the Holy Spirit is a treasure. We are not special in ourselves, but it is God who has placed His glory in us for us to treasure.

This teaching keeps my spiritual nose in place. When I wake up and feel as if I am something- God reminds me, "Apart from Me, you can do nothing." When I wake up and say, "Oh, Lord, not me, please not me." He reminds me, "I will equip you." It isn't the container but the power inside that will do the job.

There is an illustration I once read in a book about clay jars. These jars were used to carry water from the well up to the master's house. One jar was so sad, and the servant asked, "Why are you so sad?" The jar replied, "It is because I'm cracked, and every day when you take me down to the well and fill me up on the way back, the crack leaks half the water before I ever get to the Master's house. I want to be pleasing to my master. I need to be fixed."

The servant took the jar and took him down to the well. He said, "Look up along the path leading to the master's house. What do you see?" The jar said, "I see beautiful flowers on one side of the path but not on the other."

"Our master had a plan," the servant said, "He had me plant those seeds along the right of the road. Every day, when I take you down to the well, I always carry you up the right side. He knows that you will water the seeds, making the countryside beautiful, and I will carry you home to your master."

What a wonderful illustration to let us know that God uses ordinary people to carry out His plans. He doesn't need extraordinary people when He resides in us. In fact, He receives glory when He works through our weakness and our brokenness.

Aren't you thankful that no matter who we are in this world, He can use us? I know that is true in my experience. When I look back over my life, I see His grace and mercy. Jesus has equipped me to do things I never would have dreamed possible.

Ponders of the Heart

We are all broken jars, but do you know God wants to use you?

What patterns of this world do you need to let go of?

Read Romans 12:1-6.

Prayers of the Heart

Dear Father,

We give ourselves to You, broken and cracked. Lord, use us by Your mighty power. Transform our thinking about who we are and look to You for our identity. You can use us despite our weaknesses. How we thank You for using ordinary people to be involved in Your supernatural work. Lord, we love You. In Jesus' name, amen.

February 24 ~ The Bread of Life

In our on-the-go world, junk food and fast food take the place of balanced meals.

I, on occasion, run out of time or energy before a balanced meal is prepared. My husband is not a fussy eater and does not complain if I take the easy way out. If I'm not careful, we eat unhealthy food and too many snacks. We lose our appetite for healthy meals, and our bodies begin to show it.

In Exodus 16, the Israelite community was introduced to manna, which translates as "What is it." God fed the Israelite people with manna each day. The food God provided lasted one day, except on the day before the Sabbath, they collected for two days, and it lasted.

Jesus tells us He is the true manna, the Bread of Life. How well are we collecting our daily portion of spiritual food?

Spiritual food, like the manna of Moses' day, only lasts one day at a time. When we try to go without His Word, we become weak, for only Christ satisfies the deep spiritual hunger in us.

After a healthy meal, our bodies are refreshed, and we are reminded of our need for nutritious food.

This is also true for our Spiritual health. After a feast on God's Word, our spirits feel the satisfaction that only He can bring. Putting ourselves on a healthy diet of God's Word refreshes our souls, and it is especially wonderful to find a good company to feast with.

Conversation over God's Word is the best fellowship we can ever find.

"And Jesus said to them, 'I am the bread of life. He who comes to Me shall never hunger, and he who believes in Me shall never thirst'" (John 6:35 NKJV).

Ponders of the Heart

What is your spirit feasting on today?

Have you found others to fellowship with as you study God's Word?

Read Philippians 4:8-9 and 1 Thessalonians 5:16-24.

I am somewhat of an introvert, but I realize I need others to walk a meaningful Christian life. We were made for the community.

Prayers of the Heart

Dear Father,

We thank You for giving us spiritual appetites. Let us meditate on the wonders of Your love and ponder on Your Word. Thank You for promising that You will complete Your work in us. Father, You are so faithful. We look upon Your beautiful face, and we marvel at Your love for us. In Jesus' name, amen.

February 25 ~Spiritual Awakening

Will we ever experience a spiritual awakening that brings us back to resting, depending, and having faith in the God we worship each Sunday across this land?

Many of us felt the horror of September 11, 2001. The visions of that day and the days that followed will forever bring tears to our eyes and a lump in our throats.

Never shall we forget the words of our President, our congress singing "God Bless America" on the capital building steps, or the open, unashamed call out to the Lord. We were united in purpose.

When we think of a spiritual awakening, we often focus on people and circumstances in the world. But change must begin in the heart for transformation to happen.

There is a story I read, and I do not remember the name of the man, but the message of the story is one I will never forget.

The man was a moral Englishman. He was swimming in a river when he saw a woman across the river coming to bathe. Even though this man had been faithfully married for years, he felt lust rise in his heart for this woman.

He decided he would swim across the river and proposition this poor woman and satisfy his lust. Part of him screaming out no, but he swam to the other side.

He had never felt such lust rise in his heart as he approached the woman. As she turned to face him, he saw she had leprosy. Her eyes were sunk deep into her head; her nose and fingers had been eaten by the disease.

His lust turned to horror, and a gut-wrenching sickness overcame him.

At that moment, as he looked at the woman, repudiated by her looks, he saw his own despicable heart. He knew he was full of evil and saw his need for a heart transformation. It was that day he experienced a spiritual awakening.

"Then I will sprinkle clean water on you, and you shall be clean; I will cleanse you from all your filthiness and from all your idols. I will give you a new heart and put a new spirit within you; I will take the heart of stone

and give you a heart of flesh. I will put my Spirit within you and cause you to walk in My statutes, and you will keep My judgments and do them" (Ezekiel 36:25-27 NKJV).

Ponders of the Heart

Read Ezekiel 36:25-27. Which "I Will" gives you hope?

How hard is it for you to remember these precious promises of God?

Read Hebrews 11:1-2, 2 Timothy 1:12, and 1 John 4:4.

Prayers of the Heart:

Dear Father,

We pray for those who do not know You. Lord, reveal to them their need for transforming grace. Help us all draw near to Your life-giving love. Father, we love and praise You. In Jesus' name, amen.

February 26 ~ Gratefulness

There are various kinds of hearts. There are broken hearts, hard, angry, evil, prideful, and tender hearts, but I have found few grateful ones. What is it that makes a heart grateful?

What are we usually grateful for? We are generally thankful for our families, friends, jobs, our money, and health. But does that give us a grateful heart? I'm not talking about the kind of grateful heart that changes when circumstances change, but the kind of heart that abides in peace and joy.

I met a gentleman about 80 years old with a gracious spirit. His joy was not in his youth; that was gone, as well as his hearing. But when he began to share his heart, it was full of thankfulness.

His life was free of worry and busyness. He enjoyed life. His hand was open to God. He didn't want to be in charge or compete with others. Being the smartest, fastest, and strongest was not his goal.

He was depending on God for all he needed, and this made him grateful.

When I visited Hospice in LaGrange, Georgia, I met grateful hearts. I know that sounds strange, but it is true. I found that the people there were grateful. It was the simple good things in life that made them thankful.

They were overjoyed when they saw a bird in a nest, flowers blooming, and a tomato plant growing. Life had become precious; time with family was the most valuable thing of all. Selfishness had turned to selflessness. Heroes were born.

Every moment counted. Every precious second.

Does accepting death make living possible, even to the point that your heart becomes grateful? Can only the old, wise and dying have grateful hearts?

My heart can be full of selfishness, that there is no room for gratefulness. A great exchange is needed. The secret is in letting go of myself and setting my heart free by trusting God. Believing in His promises and goodness.

Trusting like a child trusts their father. Seeking Him over seeking things. Loving life and people instead of trying to conquer them. We need a value exchange system. These passages say:

"Jesus replied, 'Love the Lord your God with all your heart and with all your soul and with all of your mind. This is the first and greatest commandment'" (Matthew 22:37-38).

"Whoever finds their life will lose it, and whoever loses their life for my sake will find it" (Matthew 10:39).

Ah! That could be the great exchange we are looking for. Grateful hearts are found by losing our hearts to the One who made us for Himself.

Ponders of the Heart

Who do you know that lives a life of thankfulness?

When was the last time you were grateful to God?

Did you bow your head, lift your arms to heaven, shout thank you, or do a happy dance?

Read Psalm 3:1-4 and Psalm 100.

Prayers of the Heart

Dear Gracious Father and Lord,

We praise You for Your great, wonderful love. We praise You for loving us, for saving us, and for giving us new life. Lord, we want to walk with You this day and every day. Father, let our hearts rejoice with gratefulness as we praise You with all our hearts. In Jesus' name, amen.

February 27 ~ The Price of the Kingdom

Julie, my daughter, called me in a panic. "Mom, I have lost the diamond out of my engagement ring. It is gone. What am I going to do?" I told her, "Don't panic; Dad and I will come help you look." We did, but we could not find the diamond.

Ryan, our son-in-law, had insured the ring, so a new diamond replaced the lost one. It worked out fine, but it was traumatic for Julie. She had lost something that was precious, and even though she had a new diamond, she had lost a valuable treasure. It was a gift from Ryan, and she felt she had been careless.

Julie has now moved from that townhouse; what a surprise it would be if someone found her diamond. They would think it was their lucky day because they found a hidden treasure.

Jesus tells a parable in Matthew 13 about finding a hidden treasure.

"The Kingdom of heaven is like treasure hidden in a field. When a man found it, he hid it again and then in his joy went and sold all he had and bought that field" (Matt. 13:44).

Just imagine this man working on a leased field. Hard labor, toiling day after day with no advancement in sight, just laboring for the essentials, nothing for tomorrow, just enough for the day. There is no hope or joy in a life like that. It is hard to find purpose when life seems hopeless.

One day, as he is working, his shovel hits something. He thinks he has hit another rock. He has removed thousands of rocks from the soil. Working hard, he removes a chest from the ground. When he looks inside, he finds a hidden treasure. He realizes this treasure would be his if the land belonged to him. He goes and sells all he has and buys the land.

We are left pondering the meaning of the parable. There is a Christian song entitled "He's Everything to Me." Is God everything to us?

I believe the secret of this life is found when we realize we are everything to Him. When we recognize He liquidated heaven to purchase us. Jesus left the riches of heaven to pay for our sins on the cross.

It was His blood God took in our place. We are God's treasured possession, and the price was the death of His own Son. Could there be a richer gift in all the world than this?

Once we realize what we mean to God, we can begin to realize how He can be everything to us. He loved us first, and His love is eternal. He is the author and the perfecter of our faith. When He looks at us, God sees us as treasures to be bought with the riches of heaven, Our Jesus.

Ponders of the Heart

Do you think of yourself as a treasure and a royal priesthood?

If you can imagine yourself in this way, how does it change your heart toward God?

Read 1 Peter 2:9-10.

Meditate on these truths and let them change your attitude about yourself and your attitude toward others.

Prayers of the Heart

Oh, Father,

Help us to remember that we do not deserve Your grace, but You call us worthy by faith in Your Holy Son. Teach us to love as You love and seek You every day. Thank You, Father, for loving us so. In Jesus' name, amen.

February 28 ~ Prayers of the Heart

"The Lord himself goes before you and will be with you; he will never leave you nor forsake you. Do not be afraid; do not be discouraged" (Deut. 31:8).

Dear Father,

What a promise for us today as we come to praise You. Lord, we always need to hear You say You are with us, and You will never leave us. O, but Lord, this verse tells us that You go before us. You know what will happen tomorrow, and You are already there waiting for us. How that gives us strength to face the unknown with courage. Thank You, our Father and Lord.

"The Lord our God will circumcise your hearts and the hearts of your descendants, so that you may love him with all your heart and with all your soul and live" (Deuteronomy 30:6).

Lord, Thank You for another promise from Your Word. How we pray for our hearts to be circumcised by You. We want to give you deep, rich love, and we thank You for loving us. Father, we also pray that our children and their children will know You, love You and have their hearts set apart for You. All for Your glory. Please hear our prayer. You are our Master, and You are our joy! We praise and honor You with all our hearts. In Jesus' name, amen.

march

— 66 —

And God is able to bless you abundantly, so that in all things at all times, having all that you need, you will abound in every good work.

2 Corinthians 9:8

March 1 ~ A New Disposition

My father-in-law tried for years to talk me into liking oysters. I tried them raw, steamed, and fried. I didn't like them, but because I loved my father-in-law, I would smother them with hot sauce and ketchup and gulp them down on crackers. No matter how hard I tried, I couldn't stand the taste or the texture.

The only conceivable plan that could change my dislike for oysters is a tongue transplant. That would do it if I could have an oyster lover's tongue given to me. Then, my new oyster-loving taste buds would rejoice at the chance of eating them. It would be a "get to" instead of a "had to."

When we become believers, something similar happens. God takes out our old disposition toward Him and places within us a new disposition:

"I will give them an undivided heart and put a new spirit in them; I will remove from them their heart of stone and give them a heart of flesh. Then they will follow my decrees and be careful to keep my laws. They will be my people, and I will be their God" (Ezekiel 11:19-20).

At birth, our disposition toward God was not indifferent but hostile. His ways are burdensome to us, and we do not understand Him or His people. For us to come to Him, we need a heart transplant that changes how we feel about God.

Faith in Jesus, our Savior, cleanses us from sins and gives us a taste for things of the Spirit. Things like reading God's Word, praying and worship music. At the core of our being, we want, even hunger for spiritual things. The people we used to call "Jesus freaks" we now love with a new heart and attitude.

Don't panic if your inclinations and dispositions fail you in your actions. That happens to us all, but we begin a journey toward Him and the things of the Spirit. Oswald Sanders writes,

"We must take it by faith. The moment we believe in God's promises and act upon them, we will find them true in our experience."

God brings change in our lives as we accept by faith that we are new in Him. He has given us faith to do that, and it is His job to carry out His work in us. When we walk in the Spirit, we discover we have a taste for the things of God.

Ponders of the Heart

Read Psalm 1 and Ephesians 3:14-19.

According to Psalm 1, how are we blessed as believers?

Did the prayer in Ephesians comfort you? How?

Prayers of the Heart

Dear Father,

Thank You that our salvation continues to grow. You have completely saved us. Thank You, Father, that inch by inch, glory to glory, You are transforming our "have to" to "get to." Be the real reality of our lives. We love You, Lord. In Jesus' name, amen.

March 2 ~ Spiritual Discipline vs. Spiritual Indulgence

"I have been crucified with Christ and I no longer live, but Christ lives in me. The life I now live in the body, I live by faith in the Son of God, who loved me and gave himself for me" (Galatians 2:20).

We know eating right and exercising are good things but knowing and doing are two different things. Disciplining to exercise every day is hard. Some days, I never get started, but on the days I do, I find myself delighting in the discipline.

Bill and I walk around our neighborhood almost daily, but on cold winter days, when the cold wind hits me, I say something like this: "I am freezing, and you know I hate being cold." Bill says, "It's okay you'll warm up."

So, I continued with rebellion and aggravation in my heart. Before long, I was not cold and could feel my body reacting favorably to the walk. I even felt energized. The first step is discipline, but the experience is bodily indulgence. I find I did what was good for my body and what it longed for. I wish I could say my next walk will be without a struggle, but there often is.

The Christian life is similar. We find Paul struggling in Romans 7. He does the things he hates and the things he loves he doesn't do. The inner man delights in the things of God, but he is in a power struggle with the old nature and ends up doing what he hates and not doing the very thing he wants.

Sound familiar? It sounds familiar to me.

We hear about Spiritual disciplines such as quiet times, prayer, Bible reading, attending church, fasting, solitude, etc. The list can become so long that we grow weary just hearing it. There seems to be so much to do. How in the world can we add these "disciplines" to our busy lives?

What seems like a "have to" or "ought to" can become a "get to." " I know that is true about my time with the Lord in the morning. I do not get up and make myself spend time with the Lord. I get up so I can spend time with Him.

This discipline has become a spiritual indulgence. I love this time better than chocolate. Do I sound very spiritual? I am. God has made me a spiritual person, and you also, if Christ is your Savior.

This is our deepest desire. The real us. We need to get past the first step, and then we will drink in the living water of life. Like my exercise, the first step is the hardest, but once we discover who we are, discipline becomes our intense pleasure.

Ponders of the Heart

Does the Bible lead you to praise?

What are you the most thankful for today?

Read Psalm 27:1, Psalm 30:11-12, and Psalm 37:3-6.

God's Word can lead us into praise and thanksgiving and release us from fear. His Word can even make an old girl like me start to dance and sing.

Prayers of the Heart

Dear Father,

How we delight in You, Lord. You are our delight and our strength. Father, help us take the plunge into your love with praise. We love You, and apart from You, life has little meaning.

Thank You, Father, for allowing us into Your presence with our praise. In Jesus' name, amen.

March 3 ~ A Face to Remember

It was a long-awaited day, full of anticipation, when my daughter Tracie gave birth to her firstborn. The day did not go as planned. Few do. But this was the day, and this was the time.

The curtain separating the nursery from the waiting room opened, and there stood our son-in-law, Ryan, holding a perfect little boy. The baby was wrapped so tightly that the only thing you could see was his face. A face that had none of the wear and tear of the world.

Looking at my grandson's face, I saw the image of his dad. My son-in-law, Ryan, was at the beginning of a brand-new journey, one as a father. There was also a new child that was going to face the world. He would face the good and the bad, and it would be the job of his parents to protect, teach, train, and provide. Oh, what a privilege and responsibility.

As believers, I see Jesus holding us up in the heavens. There we are, wrapped in His loving arms, covered completely from head to toe in His righteousness. He is showing us to the Father. We resemble His lovely face as He presents us to the Lord as His very own. The Father's eyes fill with tears and joy over the birth of this new creation. A re-creation in the likeness of His Son, His Son in whom He is well pleased.

The day the Lord held us up to the Father, He stood with us as a proud Savior. He knew what His job would be. Jesus for all eternity, would intercede for us at the right hand of His Father.

Jesus would protect, teach, train, and provide. We would sometimes fight against Him, but His love will be irresistible. Jesus accepted this responsibility with great joy and honor. He is our hope and refuge. It is in Him we find security in life.

Ryan held our precious Collier in his arms, and I wondered, did he realize he would not have to do this job alone?

He would need help, and God would provide. Ryan can depend on Him and rest in His sufficiency and faithfulness.

We praise the Lord for our spiritual birth and the promise that He will change us to be like Him. My prayer for Ryan and Tracie is God will draw them near, and they will depend on Jesus to help them be the parents their children will need. We are all helpless to do this job without Jesus.

As for us, let's remember that there was a day in heaven when Jesus held us up, all wrapped in the blanket of His righteousness, and God the Father looked at our little pink cheeks and said, "Ah, they look just like my Son."

Ponders of the Heart

Have you been born again?

Do you believe the promise that you will be changed into the image of Jesus?

Read Heb. 1:3, Colossians 1:15-17, John 3:3, and Romans 8:15-16,29.

Prayers of the Heart

Dear Precious Lord,

You labor over us until we are complete. Then You present us to our Father. Oh Lord, our words are inadequate to express the rich joy we feel. We are thankful that You can change us and make us new. Search our hearts so we can give You our best praise. In Jesus' name, amen.

March 4 ~ Zeroes to Heroes

When my youngest daughter was in the fourth grade, she was an angel in the children's musical titled "Zeroes to Heroes." The musical was about how God transforms His people from fear to faith. Julie was the angel who went to Gideon and told him, "The Lord is with you, mighty warrior."

We see examples in the Bible of God using ordinary people to do extraordinary things. I have a hero of faith. Her name is Carolyn Enis, my Bible Study Fellowship teacher (BFS) for three years in Peachtree City, Georgia.

Carolyn was a very classy lady, full of poise, and when she taught God's Word, her countenance was illuminating.

Looking at her was like looking at the water when the sun shines upon it. The light comes from the sun, but the beauty of the water cannot be ignored. Carolyn's teaching took my breath away. I loved Carolyn. I still do.

At the beginning of her teaching for BSF, she was a classy country club girl. Her husband was a high executive in his company, and they had the "American dream." She taught for eight or nine years, and in that time, she was transformed by the power of God's Word. She was not loved by all, for she was known as the "Bible girl." Not everyone loves those who love God.

After those years, she and her husband Mike went to Kampala, Uganda, which is in East Africa. They gave up earthly treasures to serve God as missionaries. They worked in a Rafiki children's center. She went from dressing in classy American style to sometimes dressing in *gomesi*, while Mike sometimes wore a *kanzu*, which looked like a dress. (It might be the other way around.)

I wish you could know Carolyn. She went from a zero to a hero in her life, serving God. Our God does awesome things in our lives, and I pray God will transform me into a woman who brings glory to His name.

"May the favor of the Lord our God rest on us; establish the work of our hands for us yes, establish the work of our hands" (Psalm 90:17).

Carolyn would not see herself as a hero. In fact, she said if they accomplish one thing a day in Uganda, they have had a successful day. Things move very slowly in Africa as they do in God's kingdom.

Time means little to people in Africa, and time means less to the Lord.

I remind myself of this fact so I will not grow weary in the slow movement of my transformation. But our God promises to change us, and He is faithful. Praise our God and our great King.

Ponders of the Heart

How long has it been since you focused on the work Christ has done on your behalf?

Do you feel like your transformation is moving very slowly?

Read Hebrews 10:8-14 and Hebrews 10:19-25.

Prayers of the Heart

Dear Father,

Because of Your work, we bow before You. We bow with praise on our lips and wonder in our hearts. Lord, there is none like You in all the world. Your loving kindness and Your grace overwhelm us. We praise Your Son, Jesus, and we thank You. In Jesus' name, amen.

March 5 ~ Morning and Children

"Because of the Lord's great love we are not consumed, for his compassions never fail. They are new every morning; great is your faithfulness" (Lamentations 3:22-23).

Some of my favorite memories with my children and grandchildren happened in the morning. I confess I am a morning person. I was not destined to be a morning person, but my dad made me one. He loved mornings, and he taught me to love them, especially mornings with children.

They tumble out of bed, ready for the day. Taylor, my granddaughter, wakes up ready to eat. Collier, my oldest grandchild, got up, ready to play with eating not far behind. He also used this time to charm you. A smile, a couple of hugs, and you're his. At 22, he still has me.

Bailey and Elizabeth, two of my granddaughters, loved to snuggle in the morning, and I love those times. They just wait for the opportunity to crawl into your lap. Clayton, my youngest grandson, is all about asking you questions in the morning. Each child is different, but mornings with children are priceless. Why is that?

Children, like adults, usually begin their day free from yesterday's attitudes. Rested children are usually happy children. I wonder if that is why God wants to meet us first thing in the morning. I would if I were Him. The day has a way of confusing me. I get frustrated over stupid things, and I let the lesser things of life overshadow the greater.

Mornings are new beginnings. They are fresh and unblemished by the world.

What is your favorite thing to do in the morning? Even though I love children in the morning, I like my day to begin before they get up. I need, desire, and want precious time alone with God. A new day of hope, promises, and a new day of His presence.

One morning, I woke up thinking about how He loves and completely accepts me. That was a wonderful way to start a day. I was thankful He was on my mind. There He was, smiling at me before I even opened my eyes.

Maybe that is why children are so delightful in the morning. They realize in places, we have forgotten the wonder of God's mercy. Life can be hard, but each day is a new opportunity to experience His mercy. Praise the Lord for mercy and faithfulness to His children.

Ponders of the Heart

Read 2 Peter 1:19-21 and Revelation 22:16.

Who is the bright morning star that rises in our hearts?

Do you think God is also a morning person?

Prayers of the Heart

Dear Precious Father,

What a joy and privilege it is to meet with You each day. How could we think we are too busy to meet with the Bright and Morning Star? Father, light up our hearts this day and we thank You for Your faithfulness and mercies that are new each day. In Jesus' name, amen.

March 6 ~ Patience and Perseverance

My daughter, Tracie, loves clothes and knows the style, quality, and the look she is after. Going shopping with her is like being in the wake of a master. She can enter a store and size it up with lightning speed. You can just be coming into the store as she is going out.

Tracie is our in-family fashion consultant. If you want to look good, you ask for Tracie's opinion. Be ready; she isn't shy about giving it.

I understand Tracie's heart by the clothes she wears. One area that concerned me was how she dressed Collier when he was just a baby. She wanted him to look like a big boy. I think she was always trying to make him grow up too fast. I know that sounds like a grandmother.

My concern was I wanted Tracie to enjoy Collier's baby stage. In fact, I wanted her to enjoy every stage of her son's life. It is true that he seemed older than he was, but growing up is a process, one to be enjoyed along the way.

The big boy equipment was all there. It just wasn't fully operational.

I can't point an accusing finger at Tracie, for I often get impatient with my spiritual development and the spiritual development of others.

When I dress myself in big girl spiritual attire, and my hem drags the floor, I find myself tripping and falling face-first. God gently picks me up as he reminds me I am on a journey. He whispers in my soul that all the equipment is there but not fully operational in my experience. The Holy Spirit is working in me, but it is a process.

God wants me to be patient and persevere as He works in my life, not only in my life but also as He works in the lives of others. Our growth is all in His Hands.

I not only dress beyond my maturity, but I also hold on to things I have outgrown. The Lord isn't shy about cleaning out my closet of well-worn spiritual garb. These are the times He gently reminds me to let go, for it is time to move on.

The whole thing boils down to our relationship. God wants us to enjoy our time with Him as He shapes us through the process. The process is sure, and it is in the Master's Hands. There is much to learn as we continue. The greatest part is His fellowship, presence, and love, which He gives us throughout our lives.

The clothes we wear are the righteous robes of Christ. He sizes them to fit us at each stage of development. They fit perfectly and are completely beautiful.

Our job is to stay out of His closet. He will get us there in time, but for now, as well as later, let's enjoy our relationship with Him. He doesn't want us to miss out on one second of our journey home.

Ponders of the Heart

Do you have a hard time remembering you are wearing the righteous robe of Jesus?

Are you running after the things of this world, or are you seeking after the things of God?

Read Isaiah 61:10, Romans 5:21, and Matthew 6:31-33. Also, read Revelation 7:9-12 for a picture of what is to come.

Prayers of the Heart

Dear Father,

God of heaven and earth, we praise You. You are our righteousness and our very great reward. Who is a God like You who restores our hearts to purity and robes us in the righteousness of Your Son? Thank You, Father, for Your unconditional love. Your gift of Life and Your beauty. In Jesus name, amen.

March 7 ~ Preparing for the Feast

I had a special tablecloth I used at Christmas and special times. The tablecloth was white and had a beautifully elegant design that went through the middle. Each tip of the cloth had the same elegant design. The problem with the tablecloth is it had to be starched and ironed to look its best.

After Christmas, it sat on my ironing pile for a long time, sometimes until Christmas the next year. But I loved the way the table looked when I used it. It was beautiful.

You might think such a thing should not matter to me. You are probably right, but I enjoyed doing it, along with our best dishes and the matching napkins. Some great memories happened in our dining room. We ate there on special occasions or when everyone was home, which, in a mom's heart, is a special occasion.

My family couldn't resist making fun of me when I would go to the trouble of putting my special stuff in place. Bill, my hubby, loved putting the blue salt box and the red tin pepper can on the table. Chris, my son, tried to get someone to throw him something while Ryan, my son-in-law, would join in the fun with a two-liter Coke bottle on the table.

I didn't mind because they knew I was saying this was a special occasion, and I wanted them to feel special and feel free to be goofy. We all had a good time of fun, and we still do, even if this tablecloth is not used.

Our special meals remind me of the ones Jesus had with His disciples, especially the Last Supper. What a special memory that must have been for the disciples after their Lord was gone from this earth and for Jesus as He waited for their arrival in heaven.

There is a feast waiting for us in heaven. I can picture the table. It will be arrayed with all the beauty of heaven. Can you imagine the tablecloth? I'm sure no Morton salt box or a liter of Coke will be there. All will be adorned for the Groom and His bride. You and I will be there. We will be the bride dressed for our Lord and be adorned by the beauty of His Holy Presence.

"And I heard, as it were, the voice of a great multitude, as the sound of many waters and as the sound of mighty thunderings, saying, 'Alleluia! For the Lord God Omnipotent reigns! Let us be glad and rejoice and give Him glory, for the marriage of the Lamb has come, and His wife has made herself ready'" (Revelation 19:6-7 NKJV).

It will be a very special time, one we will talk about throughout all eternity.

Ponders of the Heart

Are you ready for the feast in heaven where you will be the Lord's bride?

Are you preparing yourself for that day?

Read Rev. 19:6-10 and read your favorite Psalm, giving praise to God.

Prayers of the Heart

Dear Father,

How You have adorned Your earth with beauty. We can only imagine what heaven must be like. Thank You, Father, that one day, we will be with You and will see Your beautiful face. Until then, we pray You will give us spiritual sight to see You and hearts that love You. Worthy is the Lamb. In Jesus' name, amen.

March 8 ~ We Never Walk Alone

Julie, my youngest daughter, amazes me. When she left our home, she lived by herself. I went right from my parent's house to mine and Bill's. Julie, who is like me in many ways, surprised me in that she seemed very comfortable living by herself.

Even so, I am sure there were times when she felt overwhelmed with responsibilities. She was what the world would say, "On her own." We are led to believe that to be on our own is the mark of maturity.

In some ways, this is true, but if we embrace independence as a goal in life, where does God fit into our lifestyle? True maturity is when we realize we are dependent on God. Good parents produce children who go from being dependent on their parents to being dependent on God.

If I read my Bible correctly, the original sin was independence from God. We were never created to walk alone. Our sufficiency is to be found in Him.

"For I am the Lord your God who takes hold of your right hand and says to you, Do not fear; I will help you" (Isaiah 41:13).

One of my prayers for my children and grandchildren is that they will never walk or feel alone. I want them to realize that God is right there caring for them. We all need to know He is for us, and we do not have to feel overwhelmed in life because He is our Salvation and strength.

We are not alone. We have a faithful Father who cares about our lives. He loves His children.

Ponders of the Heart

Are there areas of your life where you try to live independently without God?

Are you willing to turn that over to the Lord?

What change would you like to see in your life this year?

Read Deuteronomy 33:29, 2 Samuel 7:23-24, and 1 Peter 2:9-10.

Prayers of the Heart

Dear Father,

Thank You that we never walk alone. You walk with us, for You are our very life. Help us not listen to the lies of the world that we are called to be independent. God, help us remember we are called to be dependent on You. We honor You, Mighty Father. In Jesus' name, amen.

March 9 ~ The Book of Life

"Nevertheless do not rejoice in this, that the spirits are subject to you, but rather rejoice because your names are written in heaven" (Luke 10:20).

Jesus had sent seventy disciples out two by two, and they returned rejoicing over the results. Jesus rejoiced with them but knew serving God should never take the place of the gift of God. He was their great reward.

The disciples were not much different than we are. They were caught up in performing and doing instead of the gift of being. God's gift to us is that through Jesus, we become His children and kingdom people.

These disciples were not men used to power or influence. They were ordinary people who had been bullied by the religious leaders and the government. Men who had been exploited by the Sadducees and rejection by the Pharisees. This mission trip had given these ordinary men power over evil spirits. They were not used to such influence.

Jesus knew the danger of power. Power in the human soul is deadly, but joy over the gift of God gives life.

How different are we? Jesus wants to do great and mighty things through us, but He knows the danger of our flesh. So, then, as well as now, He focuses our minds and our hearts back to the gift of being God's child over our serving.

The disciples' power was the work of the Holy Spirit, and the results of what they experienced were done by God. His plan to work through us is not for results but that we might come to know Him. He wants us to realize we are His, and He is working in us and through us.

God can do great and mighty things through His children, but the gift and wonder is that we have been brought into His family by the work of His Son. Praise evermore. Our names are written in the Book of Life. We are God's own people.

"But you are a chosen people, a royal priesthood, a holy nation, God's special possession, that you may declare the praises of him who called you out of darkness into his wonderful light" (1 Peter 2:9).

Ponders of the Heart

Have you ever fallen into performance for worth instead of rejoicing over who you are in Christ?

Is your identity found in your relationship with Jesus?

Read Luke 10:1-20.

Prayers of the Heart

Dear Father,

Thank You for the times You have chosen to work through us. We confess we often get carried away with performance instead of praising You for making us new. The next time You choose to use us, remind us to give You praise. Lord, in our hearts, we want it to be about You. Keep our hearts safe from the desires of our fallen nature. In Jesus' name, amen.

March 10 ~ What is Love?

When I was in the tenth grade, I had the cutest boy you can imagine in my English class. Because our school was in double session, I had an English class late in the afternoon. This cute boy was a baseball player and often missed our class. He was shy and athletic, but what I remember most about him was he wrote a poem about me. I don't know why he had to do it, but I remember the poem.

"Short, cute, sweet as a button. That's our girl, Miss Marilyn Sutton."

In the eleventh grade, this same cutie pie was in my history and English class. On the Friday after Thanksgiving that year, I had my first date with him. He wrote in my yearbook he was going to marry me. On May 10, 1969, he married me, and I married him.

Would he marry me again with what he now knows about me? I know I would marry him again in a New York minute.

God uses Bill in my life more than any person I know. He has taught me about God's unconditional love and how God does not need me but wants me.

When Bill and I married, I had wrong beliefs about myself and marriage. I married him with the opinion that someday he would leave me. I thought my only hope in keeping Bill was to perform well, look good, and behave right. It was up to me. The problem with this stinking thinking was I could not measure up to my standards. I often dreamed he would leave me.

After 50+ years of marriage, there have been ups and downs. We have had "life," but through it all, our love for one another has remained. I have confidence now that Bill loves me, and he isn't going to leave me.

Our relationship is not a relationship built on performing. Our relationship is built on mutual commitment of want, not need, and respect.

He has loved me since the eleventh grade. I am his beloved. I love him, but I must admit he loved me first. Bill knew how; I didn't.

How gracious my heavenly Father was to bring such a man into my life. A husband that has given me a taste of God's unconditional love.

My flesh continues to yell out to me that I must earn God's love, but this is a lie. A lie that, by His grace, I can learn to stand against. God's love is unconditional and not based on performance. We are His. We are loved, forgiven, secure, and made righteous by His grace.

Even though I have had a hard time understanding why Bill loves me, greater still, we often have a hard time understanding why God loves us.

"This is how God showed his love among us: He sent his one and only Son into the world that we might live through him. This is love: not that we loved God, but that he loved us and sent his Son as an atoning sacrifice for our sins" (1 John 4:9-10).

There are mysteries in life, things we will never understand. The greatest mystery of all is God's love for us. We can only appropriate this truth by faith. How I marvel and glory in His mercy and grace. Oh, Father, love on.

Ponders of the Heart

Read John 3:16-17, Titus 3:4-5.

What do these passages point out about God's love and His attributes?

How do these verses give you hope?

God's love and provision for us is beyond what any of us could hope for.

Prayers of the Heart

Dear Father,

We are thankful for the gift of Your love. We can't fully understand Your desire for us, but we accept this love by faith. Fill our minds with the truth of Your word and our hearts with hope. Open our eyes to the glory of our future. Let us enter Your rest with faith. Father, help us turn from unbelief and doubt. Let us experience Your peace. We love You and praise you. In Jesus' name, amen.

March 11 ~ Something is Wrong

My time of the month was a painful experience. After three children and countless months of agony, I decided to mention it to my doctor. After describing my problem, he suggested a test that could be done in the office but would be uncomfortable.

He said I might have endometriosis, but he could only tell by this test or surgery. I don't know if it was fear or pride, but I decided this doctor was crazy. After all, I was healthy, and nothing was wrong with me. I also was not crazy about a test that would be painful. I left that office determined never to go back.

A couple of years later, the pain got worse. I knew I could not continue feeling this way. It occurred to me that this was not normal after noticing my daughters did not have the same trouble.

I finally admitted something was wrong and made an appointment. After a sonogram, it was decided I needed surgery for fibroid tumors. I finally conceded to go under the knife, and surgery was scheduled.

My doctor was right. I had endometriosis and had a complete hysterectomy. Never in the time of recovery did I feel more pain than I experienced every month for years. The first step for the cure was to admit something was wrong.

That is where Paul's Jewish brothers were. They knew something was wrong. Paul knew they knew, for he also had rejected Jesus as the Messiah. They, like Paul, had to be willing to admit that Jesus was Who He said He was and yield to God's provision.

That is where so many people are today, inside and outside the church. We need help from God. People need salvation. The first step is hearing, the second is admitting something is wrong, the third step is admitting we need God, the fourth step is repenting, and the last step is yielding to God, His plan, and His way.

Faith comes from hearing and hearing from the Word of God. Oh, that we might yield to the voice of God. After yielding and believing, let us join the mission of sharing and proclaiming the good news to others. What a joy to proclaim the news of His great salvation.

Ponders of the Heart

Have you admitted that something is wrong with you?

Have you called on the Lord for His salvation?

When was the last time you shared the good news?

Read Romans 10:9-10 and Romans 10:16-17.

Prayers of the Heart

Gracious Lord,

Thank You for the gift of our salvation. Thank You, Father, for the privilege of being Your children. There was a sweet day when we admitted that something was wrong and we needed You. Father, the day we came to You was a day You had planned before the foundation of the world. Your goodness and grace are worthy of being praised, honored, and adored. We love You, and we praise you. In Jesus' name, amen.

March 12 ~ New Pages

Today, I begin a new journal, a fresh book with blank pages. I have books and books of prayers to the Lord. Who knows if they will probably ever be opened again, and yet they record years of the prayers of my heart.

When I run across one of these books, I am often surprised at what I find written inside. So many of my prayers are like the one I prayed yesterday, and yet I am also surprised at the words that flow from my heart.

My journal has the voice of God coming through to me. I have evidence that He was right there with me. The entries make it so clear that I am never alone. When we belong to God, He is always near.

This new journal reminds me of the toy you write on with a plastic pencil. You can write and write, yet with one pull, you erase your words or pictures. You face a blank page to record or draw on. No worries, though, for with one zip, you can erase any mistakes you make.

Even though I like to start over with blank pages, I do not want to begin without the insight and revelation the Lord gives me. The Lord has given me some wonderful moments. He speaks to me in such a gentle voice that I often forget as the day takes me away. As I said before, I am amazed at the repetition of my prayers and yet amazed at His presence.

The toy writing pad I wrote about has a hard black cardboard piece that seems to have some type of waxy cover. If you look very closely in the light, you will see something you wrote on the permanent cardboard. You can't erase that. It stays, no matter how many times you start over.

If you keep your magic pad long enough and use it often enough, you will begin to get little grooves in the underneath section, and your plastic pencil will go down into the grooves.

The revelation of the Lord is like that. He often has us start over. We often make mistakes and want to start over. If we come to Him and confess or agree with Him about our failures. He picks us up, and we will start our journey again.

Even though we start again in the depths of our hearts and the permanent places of our souls, He begins to write and engrave into us His ways and His Words. His engraving is an insight for today but will be with us for all eternity.

"The secret things belong to the Lord our God, but those things which are revealed belong to us and to our children forever, that we may follow all the words of this law" (Deuteronomy 29:29).

Ponders of the Heart

What secret things has God revealed to you?

What do you know that you are sure of?

Do you know who you are in Him?

Read Hebrews 10:14, Romans 15:7, Romans 8:30, Romans 6:6, Ephesians 4:24, and Ephesians 2:6.

Prayers of the Heart

Dear Gracious Lord,

How we praise Your holy name. You have given us reason to shout at all the blessings that are ours because of our beloved Savior. Joy floods our souls at the wonder and graciousness of Your great love. Help us to shed the old clothes of shame and walk in the newness of our new identity in You. Lord, we love You. In Jesus' name, amen.

March 13 ~ Communications

My son-in-law, Ryan, works with computers. I am not sure what he does. Computer lingo is a foreign language to me. I just don't speak computer. I did find out, however, that all computers don't speak the same language.

When I asked someone who is a computer expert about languages, I was confused again. I just don't speak fluent computer. It is, however, very important for Ryan to know what language a computer speaks to understand how to write a program. It is a must for communication's sake.

At one year old, my granddaughter, Bailey, had a language all her own. I could usually get the general jest of what she was saying, but the specifics were somewhat of a guessing game. For instance, she would let me know she was unhappy. My job was to figure out why. Is she wet, hungry, or tired? I wanted to understand because she is important to me.

Communication is hard, even if we speak the same language, but when we don't, it complicates things. Do we listen and understand God?

When it comes to computers, I don't try very hard to understand; I really don't care, nor do I think I can. So, my attitude is, why try?

Bailey is another story. Understanding Bailey is a top priority. I want our relationship to be strong, and if we do not understand one another, our time together will not be good. As her grandmother, I want ears that hear her words and her heart. She is my Bailey girl.

What is our attitude when it comes to understanding and responding to God? Do we have the mindset we can't communicate with God, our Father, so why try? The truth is God is a mystery. We can't understand the things of God with our finite minds. Just as I knew that at one year old, Bailey could not understand all that I was saying, God realizes our ability to understand Him is limited.

He knows our limitations, but He also knows how to speak to us despite them. God has given us His Holy Spirit and His written Word. The Holy Spirit can give us understanding and revelation about the deep things of God. That's His job. God wants us to hear and understand Him. We are His priority. Why God loves us is a mystery, but His universal language is love.

"We love Him because He first loved us" (1 John 4:19 NKJV).

Ponders of the Heart

What qualities of love do you lack?

Do you have someone in your life you need God to help you love them with His love?

Read 1 Corinthians 13:1-8.

Prayers of the Heart

Dear Precious Lord,

Thank You for the language of love. A love that comes down from Your heart to ours. A language that cannot be given or communicated apart from Your life in us. Father, thank You that Your Word promises that Your love never fails. We praise You, our Lord and life-giver. In Jesus' name, amen.

March 14 ~ What is Our Purpose?

What is the chief purpose of man? The Westminster Catechism answers:

"Man's chief end is to glorify God and enjoy Him forever."

I have been struggling with joy, and so I have been asking the Lord to show me where is my joy? He has pointed me to this chief purpose.

There was a lady in the church who is now with the Lord. I never knew her very well, but I heard about her. She was well-loved by the ladies in her

Sunday school class. They would tell me she was a great teacher and a wonderful, godly woman. I would also run into women who had been in a Bible study with her and would sing her praises as a woman of God.

She had a 2-year battle with cancer. The last time I saw her, you could see how cancer had overtaken her body. The sickness hung over her, and yet there was humbleness and gentleness about her. Even with all she was going through you sense joy.

I saw this dear lady days before her death. She had gone to the hospital because her pain was so severe, and she needed relief. Again, I was struck by the kindness and gratefulness she showed me even as she struggled with her pain. They moved her to Hospice, where she died just a couple of days later.

A friend who worked at Hospice at the time told me something I will never forget about this dear saint. She said that she came to hospice facing death with peace. She died peacefully with joy.

For to me, to live is Christ and to die is gain " (Philippians 1:21).

The Apostle Paul understood his chief purpose was to glorify God and enjoy Him forever.

Another way to put it, Paul understood that God is glorified when we are satisfied with the gift of His closeness. "To live is Christ." He can take our hands and use them. Christ can use our legs and feet to walk the path of life with Him. We will be satisfied when we walk where He wants us to go and use us however He wants. We need Him to fill our hearts with His love and fill our minds with wisdom from above.

Our lives can be for His glory.

Paul also says, "To die is gain," for He was looking forward to heaven. Paul would not just be a vessel through which Jesus was working. He would see Jesus face to face. That, to Paul, was the ultimate treasure to glorify God and enjoy Him for all eternity.

Our joy comes in glorifying God, and God is glorified when we enjoy Him. You can't have one without the other.

"The joy of the Lord is your strength "(Nehemiah 8:10).

Ponders of the Heart

Do you struggle with having joy?

What is your chief purpose in life?

Read Philippians 1:20-21 and Galatians 2:20.

Prayers of the Heart

Dear Father,

Fill our hearts with a desire to enjoy You and pursue You with great joy. We want to glorify You and be vessels You can use. You are our wisdom, strength, and joy. Seeing You face to face and being with You forever more will be our great reward. In Jesus' name, amen.

March 15 ~ Single Mindedness

I like to watch golf on TV. Some might think this is a boring sport to watch, but I much prefer it over other sports. You could say I am very single-minded in most things. I like to do one thing at a time and prefer to know a few people well instead of many.

Maybe that is why golf is for me. It is a slow-moving game that demands quietness, and one person plays at a time. The crowd, for the most part, is silent except for the announcers. It is a hard sport, and I like it.

That is probably an indictment of my personality and intelligence, but I'm really okay with that. My husband is so different. He can think in 40 directions at once, and so can Tracie, my daughter. They are both good for me, for they rush my life. I enjoy them, but I also like people who ponder, determined people like my son, Chris, my other daughter Julie, and my grandson, Collier.

Let me share with you a verse that "floats my boat." This translation is from the Amplified Bible.

"[For my determined purpose is] that I may know Him [that I may progressively become more deeply and intimately acquainted with Him, perceiving and recognizing and understanding the wonders of His Person more strongly and more clearly], and that I may in that same way come to know the power outflowing from His resurrection [which it exerts over believers], and that I may so share His sufferings as to be continually transformed [in spirit into His likeness even] to His death, [in the hope] That if possible I may attain to the [spiritual and moral] resurrection [that lifts me] out from among the dead [even while in the body] (Phil. 3:10-11).

What a verse! Paul knew his purpose. He was single-minded and determined to know Christ. Can you grasp those verses with your heart? Just thinking about knowing Christ more deeply and intimately should produce chill bumps in each of us. We need to be careful because we can become so focused on the goal of knowing Christ that we miss the object of our goal, Christ.

Jesus cannot be managed through a 12-step program of "How to Know Christ." He is beyond any earthly system of understanding, and yet He wants us to know Him. We must make room for Him as we pursue to know Him, knowing all along He is the one who put that desire in us in the first place.

What a great, worthy God we serve. He cannot be managed, but in His compassion, He comes to us. We can know Him progressively, only to realize He is beyond our ability to understand Him. He is awesome and powerful, and yet tender and intimate with His own.

How do we serve such an unfathomable God? Only out of His great mercy and excellent provision can we approach His throne. If it were not for His great love, we would be consumed. Don't you just want to shout glory?

Go ahead. Let's do it on the count of three. One, two, three, Glory to the Lamb.

Ponders of the Heart

How do you go about making room in your life to know God?

What question about God would you like Him to reveal to you today?

Read Psalm 47.

Prayers of the Heart

Dear Father,

We shout with joy as we ponder You. Lord, You are beyond our wildest dreams. You are more wonderful than all this earth has to offer. In You, we have hope for our lives and salvation for our souls. Jesus, You are our solid Rock, and we praise You, for You alone are worthy of all praise, honor, and glory. We love You, and we will praise You forever. In Jesus' name, amen.

March 16 ~ He Makes Things Beautiful in His Time

"He has made everything beautiful in its time. He has also set eternity in the hearts; yet no one can fathom what God has done from beginning to end" (Ecclesiastes 3:11).

There are days when you can only hang your heart on the promises of God. We can go to the New Testament and see Romans 8:28 and realize that because we are in Christ, God will work all things together for our good and His glory. We can rest in the sufficiency of His power, mercy, wisdom, and love.

Today, as I write this, my friend, Sharon, lost a loved one. Her father stepped into eternity while his family circled the bed singing hymns. How precious. Nothing affects us so much as death and birth. I think that is true in heaven, too. Only in heaven, the death of a saint is precious, and the death of a sinner brings great mourning. We mourn the loss of friends, parents, spouses, and children while heaven is rejoicing when they finally make it home.

For years, I asked the Lord to tenderize my heart. The death of my father and the birth of my first grandchild indeed did that. These events gave me compassion that was never there before. I felt compassion for families who mourned the death of loved ones, people who were battling cancer, and those who cared for those fighting that disease. I have been able to reach out to others with compassion and the love of Jesus.

When Collier was born, my heart grew bigger than the size of Texas. I understood more clearly the way the grandmothers in my Sunday school class felt about their grandchildren. But I was also sensitive to those who had not joined the grandmother club. It was not so long ago that I felt the same way. But now that I have experienced this great happening, children have captured my heart in a fresh new way. I am grateful for this new tenderness. The grandmothers in my class were so right about how great it is to be a grandmother, and I will enjoy their bragging rights. Hopefully, they will enjoy mine.

God hears and responds to our prayers. In fact, He wants to reveal to us our need for more tender hearts. Oh, what a Savior. He takes our brokenness in His Hands, knowing life is full of hurt and pain, and gives us a heart like His.

Ponders of the Heart

How has God been working in your life?

How have the difficulties of this life helped you identify with others?

Read Isaiah 61:3, Isaiah 66:13, and Mark 10:13-16.

Prayers of the Heart

Gracious Father,

You have given us a new heart. Lord, make them tender and compassionate like Yours. Use all things for Your glory and use all things in life to change us to the image of Your Son. We love You, Lord, and desire to be transformed by Your grace. In Jesus' name, amen.

March 17 ~ If This Were the End

The last days of my dad's life were bittersweet. Dad took this time to tell us things he wanted us to remember. He had a list of things he wanted to do and wanted to spend as many hours as possible with his family.

Dad had a hard time expressing his feelings and being in front of people.

The day I got married, he almost choked trying to say, "Her mother and I." So, for him to freely tell us that he loved us was very meaningful. He also took time to tell us, his stepchildren, where he had failed and made sure we knew that we were his children in his heart. It was a bittersweet time.

If we were facing the last days of our lives and we had only one more day to talk to our loved ones about the Lord, what would we want to share with them?

Would we tell them because we were born with a sinful nature, we are sinning machines in need of forgiveness? Would we share with them that Jesus is God's provision for salvation?

It is true without forgiveness, we are doomed. But we needed more, and salvation offers more.

If these were the last days of our lives, would we want to proclaim we were cleansed from our past, present, and future sins? Would we tell them that Jesus offers us a new life with a new nature, a new family, and a home in heaven? What would our final words be?

We are children of God, heirs to the throne, clothed in the very righteousness of Christ. We are seated in the heavens. Oh, what a great salvation. A great exchange has taken place in our lives. We give Christ our filthy rags, and He gives us His righteous robes. He takes our sins and nails the old man to the cross. We are justified, just as if we never sinned.

"Grace and peace be multiplied to you in the knowledge of God and of Jesus our Lord, as His divine power has given to us all things that pertain to life and godliness, through the knowledge of Him who called us by glory and virtue" (2 Peter 1:2-3 NKJV).

Our new life is one we appropriate by faith in the one who has called you out of darkness into His wonderful light. What a great salvation we could proclaim.

Ponders of the Heart

Who would you want to share the gospel with if this was your last day on earth?

Why would you choose that person?

Read Ephesians 1:1-14 and Ephesians 3:20.

Prayers of the Heart

Dear Holy Jesus,

We bow before You with praise. We open our mouths with praise and adoration. We bow our hearts and our lives before You in gratitude and wonder of Your great salvation that is ours by faith. In Jesus' name, amen.

March 18 ~ Serving with Love

My husband, Bill, won't let me wait on him. He is an independent man. I love to do little things to please him that he would never ask me to do.

One day, not feeling well, he did not get out of bed in time for his morning run. For a man who ran six days a week for twenty years, that was a big deal. He jumped out of bed and into the shower. With his routine a mess, it was my turn to help.

When Bill got out of the shower, his paper was on the table with his coffee. He was pleased, but not as much as I was to slip in an act of love to my self-reliant man.

I didn't go get his paper because I had to or because he expected me to, but I wanted to. Because of my love for this man, I want to do things for him.

The Bible tells us that one day, we will all stand before the judgment seat of Christ. That thought can produce uncomfortable feelings. I can see Christ standing above me, waiting to whack me over the head for my stupidity, laziness, and sin. Is that what the judgment seat of Christ will be like? Didn't Christ die for all our sins? What will that day be like?

I don't know, but I think it will be a time when all those things we do because we love the Lord will be brought to light, including things Christ did through us. We yielded to Him because He made us new. He didn't need us, and yet, in His love, He chose to use us.

We will stand as Olympians receiving a crown for those eternal works. He will be pleased because they were done out of devotion, love, respect, and adoration. He will say, "Thank you for showing me your love, trust, and faith in me. I know it was hard, and sometimes you were afraid. Yet, you trusted Me. I love you, and you are Mine."

Because Jesus is the greatest gift we could ever ask for, in His presence, we will fall before Him and lay praises at His feet. Then, we will rise to serve Him for all eternity. We might even find ways to slip out and bring Him His paper and coffee. Our biggest problem will be that eternity will not be long enough to show Him our thanks, love, and praise.

Pondering heaven is exciting. I love thinking about seeing my mom and dad again. My friend, Sharon, has promised that she will save a place for me beside her. We want to sing praises to God for eternity. I can't wait to see the beauty of heaven. There will be streets of gold and God's throne with light brighter than the sun. Hearts will be full of love flowing like a river.

Can you imagine seeing the angels? But at the end of the day, it will be the face of Jesus who will take our breath away.

Ponders of the Heart

How do you picture the Judgement seat?

Do you look forward to the day you stand before the Lord, or do you fear that day?

Read 1 John 4:17-19 and Revelation 22:1-5.

Prayers of the Heart

Dear Precious Father,

How we thank You for our heavenly home and how we praise You for Your great love for us. Cast from our hearts all fear and replace that fear with joy. Help us see You as our loving Father who has made a way for us to live with You forever. In Jesus' name, amen.

March 19 ~ Listening and Conversation

A man told me about an argument he had with his wife. He said his wife said, "You never listen." We have all heard complaints like that one from friends about their marriages. It seems to be a universal rub in marriages. What makes a man not listen? But we need to be fair; men are not the only ones who don't listen.

How many teenagers say to their parents, "I told you that, but you didn't listen." I can relate because I have said to my children, "Would you please be quiet and listen to me." How many little children tug on their mommy's sleeve or daddy's pant leg, trying to get someone to listen to them? It is a universal problem. Why is listening so difficult?

Of course, there can be countless reasons, but one is we often talk to people, not with them. They become our sounding board, and they feel it. Communication is a two-way street, not just the opportunity for us to hear ourselves talk.

We talk with ourselves for ourselves. The universal problem is self, and because self is the problem, we only want to listen to people who love us the way we love ourselves. Ouch.

Prayer can also just be about us. We can talk about God and not with Him. Our listening skills can be completely turned off. If we are still under the notion that we are the center of the universe, we will not be interested in what God has to say. I will admit that my prayers of often a one way conversation. Me talking to God and me wanting Him to listen.

If you feel beaten up, do not worry. We all fail to have a perfect prayer life. The encouraging information is our deepest longing is to know God. Our most profound need is to hear Him; His deepest desire is to fellowship with us. He wants to communicate with us.

Oswald Chambers says, "Sanctification means being made one with Jesus so that the nature that controlled Him will control us."

Our preoccupation with us is constantly getting in our way and keeps us from communicating with those we love and listening to those who love us. Self keeps us from listening to God. We talk at Him instead of with Him. Oh, how we rob ourselves of His company. May it never be said in the throne rooms of heaven that we do not listen to our God.

Ponders of the Heart

Do you feel you talk at God more than you listen to Him?

Do you need God to speak a fresh word into your soul?

Read Isaiah 53:2-3, 1 John 4:6, and James 1:19-20.

Prayers of the Heart

Father, God,

Help us know how much you love us. Please communicate with us and help us learn to talk with You and not at You. Lord, give us insight into our self-centeredness. We long to be more like Your Son, Jesus. Father, we belong to You and not ourselves. In Jesus' name, amen.

March 20 ~ Sticks and Stones

Pop-up ads can be so frustrating. Games on your phone and Facebook have pop-up ads all the time. We can also be bombarded with scam calls on our phones. People are calling to sell you something. It seems television ads and shows are so filled with language and scenes that dull our consciences. Our culture takes a toll on the purity of our lives with words and sights.

"Sticks and stones can break my bones, but words can never harm me." Whoever wrote that was wrong, and if I say that to someone, I'm wrong. Words destroy people. Most of the unhealed places in hearts are caused by them, not sticks or stones. The harm we cause others is done by our words.

Our words break hearts. Lies fill our world, and impurities fill our hearts from the inside and the outside.

Words hang in our minds so they can come back and assault us when we are vulnerable. They can destroy our relationships, reputation, our witness, our godly thinking, and well-being. Words can be far more damaging than sticks and stones.

On the doors of our houses and cars, we have locks to keep predators out. We need locks on our mouths to keep harmful words from hurting others. James is right when he warns us that the tongue cannot be tamed.

"The tongue also is a fire, a world of evil among the parts of the body. It corrupts the whole body, sets the whole course of one's life on fire, and is itself set on fire by hell" (James 3:6).

What can we do about our words that come from hell and fight the wrong messages we hear? How do we protect ourselves and others from hurtful messages that destroy? Are we without hope? We cannot control our tongues.

The only way is to let Jesus have control of our lives. His Living Word can restore us, heal us, and others. Only the Holy Spirit and prayer transform our minds so we can recover from the pain and the suffering we have inflicted on others and the pain that has been inflicted on us with harmful words.

Let us not become full of despair but of hope, for the One who gave Himself for us is the One who will keep us till the end. Praise the Lord, we are not doomed. We have the Great Physician for the healing we need.

Ponders of the Heart

Do you have trouble taming your tongue?

Have you been hurt deeply by the words of others?

Ask God to give you His power over your tongue.

Read 2 Corinthians 12:9, 1 Peter 2:24, and Psalm 147:2-3.

Prayers of the Heart

Dear Father,

Heal our hearts and our minds today from the harm this old world inflicted on them. Lord, help us forgive those who have harmed us with words. We pray for the power of the Holy Spirit to help us control our tongues. Forgive us for the harm we have caused with our words. Give us words that encourage others. Father, thank You that our lives are hidden in You. In Jesus' name, amen.

March 21 ~ The Work vs Our Tasks

I prayed for my husband and asked the Lord to release him from the frustration of his work. Bill was overburdened with his job and felt responsible for too much.

He is a man who is responsible and willing to help, but he is not responsible for everything and everyone. I have been guilty of using him to do things I should handle. I was wrong for doing that, and he was wrong for thinking he should.

Bill has God-given discernment. He can see a problem, but that does not mean he is always the one to fix it. We all have responsibilities that include tasks, but God controls the results. This is such a major lesson to learn.

When I prayed for Bill's release from the burden of work, I was not praying we go on welfare, win the lottery, or inherit a million dollars. I was praying for him to discover his dependence on his heavenly Father for guidance, wisdom, and boundaries. God enjoys carrying out His work through His people. We do the tasks; God does the work, and it is hard to know the difference.

It is the Lord who is in control of the outcome, and He is the only One who can change a heart, move a mountain, and bring good out of bad. There is a sweet release in surrendering control, believing that there is a power beyond us that brings about eternal results of our labor.

When we weed a garden or water the plants, it is still God who makes the plants grow. The Lord can plant a seed and water the plant without us. He could have a flower grow in the middle of the desert, but, in His great compassion, He allows us to be involved in the task of gardening.

Thinking it is up to us is prideful. We play a part, but we need to see ourselves as vessels God can use. The results are in His Hand. The bottom line is life is short, results are slow, but God is eternal.

I am thankful the Holy Spirit places integrity into the hearts of His own. His integrity helps us discern the wrong around us as we speak the truth, but the outcome is God's. We are responsible for our task, but we are only vessels for His glory. Our love for Him and service for Him is a privilege.

Ponders of the Heart

What task or responsibility are you trying to do apart from God?

Are you frustrated enough to ask God to take control?

Read John 15:1-7, 2 Corinthians 3:5, and 1 Corinthians 15:10.

Prayers of the Heart

Dear Lord,

Release us from self-control into Your wonderful care. Lord, life is hard, and we cannot do it without You. When we try, we feel overwhelmed. We want to pray and love others. We want to help and serve but trust You with the results. Help us trust You with our families, professions, and spiritual growth. You and You alone are our hope. Lord, God, You are our joy and our crown. In Jesus' name, amen.

March 22 ~ Senses

We were created with five senses. These senses help us to relate to the world around us. Like the sense of smell. Is there a smell so wonderful as coffee and bacon in the morning or a smell as gross as a wet dog? What about the sense of sight? Can you still recall the first time you saw the ocean, mountains, or your child's face? There is beauty and wonder in God's creation.

I love to look at old pictures of my children and remember those days. Seeing a beautiful sunrise or sunset can lift us when we are sad. I think October sunsets are the best. What about the taste of ice cream on hot summer days or hot chocolate on winter nights? Such pleasure and wonder we see, taste, smell, touch, and hear with our senses.

A strange thing about me is I hear both with my ears and my eyes. I tend to read lips while I listen. We also pick up on attitudes by the sound or tones of voices and body language. It is true we relate to our world through the beautiful senses of our bodies.

These senses are wonderful, yet the evil in our world and the lust of our flesh can turn God-given senses into trouble. One night, I was watching TV, and for once, I was holding the remote control. Because the remote is usually in the hands of another, I don't often know what station a program is on.

While searching for a particular program, I was trying to go to the guide channel to find it. I wanted to scroll down, but instead, I hit the wrong button, and boom, I was watching what looked to be a pornographic movie.

I don't have movie channels, but this was pornography all the same. I quickly hit a button to get off that channel, but in my mind was this image I wanted gone, but it was there. I was fighting to recover from something I didn't intend to see. The sense of sight is very penetrating.

What happens when young minds see the things that are pumped into our homes every day? There is violence and sex on television, and it is hard to avoid. A God-given sense used for such ungodly things. That is the result of sin and the path of man apart from God.

For us, we can fight with the Holy Spirit that lives inside us. For the world at large, they are stuck in the web of destruction. We need to ask our Heavenly Father for His help to open the hearts of this lost world and help us stand in the gap for them.

"Therefore, I urge you, brothers and sisters, in view of God's mercy, to offer your bodies as a living sacrifice, holy and pleasing to God—this is your true and proper worship. Do not conform to the pattern of this world, but be transformed by the renewing of your mind. Then you will be able to test and approve what God's will is—his good, pleasing and perfect will " (Romans 12:1- 2).

We want to protect our senses because it is through the senses that the world enters our minds. Our need is to be transformed by God. We will be held by one or the other. Either the world will control us, or God will transform us from within. There is no neutral ground.

Ponders of the Heart

What is the best way to protect your God-given senses?

Do you have an area in your life that you need help resisting?

Read 1 John 2:15-17.

Prayers of the Heart

Dear Father,

How we thank You for the wonderful gift of senses. Thank You for allowing us to enjoy life through them and with them. Protect these senses and protect us from using them in any way that dishonors You. Help us reflect Your glory, purity, and peace so others will be drawn to You. Cleanse us, Father, protect and set us apart in Your pure, wonderful light. In Jesus' name, amen.

March 23 ~ Exhausted

As I write this, I am dealing with grandmother's exhaustion. This past weekend, my husband and I took care of our grandson. It was wonderful. The reason this exhaustion was wonderful is that it was a "get to," not a "have to." After a weekend like this, I think it would be wise to set up an exercise program and get this grandmother physically fit.

Grandmothers do not want to give out physically. They want to give attention and love to their grandchildren. That can be very hard when you get tired. Even if this weekend was fun, this old GiGi is ready to get some rest and revive. Ecclesiastes 5:12 says the sleep of a laboring man is sweet, and so is the sleep of a laboring grandmother.

Bill and I have great joy in caring for our grandchildren. Our exhaustion is sweet. As I reflected on this, I asked myself if I enjoyed serving my Lord with the same joy and excitement. Have I adopted the attitude of "have to" instead of "get to"? I wonder if that is what Paul was thinking when he wrote.

"No, I strike a blow to my body and make it my slave so that after I have preached to others, I myself will not be disqualified for the prize" (1 Cor. 9:27).

Was his love for Christ so strong that he served after his body wore out?

When our grandchildren come, we delight in the things they say and do. We work to please, teach, and show them our love. Bill and I are fools when it comes to them. As I reflect on the things the Lord has done and continues to do, I am amazed. Oh, Father, open our eyes to Your wonder.

"Yet I hold this against you: You have forsaken the love you had at first " (Revelation 2:4).

Let it never be said that we would leave such gracious love. When we do stray, may the Lord bring us back with cords of His love. May we delight in Him and stay spiritually and physically fit so we do not "give out." We want to love Him well all the days of our lives. Revive our hearts and service, we pray.

Ponders of the Heart

Are you in need of a revival?

Has it been a long time since you enjoyed being with the Lord?

Read 1 Corinthians 15:58, 1 Corinthians 13:1-3, and Revelations 2:4-5.

Prayers of the Heart

Dear Precious Lord,

How wonderful You are and how much we love You. Touch our hearts, stir our minds, and give us a thankful heart for our salvation and the Holy Spirit. Father, put Your love in us and love through us. In Jesus's name, amen.

March 24 ~ The Age of Technology

The computer age is moving at the speed of light. I have a good computer, but it has a poor operator who is walking when she needs to be running.

Recently, in getting this book ready to publish, I have been overwhelmed by the tools available. My friend Sandi amazes me. She has helped me set up the styles of the book. She is incredible.

Our granddaughter, Elizabeth, who is five as I write this, can do more on her iPad and computer than I can. The other day, she cast a program from her iPad to our TV. I can't do that. Folks who are efficient with computers tell me my computer can do all sorts of things. It is not the machine that is the problem.

There are Christians who are illiterate in God's Word, as I am computer illiterate. They don't know the full gift of salvation that has been given to them. So, their Christian life is limited. Some Christians know God's Word but refuse to appropriate the truth by faith.

I was talking to a young man who was trying to live a Christian life in his power and self-will. He was failing and was frustrated. Yet he wanted to live this new life. I told him to give up. The Christian life is impossible to live. Only Christ could live this life through him. That sounds so lame to so many people, but it is a true nugget to ponder. Paul put it this way:

"I have been crucified with Christ and I no longer live, but Christ lives in me. The life I now live in the body, I live by faith in the Son of God, who loved me and gave himself for me" (Galatians 2:20).

Paul knew that apart from Christ, he could not live the Christian life. Paul tried to live God's law. He had been a Pharisee, but after meeting Christ on the Damascus Road, everything changed. He needed the life of Jesus alive in him, and so do we.

It is possible to learn things about computers, and it is possible to learn things about God through His Word. But to understand His ways, we need His Spirit. His ways are higher than our ways, and His thoughts are beyond us. He is more than a great computer in the sky; no one can fathom His worth.

You know what is the biggest wonder of all? God loves us and desires to have a relationship with us. He gave His Son for our redemption, so by faith in Jesus, we can become His children.

Today, as we live and breathe, we need the Lord to live through us. We can do nothing of eternal value without Him. He offers us spiritual eyes to see how He works in the world around us.

Ponders of the Heart

Are you frustrated with your Christian life?

Do you long for a fresh encounter with the Holy Spirit?

Read Galatians 2:20-21, Colossians 2:20, and Colossians 3:4.

Prayers of the Heart

Dear Precious Jesus,

You are our life and our wisdom. We need You, Jesus. You are our hope for today and all our tomorrows. Apart from You, there is no joy or meaning to this life. You are the Alpha and Omega of our souls. Use us for Your work and Your glory. Lord, open our eyes and let us see the wonder of how You work in and through Your vessels of clay. In Jesus' name, amen.

March 25 ~ Trust

Our grandson enjoyed eating baby food. With each bite, he would say, "Mumm." He liked the different foods we gave him. He loved carrots and squash as much as applesauce and bananas. Each bite was a delight to him, and I am thankful he did. I have seen poor mammas all but stand on their heads to get their little ones to eat.

There was a time I cared for him when he was sick with an ear infection and was on medication. He was like a little bird taking his medicine. He opened his mouth wide, and down it went.

I had three different types of medicine and ear drops. Each bottle of medicine had a different dropper, and the prescription had a different amount to be taken. I was very careful to read each label each time to make sure I gave him what was prescribed. He would have taken any amount I gave him. The companies that make medicine for babies must have seen "Mary Poppins." You know, "A spoonful of sugar makes the medicine go down."

Collier was so trusting, and it was important I was careful with that trust. We all have had people in our lives who were not careful or trustworthy. As I watched him, I trembled at the thought of anyone hurting this little one or any baby.

This world can be hard and mean. Who or what can be trusted? Is there anyone we should open wide and accept what they give us with childlike trust?

Trust is hard to come by in this fallen world. The trust we give has often been shattered. This has made it difficult to trust even the Lord. He is faithful and can be trusted. We must fight our flesh and the experiences in this life and not judge our heavenly Father by what has happened to us in this world. The Lord says:

"I am the Lord your God, who brought you up out of Egypt. Open up your mouth and I will fill it" (Psalm 81:10).

When we read verses like this, do we wonder what God wants to give us today that we are not accepting with trust? I wonder if we respond with "yum" to the good life He has bestowed on us. In discipline and hard times, we can still open wide and receive needed help.

We can trust God with all that comes our way.

Ponders of the Heart

Have you had something happen in your life that makes it hard to trust?

Do you know that God is trustworthy?

What is something we can do when it is hard to trust the Lord?

Read Proverbs 3:5-6, Heb. 2:13, Rev. 19:11, John 17:3, and 1 Thess. 5:24.

Prayers of the Heart

Dear Father,

You are Holy and True. You are the one we can open our mouths and receive anything You want to give us. We can trust You to know what is right and good. You know what heals, corrects, and guides. We can have confidence in You, our Heavenly Father. Help us trust you with our whole hearts, minds, and souls. In Jesus' name, amen.

March 26 ~ Well Water

When we lived in South Georgia, we lived in a neighborhood with wells. It was a new subdivision with new houses being built around us. My husband was in the real estate business, and his company handled the sale of these homes.

The neighbor across the street started complaining about his well water. He complained that the water tasted funny. Mortgage Company underwriting rules demand that wells are tested before closing. Since this well had been tested with no problems, no one thought too much about there being a problem.

Our neighbor talked my husband into coming over and tasting the water. Bill is a city boy, but he had to admit something was wrong with that water. They did whatever you do to wells; chlorinate or something, who knows. Anyway, the water tasted better for a few days. Then it was worse than before. They decided to drain the well and found a dead rabbit. Bill was sick for a week; he thought for sure he was going to die.

They dug the rabbit out, and the water was great after that. Those poor people. That could take the joy out of a new house in a New York minute. You notice I didn't say a South Georgia minute. That moves much slower.

The day the Lord revealed that I had been made new in Christ and the old man was dead was greater joy than a new house. It was more precious than silver and sweeter than honey to my heart. I rejoiced as I drank in that sweet water of acceptance. This was great, wonderful news. Hope I can hang my heart on, but I find the old dead man polluting my spiritual water.

After a day in this world, I often come away with a bad taste in my mouth, and I know something stinks in me. I can just picture that old me, dead in the water and polluting my life with its decay.

I know it will never be any good. I can go to that old dead flesh, wash it, dress it, but it will still be dead and full of decay. What can be done about this body of death that lies in the new me?

Paul found this to be true in his life. At the end of Romans 7, he expressed, "O wretched man that I am! Who will deliver me from this body of death? I thank God- through Jesus Christ our Lord" (Romans 7:25).

When my neighbors had their well chlorinated, the water was purified for a while. Then, the rabbit's carcass polluted it once more. In my life, this dead man or the flesh continues to pollute my life with its decay, but I have a purifier that is stronger than any decay, in fact, stronger than death, and that is the sweet purity of Jesus.

One touch from Him, and all is clean. Every day, I need His touch to purify my life with the refreshing bath of His Word. I will always be His, and I am acceptable to Him, but I want to walk this life with the sweet-smelling fragrance of my Lord, not the stink of my old flesh. Praise God that He is willing to plunge me into His purifying Spirit. He is our hope.

Ponders of the Heart

What do you do when the old man shows up in your day?

Does it give you hope when you realize Paul the apostle fought the old man also?

Read Romans 6:6-14 and Hebrews 10:22-25.

Prayers of the Heart

Dear Father,

We praise You for making us clean, not by our works, but through Your grace. Father, we are thankful You have given us Your Spirit to continually purify our lives. Precious Lord, plunge our lives deeply into Your purifying love and make us a sweet-smelling fragrance of Your grace. In Jesus' name, amen.

March 27 ~ Nascar

Nascar, in the 90s, was named the most popular spectator's sport in America. During that time, my family was part of a group that loved racing. My husband was a jock in high school, and I always thought of car racing as somewhat, excuse the expression, a red-neck sport.

When Bill said he was going to Daytona, I was certain he would not like it, but he was hooked from the start.

He started going to Daytona in 1987. During his Nascar obsession days, he made racing fans out of all my kids. Even the people at his company knew more about Nascar than they could believe.

Nascar is a sport that can take up the best part of the day, in fact, the best part of a weekend. The big race is usually on Sunday, but they have other races on Saturday, the truck race sometime during the weekend, and qualifying sandwiched in there somewhere.

My girls knew the names of all the Nascar drivers and the numbers on the cars they drove. They knew where all the racetracks were located. As I said, they were fans. The race was something they watched at the beginning, did other activity in the middle, and was glued to the TV at the end.

Just because you start at the front doesn't mean you'll end up there. You can also start at the back and win, but not always. It is a funny sport in that there is no telling what the outcome will be. There are a lot of things that can go wrong. You can have a wreck, engine trouble, tire trouble, a bad pit stop, or your engine can blow up. It is risky, dangerous, challenging, and exciting.

Like Nascar, the end of life is hard to predict. Sometimes, people begin with good families, each having a good start in life, only to finish life badly. There are other people who have a bad start and win, but not always. Life is risky, dangerous, challenging, and exciting.

What makes a person a winner in life or a loser? Can you win the game of life? Is there any guarantee that you can finish up front?

Paul tells the Corinthians to run the race to win. The audience would relate to his instructions because games, like the Olympics, were held there every other year.

"Do you not know that in a race all the runners run, but only one gets the prize? Run in such a way as to get the prize" (1 Corinthians 9:24).

It sounds as if Paul is instructing us to run the race of life to win. But how?

"For whatever is born of God overcomes the world. And this is the victory that has overcome the world- our faith. Who is he who overcomes the world, but he who believes that Jesus is the Son of God" (1 John 5:4-5 NKJV).

We only need to believe in Jesus. We believe He is the Son of God, that He is our Redeemer, and our hope and glory. If we believe, then we are more than conquerors.

Belief is more than head knowledge. Belief is to trust, rely on, submit to, have faith in, and turn to Jesus for forgiveness and life. He is the one who forgives, saves, and gives us victory.

Ponders of the Heart

Read 1 John 5:6-13, 2 Corinthians 5:21, and Romans 8:27.

What has Jesus done for us according to these verses?

Do you want to praise Him right now? Go ahead, praise the Lord.

Prayers of the Heart

Dear Father,

    We often feel defeated in life and lose our focus. Lord, help us realize and regard ourselves as victorious children of God. We can find ourselves in front, running with faith, only to fall into the pits of discouragement. Help us keep our eyes on You, running with faith and knowing that the victory is ours because Jesus is our victory. In Jesus' name, amen.

March 28 ~ The Game

    The game "He loves me, he loves me not" has been around as long as I can remember. How many flowers have come to an early doom so I could find out if he loves me? The great part about the game is if things don't work out to suit you, you just grab another flower. How long has it been since you played this game? Don't laugh; I think we will play it more than you think.

    We often play this game, not with flowers, but with circumstances.

    "God, if you love me, don't let this happen."

    "Lord, show my son you love him by letting him have his way."

    Circumstances are how we often measure God's love for or against us. We might put a holy twist to the game by thinking we have failed, and that is why things have gone awry. Sometimes, we have failed, but not always.

There are times when God causes or allows the circumstances, but He is always aware. We might say to someone hurting, "If you will just go to church more, give more money, or serve more, then God will help you, and if you don't do these things, your life will always be a mess."

What terrible theology, but in some ways, I have used it. It makes sense to me, but I'm afraid we are selling God for the purpose of making our lives work. It is really the fear factor. I use it on my children. It never works, and it gives them a terrible concept of God.

His ways are not our ways, and His plans are for eternity. We only see the temporary circumstances. God wants us to rest in Him and have faith. Do we want to use God, or do we want to rest knowing He is good and faithful? He is in control, He is good, and He loves us, for we are His children. God cares about our lives, and He does not want to harm us, but His sights are set on eternity, not earthbound happiness.

The circumstances can be good or bad, but the love of the Lord stays. He will see us through, lead us around, or change the whole mess. The truth is we can know Him, follow Him, and see how He works in and through us.

It is my prayer that God gives us hearts to trust, eyes to see, and wisdom to obey. We need help to live each day of our lives with the knowledge and confidence that the victory is already ours in Christ Jesus.

Don't play the game, "He loves me, he loves me not," with the Lord. He loves us. God gave His life for us, and He gave us a new birth, a new family, and a new home. We can rejoice in the Lord. We can be content in all circumstances, for the Lord God will never leave us or forsake us. He will work through our circumstances to give us Himself. These are excellent results.

Ponders of the Heart

How do you see God? Do you think He is keeping score?

Do you know as His child, He will never love you more or less?

Read Isaiah 55:8-9 and Romans 8:31-39.

Prayers of the Heart

Dear Father,

We honor You for Your love, control, wisdom, and promises. Circumstances are hard, and sometimes we doubt Your love, but give us the wisdom to trust You and rest on Your truth. Help us be so satisfied that the circumstances of life fade in comparison. Lord, we love You. In Jesus' name, amen.

March 29 ~ One Hundred Percent

The older I get, the dryer my skin becomes. One author said that his skin looked like it needed ironing. I understand. Mine doesn't only need ironing; it needs greasing.

After a hot bath, my skin doesn't look so parched. It is smoother and not so crackly if crackly is a word. The best time to put on lotion is after my bath because it seems to seep in deeper and moisturize my skin longer. The problem is when I see my skin wet, I think it doesn't need moisturizer, so I skip the lotion. This is a bad idea as I need the moisture.

In our Christian life, we often see the dryness of our hearts, and we seek the refreshment of the Lord. Other times, when we are having a particularly good or busy day, we begin to think we can go without Him.

The longer I live with Jesus, the more I realize I will never mature to the point that I don't need Him 24/7. I will always need Him 100%. The good news is that it is exactly the way He planned it. He hates independence. In fact, it is a sin. He made us dependent on Him and interdependent with each other.

I know we all go through hard times. Each of us will face bad circumstances. A fallen world with fallen people will always have dreadful times. We don't have to face them alone or without victory. We don't have to pretend. We can share our burdens first with God and then with each other.

We have times when we all go through similar situations. How do we support each other without having pity parties? Can we have joy in the middle of trials and trust God when our lives are falling apart? These questions don't have quick answers. I do not pretend to know the answers. Only God knows the solution when we face evil and hurt. Let's look at some encouraging words together.

"He who dwells in the secret place of the Most High shall abide under the shadow of the Almighty. I will say to the Lord, 'He is my refuge and my fortress; My God, in Him I will trust" (Psalm 91:1-2).

"My flesh and my heart may fail, but God is the strength of my heart and my portion forever" (Psalm 73:26).

Ponders of the Heart

Do you have a hard time sharing your heart with God or others?

Are you trying to walk alone through life?

Read Micah 7:18-19, John 1:3-5 and John 10:10-11.

Prayers of the Heart

Dear Lord,

Life is hard and sometimes very hurtful. We thank You that nothing is too hard for You. We thank You that You will deliver Your own. God, we are Yours, and You are our hope and our refuge. Thank You that You never leave Your children, and You never shame Your own. Father, hide us in the palm of Your hand. In Jesus' name, amen.

March 30 ~ Springtime

I have a few great memories of Douglas, Georgia, but springtime is one of my favorites.

It was beautiful there. We lived in a neighborhood called Touchton Woods. The yards were covered with dogwood trees and azaleas. It was a stunning time of year. Near our front door was a flower bed that was loaded with azaleas. This was the spot we took our Easter pictures. Chris complained about the sun in his eyes while Tracie and Julie posed for the camera. How fast these years flew by, but they are etched in my mind forever.

Excitement engages us in springtime. Winter can have its toll on us, and we are ready for outside activities and fun. The grass turns green, the flowers bloom, and our lily-white legs call out for the sun.

March is one of those months that can fool us. One minute, we pack away the sweaters just to pull them out again. We are ready for change, but sometimes, change is not ready for us. The greatest thing about spring is that it offers hope. We know warm weather is coming. God has been faithful in the past, and He will be faithful again. Seasons are reminders of His faithfulness.

Where do you find your life today? Are you living hot or cold? Do you have warm days of hope just to have them turn cold on you the next? Has your family bloomed in one area just to be somewhat dead in another?

In the middle of your spring cleaning, if you do such a thing, allow the Holy Spirit to dust off your hope and your dreams. Sometimes, I think I am too old for hopes and dreams, but when I look at God's Word, I see no age limit on that.

As you look at new life on all the plants, look to God and let Him put new growth in you. Allow Him to prune the dead areas and let life come busting out. See yourself not as old, used up, or messed up but alive in Christ. Go ahead, take a deep breath of the Holy Spirit. Feel your spiritual lungs expand as He fills you with life.

Ponders of the Heart

Where do you find yourself today? Hot or cold?

Are you hopefully living or living with hope?

Read Colossians 2:6-15.

Spring is beautiful, but you are far more beautiful when our Savior shines in your heart.

Prayers of the Heart

Dear Father,

What a joy to see Your faithfulness in the seasons each year. Thank You, Father, that You have given us new life, and You will faithfully bring us the fullness of that Life in Christ. We can never understand the fullness of Your love and the completeness of our salvation, but glorious Father, we praise You for Your Word that helps us get a small revelation of Your work on our behalf. In Jesus' name, amen.

March 31 ~ Prayers from the Heart

Dear Gracious Lord,

We bow before Your throne with praise and awe of You. We come to praise Your name and Your presence and to adore You. In our hearts, we want Your presence. You have graciously given this desire to us. We are new creations because of Your provision. Creatures who adore You, and we are thankful for the new spirit within our souls.

God, break the chains that bind us. Break those attitudes and traps that steal our lives. We often leave our first love and chase after things in this world. We replace You with worthless things, making us feel so worthless. We agree that they are not what our hearts were made for.

Thank You for the beauty of creation, the wonder of children, and the gift of family and friends. Father, mostly, we thank You that we are safe in the palm of Your Hand. We are grateful for this day, for Your Word, for Your people, and for the future that is ours. We bow again in praise, for You are worthy, and You are enough. Oh, Lord, You are the fulfillment of all we need. Yet, by Your grace and mercy, You have given us much more. Lord, receive our heartfelt praise and gratitude for Your love for us.

Use the good, the bad, and the in-between to bring us closer to You. Let our faces shine with Your glory. Let our hearts care deeply for others. Help us forgive completely, love with no thought of vulnerability, and give, knowing we have the resources of heaven. Let us live each day in sweet fellowship with You.

Father, bind Your people together. Mend broken families. Protect our children and grandchildren. Help us experience Your love as we love others.

Use us to care for the weak and lead others to Your throne.

Father, we love You. We want to use this time to linger in Your arms. What a wonderful Savior You are. In Jesus' name, amen.

> " —

Very truly I tell you, whoever hears my word and believes him who sent me has eternal life and will not be judged but has crossed over from death to life.

John 5:24

april

April 1 ~ April Fools

How did the holiday of April Fools begin? Most believe it came about because of the calendar change during the sixteenth century. April 1st was the beginning of the New Year and, therefore, was celebrated much like January 1st. There were parties, with people staying up all hours of the night celebrating.

This was long before modern technology and news of the calendar change traveled slowly. Many people were not aware, and even some who heard of the change refused to believe it. These folks were labeled fools.

Folks continued to have parties celebrating the New Year, and some people sent out invitations to parties that never took place. Other jokes were played on those who either didn't get the word or didn't believe it. Mark Twain once wrote, "The first of April is the day we remember what we are the other 364 days of the year." I'm not sure about that statement, but I have felt like a fool and, at times, acted like one. Paul in 1 Corinthians 1:26-27 has a play on words that tells us how God uses our foolishness.

"Brothers and sisters, think of what you were when you were called. Not many of you were wise by human standards; not many were influential; not many were of noble birth. But God chose the foolish things of the world to shame the wise; God chose the weak things of the world to shame the strong."

And when we feel foolish and want to go back to our old habits and thought patterns, Paul writes:

"You foolish Galatians! Who has bewitched you? Before your very eyes Jesus Christ was clearly portrayed as crucified" (Galatians 3:1).

In those passages, we are told the truth of how our feelings can lead us into foolish acts and how God views the wisdom of this world. We see the heart of Paul and his security as he lived in Christ.

"We are fools for Christ's sake" (1 Corinthians 4:10).

In our Christian Walk, we will appear foolish in this world, for the world is caught in the wisdom of this age. We will sometimes listen to the world and have the Lord call us back to Himself. Today, on this holiday set aside for fools, let's proclaim with the voice of Paul, "We are fools, for Christ's sake!"

Ponders of the Heart

Has God revealed to you the places where you have become wise in the world and foolish in God's wisdom?

Do you need to come back to your first love?

Read 1 Corinthians 3:18-23 and Colossians 1:21-22.

Prayers of the Heart

Dear Father,

We have all felt and acted like fools at times. But in You, we are redeemed and have the righteousness of Christ. God, what a gift of Your grace. What a wonderful thing to belong to You. Jesus, help us give up the wisdom of this world and embrace Your wisdom. We praise You in the name that is above every name. We lift the name of Jesus. In His name, we pray, amen.

April 2 ~ What the World Needs

We have all heard it said what the world needs is more love, but where does this love come from? Truly, since the time of Eden, sweet love has been hard to find. How does one explain love? There are those who think it is an emotion. I have heard and believe it is also a decision. Where do you find this thing called love, and are we capable of it?

When I was in the first, second, or third grade, my brother had a friend named Richie Jordan. I thought he was the cutest thing I had ever seen. He came to one of my birthday parties, and I slept with his birthday card under my pillow for days. I thought that was love. As a young teenager, I went to a Beatles concert in Jacksonville and screamed with all the other girls. That must have been love. You say, "How silly, of course not." Love is hard to explain and harder to experience.

After Peter denied Jesus and while Jesus was in the grave, Peter must have asked himself a few questions about his ability to love. He thought, and had even proclaimed, that he loved Jesus. How could he deny who Jesus was?

Have you ever done something to someone you loved and asked yourself, "How could I do such a thing?" Has someone who said they loved you ever done something horrible to you? At that moment, you were sure they didn't know what love was. Our actions can damage the people we say we love. This is a discouraging thing.

The Greeks were wiser than us. They had different words to describe love. They had a word that described love between a woman and a man, a word for friendship love, and agape was the word that described the unconditional love God has for us. His love is a quality that dwells in His being. He is the Author of love, and it needs no response from us.

Think about that for a moment. God's character is love, and it is unconditional. It is more than an emotion, for it does not change according to our response or changes according to circumstances. It is grounded in who He is.

Who is this God? He is the One who is all power; therefore, His love is all-powerful. Our God is all-knowing; therefore, His love is all-knowing. He knows our failures before we do them. He is everywhere; therefore, His love can be and go everywhere. We cannot escape His reach.

I would rather have this love given to me than the mushy or passionate kind I see on TV or read about in novels. I'm not against mushy or passionate love, but the greatest kind is the immovable love of God. We can long for it with boldness.

Why did Jesus ask Peter the question, "Do you love Me?" He knew the answer. He asked Peter the question to restore him. From that point on, Peter didn't doubt his love and devotion for Jesus. The Holy Spirit had poured God's love into his heart.

Peter was unaware of the depth of his great exchange in Christ. He knew of human love, and now he was ready to discover the supernatural love that was his because of his new birth in Jesus.

The day Jesus died, Peter died on the cross. (Galatians 2:20, Romans 6:3) When Jesus was resurrected, Peter was resurrected. (Romans 6:9-11) He was a new creation, created in Christ Jesus. He now could love out of the character of God.

This is a gift from the Holy Spirit. We can love with *agape* love, which is supernatural because it is Christ's love that we have received.

Our godly love can transform the way we love our husbands, children, and our grandchildren. We can extend this love to friends and even our enemies. It is truly supernatural. Our care is not tied to our circumstances or how the ones we reach out to respond. It freely flows in the lives of those who walk in the Spirit and not the flesh.

We now know what kind of love our world needs: *agape* love.

Ponders of the Heart

Can we ask God to give us His love for others?

Who are you having a tough time loving?

Read 1 Corinthians 13.

His love is mighty and tender and all-consuming and gentle; His love is eternal and for today. Spend time praising Him and drinking in His love. Then, go forth and love others.

Prayers of the Heart:

Dear Father,

You are the source and power behind true love, and we thank You for filling us and surrounding us with Your love. We are now free to love You and others with our whole hearts. We are safe in Your goodness and secure in being wanted and loved by You. In Jesus' name, amen.

April 3 ~ The Cave of Protection

Bears hibernate in dark caves in the wintertime. Their purpose is to get a good winter nap in a protective environment. This would not be my choice, or would it? Let's see, a cave is dark and quiet, is a cover from weather and enemies, all that seems good to me. Caves are also wet, dingy, nasty, muddy, and ugly, and that doesn't appeal to me at all.

The Bible tells us Obadiah hid one hundred prophets in two caves, providing for them food and water (I Kings 18:4). Elijah spent the night in a cave hiding from Jezebel (I Kings 19:9). Jesus was born and buried in a cave. It looks as if, throughout history, caves have been somewhat of a dwelling place.

My biggest problem with caves is the fear of being trapped there, unable to get out. Miners go deep into them looking for coal, silver, gold, etc.; they blast rocks away and sometimes end up stuck there. I will need to stop typing for a moment so my hands will stop sweating at the thought of being stuck in a cave.

I know people who have been stuck in caves and are unable to get out. They go there for protection, rest, and to lick their wounds, but they end up trapped there. They are even afraid to come out, for they do not know if they can handle life outside their cave of protection.

Now, I am not talking about a physical cave, but a protective one they erected around their hearts. They have their love, compassion, and tenderness hidden deep in their cave of protection. If you touch the wall of their cave, watch out, for the walls are covered with bitter and angry words. The light is dim at best, and the doors to their caves are hard to find.

Men are famous cave dwellers, but women dwell there too. Men are afraid of failure, especially in relationships. This fear will send them deep into their cave, and they will not let you in. Knock, shout hurtful words, call them every name in the book, but you are not getting in. Your knocks, words, and name-calling only cause them to go deeper so they cannot hear you.

Do you know any people like that? Women go in for protection also. They like to look out the window just to see you act like a fool. Then they say, "I knew it. I knew I could not trust you. You are not getting in." We become cave dwellers of the heart. That is sad, isn't it?

What can get us free so we can start living again? If failure or lack of trust sends us there, then acceptance and trust of someone can get us out.

"Here I am! I stand at the door and knock. If anyone hears my voice and opens the door, I will come in and eat with that person, and they with me" (Revelation 3:20).

Only Christ can give us perspective about our situation. He can show us His acceptance and faithfulness. Christ can show us how to live out who we are in Him, not how we feel. The two most critical issues of life are knowing who God is and what He says about us. If we are "in Christ," then we can live out of the truth of who we are. If you are not "in Him," then by faith, receive His forgiveness and His new life.

We are to live in this truth, not our feelings. Even when life is unsettling, and we feel alone and abandoned by Him, we can stand on the truth of His Word. God tells us He will never forsake us, and this helps us change our wrong feelings.

For those cave dwellers you know and love, tenderly love them. Pray for them that the tenderness of God will reach their hearts. Be a vessel He can use to woo them out. God's love is powerful enough to blast the walls of our caves, and His love can reach the darkest, deepest part. God wants us to come out into the light and live a joyful life. Praise the Lord.

Ponders of the Heart

Read Colossians 2:11-15, Colossians 3:1-4, and Ephesians 1:3-8.

What does God's Word tell you about who you are in Christ?

What directions does His Word give you on how to live the Christian life?

Prayers of the Heart

Dear Father,

You have taken us out of darkness into the kingdom of Your Son. You have redeemed us from being cave dwellers to kingdom dwellers. Help us keep our eyes on things above, not on things below. Flood our lives with Your powerful love and blast us free from the caves of gloom and destruction. In Jesus' name, amen.

April 4 ~ Protection

When my son was in his teenage years, he loved skateboarding. Before he got his driver's license, I would load up the car with the boys and head to Jacksonville, Florida, to a skateboard park. At the time, we lived about two hours away. The trip to the skate park wasn't bad, but the trip back with a car full of sweaty teenage boys was unpleasant for the nose.

These boys would have all kinds of equipment. They had helmets to protect their heads, knee pads for knees, elbow pads, gloves, and just the right kind of skateboards. All this equipment was for protection, but I carried home some banged-up boys. We all realized there was a risk to the adventure. However, their bangs and bruises never deterred them from the love of skateboarding. The battle scars were part of their manhood display.

Yesterday, we talked about cave dwellers. People who have covered their hearts with walls of protection to keep themselves locked in and to keep others out.

In the Christian life, we are given a lot of protection equipment. First, we are covered by the blood of Jesus, giving us purity, forgiveness, and access to the throne room of heaven. We are given the Holy Spirit to mark us, instruct us, and give us new eternal life.

God has given us His Word so we might know and live in a relationship with Him. The Spirit uses the Word to transform our minds where the battle rages. We receive protection from God's grace, His love, and fellowship. All of this plus the guarantee of an eternal home with the conveniences of peaceful living. Our home will be void of evil, sin, worry, sadness, and shame. Even if we get banged up in this life, we will arrive home safely.

If we are to be cave dwellers, let's dwell in caves of His making, formed by His hands and not ours. A cave of His grace and the blood of His Son that will give us freedom and adventure.

"You will be a crown of splendor in the Lord's hand, a royal diadem in the hand of your God" (Isaiah 62:3).

Ponders of the Heart

Do you hide your heart and limit your love to protect yourself?

Do you love someone who is a cave dweller?

Read Job 5:18 and Isaiah 61:13.

Prayers of the Heart

Dear Father,

We come with no answers, only hope in You. Life is hard and sometimes painful, but You are our hope. Father, fill us, mold us, and use us for Your glory. You, and only You, can give us Your peace and joy. Come and fill us. It is in Jesus' name, amen.

April 5 ~ Birth

Fears keep me far away from anything medical. God has a way of helping me deal with fears, and love is a great motivator.

I recall the day my daughter, Tracie, went into labor. Neither of us intended for me to be in the labor room, but something about pain and fear changed our minds. She didn't want me to go, and I was not leaving my girl's side.

Together, we pushed, panted, and held on for dear life, but all for naught because, with the help of a c-section, Collier came into this world with screams of life and a great need for a bath. As a little boy, he will repeat that need many times.

Ryan, my very efficient son-in-law, videoed the birth. With a screen in the proper place for privacy's sake, we were all privileged to see Collier's birth.

I will always be thankful for this day. It was a day that sealed love from one generation to another, with Collier as the common link. He received love from both the older generation and the younger one. This is not the case for all babies.

Ezekiel 16:1-6 describes the birth of an unwanted child. The baby is biracial, the father of one race and the mother of another. How can a baby be unwanted? We can be such cruel people with strange, unloving ideas.

In this story, they left the baby for dead. No bath for this little one like our Collier received. No joy from grandparents or parents over this birth. The scriptures say the baby was "left in his own blood; no eyes pitied this child." They threw the baby out in the field to die because they loathed the child from the moment of its birth.

How many children enter this cruel world unwanted? Babies are aborted before they take their first breath. I hate to think about such terrible things. Yet, this story in Ezekiel gives us hope.

If you haven't stopped to read Ezekiel 16:1-6, now is the time to do it. Verse six is the verse to ponder.

"Then I passed by and saw you kicking about in your blood, and as you lay there in your blood I said to you, 'Live!'" (Ezekiel 16:6).

God has just given us a picture of ourselves apart from His mercy and grace. We were dying in sin with the plague of humanity, struggling, and death. But the King of all kings and the Lord of all lords saw us struggling in our death, in our blood, and said to me, "Marilyn Collier, live." He said to you, "Live."

Oh, that we might see the glory of our new birth in Him. Glory, honor, and praise to our King.

Ponders of the Heart

Are you living in the power of the Lord?

Are you eating and drinking His Word?

Read John 15:1-5 and John 6:53-57.

Prayers of the Heart

Dear Father,

Could our praise be more? Could our love be more overwhelming than when we realize that one day, you called us from death to eternal life? Father, God, Your compassion is more than we can bear, and Your mercy is a consuming fire. Precious Lord, giver of eternal life, we praise, adore and honor You. Father, teach us how to live. In Jesus' name, amen.

April 6 ~ The Betrothed

We started reading Ezekiel 16 yesterday. In it, God uses the birth of an unwanted child to relate to His people, the Israelites. They were a nation born from the Amorites and the Hittites, whose father was Abraham.

He reminded them they were a hated nation in Egypt by the example of an unwanted child and the disdain the world held for this child. He, however, had a different heart and showed compassion.

We marveled over the fact that it was also our calling. In Ezekiel 16:7-8, God paints another picture for us of a young woman who grows into a beautiful one and enters the covenant relationship of marriage.

This scripture reminds me of one of my favorite fairy tales, Snow White. I call it a fairy tale, for this was not my experience as a young woman. Somewhere in my youth, I became plump. I was also short, so being plump and short was a double whammy. I was cute but not a beautiful, budding flower like so many girls in my school. Of course, in this comparing game, I wasn't the worst either. Could life be more shallow?

Ezekiel 16:7 talks about the young woman's beauty but also her nakedness and emptiness. Outward beauty does not meet the needs of our souls. Only God can do that. The story continues, and the Lord looks upon her beauty and need. At just the right time, He makes her His.

As I related to you, in my eyes, I was not a beauty, but my Bill thought I was. When he saw me, he said, "That's the girl for me." I call it grace. I could not believe his love for me. I also believe that those I thought had it all together felt inadequate. You might have been one of those beauties. You are probably shaking your head right now. For you, like me, were so afraid life would pass you by. Some of you still do.

Remember the covenant where God said to us, "Live!" He looks at us and takes us into an everlasting covenant with Him. We become His, and He becomes ours. He looks through all the outward beauty or lack thereof and sees His soon- to-be-bride. He uses His wing to cover our nakedness and fill our emptiness with His Holy Spirit. He does not miss the void of our souls; He fills them with Himself.

We marvel over the wonder of His all-sufficient love. He, the lover of our souls, satisfies us completely. He has not passed by us. He has clothed us with His righteousness, preparing us for the wedding of the Lamb.

I love my husband, but there is no way our marriage will be like this one. You might think, "A bridesmaid, but never a bride." Your marriage here on earth might be a disaster, but this one will be more than we can imagine. Earthly marriages can indeed be awful, and some are wonderful. They can be hard, impossible, and some are great.

Marriage on earth has an earthly purpose. One purpose is to be an example of the marriage that is to come. We can rejoice over earthly marriages that bring praise and honor to God. Rejoice, knowing one day we, too, will be at a marriage feast. We will be center stage, praising the Lord for seeing us in our nakedness and our emptiness. We will fall before Him in praise for filling our hearts with His Spirit and giving us Himself. What wonderful joy.

Ponders of the Heart

If you are married, what was your wedding like?

How would you describe your marriage?

Read Exodus 19:4-6, Isaiah 61:10, and 2 Corinthians 5:21.

Prayers of the Heart

Dear Father,

You have covered us with Your beauty, clothed us with Your righteousness, filled us with Your Spirit, and someday You will bring us home to be Your wife. Praise and glory to Your name. Which is to say, praise and glory to Your nature, which is love and compassion. So worthy are You to be praised. Worthy is the Lamb. In Jesus' name, amen.

April 7 ~ The Marriage

Looking back at Ezekiel 16, we discovered that God saw us dead in our sin and said to us, "Live!" We also discovered that in our youth, outward beauty was not enough because we were naked and empty. God looked upon our souls and covered us with His wing, filled us with His Spirit, betrothed us to Himself, and made us His. Today, look at Ezekiel 16:9-14, a perfect picture of the consummation of our lives with Him.

In this passage, we see the gifts the groom gives to his bride. These were gifts portraying how special she was to him. Her body was cleansed as our Lord cleanses us with His blood (Heb.9:13,14,22). After she was cleansed, he clothed her with fine garments and adorned her with ornaments and jewels. Placing a crown on her head, then feeding her with fine pastry. She was taken from being an ordinary woman to royalty.

I remember my wedding day. Not because I was so beautiful but I remember how excited I was. Our love was passionate and innocent. We had waited for this day for so long and could not wait to consummate our love. I wasn't especially nice to the people who came. Maybe I was, I hope so. I do not remember the flowers, the cake, or what anyone said or did, but I remember the anticipation of being Mrs. Bill Collier.

We did marry, and because of the innocence of it all, we spent the next months, even years, going on decades, discovering the wonder of our love.

That is what it will be like in heaven. We will discover our love. Jesus will have no sin attached to Him. The wonder of Jesus will exceed our expectations. All disappointing relationships will be crushed under His perfection. He will be our perfect match. The "what ifs" will be overshadowed by the "what is." The glory of His presence will light the sky with the glowing light of His love. We will be as queens to Him, and our hearts will be safe and full of love.

I know it is hard to imagine. It sounds too good to be true. I know you are afraid to think of such wonder, but it is true. You just read it in His Word. If not, stop and read it. Drink what is true, regardless of your experiences and how you feel right now. Our motivation is found right here, in the truth of His Word, the truth of our future.

If we have been cleansed by the blood of the Lamb, covered in His righteousness, and have received the Holy Spirit, we are on our way to glory. We are going to be brides. His bride.

I find it funny that not only will I be His bride, but so will my husband.

When I read passages like these, I realize how wonderful it is to be a woman and how much God loves women. We have been given special insight, and we can picture with our hearts the future. How I praise the God of our birth. I am thankful and proud to be a woman. Thank you, Father, God.

Ponders of the Heart

Read Ezekiel 16:9-14 and Revelation 19:6-10

Has this world made you feel ugly and unworthy?

How have these verses helped you see yourself differently?

Prayers of the Heart

Dear Father,

Our Husband and future, how we love You, and how excited we are to have the fullness of our relationship consummated. You are still preparing us to be Your bride. She will be the full manifestation of Your glory, and she will be presented to You complete. Father, who around us needs to hear of Your love? We are here; send us. We are ready, use us. Lord. We love, praise, and adore You. In Jesus' name, we pray, amen.

April 8 ~ My Splendor

"And your fame spread among the nations on account of your beauty, because the splendor I had given you made your beauty perfect, declares the Sovereign Lord" (Ezekiel 16:14).

In Ezekiel 16, God describes His beautiful bride. He says she is exceedingly beautiful and perfect, which means complete. Then the verse says something fantastic. It says that she, which means us, was made perfect by His splendor, which He bestowed on her.

I want us to picture this one more time. We are all at the wedding feast, and Christ has prepared us. Our bodies are clean, pure by His blood. Our souls are filled by His Spirit, and we are adorned with the beauty of Christ.

We have changed from ordinary and corruptible people to queens and incorruptible people. Our splendor is the very work of our Lord.

I wanted to stay here one more day for this very purpose. When God saw us in our death and said, "Live." He betrothed us to Himself; He began working to make us ready to be His bride, and He is working our splendor out day by day.

Let me give you an example. My husband's brother, Rick, married my best friend in high school. Pat is an extremely brilliant and talented person. She made her daughter's and daughter-in-law's wedding dresses. They were beautiful.

She also made a doll for each of them with a perfect replica of their dresses. I told you she is incredibly talented.

At weddings, we all marveled at the beautiful brides. They walked toward their grooms, looking radiant. Their eyes were aglow with love, their faces were full of anticipation and excitement, and they were dressed in splendor.

We all knew who had made these spectacular wedding gowns. Pat had worked for months on each dress. We all knew the love, the talent, and the sacrifice Pat had made so these girls could be so beautiful. Rick was proud of Pat and the work she had done. We were all proud of her.

I was also a little jealous. If my girls had to wear a wedding dress I made, well, they couldn't. That would just be impossible. But don't you know how loved and how special Pat made each of these girls feel?

This is how we will feel on our wedding day in heaven. We will be dressed in the fruit of His labor. Our splendor will be the beauty He bestowed upon us.

Our eyes will be full of love, and our faces will be aglow with anticipation and excitement. We will be dressed in the splendor of His work He did through us.

Can you imagine how we will feel? We will know we are truly the work of His Hand. It will be wonderful to be completely understood and treasured. Completely loved. That is going to be a glorious day.

Ponders of the Heart

When you think of God, do you realize you are completely loved?

Do you look forward to Heaven, or are you more earthbound?

Read 1 Corinthians 15:54-58.

Prayers of the Heart

Dear Father,

We look forward to our heavenly wedding. We will be dressed by Your glorious work in and through us. Lord, thank You for pouring Your love into our hearts. Fill us with passion for You. Open our eyes so we might see all You have for us. Open our ears so we might hear Your voice. Father, God, we love You and adore You. We praise You. Help us shine with the glory of Your presence. In Jesus 'name, amen.

April 9 ~ Hanging On

Way back when my middle child was about three, we were taking a walk around the neighborhood. Chris, my oldest, and Tracie were goofing around when Tracie fell and rolled right into a drainage hole on the side of the road.

She caught the side and hung on. I sent Chris running home to get Bill for help. I held her hands as I tried to pull her up. We were terrified, and I didn't know the depth of the hole. The fear was she would fall before her dad got there. But Bill, our in-house "knight in shining armor," arrived to save the day.

In the devotional book Utmost for His Highest, Oswald Chambers gives us a wonderful definition of perseverance.

"Perseverance is more than endurance. It is endurance combined with absolute assurance and certainty that what we are looking for is going to happen. Perseverance means more than just hanging on, which may be only exposing our fear of letting go and falling."

That quote hits me hard. Because of fear, I will hold on too long for the terror of letting go and falling. I admit there are times when I struggle with weak faith and trust.

When Tracie was hanging on for dear life, I was afraid she would fall. The funny part was she wasn't a foot from the bottom. Her feet were almost touching the ground. Our fear was unfounded.

How often do I let the fear of nothing control me? Oh, that I would learn to trust Jesus with all the circumstances of this life. Can you relate?

For God has not given us a spirit of fear, but of power and of love and of a sound mind" (2 Timothy.1:7 NKJV).

My fears can get the best of me. In my weakness, the Lord is strong. It is not my faith that will carry me through. It is the object of my faith, and that is Jesus. He is the one who can keep me from falling.

Ponders of the Heart

Do you have an issue with fear?

What helps you deal with fear?

Read Romans 8:15 and 2 Peter 1:2-8.

Prayers of the Heart

Dear Lord,

We praise You as we surrender our cares to You. We bless Your name that we are safe in Your Arms. Lord, help us hold on to You as we let go of fear and false securities. You have not given us a spirit of fear, but You have given us all we need to live a good life by giving us Your Spirit. In Jesus' name, amen.

April 10 ~ The Anchor Holds

Richard Shiver was a minister at a church I attended. When he passed away, the song sung at his funeral was "The Anchor Holds." What a proper song to be sung at the funeral of a saint. What a testimony of faith says, "Regardless of what you think about my life, God held me to the end."

Richard wanted us to know that Christ has been faithful to him. The anchor of his life was very real. This is a message we all need to hear today. No matter what we face, the loss of a job, the end of a marriage, the death of a loved one, or our death, our anchor will hold if the Lord Jesus Christ is our anchor.

Imagine with me a ship in a stormy sea being held tightly by an anchor. The ship bounces and moves up and down, taking on water, but the anchor holds. The sailors can only hold tightly by faith in the strength of the anchor to hold them until the storm ends.

I sit here thinking about the countless hours I have spent in God's Word, studying them and teaching them, but the point of Scripture is to draw us to Jesus. He is the One I put my hope in, not in my knowledge.

When all fails, it is Jesus who will hold us. We stand on faith in Him and nothing else. He is our salvation, future, and our hope. Only He will carry us from this world to the next. Richard's testimony is that Jesus is our anchor.

When we find ourselves with troubles and uncertainties, how do we lean on Jesus? By faith. Let me quote a good definition of faith found in Hebrews 11:1.

"Now faith is confidence in what we hope for and assurance about what we do not see."

It is not only our faith that holds us, for we could have faith in an idol in South Africa. It is the object of our faith, and Jesus is the certainty of our hope for salvation.

I am sure Richard had his doubts and fears in life. We all struggle with fear and doubt. But isn't it wonderful to know whatever we face, we do not face it alone? God is the faithful One.

Somewhere in heaven, our faith was carved out of the heavenly rock on which we stand. This faith will hold us until our eternal feet rest on this heavenly Rock. Praise to the Son and the wonder of His faithfulness. Jesus held Richard to the end, and He will hold us until we reach the peaceful shores of heaven.

Ponders of the Heart

When you are being tossed about in life, who is your anchor?

Can you picture walking into heaven with Jesus by your side?

Are you confident that Jesus will complete the work He began in you?

Read Romans 8:18-27.

Prayers of the Heart

Dear Father,

You are our rest and the sum of all our hope and goodness. You are the anchor that holds us during any storm. You are the great I Am, and we are Your children. Precious Father, hold us closely and do not pass us by. In Jesus' name, amen.

April 11 ~ Life and Death

In the spring, you often see life and death beside each other. As I travel the road, I see the trees with fresh green leaves beside trees with winter's death. My eyes are drawn to the new life.

Green is a color of hope to me, and I love to see the wonder of spring each year. I do not know what captures my heart more than new life or the contrast between the death of some trees and the life of others.

We see that contrast in people, too. I am often amazed at the contrast between the darkness living in one person and the life of Christ in another. Sometimes, when I listen to the media or watch television, I wonder about the minds of these people. I wonder if we are living in the same world. I'm aware if they heard me talk about certain things, they would think the same about me. Our perspectives are so different.

Please don't misunderstand me. I don't have the corner on all wisdom, but I know the One who does. My knowledge is so limited. There are so many brilliant people in this world, but as exceptional as they are, they are no match for the Alpha and Omega. He is my Lord, and His grace has given me a new perspective. One not of this world. No wonder I feel so odd.

In Revelation 22:1-5, we see a partial picture of heaven. John talks about the river of life that flows from the throne of God and the Lamb. He also talks about the tree of life that produces fruit for the healing of the nations and the light of heaven that comes directly from His presence. We will see the Lord's face, and His name will be on our foreheads.

We only see life in heaven, no death, just eternal life. This life comes from the Hand of God through the sacrifice of Jesus and the faith we placed in Him.

He is the provider of our life now and the provider of our eternal existence. The difference is there will be no death, for the presence of sin will be no more.

Spring is a reminder that life comes from Him. Look around and see the life that surrounds you. In our condition of death, He gives us hope for a new day. Our future is sure if our faith is in the One who promises to make all things new for eternity. Now, that is something to look forward to. I can't wait to see you there.

"He who was seated on the throne said, 'I am making everything new!' Then he said, 'Write this down, for these words are trustworthy and true'" (Revelation 21:5).

Ponders of the Heart

Can you picture heaven and you being there?

Do you try to understand the wonder of God's love for you now and His love for you in heaven?

Read Revelation 21: 1-6 and Revelation 22:1-5.

Heaven is our sure hope because of Jesus!

Prayers of the Heart

Dear Father,

Thank You for our lives being hidden in You. We praise You that our provision for life is eternally secure. Father, You light our way until we reach the foot of Your throne room. Praise You, Lord, for the hope You have given us, Your children. Hold us tight so we can feel Your mighty Hand leading us home. In Jesus' name, amen.

April 12 ~ What Are You Wearing?

What are you wearing? I have on an old tee shirt and sweatpants. My hair is a mess, but I do have on makeup. What to wear is one of the first questions I face in the morning. I go to my closet, look over the same things, and try to come up with a suitable outfit. I have two closets, and I will walk from one to the other, looking for something to put on. Sound familiar?

We are told in the Bible to put on Christ:

"Rather, clothe yourselves with the Lord Jesus Christ, and do not think about how to gratify the desires of the flesh" (Romans 13:14).

"For all of you who were baptized into Christ have clothed yourselves with Christ" (Galatians 3:27).

Have you ever thought about how we are to dress spiritually?

We all have a closet with our old fleshly clothes in it. I have a shirt that says, rejected. I also have some that say, "You don't measure up "and "You're not smart." Old shirts of mine remind me of the old me before I was clothed in Christ. Some of my shoes are marked insignificant and dirty. I washed them, trying to clean them up, but the old words kept bleeding through. I have a dress that says unlovely and unwanted. A suit that says, "Sinner."

That closet is full, but I do not have to dress there, for when I was baptized into Christ, I was given a brand-new wardrobe.

My new closet has clothes with new names. I have a new shirt that says righteous, holy, forgiven, and justified. I have shoes that say clean and treasured and a dress that says the Bride of Christ. And a suit that says, saint.

For the life of me I do not know why I go back to that old closet. I don't like those clothes. Often, I will think about putting on the shirt that says righteous but, instead, get the shirt that says rejected. When I dress like that, I have a miserable day.

We have a choice. I think I will go to Wal-Mart right now, get a lock for that old closet, and throw away the key. Do you want to come with me? Come on, put on your shoes that say clean and treasured, and go with me.

Ponders of the Heart

Do you struggle with your old wardrobe?

What are the names you call yourself?

What does God say about you instead?

Read 2 Corinthians 6:11-18 and 2 Corinthians 5:17-21. Don't wear those old clothes.

Prayers of the Heart

Dear Father,

You have clothed us with Your Son's righteousness. You have given us new life and a new identity. Lord, help us walk and dress out of the spirit and not go back into the closet of our old self. Help us dress for success. We are Yours, and we want to dress as Your children, dearly loved and totally accepted. We love You, Lord, and we praise You for loving us. In Jesus' name, amen.

April 13 ~ Solid Faith

Do you have faith that keeps you in times of trouble? Let me tell you an interesting story about faith.

There was an expert ice skater who lived near a small pond. Each year, he looked forward to his first skate of the winter season. One fall, the pond, because of the wintry weather, had iced over early. He was sure the pond was frozen solid and headed to the pond with expectation and confidence.

As he skated, all went well for several minutes, but then the ice gave way, and he plunged beneath the water. With the weight of the skates and his clothes, he could not pull himself up, and he died in the icy pond just yards from his home.

In this story, the man has self-confidence; but it was not his confidence that failed him. It was the object of his faith. The object of our faith is more important than the amount of our faith. Who or what are we putting our hope in? If, like this story, we place our hope in ourselves or an icy pond, we might find ourselves underneath the water about to drown.

I think Jesus might say to this man, "You study the Scriptures diligently because you think that in them you have eternal life. These are the very Scriptures that testify about me, yet you refuse to come to me to have life" (John 5:39-40).

If we are not careful, we can find ourselves putting our confidence in anything and everything other than God.

We will use every resource available to us, and if we happen to have outward success, we can start to think we are okay. The problem is we have placed our faith on flimsy ice.

The Lord wants us to put on our skates and face life with excitement but to be sure the ice can bear our weight. The ice may be slippery, and we might fall, but if the weight is on the Solid Rock, Jesus Christ, we can be sure He can handle the weight of our lives.

Ponders of the Heart

Do you relate to this story, or do you know someone who would?

Are you skating through life on thin ice?

Read Matthew. 7:24-27 and Psalm 20:7. Ask God to reveal to you who you are trusting.

Prayers of the Heart

Dear Father,

Let us not depend on this world but depend on You. Be our all and all. Oh, Father, we often build our lives on sinking sand and thin ice. Save us, Lord. You are our only hope. In Jesus' name, amen.

April 14 ~ Weak Faith

There was a man who lived in the wilderness, and the trading post was across from the lake near his home. He traveled to the trading post by boat, except when the lake was frozen.

It was late fall, and the lake was completely frozen. His wife became sick. He recognized her symptoms and knew the medicine she needed was across the lake.

He was sure the lake would not hold his weight. It was too early in the fall, but this was the only chance his wife had. He kissed her goodbye, doubting he would ever see her again, but he had no choice; he had to try.

Laying on a board, he pushed it in front of him, sliding over the icy lake. He inched his way ever so slowly across what he thought to be his deathbed. All was going well, and the ice seemed to hold his weight. Then he heard a groaning sound. He held his breath, waiting to crash into the water, but to his surprise, he stayed dry. If only he could reach the shore before the ice gave way.

Just then, he saw a wagon beside him with a man heading for the post. The wagon made it to the shore, and the man jumped off and ran into the trading post. Our man also jumped up, knowing if the ice could hold the wagon, it could hold him. He ran to the shore, bought the medicine, and rode back across the lake on the wagon with his new friend, who had proven the ice would hold. He gave the medicine to his wife, and all was well.

The story we read yesterday, our man had faith, but the object of his faith could not hold his weight. In this story, the man has little hope that he will make it across the lake, but the object of his faith proves him wrong. He inched away, consumed in fear, for he did not know the strength of the ice. Personally, I relate more to this story. I find myself inching along, not trusting I will make it to the other side.

Jesus would say to those who trust too much in themselves what He said to His disciples, James and John when they wanted to be elevated to the right and the left of Him when His kingdom came.

"But Jesus said to them, 'You do not know what you ask. Are you able to drink the cup that I drink, and be baptized with the baptism that I am baptized with?' They said to Him, 'We are able" (Mark 10:38-39 NKJV).

I have found faith in myself can get me into icy water. If we want to live a life of faith, I must seek the Lord in all I do. He is the faithful One, and only He can give us peace and direction. We cannot do this life without Him.

"Do not let your hearts be troubled. You believe in God believe also in me" (John 14:1.)

Jesus does not want us to inch through life with fear; rather, He wants us to have confidence in Him.

Ponders of the Heart

What story do you relate to more?

Are you skating through life on thin ice, or are you inching your way through life, not knowing you are on solid rock?

Read Hebrews 1:1-4, John 1:14, Colossians 1:17, and Phil. 2:9-11.

Prayers of the Heart

Dear Father,

You are worthy of all our faith and trust. You are worthy and able to hold us, for You alone are faithful. Father, You are our strength and our refuge. We thank You that even in our fear and our lack of faith, You are sufficient. Lord, help us rest completely in You. In Jesus' name, amen.

April 15 ~ Managing Fears

Since we all experience uncertainties and fears, here is an article from Lifetime Guarantee Ministries on managing fears.

"We stand today on the brink of war, so let me ask you, my friend. How are you managing your fears? I was reminded recently that the first thing Adam said to God after he and Eve declared independence and sinned was, 'I was afraid.' It is noteworthy that the first thing God said when Christ was born was, 'Fear not.'"

In simple terms, the struggle in our lives is between independence and dependence, fear and faith, flesh and Spirit, self-sufficiency, and reliance upon the Father. When we live independently, we are controlled by our fears. Walking in the Spirit, depending upon our Heavenly Father, is living beyond our fears in perfect love.

The Bible says, "There is no fear in love. But perfect love drives out fear, because fear has to do with punishment. The one who fears is not made perfect in love" (1 John 4:18).

If I ask how you are managing your fears, I'm inquiring about your walk with the Spirit. How are you living in perfect love, thriving in His grace, and basking in our Father's love?

When you get right down to it, at the heart of every fear is the presupposition that God is not present, in control, or sufficient. This contradicts who God is and how He designed us to live. Regardless of what happens, our Father promises to be sufficient and never leave or abandon us. There is no one, and no concern is greater than He is. We are secure in the knowledge and fact of His love. What is there to fear?

There is an Arab parable that says, "All sunshine and no rain make a desert." If we never experienced difficult circumstances, our dependence on God would be all dried up and our lives would never enjoy the wonder of His presence.

Ponders of the Heart

What do you fear?

Why do we have such a tough time trusting God?

Read John 14 and John 15:1-7.

Prayers of the Heart

Dear Father,

We confess we often forget the magnitude of who You are. Father, we confess we get so worried about circumstances we forget to look up and see Your face. You are right here, and nothing is too hard for You. Help us remember that You are for us and not against us. We long to live in the light of your path. Help us rest in Your love and grace. We love You, Father. In Jesus' name, amen.

April 16 ~ Who Am I?

What did you want to be when you grew up? Did you want to be a movie star, ballerina, nurse, schoolteacher, mom, or all the above?

As a child, we can spend countless hours pretending. I always wanted to be a schoolteacher, a cowgirl, a mother, and a wife. I made two out of four.

That is what I wanted, but what was my motivation? As a cowgirl, I wanted to be adventurous, brave, and free. As a schoolteacher, I wanted to be important; to a little girl, a schoolteacher is important. I also wanted to be loved and give my love to others; that is why I wanted to be a wife and a mother. Who knows? But one thing is sure: I wanted to be significant and loved. I still do.

In my journey through life, I have tried different things in search of who I am and my purpose. Have you found your place, or are you still searching for your purpose? What I have found is I am not far from that little girl who spent hours pretending, searching for her heart's desire.

Here are two important questions to ponder: Who have you discovered that you aren't, and who have you discovered you are? God has opened my heart to these questions in a fresh new way.

He has created us for His kingdom, and we fit perfectly. At times, I jump into things that are not for me. God helps me see He has a better plan. The challenge is finding true peace and joy in His design, timing, and way. As I said before, I am not far from that little girl who spent hours pretending and searching for my heart's desire.

Releasing myself to His perfect will is a daily challenge, but that is my desire, and yet I cannot get there without His grace.

You also have been created by the perfect Architect, and His will for you is flawless. Our job is to praise Him and ask Him to lead us and help us find our way.

Ponders of the Heart

Have you found your purpose in this life, or are you still searching?

What have you learned about who you are on this journey?

Read Genesis 1:26-27, John 3:3, 5-6, and Romans 8:28-29.

God's design purpose for us is to be conformed to the image of His Son by our new birth. Ponder this truth and ask God to free your heart into His will and way.

Prayers of the Heart

Dear Father,

You have created us for Yourself, and we belong to You. Father, conform our hearts to Your will; it is there we will find peace and rest. Thank You for the times You have called us from our wandering and captured our hearts fresh and new. Thank You that Your power is made perfect in our weakness. Your grace and love overwhelm us. We praise You. In Jesus' name, amen.

April 17 ~ Freedom and Failure

Our grandchildren went through the process of learning how to use their hands and bodies. They had to learn how to pick things up, crawl, stand, and walk. There were many bumped heads. This thing called coordination is not easy. Little bruises started showing up on their cheeks, legs, and arms as they tried to master walking and crawling. We were there to help them, but too much protection equals slow learning. There is a balance of living and growing.

Their parents, as well as Bill and me, tried to set up boundaries so their skills could equal their determinations, but they continued to go beyond our safety net. Oh, if it were not for God's grace, would anyone live past the baby stage?

As a grandmother, I didn't want them to get hurt, but I realize that if the restriction becomes too strict, it hinders their natural growth. That is also true for us. In our lives, we learned important things from failure and pain.

I thank the Lord for the freedom He gives us to fail. I surely don't like the pain that comes with failure, so I have often set up strict guidelines to protect myself, only to find myself enslaved by my own boundaries.

Eugene Peterson said, "Any formula that prevents failure also prevents freedom." God came to restore us to freedom. We were given the boundaries of the law until we were restored by His Spirit into freedom. Our shaky spiritual legs and our uncoordinated spiritual hands are to be used and exercised into maturity.

Too often, we set such strict boundaries for ourselves or others we become more enslaved than free. God's Spirit came to set the captives free. We can fail because God will pick us up and set us on our feet. There can be bruises on our cheeks and our legs, but His boundaries are in perfect balance with our needs.

God calls us sons and daughters, not slaves. We are heirs and kingdom people, not to be enslaved by fear and stunted growth.

Let us pray that God will restore within our hearts the determination to be free in Him and the determination to walk, grow, and even fall, remembering God's mighty Hand is near enough to catch us.

Ponders of the Heart

Read Psalm 145:14, Psalm 116:8, and Galatians 5:1.

What do you learn about God in these verses?

What lessons do you learn about living?

Prayers of the Heart

Dear Father,

You have given your children the freedom to live and walk in Your Spirit. Father, Creator, and Sustainer, let our lives be hidden and free in You. Help us proclaim freedom and acceptance, and if we fall, lift us with Your mighty Hand and restore us. Thank You for the freedom to fail, the freedom to mature, and the promise of Your protection and everlasting love. In Jesus' name, amen.

April 18 ~ Life and Sight

The day I got my glasses was not fun for me. I would put them on and quickly take them off. The problem was I couldn't see well without them. Later I wore contacts, and I could see except at night after I took them off. After cataract surgery, I can see without glasses or contacts. Who says getting old doesn't have some advantages? Regardless, sight is a valuable thing.

One Sunday, our Sunday school lesson dealt with Jesus being the Good Shepherd. We talked about two miracles. One miracle was giving sight to a blind man (John 9) and Jesus calling Lazarus from death to life (John 11). Jesus showed his power to give sight to the blind and life to what was dead.

His miracles reveal His power over the natural so we might understand His power over the spiritual. He is the One who gives us spiritual sight and spiritual life. Without Jesus, we are blind and dead. If that doesn't humble you, remember He is our good Shepherd, and we are His sheep. That should help us all recognize our condition and His grace toward us.

"The thief comes only to steal and kill and destroy; I have come that they may have life, and have it to the full. 'I am the good shepherd. The good shepherd lays down his life for the sheep'" (John 10:10-11)

As we read these verses, they remind us that we have an enemy. He is a thief, and he came to steal, kill, and destroy us. We also have a friend who came to give us abundant life. Do we realize how the enemy has stolen from us and works to destroy us?

We need sight to see the destruction the enemy has wrought in our lives and the ones we love. What grave clothes are we still wearing? We often become comfortable in the old rags of this world.

Jesus wants to give us a new wardrobe. Only He can give us the understanding of what has us bound. Jesus is our deepest need and our greatest gift. Only He can give us spiritual sight and eternal life.

"Jesus said to her, "I am the resurrection and the life. The one who believes in me will live, even though they die; and whoever lives by believing in me will never die. Do you believe this?" (John 10:10-11).

Ponders of the Heart

Do we see and hear our Good Shepherd?

Are we experiencing the abundant life He came to give us?

Read John 9 and John 11.

His greatest miracles are when He gives sight to the spiritual blind and life to the spiritually dead.

Prayers of the Heart

Dear Jesus,

You are our Good Shepherd, and we are Your sheep. Thank You for calling us and giving us life, Your life. Father, "When I consider Your heavens, the work of Your fingers, The moon and the stars, which You have ordained, what is man that You are mindful of him, and the son of Man that You visit him?" (Psalm 8:3-4). We love You, Lord. We pray in Jesus' name, amen.

April 19 ~ The Light

I woke up during the night, and after weeks of traveling and being half asleep, I wasn't sure where I was. What I needed was light. There have also been times when I got up in the night trying to find the door and ended up lost in my own bedroom. Light in a room can change everything.

For sixteen years, I lived in spiritual darkness. I was lost and blind and needed light. That was the year I found the Lord, or should I say the year the Lord found me. In a conversation with a man named John Smith, he shared the gospel message with me, and my life was changed.

God, who said, "Let there be light," shone His light into my heart so I could see Him and receive Him. I love the passage in John 9 where the

Pharisees are questioning the blind man who had received physical and spiritual sight, and his answer went like this:

"He replied, "Whether he is a sinner or not, I don't know. One thing I do know. I was blind but now I see!" (John 9:25).

The day the light came on for me, I could not have a deep theological discussion with anyone. All I knew was I was blind, but now I see. There have been days when I did not know the answer to a spiritual question, but I knew I belonged to God.

I do not understand the vastness of God, nor will I. There are unknowns, but Jesus is the answer. His perspective gives us light in the darkness, His presence comforts us in grief, and His glory brings joy to our hearts.

When we are in the middle of frustrating situations we don't understand, Jesus is our hope and the help we need.

"While I am in the world, I am the light of the world" (John 9:5).

Ponders of the Heart

Do we allow Him to illuminate our eyes so we can see the truth?

Do we allow Him to illuminate our hearts so we can care?

Do we allow Him to be the Master of our world?

Read John 9:1-5 and John 9:35-41.

Prayers of the Heart

Dear Father,

In Genesis one, verse three, You said, "Let there be light," and there was light, and You saw that it was good. Father, You sent Jesus into the world to illuminate our hearts. You said,

"While I am in the world, I am the light of the world" (2 Cor. 4:6).

We thank You for illuminating our hearts with light so we could hear the gospel. You have made a way for us to live with Jesus, and it is in His name we pray, amen.

April 20 ~ The Resurrection and the Life

It was Easter Sunday, the first time I sat in church with my parents. They were in their seventies but babes in Christ. This would be my only Easter Sunday in church with them because they now worship Christ in heaven.

This was a resurrection Sunday. Mom sang with tears streaming down her face, and Dad sang unfamiliar hymns with a determination to praise his Lord.

I never felt more ashamed of my worship as I watched these new saints of the Lord. Where was my awe of God and my heart of thanksgiving? Could it be I had grown cold? Where was the wonder of my salvation? As I sat there, God began to stir my heart to remember His gift of grace. 1 Corinthians 15:20-22 began to teach me again of my condition without Jesus.

"But Christ has indeed been raised from the dead, the firstfruits of those who have fallen asleep. For since death came through a man, the resurrection of the dead comes also through a man. For as in Adam all die, so in Christ all will be made alive."

God reminds us we are born dead in sin, separated from Him. We can have physical life without ever really living. It is by grace through faith we can be given true life. In Adam, we are sinners, but in Christ, we are born again. We need forgiveness for sin, but we also need new life.

I was thankful to God for reaching into my parents' hearts and saving their souls. Peace and joy replaced their old hearts of stone, but that Sunday, I realized I needed a fresh touch of wonder and thankfulness back into my life. We grow away from loving God one degree at a time. My soul cried out that morning for Him to refresh my heart. I needed to come back to heartfelt worship.

Only God can transform our hearts and refresh our souls. He is the only One who can show us how far we have fallen. God does all those things and more for His children. If we have walked with the Lord for a long time or a short time, we all need tender hearts of worship and gratitude.

Join me in praising God for our wonderful salvation in Jesus.

The death he died, he died to sin once for all; but the life he lives, he lives to God. In the same way, count yourselves dead to sin but alive to God in Christ Jesus" (Romans 6:10-11).

Ponders of the Heart

What about you? Has your worship become cold, half-hearted?

Has the worship of the Almighty become common in your heart?

Read John 11:1-44.

I pray God's mercy will fall fresh on us today.

Prayers of the Heart

Dear Father,

We praise You for the gift of resurrection. You have defeated death for us so we can have life. We praise You with a fresh look at the wonder of Your grace. Thank You, Father. We love You. Only You are worthy of our praise and our worship. In Jesus' name, amen.

April 21 ~ The Bread

Betty Crocker says the way to a man's heart is through his stomach. Her point is that a man likes tasty food.

With my husband, good food is not as important as just food to satisfy his hunger. He eats to live, not live to eat. I could give him the same thing every day, and if it filled him up, he would be fine.

I wish that were true for me, but I like tasty food and variety. Food is necessary, for hunger is real, and this hunger reminds us that our body needs nourishment. I can go overboard with food as well as other things. In the gospel of John, Jesus makes seven "I AM" claims; one claim being that He was the Bread of Life; Jesus is our substance for spiritual life. He came to give us His life.

In John 5, He tells the Jews that they search the Scriptures to find eternal life, but the Scriptures bear witness to Him, and yet they refuse to come to Him for life (v39-40). The source and substance for eternal life is found only in Jesus. In chapter 6 of John, He feeds the five thousand with the miracle of fishes and loaves. Jesus says we must eat His flesh and drink His blood for the true food we need (47-69).

The Bible tells us there is a hunger deep inside that only He can satisfy. Jesus can provide our physical substance as He did in John 6, but we need much more. We can fill our stomachs with bread, but filled stomachs will never satisfy our deepest hunger. Only the Bread of Life can do that. We live in a culture where people battle weight and eating disorders. I wonder if they are trying to satisfy the soul's hunger with physical food.

It may be the disorders we encounter are spiritual. We are hungry, not for Betty Crocker rolls, but for the Bread of Life. Sorry, Betty, but our deepest need is not satisfied through the stomach but by feasting on Jesus. No variety, please.

Ponders of the Heart

Have you been trying to fill your soul with the things of this world?

What eternal thing does God want to give you?

Read John 6:35, John 6:47-51, and Job 8:21.

Ask Him to fill you with His desires.

Prayers of the Heart

Dear Bread of Life,

Come and fill our souls with rich satisfaction. Lord, help us see the substitutions in our lives that keep us far from feasting on You. Forgive us for the things in this world we hold up as life. You are our deepest hunger. Come, Bread of Life, and fill us. In Jesus' name, amen.

April 22 ~ The Door

In the television game show, "Let's Make a Deal," the winner of the day chose prizes behind three doors. "Do you choose door number one, two, or three?" The game host would ask. The contestant was always nervous because they had to live with their choice. There were good prizes, great prizes, and junk.

I wanted the contestants to choose the right door and go home with a great prize, and I hated it when they ended up with chickens or something worse. But that was the game. It was a gamble of choices. Our lives can feel like that. We have all made choices in this life that have turned out awful and, at times, great.

John 10 says Jesus is "The Door," the grand prize, the only opening to the Father. I know other religions claim to have another way, but Jesus is clear: He is The Door.

"I am the door. If anyone enters by Me, he will be saved, and will go in and out and find pasture" (John 10:9 NKJV).

What joy to realize by placing our faith in Jesus, we have entered the family of God by His provision. Jesus' great promises are for those who enter "The Door" by faith. He promises salvation and abundant life. We are warned if we choose another, we will end up with the thief who has come to steal and kill.

Behind door number three is destruction. Our downfall can come in different ways, but in the end, destruction is destruction. The only right choice is door number one, the door that says Jesus Christ. The other choices offer only a substitution for the real thing. Gambling on a game show is one thing, but who wants to gamble on their eternal destiny?

I remember the day I entered "The Door" of salvation by faith. He was much more than I could ever dream. He gave me peace and security that day. I have made poor choices and suffered because of those choices, but Jesus is my grand prize.

He is the One who takes away my shame and guilt and welcomes me into His family. Jesus gives me hope, a new identity, and righteousness. He is not only that for me but for all who have placed their faith in God's grace.

If you haven't chosen Jesus, don't delay; He is waiting for you behind door number one. Jesus will exchange the junk of your life with the real thing. He is our entrance into the kingdom of God. Jesus is the grand prize of the ages.

I boldly choose Jesus. What about you?

Ponders of the Heart

What would you say if someone said all religions are good if you are sincere?

How important is it for someone to understand that Jesus is our provision for salvation?

Read Ephesians 2:18 and Acts 4:12.

Prayers of the Heart

Dear Father,

We can come before You because of the provision You made. We come through Your Son, Jesus. He is our entrance, our salvation, and our righteousness. Lord, thank You that we can come into Your Holy presence. We praise You for Your grace and mercy. In Jesus' name, amen.

April 23 ~ Darkness

"The people who walked in darkness have seen a great light; on those living in the land of deep darkness a light has dawned" (Isaiah 9:2).

We live in a world of darkness. Evil hides in the dark along with its deeds. This evil power can have control over us and hold us captive.

In counseling, one of the counselor's jobs is to help expose the secrets of the soul. What lurks in the darkness of our past that we don't realize is amazing. Our past has so much to do with how we cope in life.

We have situations in our past that are true, and some are perceived. We bury our past in the dark corners of our minds, not wanting the light to expose them. The darkness hides the chains that bind us, and we don't realize the hold they have over us.

"When Jesus spoke again to the people, he said, "I am the light of the world. Whoever follows me will never walk in darkness, but will have the light of life" (John 8:12).

Jesus is the light of the world. If we are ever to see what is in the dark, we need His light to shine and expose what is lurking there.

The first step in healing is self-revelation. Jesus illuminates the darkness so we can see the deceptions, the lies, and the chains that hold us.

The variety of evil is so vast that every person can deal with different things, but there is only one truth. His name is Jesus. We need Him to come and shine His light into our past.

It hurts when we are exposed to things we do not remember or do not want to remember. The process hurts, but it also brings sweet relief. A good counselor allows the pain and horror so healing can begin.

Self-revelation is the beginning, but it is not enough. Jesus is the great Healer. He will heal and light our way, but we must submit to Him. We cannot turn the light on, then quickly turn it off and expect what lurks in the darkness to lose its control.

If a roach or a rat is found in your kitchen, you want more than to see it. You want to get rid of it. The same is true of our healing process. We want more than to see the chains. We want to be free.

Jesus is the "I Am." He is the all-powerful healer who lights our path to freedom. He is our light and freedom.

Ponders of the Heart

Do we dare ask Jesus to show us what is hidden in our souls?

How do we deal with the hidden evil in our lives, according to Isaiah 50:10?

Read Isaiah 42:16 and Ephesians 5:8-13

Prayers of the Heart

Dear Lamb of God,

You are the light that has come to help us see. You are the great Healer and Redeemer who comes to redeem us from our past. Jesus, come with Your marvelous light so we can walk free from our past and the chains of darkness. Lord, expose the evil in our lives so we can experience the great blessing of purity in You. Protect us and expose the evil one. Thank You for the wonder of Your love and Your protection. In Jesus' name, amen.

April 24 ~ The Way

"I am the Way, the Truth and the Life" (John 14:6 NKJV).

One wintry day, my daughter, Julie, and Bill, my adventuresome husband, decided to take a boat trip around the lake. They both love fighting the elements, so off they went fishing for adventure and came home with quite a fish story.

As they took their excursion around the lake, a deep fog rolled in, and they were lost in a sea of fog. The shore was unseen, but they thought the boat ramp was straight ahead. They steered the boat in that direction, ending up on the opposite side of the lake, not knowing how in the world they got there. They carefully followed the shoreline until they reached the boat access. They were wide-eyed and shaking by the time they got home.

I do not know my way around the lake, but Bill does, which means he can get us back home. However, on this day, he couldn't see the way. According to John 14, Jesus is not a way but "The Way." What does that mean to us? It means that Jesus is our way to salvation.

"For there is one God and one Mediator between God and men, the Man Christ Jesus" (1 Timothy 2:5 NKJV).

Jesus is also our way of handling life.

"For we are God's workmanship, created in Christ Jesus for good works, which God prepared beforehand that we should walk in them" (Eph. 2:10 NKJV).

Do you ever feel lost in life, covered with a blindness that leaves you foggy? I surely do.

I recall a time when we moved to a new town. This was exceedingly difficult for us, especially for our children. My son, who was in the eleventh grade, refused to go back to school after the second day. I didn't know what to do. I was afraid, angry, and frustrated.

In desperation, I asked Jesus to help me, and He did. He helped me understand my son was not trying to cause trouble; he was afraid. Just like Bill and Julie kept their eyes on the shoreline as they carefully found their way, I kept my eyes on Jesus. He helped me overcome my frustration and gave me compassion for Chris until we muddled through fear, and home felt like home again.

Life has a way of rolling a deep fog over our minds, and before we know it, we are lost and feeling confused. We do not know where to go or what to do, and just do something, we can find ourselves on a shoreline opposite of where we were headed.

Our loss of direction does not have to be permanent. We can take control of our situation by calling out to Jesus. Thank goodness, He is more than willing to help. He will give us balance and vision. It is through our personal relationship with our Savior that life gets back on track. I praise Him for being our Salvation and Holiness, our Hope and Vision. Jesus is the Way.

Ponders of the Heart

We are told in Hebrews 10: 22 to draw near to God. What are the benefits listed in these verses?

Read Hebrews 10:19-24.

Which "Let Us" does God want you to work on in your life?

Prayers of the Heart

Dear Father,

Your Son is the only way into Your presence. Thank You that we can come covered with the precious blood of the Lamb. We can come and listen to You and give You our praise and worship. Your provision for us, Your children, is Jesus. One day, You will call our name, and Jesus will bring us home. In Jesus' name, we pray, amen.

April 25 ~ The True Vine

"I am the vine; you are the branches. If you remain in me and I in you, you will bear much fruit; apart from me you can do nothing" (John 15:5).

The work of the vine is to give life to the branches, and through the vine and the branches, fruit is produced. In John 15, Jesus said, "I am the True Vine."

There are many vines, but He is the true vine. People can live from other vines and even look as if they are doing well, but Jesus said He is the true vine. Only through Him can we produce lasting fruit.

There are substitutions on the market today—butter, sugar, and more. I have settled for some and say they are good. I'm lying. I might adjust to diet drinks and butter substitutions, but they do not measure up to the real thing.

People have settled for substitutes in their marriage relationships. That is what we call affairs, sexual rendezvous, and pornography. These substitutes do not satisfy; they destroy.

We often try to get life from sources that are not true life—things like jobs, pleasure, power, prestige, and even our children. The vines of life are out there, but Jesus said, "I am the True Vine."

In counseling, people come face to face with the fact they have missed something. They know something has gone wrong, and they need help finding their way out of the maze of confusion. The guilt of the past and the present are reminders that they have missed true life. We are creatures that were made to live. We need the life Jesus offers.

We face temptations every day that lead us to false vines and away from the True Vine. My life has produced some fruit, but I wouldn't want you to eat it. Only the fruit from the True Vine produces eternal satisfaction. I want to abide constantly in Him. What a gift He has given. He has given us His life.

Ponders of the Heart

Do you regret the ungodly fruit in your life?

Have you asked God to restore you to who He has called you to be?

Read John 15:7-8 and 2 Corinthians 3:4-6.

Prayers of the Heart

Dear Father,

Help us hear as You speak to us today. Without You, we can do nothing. Father, we are Your children, and we do not want a substitution. We want to be a vessel that produces good fruit, fruit that lasts and brings You glory. Teach us how to abide in You. In Jesus' name, we pray, amen.

April 26 ~ The Good Shepherd

"I am the good shepherd. The good shepherd lays down his life for the sheep" (John 10:11).

"My sheep listen to my voice; I know them, and they follow me" (John 10:27).

A shepherd and sheep take my mind back to rolling pastureland, quiet streams, blue skies, and warm sun. Personally, I've not visited such a place, but that is what I see when I think about shepherds and sheep. A peaceful countryside where voices are heard and recognized. I picture a man calling for his sheep and them lifting their heads to run toward the shepherd's voice for food.

Never in the history of the world have we had more resources available to teach, train, and shepherd us in our Christian Walk, but for every resource, there is a distraction. This is a sign of our times. Noise and "busyness" are inhibiting us from hearing or seeing nature.

Jesus tells us He is the good Shepherd, and His sheep hear His voice. That really encourages me as I wonder about all the "noise" and "busyness" around us. Children especially are bombarded with noise. All toys sold today must make some kind of sound. A recent visit to a toy store made me thankful for quiet walks near the lake.

Regardless of how old-fashioned this might make me sound, I am convinced all people, young and old, are drawn to nature.

Romans tells us that nature is God's general revelation to us. Satan is busy distracting us away from nature because he does not want us to see our Creator in the beauty of creation. He tempts us and distracts us in every way he can.

I do not want to be distracted from the voice of our good Shepherd. I rest in the knowledge of John 10:29.

"My Father, who has given them to me, is greater than all; and no one can snatch them out of My Father's hand."

We are safe and secure, but I do not want to miss even one tender call. If we hear His voice, let's all lift our heads and run to God.

Ponders of the Heart

Do you long to hear from the Good Shepherd?

When was the last time you discerned His voice?

Read 1 Peter 1:16-18 and 1 John 1:1-4.

Prayers of the Heart

Dear Precious Father,

We bow before You, wanting to hear Your voice calling us and drawing us near, Lord, help us know You intimately. Keep us away from the distractions of this world, but draw us close to You. So close that we could hear You even if You whispered. In Jesus' name, amen.

April 27 ~ The Real Thing

On the streets of Jerusalem and Bethlehem, there are people who sell goods. They follow you and repeat, "One American dollar." These people seemed desperate, but our guide warned us to wait for the shops he suggested. I'm not sure if the merchandise was faulty on the streets or if our guide had a kickback scheme going. Regardless, we know there are substitutes for the real thing.

In John 15, Jesus said He was the True Vine—no substitute. He was the sap of God's life.

On the road of life, Jesus knows we encounter enticing shouts to buy their goods. Some enticements deal with a darker, sleazy substitution for living, like sex, drugs, thievery, and violence. While others deal with power, prestige, or material gains. In our need for substance and meaning in life, we can fall into these traps, but they will leave us empty.

Even religion can be a substitute for hearing and knowing Jesus. During my pilgrimage to Jerusalem, this was never clearer. There were religious people there, but few who were enjoying the sweetness of the vine, Jesus. It was their lack of joy and peace that convinced me they had a substitution for the real sap of life.

Here in America, our substitutions may look more appealing, and yet the emptiness of the soul is the same.

Jesus, being the True Vine, offers us fulfillment in one of our basic needs. We all need to feel our lives have a purpose. Jesus tells us if we abide in the True Vine, we will bear much fruit. Our God-given need for purpose will be fulfilled by abiding in the vine. The opposite is also true, for Jesus says, "Without Me, you can do nothing" (John 15:5).

He also gives us a picture of our lives if we don't abide. In verse six, He says:

"If you do not remain in me, you are like a branch that is thrown away and withers; such branches are picked up, thrown into the fire and burned."

No doubt, I have days where I feel like a withered-up branch. Praise the Lord, I can return to the sweet life-giving sap of Jesus and fill my withered soul with Him.

Ponders of the Heart

Who would you say you love more, the world or Jesus?

Who would Jesus say you love more?

Read 1 John 2:15-17.

Prayers of the Heart

Dear Lord

Thank You for being our source of life. Fill us up with Your compassion and Your sap that produces fruit for Your kingdom. Father, God, show us the substitutions that steal our hearts away and give us a burning desire for Your life. Nothing else will do. Thank You for Your love. In Jesus' name, amen.

April 28 ~ Row, Row, Row Your Boat

"A strong wind was blowing and the waters grew rough. When they had rowed about three or four miles, they saw Jesus approaching the boat, walking on the water; and they were frightened. But he said to them, "It is I; don't be afraid." Then they were willing to take him into the boat, and immediately the boat reached the shore where they were heading" (John 6:18-21).

What storm is brewing in your life? Maybe it isn't your life, but there is one brewing in the life of someone in your family or friend. Let's imagine for a minute. I would ask you to close your eyes, but then how could you read?

Whatever your storm is, I want you to imagine you are in the middle of this storm in a boat. You are tossed about with the wind and rain. You cannot see, and your stomach isn't feeling too good, either. You row as hard as you can to get to the other side of this circumstance, but you seem stuck in the mess.

Just then, you see a figure walking on the water. You blink your eyes to focus. You know it can't be a man. Men do not walk on water. The figure comes closer, and you feel the hair on the back of your neck stand up as you realize it is a man. But then, you hear a voice say, "It is I; don't be afraid." It is Jesus. You are faced with a choice.

You can believe your mind, which is saying, no way. You can believe your emotions that say, be afraid. Or you can believe Jesus.

If you believe it is Jesus, your fear will subside.

Have you ever had Jesus show up in the middle of the circumstance saying, "It is I; don't be afraid?" If so, what did you do? You can believe Jesus or not believe Him. I wish I could say I always believed Him. I can't. My fear froze me: fear of the circumstance, fear of the unknown, and fear I wasn't really hearing or seeing Jesus.

Verses in John 6 tell us the disciples willingly take Jesus aboard. The Greek word for willing is *thelo*, which means not only willing but pressing on to action. They believed it was Jesus, so they reached out and pulled Him aboard. They were immediately at the place they were trying to go. What a great lesson for me, and I hope for you. Jesus can do the impossible.

There is no place on earth where He can't go, even the deep, hidden recesses of our hearts. He is in the middle of our storms and of those we love saying, "Don't be afraid." Are we willing, and also *"thelo"?* When Jesus comes, He comes to get involved. We can believe Him and take Him aboard. He will get us to the other side.

Ponders of the Heart

Read Matthew 14:22-33.

What interesting information do you find in this passage?

How can God use it in your life?

Prayers of the Heart

Dear Father,

We need to see You walking over the storms and fears of our lives. Father, how we need to believe You. Believe You know where we are going and how to get us there. We are thankful that it is not our rowing that will get us home; it is Your grace. We want to hear, see, and be with You all the days of our lives. We confess You are our only strength, our only hope, and You are our desire. We pray in Jesus' name, amen.

April 29 ~ Certain in Uncertainty

Oswald Chambers says in his book My Utmost for His Highest, "The nature of the spiritual life is that we are certain in our uncertainty." The day I read these words, they were heaven-sent. If I am certain about God, then I can live with uncertainty. Do you need to hear that message? In 1 Corinthians, we read:

"But the natural man does not receive the things of the Spirit of God, for they are foolishness to him; nor can he know them, because they are spiritually discerned" (1 Corinthians 2:14 NKJV).

In our natural state, we cannot know the things of God, but not so for the spiritual man. We can be certain of our God during our uncertainty.

One example in my life was the day I resigned from the staff position I held at our church. I had nothing lined up, but. I knew it was time for me to let go.

After struggling for an answer from God for over a year, I went to a writer's conference, and God answered my prayer. One of the conference leaders challenged us to make a personal mission statement. I had never heard of doing this, and personally, I thought it was silly.

Her mission statement was a confession to God that she needed Him to give her focus. She needed His help to know what to say yes to and what to say no to. Her advice I heard loud and clear. I prayed, and God began to answer. He called me to teach. But to teach others, I had to first be taught by Him.

I resigned from my staff position to follow my Father. If I was going to follow His lead, I needed time to devote myself to Him. To grow healthy in my relationship with Christ, He must be my priority.

The natural world could not understand my decision to give up my job to follow Christ because it was a spiritual decision. I didn't know what the future held, but I was certain God knew.

Ponders of the Heart

What are you struggling with today?

Have you been seeking God's answer?

Read 1 Corinthians 1:20-30.

Keep seeking Him. Desire to hear and obey Him. Remember that in all your uncertainties in life, you can be certain of Him.

Prayers of the Heart

Dear Father,

We are thankful that nothing is impossible with You. Lord, You know the beginning and the end. Nothing is hidden from Your eyes. Your plans for us are perfect. We acknowledge our ways are not Your ways, and yet, because of Your character of love and mercy, we can trust You. There are uncertain things in this world, but we can be certain of You. We praise You. In Jesus' name, amen.

April 30 ~ Time of Praise and Prayer

"I will bless the Lord at all times; His praise shall continually be in my mouth. My soul shall make its boast in the Lord; The humble shall hear it and be glad. Oh, magnify the Lord with me, And let us exalt His name together" (Psalm 34:1-3 NKJV).

Dear Father,

We come praising You and thanking You for life. As we look at spring, green grass, flowering plants, and warm blue skies, we are reminded of Your goodness to us. Father, You are so faithful with all You do, and all things have a purpose. Lord, as we go through the days ahead, teach us to see You everywhere. Help us hear Your voice and see the beauty of Your Hand. Draw us near, and let us truly feel Your presence.

Father, love our children through us and our husbands. Do kind, compassionate things through us; also help us receive kind, compassionate things from others. Speak Your Word to us and through us and be our very lives. Let others see Jesus. Lord, we are Your children, and we want to represent You in our lives.

We thank You for giving us Your righteousness and a new identity. Help us walk in the spirit and not in the flesh. Father, wake us each morning with You on our minds. Set our hearts on You.

You alone are worthy of praise. Lord, You are altogether beautiful and kind, and You are our only hope. We love You because You first loved us. Why You love us will always be a mystery. We praise You and You alone. May our praise be a sweet sound to Your ears and have a pleasant aroma to Your nose. We give ourselves to You, for we can trust Your wisdom, love, and goodness. We pray in Jesus' Holy name, amen.

— 66 —

May the God of hope fill you with all joy and peace as you trust in him, so that you may overflow with hope by the power of the Holy Spirit.

Romans 15:13

May 1 ~ First Born

My firstborn was a son who is now in his fifties. I loved that boy from the very first moment I held Chris in my arms. I knew this love I felt for him would never change. If hearts grow, mine grew that day. My life changed forever because of a little baby boy. He is a big boy now, but my heart continues to react to his hugs, his smiles, and his face, shaven or not, just as it did so many years ago. There is nothing as powerful as love.

Mary's firstborn was Jesus. She also had a special day in time when her life changed forever. Luke tells us she brought forth her firstborn Son, wrapped Him in swaddling clothes, and laid Him in a manger.

As I remember the wonder of that moment for me, I can only imagine the awe of that moment for Mary. She counted toes and fingers. She smiled at that soft, cuddly bundle of humanity and thought her heart was about to explode. Something about a baby can soften the hardest heart. Oh, but what it does to a mother is unbelievable.

Mary treasured the years with Jesus, much like I have treasured all the days with my children.

I have saved notes, cards, shoes, and pictures and pondered them in a special box called memories. Even the hard days, days of sickness and trials, I keep safe in my box. Like Mary, we ponder our children's lives in our hearts.

What mistakes did Mary make? What days did she wish she could do over? I am sure the day she wanted to take Him home after his ministry began must have been one of them. The day she wanted to forget was the day her beloved Son hung on the cross for humanity. He was still her Son who somehow had become her Savior.

Mary's intimate relationship with Jesus would take her to the height of love and the depth of sorrow. Jesus, her Son, would travel a perfect road, but the road would affect her deeply. God does mighty things with His people, but they can still be hard.

He did powerful things in Mary's life, but apart from His grace, she could not have endured them.

What road did you walk today? Is there a sorrow you can hardly bear? Jesus, Mary's Son, came to walk the most demanding road so we would never need to walk alone. Praise Jesus for His sacrifice, and we bow with humble understanding for His mother. Her precious Son, given for us.

Ponders of the Heart

Can you put yourself in Mary's life and imagine the emotions, good and bad, she must have experienced?

Have you ever had to watch your own child suffer? Why would God allow His own Son to suffer for us?

Read Luke 2:1-20 and John 19:25-27.

Prayers of the Heart

Dear Father,

As we look at Your servant Mary today, we imagine the emotions she must have felt. Father, in Your perfect plan, You chose Mary, and in Your perfect grace, You sustained her. Thank You for giving us Your grace to sustain us in tough times. We thank You for special grace when we cannot see You working. Father, thank You for Your faithfulness. We praise Your perfection, and we rest in Your goodness today. Hold us close. In Jesus' name, we pray, amen.

May 2 ~ Youth Camp

The first year I went to youth camp was remarkable, even though I felt fear before going. How could a grown woman be so afraid of teenagers? I see myself as not "Mrs. Fun Girl" but more like "Mrs. Serious One," and I was worried the kids wouldn't like me.

At camp, we were divided into groups. Each group consisted of two adults and eight or nine students. I was the mother of my family group, and our pastor was the father.

Our group was impressive despite their camp parents. These kids had wisdom and a heart for God. I was overwhelmed by them. God taught me not to underestimate the depth of maturity He can give a teenager.

Those in our family group who were serious about God wanted to meet adults who would understand their seriousness. In Luke 2:41-52, we see a story about Jesus in His early years when He amazed the teachers in the temple.

"Everyone who heard him was amazed at his understanding and his answer" (Luke 2:47).

The life of God in the heart of a young person, a middle-aged person, or those of us dealing with wrinkles is amazing. Even the old teachers of the law could not help but admire the depth of the questions and answers of young Jesus. His wisdom and depth were and still are life-changing.

We tend to think our kids need entertainment and boundaries while we need pleasure and freedom. What we all need, young or old, is Jesus. We need a deep sense of His presence and His love, not to mention His truth, in a crooked, depraved world. Some of those young people fell in love with me that summer because I was in love with Jesus. How thankful I am for that amazing experience.

Ponders of the Heart

What do you think was going through the minds of the teachers of the law as Jesus asked questions?

Can you imagine what Mary and Joseph felt when they discovered Jesus was missing?

Read Luke 2:41-52.

Prayers of the Heart

Dear Father,

We come to praise You for the difference You make in our lives. You make us special because You are special. You set us apart, for You are set apart. Father, God, what a gift of grace to be Yours. Thank You, and help us see You in others. In Jesus' name, amen.

May 3 ~ Be Thou My Vision

"Be Thou my Vision, 0 Lord of my heart; Naught be all else to me, save that thou art- Thou my best thought, by day or by night, Waking or sleeping, thy presence my light.

Riches I heed not, nor man's empty praise; Thou mine inheritance, now and always; Thou and Thou only first in my heart, High King of heaven, my treasure Thou art."

This old hymn by Mary E. Byrne touches me deeply. The words of this song are a cry to the spirit in us. Oh, how our new nature loves the Lord. My words often fail me. They don't seem to come, but God has given us many avenues to express the depths of our love to Him. This precious song does that for me. Read and take in another stanza that I love.

"Be Thou my battle shield, sword for the fight Be Thou my dignity, Thou my delight, Thou my soul's shelter, thou my high tower: Raise Thou me heaven-ward, 0 Power of my power."

As I read or sing this hymn, I realize it is by His grace that I feel the way I do. These words stir the flame of love in me. He placed that love and flame there, and He has used people, places, and things to stir my heart. That is true for you, also my friend. That is true for all His children. The very warmth of these truths is ours because of His mercy and grace. The passages from Romans show our desperate need for His grace in our lives:

"As it is written: 'There is no one righteous, not even one; there is no one who understands; there is no one who seeks God'" (Romans 3:10-11).

But God has poured His grace out.

"But now the righteousness of God apart from the law is revealed, being witnessed by the Law and the Prophets, even the righteousness of God, through faith in Jesus Christ, to all and on all who believe. For there is no difference;" (Romans 3:21-22 NKJV).

Ponders of the Heart

Do you think you are a good person?

Have you come to realize your need for Jesus?

Carefully read Romans 3:10-24.

Prayers of the Heart

Dear Father,

Be our vision, Lord of our hearts. Stir up the flame of love and devotion in each of us. Teach us to be who we are by Your grace. Father, use all creation to stir our hearts of love for You. We long to live as close to You as we can get. You are our Vision and our great Reward. In Jesus' name, amen.

May 4 ~ Steps 1, 2, 3

I am the fix-it queen of my home—the fix-it queen of meals, messes, and dirty clothes. I fix people or try to; I am the fix-it queen for hair, arguments, and hurt feelings. I am the fix-it queen, and my husband is the fix-it king. He fixes deals, broken doors, cars, and overdrafts at the bank. He is the fix-it king.

Are you a fix-it queen at your house or work? I am glad God allows us to help in certain circumstances, but we need to be careful of our motives when we are able to help. We might just be using the situation to build ourselves up.

Sometimes, when we can't fix it, we use God's Word to fix people and circumstances. We say, "It's as easy as 1, 2, 3." Understand me, please. God's Word is alive and full of truth, and His Word is given to us. But God's ways are not our ways, and if we reduce His ways to "1,2,3," we might be giving false hope, which leads to disappointment and doubt.

"Therefore submit to God. Resist the devil and he will flee from you" (James 4:7 NKJV).

Step 1: Submit to God.

Step 2: Resist the devil.

Step 3: The devil will flee from you.

We might say, "Whatever you are going through, don't worry. We have three easy steps." The problem is that verse seven of James starts with, therefore. When a verse begins with therefore, it tells us to look before to see what comes before.

"But He gives more grace. Therefore He says: 'God resists the proud, but gives grace to the humble'" (James 4:6 NKJV).

Therefore, the Bible makes a huge difference, for it tells me I need His grace to claim His promises. God gives more grace. If I can stop and ponder the wonder of His grace, I will be overcome with humility. This humility enables me to surrender to God. That attitude leads me to peace and joy.

I can be a control freak, and when I am able to really submit, I find my rest. Even as I type these words, I feel relaxed.

Pray for God's grace to make everything about you humble. God gives more grace to the humble, and we can surrender to His authority. We can then resist the devil, and the devil will flee. He can't stand a grace-filled child. When he meets a person who has surrendered to God, he runs. We can't do 1,2,3 apart from God's amazing grace.

Ponders of the Heart

Read James 4:1-10 and 2 Corinthians 7:10.

There is a better way to live. How do the verses in James help us understand what is needed?

When was a time you experienced godly sorrow over worldly sorrow?

Prayers of the Heart

Dear Father,

How we need Your grace. We know others who need Your grace. There are people who need salvation by Your grace and others who need to be led out of destructive living patterns by Your grace. There are no steps to lead us into right living apart from Your mercy. We thank You, Lord, and pray for more life-changing grace. In Jesus' name, amen.

May 5 ~ My Man

My husband, Bill, is the love and joy of my life. Right after Bill comes our children and grandchildren. What a precious gift God gave when He gave us families. How sad it must make Him when He sees how often we take for granted, even misuse and abuse, His great and wonderful gift.

Today is Bill's birthday. I have no problem spending time with him and celebrating his life, but I must stop and ask myself if I pay attention to the people in my life that God has given me. Why do we spend so much time taking care of things and not taking care of our close relationship?

When was the last time we let something go so we didn't have to let someone go? We might all need to turn off the television so we can hear our spouses or children talk about something important to them. Our work is essential, we should pay attention to it, but the people in our lives are more important. I am talking to myself because I can be task-driven. When was the last time we gave someone we love more time and attention than our phone calls, housework, or yard work? Powerful questions.

Christ wants to be the center of our lives. His Lordship is our balance that helps us have healthy relationships with others. How are we doing with our relationship with Jesus? If we go to bed each night talking with Him and waking up seeking Him, then we have given Him His proper place. It is so easy to forget the privilege of being His child.

Jesus wants us to know Him, ourselves, and those we love. Relationships are everything in His kingdom. He has the power to heal the brokenhearted, give joy that surpasses circumstances, and the strength to hold us together when our lives are torn apart. God is the center of the universe and is willing to be the center of our hearts. What a Savior. I stand amazed at the man from Galilee.

Ponders of the Heart

Was there a time you struggled to believe God loved you?

Will you pray and ask God to show you the depth of His love today?

Read the prayer of Paul in Ephesians 3:14-21.

Prayers of the Heart

Dear Father,

Help us live knowing You love us, and You are in us. It is You that holds us together. Help us not only give our hearts and lives to You, but, Lord, help us give ourselves away to love others as You have loved us. Thank You for the opportunity to love You and be loved by You. Father, pour real love into our hearts so we can love You and others. In Jesus' name, amen.

May 6 ~ Burn

Have you ever burned your hand with grease? It hurts so bad. The day I burned my hand was pure agony. I ran around the house blowing and jumping until I discovered ice water. My hand stayed in ice water until eight o'clock the next morning. My night was spent sitting on the couch with my hand buried in ice water.

As I sat there, I decided to use the time wisely and do my Bible study. I wrote the answers with my left hand, so I had to make my answers very precise. It was interesting. In the Bible study, we were told that historical tradition says that the persecutors of the church tried to kill John by boiling him in oil, but he wasn't hurt, so they sent him to Patmos.

Later in the study, they said that Polycarp of Smyrna was burned at the stake because he would not reject His Lord. I was not suffering for my faith in Christ but for frying steak. I was, however, living a small object lesson.

God's grace is sufficient for His children in their time of need. God cared for John and supplied grace to Polycarp. He cares for His children in miraculous ways when they suffer for their faith. If you are a baby like me, this should give you hope.

When my dad was dying of cancer, I knew God would take him home. I prayed that dad would be faithful to his Lord and that God would be glorified. I didn't question God about dad's cancer, but I questioned God for not letting me be the first to die.

I had walked with the Lord longer, and dad was such a baby in his faith. God showed me many things through the death of my dad—more than I could have imagined. But the one that stands out the most is that it was not our faith, our knowledge, or the length of time we walked with the Lord that counted. It is the object of our faith that holds us.

If our faith is in Christ, we can even be boiled in oil, and He will hold us. He is all we need. So much is in His hands, and so little is in ours; how I praise Him for that. In this uncertain world with things that can destroy us, we need not fear. He is faithful, trustworthy, and powerful. He is for us and not against us. Christ, the object of our faith, is enough.

Ponders of the Heart

Have you ever suffered because of your faith in Jesus?

How have you experienced His faithfulness in your life?

Read 2 Timothy 1:8-13.

Prayers of the Heart

Dear Father,

In our flesh, we are weak and afraid. Thank You, Lord, we can take our fears and nail them to the cross. You are our strength, and we can be strong in Your strength. You are our protector and our courage. Father, we come before You with praise and honor. You are so wonderful, and willing to keep us no matter what. In the name of Jesus, we pray, amen.

May 7 ~ God's Mercy

I know stubborn people. To be honest with you, I can be stubborn myself. I get on an "I'm right" kick, and I can be unreasonable. This attitude can overflow into my relationship with God. It is like He is standing at the door of my prison saying, "Marilyn, come here. Marilyn, come out of there." And I say, "No."

We are at a standstill, so it seems. I have dug in, planning to stay in my misery, and I refuse to yield to His call. Is that not ridiculous? It is completely crazy, but human flesh is crazy. I don't always realize that about myself, but I could tell you about those I love. The answer is as clear as day, but their minds are clouded. What can we do with ourselves or with others?

When a child of God is being stubborn, He might let us stay there, but after a while of suffering from our bad attitudes or actions, He comes to us in His mercy.

"Humble yourselves, therefore, under God's mighty hand, that he may lift you up in due time. Cast all your anxiety on him because he cares for you" (1 Peter 5:6-7).

This passage grabs hold of my heart and reminds me of how merciful God is and how much He loves us. The promise is God cares for me, and those I love. This puts my soul to rest. When we turn to Him, He can do more in an hour than I can do in a lifetime.

I hope these words comfort you. God's grace is our hope for those in Christ. He does set the captive free; how I marvel at this promise. God's Word is our refuge when we get stuck in misery and stubbornness.

"The Spirit of the Lord is on me, because he has anointed me to proclaim good news to the poor. He has sent me to proclaim freedom for the prisoners and recovery of sight for the blind, to set the oppressed free, to proclaim the year of the Lord's favor" (Luke 4:18-19).

When Christ finished reading the passage from Isaiah in Luke 4, He said in verse 21, "Today this Scripture is fulfilled in your hearing." Jesus is telling us the promises of these words are found in Him. What great hope for us as we struggle with captivity, spiritual blindness, and oppression. When He says, "Come here," let's not just come, let's run into His waiting arms. All who come will be welcome.

Ponders of the Heart

Do you remember a time in your life when you were stubborn?

How did God get you to come, let go, and trust Him?

Read Isaiah. 61:1-3 and Isaiah 42:1-9.

Prayers of the Heart

Dear Father,

We come seeking help and find You are our greatest need. Father, it is amazing that You come for us. Help us hear You and run to You when You call. You are everything we will ever need. You are our Sufficient One. Your mercy is so wide it can find us wherever we go, and we can experience You. Thank You, Lord, in Jesus' name, amen.

May 8 ~ Understanding

"I understand." These are wonderful words when they come from a sincere heart. Oh, to be understood, really understood. It is difficult to express in words things of the heart. In fact, many things we see others do are direct manifestations of being misunderstood. I once heard a statement that spoke volumes to me. "Hurt people hurt people."

Let me add a few of my own. Used people use people. Rejected people reject others. Let me add some positive statements. Loved people love people and accepted people accept people. Helped people help and healed people heal others.

These statements are statements that help us understand one another. If I can remember that when someone is trying to hurt me, it is because they have been hurt, I can forgive. If someone hurts me by rejecting me, and I realize they are rejecting me because they have been rejected, I can cope with their rejection. Knowing and accepting the depth of God's love for me will help me value and love others. As God heals me, I then, in turn, can share with others so they might also receive healing.

We are all in the same condition. We all have harmful flesh in a fallen world with an evil adversary. Yet, we are not without hope, for God wants to shower His love upon us, heal, and accept us fully through His Son. What hope and understanding we can have for one another. If we stop and try to understand others and not just think about ourselves.

Why don't you write some statements of your own and use them to understand those around you and maybe even yourself?

Ponders of the Heart

Read Romans 7:15-25 and Romans 8:31-39.

Do you relate to these verses in Romans 7?

How does accepting God's love and promises help us heal from our hurts and wounds?

Prayers of the Heart

Gracious Father,

We come longing to know Your love, healing, and acceptance. Father, by Your glory and grace, heal us. Help us understand others so they can feel loved and accepted. We live in a fallen world, and we are all broken. We are desperate for You. In Jesus' name, amen.

May 9 ~ Stir the Spirit in Me

"For this reason I remind you to fan into flame the gift of God, which is in you through the laying on of my hands. 7 For the Spirit God gave us does not make us timid, but gives us power, love and self-discipline" (2 Timothy 1:6-7).

When my children were little, they would often get frustrated with things like tying their shoes and saying, "I can't do this." Most of the time, I would tie their shoes for them. But when I had good mother sense, I would say, "Yes, you can. Remember, you do this and then that." They would, with encouragement, try again.

Paul's heart towards Timothy was that of a father. In fact, Paul calls him his son. Timothy dealt with insecurities, especially as Paul's imprisonment and his death became so real. I can hear Timothy say, "I can't do this." Paul, being much wiser than I, told Timothy to stir the gift of God which was in him. In verse five of the same chapter, Paul answers the "therefore" in verse six. He said,

"I am reminded of your sincere faith, which first lived in your grandmother Lois and in your mother Eunice and, I am persuaded, now lives in you also" (2 Timothy 1:5).

These are great words of encouragement. In essence, he is saying, when I remember the genuine faith in you, I know you can do what God has equipped you to do. God has given you, His Spirit. His Spirit is not a spirit of fear but of power, love, and a sound mind. What a great reminder to Timothy and us that maybe we can't, but boy, oh, boy, He can.

God makes impossible things possible for us and those we love. He has poured Himself into us, and His Spirit is able. Maybe we need to give ourselves a good history lesson on our salvation and encourage others to remember, also. What a powerful gift the Spirit is in us. What junk do we believe in our minds? We forget His power is in us, His love for us, and the sound mind His words give us.

Let us stir up the genuine faith that is in us because of the Lord, Jesus.

Ponders of the Heart

Do you struggle with fear?

Do these verses help you remember the power God has given His children?

Read Romans 8:14-17 and Acts 1:8.

Prayers of the Heart

Dear Father,

The gift of Your Spirit is the hope of victorious living. We do not ask for success as the world determines success. We pray for victorious living. Living based on Your truth. Let us stir the flames of love, power, and sound mind so that our lives give You glory. In Jesus' name, amen.

May 10 ~ Rocking Chair

I married in 1969, and I was no more than a baby. Bill was 19 by five days, and I was 18. I was sure we would grow old together. I just didn't think the growing would take place so fast.

Today is our anniversary, and I am giving him a rocking chair. He wants one so he can rock on the back porch. I could say that our lives are rocking right along, or should I say, life is sometimes rocky.

We picture a rocking chair as something older people want and use. A time in their life when they have nothing to do but rock, a slow and calm life. I am beginning to realize that there is always something to do and someone who needs our help. The only way to have rocking days is to make time for them.

What is so good about rocking days? These are days to kick back and allow the pleasure of "being" to take priority over the tasks of doing. I can get so involved in my doing and miss the pleasure of just being a child of God, fully loved and accepted. I think I would take more rocking days if I really knew and believed in the full value of salvation.

Unfortunately, I realize that much of what I do and derive self-worth from is idolatry. My god is me. Yuck. God wants to give me something better. Himself. What an unattainable gift He gave to us by His grace.

I wonder about the pressure I place on others to perform. I see how driven I can be, and it concerns me that I have put pressure on others. I wish, as a mom, I had spent more time showing my children how to enjoy God as I slowed down and enjoyed being with them.

My grandchildren see a different person. I slow down, enjoy them and they do not feel pressure from me; they feel loved and accepted. I should have bought us rocking chairs years ago.

Ponders of the Heart

When was the last time you had a rocking day?

Are you able to accept that God loves you and that you do not have to earn His love? It was probably the last day you had sweet peace.

Read Psalm 46:10-11 and Psalm 63:1-8.

Take time to praise the Lord and drink in the essence of His presence. Don't hurry. Drink in the wonder of His love for you.

Prayers of the Heart

Dear Father,

Today, we thank You for allowing us to be Yours. We thank You that we can love You and enjoy being with You. Teach us to kick back and enjoy the essence of You. Help us, Lord, take time to be satisfied. We love You, and thank You for loving us. In Jesus' name, amen.

May 11 ~ Bird on the Porch

Occasionally, at our old house, a bird would get caught on our screened porch. One of the doors was always open, and even though the bird went in, he couldn't find his way out. Our dog sometimes would solve the situation in a manner I would rather not discuss, but we often interceded to guide the poor bird out into the open.

The bird doesn't see us as friends as we wave our arms and maneuver him outside; he thinks we are his enemy. I wonder when he finds himself free if he realizes we were for him and not against him.

We often find ourselves trapped in struggles. We entered the door of temptation, but we could not find our way out. We keep running into what we think is an open door just to find ourselves knocked down by an illusion of escape.

When was the last time you found yourself caught in a trap? Did you get tricked inside? Is it now an addiction? The question is: Do you want to be free?

This reminds me of a puzzling question Jesus asked a paralyzed man who waited each day at the pool of Bethesda. The belief was that when the water moved, an angel was there to heal the first person who entered the pool (John 5:1-15).

Jesus saw the man and asked him this question: "Do you want to be made well?" The man answered with an excuse, and Jesus told him to pick up his bed and walk. The lame man did what Jesus said which shows he wanted to be healed. What a strange question to ask a lame man, or is it?

The reason Jesus came was to set captives free, to bind up the brokenhearted, and to heal the hurting. Many refuse Him. We often refuse Jesus because of a false impression of Him and ourselves. Where do you find yourself? Do you need to be healed emotionally, physically, or spiritually? Jesus is willing and able to heal us if we are willing to come to Him. He is close to us and ready to help. Our part is to draw near to Him. He is not our enemy; He is our friend.

Ponders of the Heart

Do you see God as your foe or your friend?

Is it time to ask God to help you with a part of your life that is out of your control?

Read Isaiah 1:18-20 and Matthew 11:28-30.

Prayers of the Heart

Dear Father,

We confess we are easily tempted. We need You every minute of every day. Father, we have no wisdom apart from Your grace. We have no way of escaping without You. Our desire is to have only one addiction, and that is a healthy addiction for You. Thank You that You came to set the captives free. We come to You for only You can release us from the traps of this life. In Jesus' name, amen.

May 12 ~ Who is Rich?

"You say, 'I am rich. I have everything I want. I don't need a thing!' And you don't realize that you are wretched and miserable and poor and blind and naked. So I advise you to buy gold from me—gold that has been purified by fire. Then you will be rich. Also buy white garments from me so you will not be shamed by your nakedness, and ointment for your eyes so you will be able to see" (Revelation 3:17-18 NLT).

Nicolas Cage, a wealthy uptown businessman in the movie "Family Man," believes that he has everything he needs in life. In an interesting turn of events, he is given a glimpse of life if he had married his college girlfriend.

He wakes up one morning and finds out he has been married to her for 13 years and has two children. He traded his uptown prestige for a manager's position with his father-in-law's tire business and his penthouse for a four-bedroom home in New Jersey. His stock portfolio is traded for the great commodity of friends, and his uptown suits for jeans and sweats. As he learns that life is more than money, his self-pity episodes are soul-reflecting.

We all have times when self-pity overcomes us. We begin to measure our lives based on a fallen culture, and we come up short. Out of desperation, we will try to maneuver or manipulate our own way or at least get sympathy.

Oswald Chambers says,

"No sin is worse than the sin of self-pity because it removes God from the throne of our lives, replacing Him with our own self-interest."

What a sobering quote. One that makes me stand up and take notice. I don't think I have ever thought about self-pity that way, have you? We can develop entitlement in this sin. We often wallow around in ungratefulness.

"These things says the First and the Last, who was dead, and came to life: 'I know your works, tribulation, and poverty (but you are rich);'" (Rev. 2:8-9 NKJV).

There are so many delusions in this world. People try to fill the hole in their hearts with things, money, power, and fame. The problem is they do not satisfy our souls. These myths leave us empty and void of fulfillment. If we have God on the throne of our lives, then we are rich beyond compare.

I want my life to reflect praise to the Lord for His wonderful love. He is our treasure, and we are rich because of Him. There is no room in our hearts for self-pity. He is our eternal satisfaction. We need hearts and lives to understand what true success and riches are. Teach us, Father, give us heavenly vision.

Ponders of the Heart

Read 2 Peter 1:2-11.

What are the gifts and promises you see in the verses in 2 Peter?

What is your responsibility in appropriating these gifts and promises?

Prayers of the Heart

Dear Father,

How we love and praise You for Your love and Your provision for us. You have given us all we need for life and godliness, for You have given us Yourself. Lord, may we never be so blind as not to see the wonder of You as our treasure. May we never be so cold that we would choose things over You? Let us live for Your glory and bask in Your love. In Jesus' name, amen.

May 13 ~ Living Water

"For God has not given us a spirit of fear, but of power and of love and of a sound mind" (2 Timothy 1:7 NKJV).

I found myself intrigued by waterfalls on my recent visit to the mountains. They were so beautiful, full of power and energy. The sound of rushing water was soothing but also held a dangerous presence. I wanted to get as close as possible, but fear kept me a safe distance back.

Their beauty was not diminished by distance or closeness. They are so majestic. Water fascinates me and always has. I love the quiet babble of a brook and the rushing water of the waterfalls. Riding over waves in a boat and floating along the river at a snail's pace are both fun to me.

The sound, the feel, and the natural beauty of rivers, lakes, streams, and seas capture my eyes and emotions. I enjoy each body of water's uniqueness. As I stood on the edge of the river looking over at a waterfall, I thought of God. His beauty and power are beyond anything we can imagine.

As I watched the water rush over rocks, I thought of God's purity. The majestic power of the falls and even the danger I felt reminded me of the awesome privilege we have to come into His presence. Only the blood of Jesus makes this possible, and yet God, the Powerful One, bids us to come.

I also watched the rapids, wondering what it would be like to plunge over the side of the fall into the water below. The thought of this adventure made me shake with fear, but I still wondered.

If the Lord reached out to me to take an exciting new plunge with Him, I would want to say, "Yes," but would fear keep me on the sidelines?

I have missed opportunities with God because of my cautious nature. There are those I could have shared my God with, but I let those moments pass me by. Fear is a killjoy, a backseat driver in my mind. I want to hear just One voice that leads me away from fear into joyous living.

God, my heavenly Father, knows me well, and He is patient with me. One day, the fear of humanity will be peeled away, and with sweet abandonment with Jesus as my kayak, I will take the plunge, ride the rapids of His love, and feel the freshness of His purity. I will know the completeness of being His. Oh, Lord, how majestic is Your name.

Ponders of the Heart

What do you want to praise Him for today?

What word picture would you use to describe God?

Read Psalm 93 and praise the Lord.

Prayers of the Heart

Dear Father,

What a wonder You are to us. What a treasure. Father, reach out Your hand to us and bid us come. Let the wonder and adventure of You take us into the wonder of full living. Let us not be afraid, but give us the courage to respond to You and You alone. You give life, and You give it with great abundance. In Jesus' name, we praise and thank You, amen.

May 14 ~ Running from Shame

"Blessed is the one whose transgression is forgiven, whose sins are covered. Blessed is the one whose sin the Lord does not count against them and in whose spirit is no deceit" (Psalm 32: 1-2).

When Bill was a small boy, he did something he thought was bad. He was ashamed and decided the best thing to do was to hide under the house. When his mom and dad came looking for him, he crawled further away from them.

They had no idea what was wrong, so they headed under the house after him. His shame was so great that he threw dirt on them. We all laugh about it now, but can you imagine how scared he was to face his parents? I have hidden shame. I have hidden under the house of my memories, but God doesn't want me to keep it there.

Nothing is more powerful than the rule of guilt and shame. Guilt-driven people are controlled by memories of past failures. We can try to hide them. Adam and Eve hid behind bushes. I am certain Satan was hiding close by, celebrating as he watched them feel the weight of their shame as they hid from God.

He does the same with us. Satan turns our minds on rewind and plays over and over the past sins and celebrates as we feel defeated.

What "mind video" marked failure is in your closet, or should I say under your house? I'm sure, if Satan has any say-so in your mind, there is no dust on that video. He keeps it close at hand and uses every opportunity to throw us into a cold sweat of memories.

God uses guilt for the purpose of repentance. Satan uses it to make us prisoners of the past. Our past can be used to mold us, but our past does not have to keep us locked up. God is in the business of making all things new, using our past to mold us and shape us into usable vessels for Him.

Whatever is on that video, take it to God and let Him have your past. Remember, He is the Alpha and Omega of our lives. He is not limited to time or space. The prophet Joel encourages us this way:

"So I will restore to you the years that the swarming locust has eaten, the crawling locust, the consuming locust, and the chewing locust" (Joel 2:25 NKJV).

Once we enter into a relationship with God through Jesus, our past is forgiven, and our guilt is swallowed up in His purity. Don't allow your life to be controlled by guilt and shame. Christ has taken our shame to the cross, and it has been crucified forever.

Ponders of the Heart

What failure video does Satan play in your mind?

How has God taken your past failures and used them for your good?

Read Psalm 85:2-3, Romans 8:1, and 2 Corinthians 5:16-19.

Prayers of the Heart

Dear Blessed Lord,

We have failures in our lives, and if our worth were based on our behavior, then, Lord, we deserve guilt and shame. Praise to our Lord, Jesus Christ, who has taken our shame to the cross. We have died to our past, and our lives have been baptized into Your Son. We give You our past, our today, and our future. Take us, Lord, and purify us for Your glory and Your purposes. In Jesus' name, amen.

May 15 ~ The Flame of Anger

"Resentment kills a fool, and envy slays the simple" (Job 5:2).

Bill and I were traveling home one night and came upon a burning car. Bill, being the superhero that he is, jumped out and ran to the vehicle to make sure no one was inside. The flames were high and out of control. Bill kept looking in, then jumping back due to the intensity of the fire.

When he returned to our car, he had soot on his face and singed hair. Angry flames of fire are something we want to keep at a distance.

People that are driven by resentment and anger remind me of the flames of fire. You can't get too close, or you will get singed by the heat. Some people smolder with anger, while others' anger burns with huge, bellowing flames. Neither is healthy or helpful.

A person whose life is driven by anger or resentment hurts themselves far more than those around them. Usually, they hold on to the hurt that has been inflicted on them and play it over and over in their heads until that is their life. They develop a sensitive radar that picks up every word and every deed done, turning and twisting them until they are consumed with anger. It is a miserable life.

People like this are avoided, or they avoid others. They are feared and ignored and seldom invited to dinner unless it is with people who suffer from the same problem.

How can such a cycle be broken? The only way is to take our past hurts, disappointments, and resentments to the Lord. We cannot change our past, but the Alpha can use our past for our good. For our own sake, we need to let the hurt go into His hands.

Some say, "I can't." Perhaps it is not because they can't but because they won't. Understanding this concept will make a big difference in their lives.

God is the Potter, and we need His powerful Hands working to redo our past, freeing us from bitterness and shame. Our job is to yield to His work as He shows us, changes us, and molds us. There is no better place to be than in the Potter's Hand. He can change our "can't" to "He can" if we surrender.

"Yet you, Lord, are our Father. We are the clay; you are the potter; we are all the work of your hand" (Isaiah 64:8).

The root meaning of my name, Marilyn, is bitter, but I have been given a new name kept for me in heaven. I don't know what that name is, but I know it doesn't mean bitter. I claim my new name today, for I was not made for time but for eternity. That is true for all of us who are in Christ Jesus.

Ponders of the Heart

Do you have trouble forgiving others for past hurt?

What bitterness is holding you captive?

Read Psalm 37:8 and Ephesians 4:26-27.

Prayers of the Heart

Dear Father,

How easy it is to hold on to old hurt and resentment until it holds us. Father, God, we want to be held by nothing except Your firm grip. Shine Your light upon us and show us the past we cling to. Show us the walls of resentment and the flames of anger so we can let them go into Your Hands. Lord, we praise You for Your patience with us. We love You, Lord. In Jesus' name, amen.

May 16 ~ Fear

"The Spirit you received does not make you slaves, so that you live in fear again; rather, the Spirit you received brought about your adoption to sonship. And by him we cry, 'Abba, Father'" (Romans 8:15).

People controlled by fear miss opportunities. They want to say "Yes," but they say "No." That kind of living is a self-imposed prison. I am a person who often lives behind those bars.

One Saturday morning, Bill and I rode to the Atlanta Motor Speedway to watch Bill's brother, Brooks, drive a race car. Little did I know that if Brooks was driving a racecar, a relative could ride in another car with a trainer. Bill stepped up to ride, but I stayed planted on the bleachers.

A lady walked up to me and said, "You need to take a ride. You will regret it if you don't." I thought she was crazy, but I started thinking how amazed my children would be if I did such a thing. So, I decided to say, "Yes."

I was strapped tight in a racecar with Bill in the car next to me. The cars took off, and it was a wild ride. My heart was pounding, and my hands were sweating as the driver drove the car with lighting speed. I had an incredible experience.

Bill's car passed our car, and then our car passed his. As I was having the time of my life, Bill was thinking, "She is going to kill me for letting her do this." He was more than a little impressed that I had been thrilled with the speed.

My children still talk about the day their mom rode in a racecar and how, for once, she moved past her fear and did something a little crazy.

I still won't ride rollercoasters, but maybe someday.

There are all kinds of fears that keep us locked up. The fear of failure, the fear of making a fool of ourselves, the fear of being hurt, and the list goes on and on. A fearful person tries to manage life and keep away from risk. The problem with fear driven lives is we can miss what God has for us. The only way to move against fear is with faith in God and confidence in His love. I would call this truth a life-changing grace.

"There is no fear in love. But perfect love drives out fear, because fear has to do with punishment. The one who fears is not made perfect in love" (1 John 4:18).

Ponders of the Heart

What causes you great fear?

Does this fear keep you from following God's purpose for your life?

Read Proverbs 3:5-6, Psalm 37:3, and Psalm 37:5.

Prayers of the Heart

Dear Father,

We bow before You, knowing that we often let fear direct our path instead of You. We come to You and confess, asking that You fill us with knowledge, trust, and confidence in You. Father, You are kind and merciful to Your children. You are powerful and mighty to save us. We come confessing that You are our need and our very great reward. We praise You. In Jesus' name, amen.

May 17 ~ Wedding Day

"Then I saw 'a new heaven and a new earth,' for the first heaven and the first earth had passed away, and there was no longer any sea. I saw the Holy City, the new Jerusalem, coming down out of heaven from God, prepared as a bride beautifully dressed for her husband" (Revelation 21:1-2).

Weddings are very romantic and magical. As a guest, you can sit back and enjoy how the planning and preparations come together. The beautiful flowers, the glow of the lights, and the joy of the bride and groom capture your eyes and heart with tender feelings.

Stepping into someone's love story and experiencing the beginning of two lives coming together is an honor and privilege. Love and hope soaring in the bride and groom's hearts is as breathtaking as an eagle in flight.

I chose to write about weddings on May 17th because my oldest grandson, Collier, married his middle school sweetheart, Izzy. We also added a special brunch on May 18th to thank our out-of-town family who came to celebrate with us.

We worked for hours preparing our house and yard for these special days. I worked my husband to death, and he went the extra mile day after day to help me prepare for the brunch.

These are the preparations we made. We had carpet installed. My son-in-law, Ryan, cut down 15 trees, and we pulled, stacked, and burned limbs and sticks galore. Sod was planted. We bought a tent that would be set up on the other side of a cute decorative bridge, inviting our family to a sit-down feast. The gutters were cleaned. The driveway was pressure-washed, and new flowers were planted. Fresh pine straw and mulch were added to flower beds and the yard. We were busy.

Of course, new clothes were hanging in the closet, and my dress had been altered and altered again to fit my short body frame. A fancy pair of shoes was bought and worn that killed my feet. But my heart is still overwhelmed with praise to God for His love and work in the lives of Collier and Izzy.

Prayers from our family and my small group covered all the preparations. We did not want Satan to have one ounce of room to cause trouble on this special day.

Believe me, he tried. He started months ago and tried to step into the rehearsal dinner, but God is stronger and kept him from ruining a beautiful night.

You guessed it. The wedding was as perfect as anything on earth can be. The atmosphere was filled with praise for our heavenly Father. Collier and Izzy took beauty to a new level. Their faces lit up the sky with love for each other and honor and praise to the Lord, their Savior.

My heart is overwhelmed with gratitude for all the Lord has done in this young couple's life.

This all resonates in my heart about another wedding where I will be a bride. Not a bride here on earth, but a bride in heaven. It is hard to imagine the wonder and beauty of this wedding. The flowers will be breathtaking, and there is even the promise of a wedding feast. This will be a perfect wedding, no distractions, no unhappy faces, or sad memories. All will be perfect.

Jesus is the groom, and to see Him face to face and become His bride—oh, what wonder and privilege to be with Jesus forever.

Like me, all who know the Lord will join together and become His bride to love, serve, and worship Him forevermore. Jesus' love for His bride will fill heaven as we, the church, join our hearts to Him for all eternity.

Collier and Izzy's wedding is just a foretaste of what is in store for all who belong to Jesus.

Ponders of the Heart

What is the best wedding you have ever attended?

Are you looking forward to the wedding in heaven?

Do you see yourself as His bride?

Read Revelation 21:3-7.

Ask the Lord to help you prepare to be His bride.

Prayers of the Heart

Dear Jesus,

How I thank and praise You for the marriage of Collier and Izzy. What a wonderful day this was in the life of our family. But, Lord, I thank You for the preparations You are making for Your bride, the church. The family of God all joined together to love and worship You forever. Such wonder is beyond even my best imagination, but I believe. You are the hope of Your people, for You are our Savior. It is in Your name, Jesus, that we pray, amen.

May 18 ~ Timeless

"The grass withers and the flowers fall, but the word of our God endures forever" (Isaiah 40:8).

Spring is here, and the lilies in the yard are blooming. The hydrangeas with sky-blue flowers have filled the flower bed, and the pool is sparkling with clean water. New life—there is nothing so hopeful as new life.

The house is filled with flowers from my grandson and my new granddaughter-in-law's wedding. Everything looks good, and I have 50 family members filling the house and the yard. But in the kitchen, which is filled with the aroma of food, stand some of my sisters in Christ. They have prepared this delicious food and are here to serve my family. Thanking them is impossible because there are no words to express the gratefulness I feel in my heart.

As I look at the flowers in the house and those that grace my yard, I am reminded that neither will last forever. As beautiful as they are, they are not timeless. Flowers in the yard and house give the home a loved and cared-for feeling. They make people feel welcome. That is my hope for the family members who are here to help us celebrate a special moment in our family's life.

The flowers are not timeless, but I am hoping the memories of these days will remain with me throughout eternity.

I do not want time to keep me from remembering the glow and beauty of my granddaughter, Bailey, as she walked down the aisle with Clayton, our youngest grandson, so tall and handsome in his black suit. Then there was Elizabeth, our youngest grandchild, tossing rose petals and preparing for the bride.

Izzy was out of my sight until she reached the front of the aisle, but I could see Collier, and his face will be edged in my very soul forever. He was overwhelmed with emotion as he watched Izzy coming down the aisle.

Then I saw the bride. Her face matched his. Oh, my soul, those faces took my breath away and gave me such hope for the next generation.

God's Words are timeless. They give us hope, life, goodness, and wisdom, but they also help us know our Heavenly Father. Our God is the Timeless One. He is eternal, and all life comes from Him. Jesus gave His life so we could share in a timeless life. Grass withers, flowers fade, but those of us who are in Christ will live forever because Jesus is the Word!

"In the beginning was the Word, and the Word was with God, and the Word was God. He was with God in the beginning. Through him all things were made; without him nothing was made that has been made. In him was life, and that life was the light of all mankind" (John 1:1-4.

Ponders of the Heart

What are some of the events and faces that are in your memory?

Do you realize God holds you in the palm of His Hand?

Read John 3:16-17, John 15:16, and Isaiah 49:16.

Our timeless God, through Jesus, makes us timeless, too.

Prayers of the Heart

Dear Father,

Grass does wither, and flowers, as beautiful as they are, fade, but because of Your gift of Jesus, we will last forever. You give Your people remarkable times in this life. It is through these times we see Your glory and feel Your loving presence. My prayer is that those who do not know You will come to know You as they watch You bless Your own. I pray that no matter how old we get, our special memories will bring us back again and again to Your love and faithfulness. Lord, it isn't because we are worthy but because You are gracious and merciful to Your children. Father, we love You. In Jesus name, amen.

May 19 ~ Take out Two Chickens

I have a relative who is crazy. Not insane crazy, but fun kind of crazy. She tells a story about herself that will help explain what I mean.

When she was a young girl, her mother called her and said, "Would you please take out two chickens and feed the pigs?" That is just what she did; she took out two chickens and fed the chickens to the pigs. Not at all what her mother meant.

Have you ever heard the right words but got the wrong message? That was what happened in the story about Gina. She completely misunderstood what her mother meant. We can laugh at the story, but what about us? What wrong messages, even lies, have we believed and acted on?

In these devotionals, we read about things that guide our lives. We all need guidance, but who is leading us is what is most important. It is the leader who dictates our direction. What I hope we see as we read, these are traps and lies the world and our flesh offer us. I could, without God's mercy, fall into plenty of them.

In my journal, the Lord and I have talked about the traps and lies I face. One is fear, another is materialism, and another is past failures. I have repented, which means the best I knew how I turned from these, and I have given them to the Lord. They have been nailed to the cross.

The power of the Holy Spirit helped me break free from destructive traps. There was no possible way to walk away on my own self-determination. We cannot live a Christian life without the help of the Holy Spirit.

I cannot trust myself or my own understanding, and you don't need to trust yourself either. We always need to put our trust in the Lord and pray to understand His Word.

Traps will continue to get the best of us from time to time, but our goal is not to be continually tricked. This Christian life is a journey in a fallen world with an evil prince looking to deceive us as much as possible. One day, we will move out of these bodies and take a giant step into another world. Until then, we have a Savior whom we can trust and rely on.

Ponders of the Heart

Read Romans 8:28-39

How do these verses encourage you?

Can you recall when God worked something out for you that you never thought could be good?

Prayers of the Heart

Dear Father,

We want to realize the things that are holding us in bondage. We want to be taught by Your mighty hand. Lord, You are the only one that can cleanse us and free us. We are Your children, and You are our mighty Father. Fill our minds, will, and emotions with Your Spirit. Thank You for making us Yours forever. Apart from You, there is no hope. In Jesus' name, amen.

May 20 ~ Middle-Aged

Feel free to argue with me, but I am indeed middle-aged. How do I know? My thighs are now resting on my kneecaps. My well-defined arms have taken up the consistency of Jello, and my skin looks more and more like raw chicken.

Yes, middle age has hit my body, but that is not all. I know I have reached middle age because I have so much in my memory bank that the times and dates of important things are all mixed up together. I can recall my phone numbers from 20 years ago, but my children's cell numbers escape me.

I have lost what is called the cutting edge. My passion is more like a butter knife. If you are relating to me just a little, cheer up; I have good news for you. We are normal. With good news comes bad news, so here is the bad news.

"Let us not become weary in doing good, for at the proper time we will reap a harvest if we do not give up" (Galatians 6:9).

Let me quote from D. Martyn Lloyd-Jones, writer of "Spiritual Depression."

"Great attention is being paid to young people today, and a considerable amount of attention is being paid to old people, but I am perfectly convinced that the most difficult period of all is the middle period."

Great, someone has finally said it. If you are like me, you are thankful for those words. I always thought this was going to be an easy time in life. I was wrong. But God says, "Don't grow weary." Oh, Lord, I am weary. I am weary of problems, weary of grown children, and weary with weariness.

What in the world do we do when we become weary? Let's start first with what not to do. Don't give up, and secondly, don't use false stimuli to overcome weariness. Okay, great. So, what do we do? Let me quote D. Martyn Lloyd-Jones one more time:

"The world is too much with us; that is our trouble. We are too immersed in our problems. We need to look ahead, to anticipate, to look forward to the eternal glories gleaming afar. The Christian life is a tasting of the first fruits of that great harvest which is to come. 'Eye has not seen, nor ear heard, neither have entered them that love Him.' 'Set your affection on things above, not things of the earth.' Realize something in mind and heart of the glory of the place to which you are going. That is the antidote; that is the cure. The harvest we reap is certain, it is sure. 'Therefore,' says

Paul to the Corinthians, 'be ye steadfast, unmovable, always abounding in the work of the Lord for as much as ye know that your labor is not in vain in the Lord.' Go on with your task, whatever you are feeling; keep on with your work. God will give the increase; He will be an abundant harvest. Look forward to it. 'Ye shall reap. 'And above all, let us consider the Master for Whom we work."

The other ways seem easier, but oh, the glory of God's way is worth it all.

Ponders of the Heart

Have you become weary of doing good?

Why do you think we become so weary?

Read Galatians 6:6-18.

Prayers of the Heart

Dear Holy Father,

Our future is sure. We praise You. Our purpose is eternal. We thank You. Our God is mighty. We bow before You. Burn Your passion in our middle-aged weariness for You. Lord, we love You. In Jesus' name, amen.

May 21 ~ Losing Heart

During Julie's first year of teaching, she kept us entertained with stories about her kids. I would ask her, "Well, do you think you are going to like being a teacher?" Julie, like me, doesn't give short answers, but the gist is yes.

She then shared a complicated thing she had to do. Julie told me about a student who was going to be held back and her concern for this child. This student should have repeated the first or second grade and holding him back now could cause him to lose heart.

I felt her pain because I have people in my life who are weary and unhappy. Almost all of us have times in life when we have lost heart. I talked with a lady today who had lost her joy, and as I listened to her story, I was about to lose mine.

Don't get me wrong, I have things going on in my life that pull me down, and I have to work at not giving up. Do you know what I mean? I'm sure you do. Each of us struggles with things that are hard.

What exactly is losing heart? My definition is when you resign yourself to something as "This is just the way it is." When you do this, you lose hope, which is losing heart. That attitude should have no place in our Christian life. It is a foothold for Satan, one he loves.

This mindset carries on with duty but no passion. This downward spiral can damage our lives. Satan is very content when he has a Christian operating in the spirit of resignation. This spirit will cover, crush, smash, and grieve a saint's soul, not to mention his spirit. This spirit can work in our marriages, family lives, jobs, and churches. What is the solution to this dilemma? Here are two verses that can set our minds straight.

"Nevertheless I have this against you, that you have left your first love. Remember therefore from where you have fallen; repent" (Rev. 2:4-5 NKJV)

We are told to remember our first love, Jesus. "How?" You might ask.

"But the Helper, the Holy Spirit, whom the Father will send in My name, He will teach you all things, and bring to your remembrance all things that I said to you;" (John 14:26 NKJV).

The Holy Spirit who has been sent to us will help us remember our salvation and the love we had for Jesus. He will refresh us if we turn from our ungrateful hearts and remember.

We do not have to live defeated with weary souls. The Holy Spirit can fill us with the wonder of God. Then our hearts will be free, and our love will flow in and through us. Oh, what a wonderful God we serve.

Ponders of the Heart

Read Psalm 21:1-7

Can you, like David, rejoice over God's great love and blessings?

Write down a list of the good things God has blessed you with and praise Him for them.

Prayers of the Heart

Dear Father,

You know the worry of our day. You know the weariness we sometimes feel, but Oh, Lord, help us be stirred by Your love for us. Let us remember the greatness of our salvation. Lord, encourage Your people this day and fill our hearts with praise. In Jesus' name, amen.

May 22 ~ Important vs. Significant

We took our youngest grandson, Clayton, out to dinner, and he asked if we would hire him to work in one of our companies when he entered high school. The company he was inquiring about is an outside job; muscle and grit are needed. We told him we would hope so. Then he said if not that company, what about your other company? Our other company is a maid service, and I have seen his room.

My husband asked, "Clayton, do you want to clean houses?" He said, "No, I want to be a manager." We could not help it; we had to laugh. He wanted to start at the top. Clayton was 12, which makes his comment understandable. But I know adults who feel the same way.

Should a Christian strive to be important? Being important is not the same thing as being significant. Take Clayton's comment about being a manager, not a cleaner. If I am a customer wanting to have my house cleaned, the cleaner is more important to me than a manager. Or should I say they are more significant?

People dream of being important. A stay-at-home mom changing diapers can dream of an exciting career. A career might be seen as important to the world, but God knows she is right where she needs to be. Raising a child is both important and significant.

We have seen in our lives people who become famous and fall off the rails into drug addiction, divorce, and self-seeking lifestyles. They have fame, they are rich, but they lose who they are. These are traps we are all subject to.

Our very athletic grandson was a joy to watch as he played sports. Watching was fun, except for wrestling. I didn't like that sport at all. We all envisioned him playing college baseball or football and Bill and I having an RV and following him around as he played.

I am ashamed to say we enjoyed his fame. But this young man was wiser than his grandparents. He played, and he was great, but he was ready to put his effort into preparing for a good job and staying close to the girl he loved. To our joy, God has led him into a deeper relationship with Him. That, to me, is a significant plan that will produce a valuable life.

In our day and time, as in Jesus' day, people strive to be important. I am reminded of the story in Mark when John and James came to Jesus and wanted Him to give them a place of honor. They asked for one of them to sit on His right and one on His left in His Kingdom. Jesus knew they had no idea what they were asking. He called the disciples together and said:

"You know that those who are regarded as rulers of the Gentiles lord it over them, and their high officials exercise authority over them. Not so with

you. Instead, whoever wants to become great among you must be your servant" (Mark 10:42-43).

I must confess I miss God's way often, and I am thankful the Bible can teach me His way, which is always best.

Ponders of the Heart

Do you see the contrast between what we think is important and what Jesus thinks is significant?

How have you, like me, missed the mark?

Read Mark 10:13-16 and Mark 10:17-22 for insight.

Prayers of the Heart

Dear Father,

Would You please open our minds and our hearts to Your Word? Holy Spirit, we need You to show us the better way. Our world is topsy-turvy. We need wisdom from above and insight into the traps of this world. Lord, You lead people into important positions. You have wonderful people who are stars in sports. You have people in all sorts of places and positions, but we need to be where You want us to be. That is the place of significance to You. We pray in Jesus' name, amen.

May 23 ~ Panic

Our dog, Tex, panics over storms, and his back porch home is not where he wants to be. He wants to be in the house under my feet as he pants and drools with fear. If he only knew I had absolutely no power over storms, he would choose someone else to depend on.

How do you act when you panic, and who do you call? What pushes your panic button? The answers to these questions reveal a lot about us.

How we act reveals our personalities, and who we call reveals who we depend on. Who or what pushes our panic button reveals what is important to us.

There are situations that can overwhelm us, and God, in His mercy, has placed others in our lives to support and help us. When my panic button is pushed, my first thought is to call on my husband. Bill protects and rescues me as much as possible, and I know he will help me in any way he can.

I'm thankful for his love and his support, but I also realize some things are beyond his control, his power, and really beyond his job. Bill, as my husband, is called to protect and care for me, and he does. He is God's provision for my earthly life as I am God's provision for his. We are to reflect God's love and provision for one another just as the moon is light but only a reflection of the sun.

God is our provision in the storms and the pleasures of life. Sometimes, God provides through another person, and sometimes, He works with us as Father to His child. There are times when God wants me to look to Bill for help and other times, He wants me to look only to Him. But He always wants me to realize He alone is my provision.

When we are sick, God is our provision, even if He provides through doctors. Our heavenly Father is our comfort, even if He comforts us through loved ones or by His Spirit. God provides all the time in all situations, even when we can't see His provision.

As I type these words, I realize I am talking way above my walking, but I am convinced that by His grace, He will carry me or strengthen my legs as I walk this Christian life. He is my Father, and I am His child when I act like it and when I don't.

Ponders of the Heart

Who has God provided to walk with you through this life?

Was there a time when you depended on God alone?

Read Psalm 16:1-3, Psalm 18:1-3, and Psalm 27:1.

Prayers of the Heart

Dear Father,

 We praise You for Your love and Your provision. We praise You for Your grace and kindness. Father, we put our trust in You. In Jesus' name, amen.

May 24 ~ Discipline

Tracie informed me the first time she popped Collier's hand that, he had to learn to leave the plant in their den alone. I know she was right, but I did not like the idea of Collier being popped. He was just a baby, but even babies push their limits.

Collier crawled over to the plant and looked back at Tracie to see if she was watching. His hand was moving, and he was getting ready to pick up dirt. "Collier," she says. He looked at her, smiled, and then grabbed a handful of dirt. This is when Tracie popped his hand. The pop hurts his feelings. My daughter picked him up, and he put his head on her chest. She took no pleasure in disciplining him, but the job of a mom is sometimes unpleasant. Does God discipline His children?

"My son, do not make light of the Lord's discipline, and do not lose heart when he rebukes you, because the Lord disciplines the one he loves, and he chastens everyone he accepts as his son " (Hebrews 12:5-6).

God is always training His children. We need His training because there are things we do not understand. There are also things we do understand; we just choose our own way. God loves us enough to train us, which sometimes means He gives us a pop. His pops hurt, and they hurt our feelings. He takes no pleasure in disciplining, but the job of our heavenly Father is sometimes unpleasant. Hebrews 12:11 gives us the results of God's training:

"No discipline seems pleasant at the time, but painful. Later on, however, it produces a harvest of righteousness and peace for those who have been trained by it."

When I read this verse, I understand God uses everything in our lives for good. He disciplines us so our lives produce the fruit of righteousness and peace, and His work yields eternal glory.

Ponders of the Heart

When was the last time God disciplined you, and what did you learn?

In hindsight, are you thankful?

Read Revelation 3:19, 1 Peter 4:12-16, and 1 Peter 5:8-11.

Prayers of the Heart

Dear Father,

Help us not grow weary even in trials and discipline. Train us so we can partake of Your holiness. Father, we surrender to Your ways, knowing Your ways are always good, always right, and always what we need. In Jesus' name, amen.

May 25 ~ All of Me

The hit country song sung by Willie Nelson, "All of Me," is one that sticks in my head. I hear him singing this song, and I have two thoughts.

One is my marriage and the relationship I have with my husband. Bill is so good to me that, without a doubt, he can have all of me. The good, the bad and the ugly. I also want all of him. We are on this journey of life together.

The other thought is, how much of me does God want? The title of this song gives the answer. He wants all of me. The good, the bad, and the ugly. He also wants all of you. The reason is He wants us to journey through life and eternity with Him.

What a wonder. God wants us, all of us. God is most pleased with us when we give ourselves completely to Him. He knows we have problems. He knows we make mistakes. He knows we will never get it right, but our God still wants us, all of us.

How do we give God all of us? Is that even possible? I do not think it is a one-time thing. It is a daily choice. Willie Nelson's song states parts of the body he wishes to give away, and we could do the same in our prayers each day to God. We need Him in every part of our days and every part of our lives.

What if we dedicated our lips to Him each day and asked him to clean up our words? What about our arms? What great service we could give. What wonderful hugs we could offer. It is so true; if we are in Christ, He has our hearts, so why not dedicate to Him each day, all of us.

I would love to make up a new praise song, dedicating every part of me to Him. But for the life of me, I cannot get Willie Nelson's song out of my head.

Ponders of the Heart

Are you holding a part of yourself away from the Lord?

Are you afraid He will reject you?

Read Mark 12:30, Romans 12:1-2, and Psalm 47:1-4.

Christ gave us His righteousness so we can come to Him and be His children. God adopts us into His family not just for time but for eternity.

Prayer of the Heart

Dear Father,

Take all of us, for we are no good without You. You are our hope and our need. We want to be vessels that You can use. Help us live lives far away from sin. We give ourselves to You and offer our bodies to You as well as our souls and spirits. Lord, take all of us for Your glory. In Jesus' name, we pray, amen.

May 26 ~ God, Where are You?

Do you have times when God insists you listen to Him? I do, and when I don't obey, He keeps reminding me.

"Whether you turn to the right or to the left, your ears will hear a voice behind you, saying, 'This is the way; walk in it'" (Isaiah 30:21).

Once, He hounded me from heaven when He wanted me to read "The Purpose Driven Life" by Rick Warren, and I didn't want to. Everywhere I turned, someone was talking about that book. I finally gave up, to my great delight, and started reading this book. It was such a blessing to me, and I thank the Lord for His persistent insistence.

However, I have times when I am sure God has lost my address. He keeps after me when I disobey, but when I do obey, He seems sometimes to go silent. Have you ever had this happen to you?

I remember when God had impressed me that I needed to give up my job on staff at our church. He would not leave me alone about it. When I had obeyed, He seemed to go silent. I woke up one night needing Him to tell me what was next. I still didn't know the next day. I had to trust what He told me in the light, but it is hard not to doubt it in the dark. When Job was experiencing the silence of God, he put it this way:

"But if I go to the east, he is not there; if I go to the west, I do not find him. When he is at work in the north, I do not see him; when he turns to the south, I catch no glimpse of him. But he knows the way that I take; when he has tested me, I will come forth as gold" (Job 23:8-10).

God never leaves us, He promises. His presence is not the same as us feeling His presence.

Rick Warren says: "God's omnipresence and the manifestation of His presence are two different things. One is a fact; the other is often a feeling. God is always present, even when you are unaware of Him, and His presence is too profound to be measured by mere emotion."

That takes my breath away, for His presence is too profound to be measured by mere emotions. He wants us to express faith, not just feelings.

Ponders of the Heart

Is God speaking to you about something right now? Explain.

Does it seem He has gone silent?

Remember, He is always with us even when we can't feel Him there.

Read Psalm 139 and see how David expressed his faith in God's presence.

Prayers of the Heart

Dear Father,

Not a single moment of our lives is hidden from You. You are always near, and You always hear. Father, God, the promise of Your presence is sure, for You cannot lie. You are a God of truth, and in You, there is no deception. You are our real and sure foundation. You are our hope and future. Lord, let us feel Your presence, but let our faith hold us true when You are silent. In Jesus' name, we pray, amen.

May 27 ~ Running Home

When you were a child, where and who did you run to when you were hurt? I always ran home to my mom or dad.

My children, when they were young, ran home as fast as they could go when they were hurt physically, but also if their feelings were hurt. They came running inside, crying, and fell into my arms.

I would ask them to tell me what was wrong, but sometimes, wisdom would take over, and I would just hold them for a while. They needed to know they could cry, and I was there. After a good cry, they were ready to talk about the hurt. They needed the security of my loving arms and presence.

When circumstances blow up in my face or the face of someone I love, I am told to pray.

"Do not be anxious about anything, but in every situation, by prayer and petition, with thanksgiving, present your requests to God. And the peace of God, which transcends all understanding, will guard your hearts and your minds in Christ Jesus" (Philippians 4:6-7).

D. Martyn Lloyd-Jones says the word prayer in this verse is a general term. He goes on to say:

"Before you make your request known unto God, pray, worship, adore. Come into the presence of God and for the time being forget your problems. Do not start with them. Just realize you are face to face with God."

Think about the wonder of that for a minute. When my children come home, they just enjoy being there. They plop down on the couch, take their shoes off, raid the refrigerator, and have no worries, but when they walk through the door, the first thing they do is hug me. Just like my children know they are welcomed at our house; we can enter the throne room of heaven assured we are welcome. We can come to Him knowing we can lay our burdens down. He is our heavenly Father, and we are His children.

Do we realize the privilege of coming and enjoying the wonder of our face-to-face encounter? We need to stop and realize where we are and Who we are communicating with. He is worthy of our praise and our affection. Then, we are ready to present our supplication, request, and thanksgiving. If we miss His presence when we pray, we have missed the best part.

If my children came home, plopped on the couch, raided the refrigerator, and didn't miss my being there, I would say our relationships needed work. We can say the same about our relationship with our heavenly Father.

In fact, those were the very words I spoke to Him today. I asked Him to forgive me for substituting our relationship for requests. He is not my "Holy Santa in the sky." What a self-centered way to treat the Lord. It is a hurtful way to treat the One who loves me.

What a lousy way to rob myself of His presence. He is the Lord, King, and He bids me to come. My Master, yet He calls me friend. Oh, that we would run home, lay our burdens at His feet, and worship Him. What joy and wonder to come into His presence and know the awareness of His love.

Ponders of the Heart

Did you remember to praise Him today?

Do you need to tell Him how thankful you are for His presence?

Ponder these words of Ephesians 3:19 in the Amplified Bible:

"[That *you may really come] to know [practically, through experience for yourselves] the love of Christ, which far surpasses mere knowledge [without experience]; that you may be filled [through all your being] unto all the fullness of God [may have the richest measure of the divine Presence, and become a body wholly filled and flooded with God Himself]!"*

Prayers of the Heart

Dear Father,

What a privilege it is to come into Your presence. Thank You that we can know You and experience You for ourselves. Father, forgive us for wanting to use You instead of loving You, treasuring and enjoying You. We do need Your help. We need to lay our burdens down, but Father, God, we want to know and love You more. Teach us to pray. In Jesus' name, amen.

May 28 ~ Agape

When I was thirty, I discovered that my real father lived in Minneapolis and worked at a TV station. He left us when I was three and never came back. I had a stepfather who was my daddy, and I was not in need of a father, but I wanted my biological father to know his children and grandchildren.

After a little detective work, I found out where he worked and wrote him a letter. In the letter, I told him exactly what I just told you. I did not need a father; I had one. But if he wanted to know his family, he could call me.

I did not hear from him, so after about two months, I thought he was not interested. One morning, I was getting ready for work, and the phone rang. It was George Sutton, my father. I asked him why he left us and why he had never contacted us. Then I asked him why he called. This opened up a time of communication between us, and I invited him to get to know our family.

We were created by God, and He wants us to be a part of His family. God did not need us because He was lonely. He was in perfect relationship with the Holy Trinity. He didn't need a family, but He desired for us to know Him and be part of His perfect, holy family.

God comes to us and offers us forgiveness for our sins so we can be holy. This offer includes a new nature and Christ's righteousness so we can come into His presence. They're gifts from God, and we can open our hearts and accept them.

In the church lingo of today, we call people looking into the Christian faith as seekers. I really think there is only One Seeker, and it is God. He seeks us with an invitation to come to Him, get to know Him, and be a part of His family.

He tells us that as members of His family, we will have new sisters and brothers, a new Father, a new home, and a new identity.

My father stepped through the door of my invitation for several years. His wife did not want him to be a part of our lives, so he contacted me when he could. I didn't call him. He even came to visit one time, but for reasons I don't know, he cut off communications. He made the choice not to be a part of our family.

In my life, Jesus is the one who has extended agape to me, and because of His agape, I was able to extend it to my real father. I accepted the gift. My father did not. I won, and he lost.

What I won is something you can't lose. He lost something he'll never understand. I'm sorry for him, but not as sorry as those who turn God's offer down. Agape is the Greek word for unconditional love. God's love is unconditional. He offers with no strings attached, and we can accept this love or refuse it.

He needs nothing from us, but He wants to embrace us with His love. How can we turn down such wonderful love? The truth is that people do it all the time. I hope my real father did not turn down God's love. It is sad enough he turned down mine.

Ponders of the Heart

Do you realize God wants to do more for you than save you from sins?

Do you know if you are in Christ, you are part of His family?

Read Ephesians 1:5, 1 Peter 1:3-5, and Romans 8:14-15.

Prayers of the Heart

Dear Father,

We come before You with thankfulness. Thanking You for the gift of salvation and the gift of being born into Your family. Gracious Father, help us always remember we are Yours not because we deserved it but because You offered us agape love. Your love is irresistible. We thank You and praise You, Father. In Jesus' name, amen.

May 29 ~ Secrets

To whom do you tell your secrets? If you are wise, you tell your secrets to people you trust, and if you are very wise, those people are few. When a friend tells their secrets to us, we feel special, close, and trusted. When we tell our secrets to them, they feel the same way. Proverbs talk about such a friend.

"But there is a friend that sticks closer than a brother" (Proverbs 18:24 NKJV).

I have a few close friends I share my secrets with. I share my sorrows and joys, and then there is Bill, who I share everything with. Oswald Chambers says:

"Many people will confide their secret sorrows to you, but the final mark of intimacy is when they share their secret joys with you."

Then, he asks an important question. He says,

"Have we ever let God tell us any of His joy? Or are we continually telling God our secrets, leaving Him no time to talk to us?"

How convicting those words are to me. It shows me how one-sided my relationship with God can be. I can be so self-absorbed.

The concept that God has secrets He wishes to reveal to His children is new to me, but it is not new to the Scriptures:

"The Lord confides in those who fear him; he makes his covenant known to them" (Psalm 25:14).

"I no longer call you servants, because a servant does not know his master's business. Instead, I have called you friends, for everything that I learned from my Father I have made known to you" (John 15:15).

When we confide our secrets to God, it shows Him how special He is to us, but when God shares His secrets with us, it shows how special we are to Him. How many opportunities have I missed to hear from God because of my self-centered relationship? How many secrets have I missed from others because of "busyness"?

It is secrets, intimate joys, and sorrows that make close friends. My mother said, "To have a friend, you must be a friend." What a friend we have in Jesus. Let us befriend Him back. He might share with us His deepest joys. Can you just imagine what a blessing that would be?

Ponders of the Heart

How can you be a better friend?

What takes up your time, people, or tasks?

When was the last time You heard a secret from the Lord?

Read Exodus 33:11, Proverbs 3:32, and Amos 3:7.

Prayers of the Heart

Dear Father,

I keep hearing the verse in my head, "Be still and know that I am God." Lord, if I could change this verse just a little, I would add, "Be quiet and hear the Lord." I want to be silent now and listen to You. By Your mercy and Your grace, let me hear You. Quiet my mind and my heart, and let me hear and know You. In Jesus' name, amen.

May 30 ~ Eternity in Our Hearts

"He has made everything beautiful in its time. He has also set eternity in the human heart; yet no one can fathom what God has done from beginning to end" (Ecclesiastes 3:11).

Why am I so sad every time my grandson returns to college? I should be thankful for the visit we had, and I am. However, the minute he leaves, I start missing him and feel a little depressed. There is something sad about goodbyes to grandchildren and children, goodbyes to good friends, and the goodbyes because of death, which is the saddest of all.

When my dad passed away because of cancer, I went through the stages of grief. During his illness, I had peace knowing my dad had become a believer. God had saved my dad when he was in his seventies. When he died, I felt relief. After watching him suffer for months in pain and knowing his eternal destiny, I was thankful he was no longer suffering.

I believe this first stage of grief was appropriate, even though I knew I would miss him. He would now be at rest in heaven with Jesus. Dad and I had some precious time together, but there was something wrong about saying goodbye. I do not like to let go, and if you are like me, neither do you.

Ecclesiastes 3:1-8 reminds us that God is busy working things out in His time. Chapter three begins with a list of things that happened in time during this life.

"There is a time for everything,

and a season for every activity under the heavens:

a time to be born and a time to die,

a time to plant and a time to uproot,

a time to kill and a time to heal,

a time to tear down and a time to build,

a time to weep and a time to laugh,

a time to mourn and a time to dance,

a time to scatter stones and a time to gather them,

a time to embrace and a time to refrain from embracing,

a time to search and a time to give up,

a time to keep and a time to throw away,

a time to tear and a time to mend,

a time to be silent and a time to speak,

a time to love and a time to hate,

a time for war and a time for peace."

We find ourselves subject to time and the seasons of life. We are born, and we do die, but we know in our heart of hearts that we were created for something more.

The more we were created for is eternity, a life that goes on and on with no beginning and no end. God created us to have a lasting, eternal relationship with Him and each other. God has placed in our hearts the desire for eternity. That is part of being created in His image.

When we lose a friend or a family member to death, it is sad. While I am on this earth, I will continue to miss my dad and those I love who have gone before me. Our promised hope is that this is not the end. We can continue to live our lives because the Holy Spirit is in us and will equip us. We live knowing that one day, we will enter our eternal home and live forever. We can rejoice because we have the promise of something more.

Ponders of the Heart

Are you ready for eternity?

If so, what are you looking forward to the most?

Read Ecclesiastes 3:1-14 and ponder this life and the one to come.

Prayers of the Heart

Dear Father,

We are thankful for the knowledge that it is right for us to yearn for something more. It is right for us to yearn for eternity. Lord, help us live our lives looking forward to the time when we will be together with You and each other, never to say goodbye again. Lord, thank You for the provision of eternal life through Jesus. Help those who ache for something more to find You, Jesus. Draw them into Your loving eternal heart. In Jesus' name, amen.

May 31 ~ Prayers of the Heart

"And may the God of peace Himself sanctify you through and through [separate you from profane things, make you pure and wholly consecrated to God]; and may your spirit and soul and body be preserved sound and complete [and found] blameless at the coming of our Lord Jesus Christ the Messiah)" (1 Thessalonians 5:23 Amplified Bible).

Dear Father,

How I pray this for all Your people. Separate us from profane things. There are so many wicked things around us. They are everywhere. We want our bodies, our souls, and our spirits to be found complete in You. We want to be faithful people of praise when Jesus comes for us. Lord, move over us and do for us that which we cannot do for ourselves. We long to be sanctified through and through.

"The one who calls you is faithful, and he will do it" (1 Thessalonians 5:24).

Father, before my prayer gets cold on the page, You have promised You will do the very thing I have asked because You are faithful even when I am not. Your promises give me hope that You will supply all the power to transform me if I cooperate with You. My loving Lord, thank You that Your desire for us is something that is possible because You give us Yourself. Help us keep our eyes on You, our Lord, and God. In Jesus' name, we pray, amen.

june

— 66 —

Do you not know? Have you not heard? The Lord is the everlasting God, the Creator of the ends of the earth. He will not grow tired or weary, and his understanding no one can fathom.

Isaiah 40:28

June 1 ~ Identity

My two oldest granddaughters were born seven weeks apart. They have been close cousins since the very beginning of their lives. As I write this, they are teenagers, and both are beautiful. Reagan is tall with dark hair, brown eyes, and beautiful golden skin. Bailey is short, with blond hair and blue eyes, and has a lovely creamy complexion. Both are stunning.

There are times Reagan wishes she could be like Bailey, who can light up the room with her smile and have the confidence to talk with everyone there, especially children. She also wishes she had Bailey's tiny feet.

Bailey wishes she had Reagan's nose and her self-confidence.

But as their grandmother, GiGi, I would not change a thing about either of them. They are both exactly as they should be.

God tells us in Acts 17:26-28 that He predetermined when and where each of us would live. He chose our parents, the color of our eyes, gifts, and our talents. He made us to be who He wanted us to be. When God looks at us through the eyes of grace, we are perfect and beautiful to Him. Just like this grandmother, when I look at my two granddaughters, God loves and sees us exactly as we should be.

To keep me from comparing and losing sight of the One who says I am beautiful, I need to remember the identity He has given me. It is fine for me to admire someone, but God could not love me more. His unfailing love and complete satisfaction should free me to be all He made me to be. It also frees me from comparing myself to someone else and encourages me to discover and live out my true identity. The identity I have because I am a child of God.

The Evil one wants us to get stuck in disappointment and envy or get us busy competing with one another. If he can get us stuck, we cannot flourish into the people God made us to be. This stuns our Christian growth.

It seems women especially start thinking everyone must look a certain way to be beautiful, but God loves blue eyes as much as brown, long legs, and short ones. He adores wit and quiet spirits, and He smiles at singers and athletes. We are all made in the image of God, with different personalities, talents, gifts, and purposes. If we live out of the identity God has given us, we can appreciate others while staying true to ourselves. Oh, God, help us live out our purpose for Your glory and our best fulfillment. We often settle for less than what our God has in store for His children.

Ponders of the Heart

How can we fight the urge to compete and compare and love who God made us to be?

How does God's complete love and satisfaction free us to be ourselves?

Read Genesis 5:1-2, Acts 17:26-28, and 1 Corinthians 12:12-20.

Prayers of the Heart

Dear Father,

Help us see ourselves and others through Your eyes. We want to be who You made us to be. Help us remember our identity in You is where we find the peace and joy we desire. Lord, help us discover the very reason we are here and live out our purpose with hope and grace. Father, thank You for loving us and making us Yours. We love You. In Jesus' name, amen.

June 2 ~ Do You Want to Be Made Well?

Bailey has constant sinus problems. Her nose is stopped up more than not, and it drives her mom crazy. Tracie hates the fact she cannot breathe.

The strange thing is Bailey doesn't seem to notice. Her sinus condition causes her bouts with sinus infections, and then she is forced to notice. She takes a round of antibiotics and antihistamines and fights through misery.

We hound her about taking her medicine because we know Bailey will forget to take it. Tracie gets frustrated with her and asks her, "Do you want to get better?"

Jesus asked the same question to a man who had been sick for 38 years. The man answered Jesus with a reason for his dilemma. Jesus just responded, "Pick up your bed and walk." Immediately, the man got up and walked.

When I read passages like this one, I wonder about my response. Would I have enough faith to try and get up? Would I turn my head in disgust or come up with another excuse? I wonder when was the man healed? Was it the moment Christ asked the question or the moment he responded?

I do not know the answers, but isn't it wonderful to know Christ is willing to look at us and heal us? We need more than physical curing. We need deep, divine healing. The man was healed physically, but was he made whole spiritually? For us to receive total healing, we must exercise faith in Jesus, who is willing to restore our souls. The question comes to us as it did to this man, "Do we want to be healed?"

Have you been praying for a healing miracle? I have. There is a marriage that needs restoring. The two people in this marriage need God's healing Hand. This can only be done by the Miracle Healer, Christ. This couple must believe He can. I am praying for someone with a broken heart. They need the heart healer, Christ, to heal them. He is willing; they must believe. In my life, I live in constant need of His touch, healing, and His love.

Ponders of the Heart

Do you see any evidence this man was healed spiritually?

Can we receive something from Jesus and yet never know Him?

When you pray for others, do you ask for temporal relief more than eternal miracles?

Read John 5:1-15.

Jesus is so much more than a physician of the body. He is the physician of our souls.

Prayers of the Heart

Dear Father,

Heal our souls, our minds, and our hearts. Lord, then we can love, think, serve and be more like You. Teach us to walk in trust and obedience. Oh, Father, we ask for miracles, miracles only You can do. We love You, Lord. In Jesus' name, we pray, amen.

June 3 ~ What If?

Are you a person who habitually plays the "what if" game? Chris, my son, had a disagreement with one of his bosses. The boss left to go on vacation the next day, and Chris played the "what if" game in his mind. After the boss's vacation, a meeting was called, and Chris thought he knew what was going to happen.

He was told the meeting would be at 8:30 the next morning. Chris spent a miserable night playing the "what if" of worry. I can just feel the knot he probably felt the next day when he walked into that meeting. As his mom, I would rather go through the conflict than have him go through it. His dad and I had prayed for him and encouraged him as best we could, but he was too focused on the "what if" for us to be any comfort.

The next day, the meeting was held, and Chris received an apology and a promotion. He was too exhausted from the emotional roller-coaster he had been on even to enjoy the news.

Have you ever been there? We all have. The mammogram doesn't look good. One-third of the staff is being laid off by the company. Bills are more than the income. On and on, we go with circumstances throwing us into the "what if" game.

Corrie ten Boom offered us words of wisdom when she said,

"If you look at the world, you'll be distressed. If you look within, you'll be depressed. But if you look at Christ, you'll rest."

The message is our focus and directs our feelings.

Only God knows what tomorrow holds. He is the only One who can see the purpose and the outcome. Do we believe He is in control and His goodness will see us through?

How often do we end up back at basic questions about our faith? If I had a dollar for every time Jesus has asked me to believe Him, I would be a rich woman. If I had to give away one every time I played the "what if" game, I would be in rags. Oh, if we would believe Jesus and focus on Him and not our circumstances, we would have fewer wrinkles, fewer gray hairs, and restful, peaceful hearts and minds.

"For our light and momentary troubles are achieving for us an eternal glory that far outweighs them all. So we fix our eyes not on what is seen, but on what is unseen, since what is seen is temporary, but what is unseen is eternal" (2 Corinthians 4:17-18).

God wants us to have the hope of eternity in our hearts and minds. Our culture has an Instamatic viewpoint. We are called to be in the world but not of it. Let's turn our eyes toward Jesus.

Ponders of the Heart

What is your greatest concern today?

Who knows the outcome?

Read Romans 8:28-39.

If you belong to Jesus, you can rest on His Words.

Prayers of the Heart

Dear Father,

Teach us to trust You and to focus on You and not on circumstances. Help us realize we grow and mature in tough times. May our hearts rest, knowing You are with us and for us. You are our strength when we are weak and our hope when things are hopeless. You, our Lord, are as close as a prayer. We bless You and thank You for Your unmatched love. In Jesus' name, amen.

June 4 ~ A Diamond

Bill and I usually take a trip for our anniversary, and that is our gift to one another. One year was different. He surprised me with a new wedding band. If he had asked me if I wanted a new wedding band, I would have said, "No."

I am a little partial to the one I already had, but when I saw this wedding band lined with just- the right-size diamonds for me, I took the other band off with lightning speed, never to think of it again. I cannot tell you how often I look at my new wedding band. It is beautiful, but the gift is so uncharacteristic of Bill because he knows his practical wife.

After seeing the diamond band, I was glad he bought it, and I felt little to no guilt. If Bill had taken one of the rings around a cigar and given it to me, I would never have taken off my original ring. The paper cigar ring is not worth anything. If he had bought me a new wedding band of equal value, I would not have wanted it over my old ring. The value and the beauty of the diamond ring made an impression on me.

How unworthy I am that Christ would want me. He wanted me when I was of no value. In fact, Scripture tells us that He paid for me with His life.

In other words, I was not a diamond. I was less than a cigar ring, and yet He wanted me and died to pay for me.

This truth is also for you. Christ saw you, loved you, and gave His very life for you. He is the One who gives us worth. What a wonderful Savior who looks beyond our worthlessness, beyond our sin, and makes us into His diamond. He paid a high price with gladness and no regret.

Ponders of the Heart

Do you realize the worth God places on you, or do you live feeling worthless?

Do you believe God is able to transform your life?

Read John 3:16, Romans 5:8, Romans 8:29, 2 Cor. 3:18, and Phil 2:15.

Prayers of the Heart

Dear Father,

Thank You for seeing beyond our sins and for loving us. Lord, we praise You for the work You are doing to change us into Your likeness. You are our hope and our future. We are Your diamonds in the rough. We praise You in Jesus' name, amen.

June 5 ~ No Satisfaction

We surely live in a world with little satisfaction. I am reminded of the old Mick Jagger song, "I Can't Get No Satisfaction."

This song is the cry of women who stay at home and those who work. Ladies with children, husbands, and homes and those without children, husbands, and homes "can't get no satisfaction."

People with money, those without money, teenagers or children, are unsatisfied. All ages share the same emptiness in this fallen world.

What is wrong with us? Jesus knows our dilemma is in our souls. In fact, God knows that life without Him leaves us unsatisfied. We were made for Him, and we find our worth, our purpose, and deep, satisfying love in Him. He wants to give us His best, so He gives us Himself.

The emptiness of our souls can only be satisfied by Him and in Him. The more we believe this statement, the more peace we will experience.

What dissatisfaction are you feeling today? If the song "I Can't Get No Satisfaction" is your theme song, change your theme. Look not to this world but look to His Word.

"As for me, I will be vindicated and will see your face; when I awake, I will be satisfied with seeing your likeness" (Psalm 17:15).

May this Psalm be our heart cry.

Ponders of the Heart

Where do you find yourself today, empty or satisfied?

How can the Bible help us refocus and find satisfaction?

Read Isaiah 55:1-3 and Isaiah 48:18.

Prayers of the Heart

Dear Lord,

We were created for You by You, and thankfully, we belong with You forever. This world has nothing to offer us that compares with You. Keep our eyes and hearts focused on You. We are weak without Your strength. We are easily distracted. Give us enough, Lord, so worry is not our master but not so much that we become cold and greedy. Father, You know us so well; do what it takes to keep us close to You. We love being Your children. In Jesus' name, we pray, amen.

June 6 ~ Shyness

For years, I would tell people, "I'm just shy; I can't do that." Then, a preacher came to town and stepped on my toes when he said shyness was nothing more than pride. Suddenly, being shy wasn't an acceptable behavior.

I started asking God to change my thinking about shyness being an acceptable characteristic. If the preacher was right, I would have to say I am not shy; I am prideful.

Pridefulness, being the root cause of shyness, is very revealing.

Admitting to myself that I am prideful is not a comfortable admission. Most likely, there are those reading this devotional who feel like their toes just got stomped on; you are not alone.

When our family gets together, we play games. One game that brings out the bashfulness is Jesters. In this game you are acting out words, trying to get your team to guess five words in a short period of time. You can't be shy. You have to go fast and crazy. Those of us who are introverted hate the game until we get past our pride and go for it.

I am prideful, in a shy sort of way, but I don't want to stay that way because I will miss living. What do we do when we have a pride problem?

The first thing I had to do was believe pride was the root cause of my shyness. That wasn't easy. Being shy was much more endearing than being prideful. Then I had to believe God, who had begun a good work in me, was working in my life, and help was on its way.

It was my heavenly Father who wanted me to know I had a problem and that I could come to Him for help. The Lord's motive was not to destroy me or to make me feel bad. His motive was to overpower this deceptive sin in my life. I first had to accept this was sin, then confess and give it to the only One who can defeat sin, Jesus.

There are times when I still act shy. I'm not comfortable in all situations and need to fight my feelings. When I feel uncomfortable in a situation, I can run to my heavenly Father, saying, "Lord, defeat this power of shyness in me so I can enjoy this moment?" Just writing these words to you and confessing this problem releases its power over me. Praise the Lord that what is revealed in the light loses its power.

Ponders of the Heart

What behavior are you explaining away as "this is just how I am?"

What sin is sneaking in the dark, keeping you captive?

Read Romans 13:12-14, Galatians 5:16-18, and Galatians 3:27.

Jesus wants to empower us to take off the old man and put on the new.

Prayers of the Heart

Dear Father,

We praise You that we can walk in the newness of life. We can rid ourselves of the old man and walk in the Spirit. We have been baptized into Jesus, and we can walk in Him. Father, what a great salvation You have given us, and we praise You. In Jesus' name, amen.

June 7 ~ Honor

Bestowing honor on someone is far more precious than gold. People can demand honor, but it has little value if not given freely. One of the first ways a bride honors her husband is by taking his name. In our society, we have few opportunities to change our names, but the day I married, I walked into the church with one name and out bearing the name of my husband. As wives, we can give special honor to our husbands as we identify ourselves with them by taking their family name.

When my daughter married, I had a tough time remembering she was now Tracie Blair instead of Tracie Collier. Not so with her, she did not struggle with her name change. In fact, she honors Ryan each time she reminds me of her new identity.

You can imagine how thrilled we were when Ryan and Tracie named their son Collier. They intertwined the love and respect they had for their families with the naming of their son.

Names identify us, set us apart, and reveal who we are. That is why kids and adults are devastated when they are called cruel names. As believers, Jesus Christ gives us new names. We bear our Savior's name, and we identify with Him. The Bible gives us a new identity by the new names it gives us:

We are children of God (John 1:12)

Christ's friend (John 15:15)

A new creation (2 Corinthians 5:17)

A saint (Ephesians 1:1)

A citizen of heaven (Philippians 3:30)

Understanding what God calls us dramatically affects our lives. We have a rich heritage, one given to us by the living God. He honors us by freely giving us His name. As we think about God honoring us by giving us His name, doesn't it make us want to honor Him by wearing His name well?

Ponders of the Heart

What name do you call yourself?

If you signed your check as Mrs. Jesus Christ, would it affect how you act?

Read Ephesians 1:3-12.

Prayers of the Heart

Dear Father,

You have given us a new identity and a new family. Thank You, Father, for the gift of Your love and honoring us by adopting us into Your family. Oh, Father, help us honor You by wearing Your name with honor. In Jesus' name, we pray, amen.

June 8 ~ Growth

My husband does not like change, and he doesn't like to throw anything away. He is what I call a packrat. Bill keeps clothes way past their usefulness, and he has old shoes galore.

His old truck is so rusty the hood bends when you lift it up. But get rid of his truck? No way.

I make fun of him about things like shoes and shirts, but I must admit, change is also hard for me. I am afraid of the unknown. As I confess this to you, it will help you understand why the quote below hit me between the eyes.

"Growth is often painful and scary. There is no growth without change; there is no change without fear or loss; and there is no loss without pain. Every change involves a loss of some kind: You must let go of old ways to experience the new. We fear these losses, even if our old ways were self-defeating, because, like a worn-out pair of shoes, they were at least comfortable and familiar" (The Purpose Driven Life by Rick Warren).

When I face changes in my lifestyle, the closer I get to the change, the more I experience fear. Rick Warren's words remind me these emotions are normal. This quote also reminds me to hang on and trust; growth is on its way.

Do you have major changes taking place in your life? Are you afraid? Do you feel a little lost? Take heart, you are okay. These feelings are normal.

We need to focus on the Lord. He knows where we are going. He is in control., and He is on our side. We are not lost, no matter how we feel.

Old ways are hard to give up. God's Word tells us that giving up old ways is part of dying to self. We can know the way through changing times if we know the One who knows the outcome. Keeping our eyes on Jesus is our hope.

Ponders of the Heart

Does it encourage you to know that, being human, you will sometimes be afraid?

How does the Bible help you remember you are not alone, God is with you, and He has a plan for you?

Read Jeremiah 29:11-13, Proverbs 3:5-6, and Romans 8:28.

Prayers of the Heart

Dear Precious Lord,

Thank You for reminding us You are bigger than our feelings. Especially our feelings of fear and loneliness. You are better than we can imagine. You are here, and we have nothing to fear. Father, we love You, and we thank You. We can trust and rest in You. In Jesus' name, we pray, amen.

June 9 ~ Changeless

There are aunts and uncles, first, second, and third cousins in my family I have not seen in years. You could say we have lost contact because of distance and busy lives. My husband has family members; I do not mind if I ever see them again. It is amazing, however, how time changes us all.

When a family event is scheduled, and there will be family members I have not seen in a long time, I usually go on a diet. Who wants to hear their family say, "You are sure looking healthy," when what they are really saying is, "She has aged and put on a few pounds." I also try to dress a little spiffy. As I reveal how shallow my actions are, please remember being honest is hard, so pray for me.

Gossip at a family reunion can go something like this, "Poor Aunt so-and-so, she is looking old. Or so-and-so sure has gotten fat. At times, the conversation might go like this, "Uncle so-and-so sure has nice grandchildren." Or maybe, "What a pretty granddaughter you have." My favorite would be, "My, how does Marilyn stay looking so young?" Those are the comments you want to hear.

Everyone realizes when they are looking older or gaining weight, they just don't want others to talk about it. All of us change over time. Sometimes for the better and at times for the worse, but don't let it keep you from getting together with your family.

People change, and things you count on to never change do. Life is a series of changes. We buy new cars and houses. We sometimes switch the church we go to, and I am famous for changing my hairstyle. Sometimes, the change is good; other times, it is not.

What about technology and the computer age? I will never catch up. Things change. In a changing world, isn't it wonderful to know that God does not? He is changeless. Progress and changes may characterize His work, but He stays the same. If God changed, He would not be perfect. He is the one solid, unchanging One.

That means we can count on Him. We can find our way if God is our guide. Our rest and our trust are in Him alone. He never grows old, fat, unloving, distant, or evil. God is our perfect, unchanging Father. Glory to our Lord, and glory to His Kingdom to come.

What a wonderful characteristic of God. Our feet are on solid ground if we are grounded in Him. If our hearts rest in His love, we can be free of fear. He loves us today and will love us tomorrow. If He forgives us today, we are forgiven. Rock solid is our God.

God is faithful, which is another characteristic we can trust. He is faithful to His Word and promises even when we are not faithful to Him. Our job is to know His Word so we can depend on His promises. The old hymn, "Great is Thy Faithfulness" says,

"Great is thy faithfulness, 0 God my Father, there is no shadow of turning with thee; Thou changes not, they compassions, they fail not; As thou hast been thou forever wilt be."

Ponders of the Heart

Are you someone who dislikes change?

Are you comforted by our unchanging God? Why?

Read Hebrews 1:12, Hebrews 13:8, and Lamentations 3:23.

Prayers of the Heart

Dear Father,

Because of Your perfection, You stay the same. If we know You, then we can count on You, Your character, presence, and love. Oh, Father, in an ever-changing world, thank You for being our unchanging reality. We rest on You, our solid rock, Jesus. We pray in Jesus' name, amen.

June 10 ~ FROG

"Therefore, if anyone is in Christ, the new creation has come. The old has gone, the new is here" (2 Corinthians 5:17).

In Christ, we have become new creations. That is great news. When teaching this verse, I have often said that we are no longer caterpillars but we are butterflies. We are no longer sinners saved by grace; we are now saints who sometimes sin. We are new in Christ.

One time, in a small group, we were reading "Growing in Grace" by Bob George. At the end of the study, I gave all the ladies a butterfly to remind them of the transformation that takes place once we trust in Christ. The men I gave frogs. I thought they would relate better to being transformed from a tadpole to a frog.

If I could give you a gift today, I would give you a frog to represent the meaning of living each day, "Fully Relying on God." F.R.O.G.

God is worthy of our trust and faith. When we trust in His attributes and natural characteristics, we find rest in our circumstances. In the days ahead, we will look at the attributes of our God. He is beyond all we can know or even imagine, but we can,

"progressively become more deeply and intimately acquainted with Him, perceiving and recognizing and understanding the wonders of His Person, more strongly and more clearly." (Philippians 3:10 Amplified Bible).

To fully rely on God, we need to know Him. This is a process, but as we come to understand our God more, we will trust and rely on His Word.

God is all-knowing. He is everywhere, eternal, holy, righteous, wise, full of truth, and He is love. As we look at each of these wonderful attributes in the next few days, I pray God will give us revelation, illumination, and insight into the wonder of who He is.

Ponders of the Heart

Which of God's characteristics are you the most thankful for today?

Why don't you thank Him right now for Who He is?

Look at Exodus 34:6-7 and think about the attributes of our God.

Prayers of the Heart

Dear Father,

You are the one true God. Your power and wonder are everywhere to be seen. We are thankful for Your power and the wonder of Your presence, but Father, we are overwhelmed by Your mercy, loving-kindness, and Your forgiveness and love. We need You. You are our hope and our dreams. In You, we find our rest and our strength. We can do nothing of value apart from You. Lord, teach us to fully rely on God. F.R.0.G. In Jesus' name, amen.

June 11 ~ God is Spirit

"God is spirit and his worshipers must worship him in spirit and in truth" (John 4:24).

What does that mean? God is spirit? The word spirit comes from the Greek word Pneuma, breath or air. God is not wind or breath but like wind or breath. He is invisible to the human eye. You cannot see Him, but you can see the works of His hands. You can feel His presence like the wind, but you cannot see His face.

I am sitting inside my house with all the windows closed. I cannot see or feel the wind blowing, but I know it is. How? The trees are blowing, and the leaves are moving by the power of the wind. Wind is invisible, but it is real, just as God is invisible, but He is very real. I wonder if anyone doubts the wind because they cannot see it. You think how stupid. I agree, but how many people refuse to believe in God because they cannot see Him with their eyes or hear Him with their ears?

Our God is invisible, but once in time and space, He came in the person of Jesus Christ. Jesus walked and talked on this earth so people could know Him. He performed miracles, fulfilled prophecy, healed the sick, spoke words of truth, and yet some refused to see or hear. Others saw with their human eyes and heard with their ears, and they believed in spirit and in truth.

God has equipped us with spiritual wiring. We can be alive in our spirit and know, hear, and see our God. He is invisible to our human eyes and ears, but we can know the invisible One. Space or Time cannot hold Him, but He works in our world of space and time. His essence is spirit, and He made us in His image. He has no measurable form, but our immeasurable God reveals Himself to us. Oh, Lord, breathe on us so we can feel and know the wonder of You.

Ponders of the Heart

Do you know God is real?

In your spirit, have you experienced Jesus?

Read Colossians 1:15, 1 Timothy 1:17, and Hebrews 11:27.

Prayers of the Heart

Dear Father,

You have made Yourself known to us. You have called us out of darkness into light. You have given us insight to see and faith to believe. You are Spirit, and You have made us in Your image. Help us worship You in spirit and in truth. Lord, thank You. We praise and love You. It is in our Lord Jesus that we pray, amen.

June 12 ~ God is All-Powerful

When my son, Chris, was a little boy, he loved the television series "The Incredible Hulk." Bill Bixby played Dr. David Banner, and Lou Ferrigno, a six-foot-five inch, three-hundred-pound bodybuilder, played the Hulk. When Dr. Banner got angry, he turned into a yellow-eyed, blazing green monster who flung and smashed everything in sight.

Dressed in his little green Hulk pajamas, Chris would stand up on a chair, red-faced, grunting, growling, and clinching his teeth like the Hulk. He would jump off the chair and chase me and his younger sister around the house as we screamed bloody murder. The game would end with us on the floor exhausted. My little guy felt very powerful.

The Marvel movies recreated the Hulk, which was even more terrifying. My two grandsons were enthralled with this character. This Hulk could smash cars with his foot, crack a highway, and send buildings to the ground with his clenched fist. After his fit of rage was over, Dr. Banner would find himself with torn clothes and full of shame because of the devastation he caused.

Both my grandsons loved the movies and had their very own green Hulk pajamas. You could say the Hulk lives on in the imagination of little boys.

Even though the Hulk is a make-believe creature, if he were real, he would be no match for our all-powerful God. Our Creator can part the waters, calm the storms, and create light. He is profoundly mighty.

"One thing God has spoken, two things I have heard: 'Power belongs to you, God'" (Psalm 62:11).

Uncontrolled power is frightening, but if controlled, power can be reassuring. Rage controlled the Hulk's force. His power was unpredictable and destructive. That is true in our world. Those with power often misuse it for self-gain. The might of others can be fueled by rage, selfishness, and desires.

Not so with our omnipotent God. He is in complete control of His power and uses it to help, save, restore, plan, and bring goodness to His children. God's power is good and trustworthy. An authority to reassure in uncertain times and is without equal. A.W Tozer says:

"Sovereignty and omnipotence must go together. One cannot exist without the other. To reign, God must have power, and to reign sovereignly, He must have all power. And that is what omnipotent means, having all power."

If God is your enemy, fear, but if God is your Savior, King, and hope, you rest in His control. He is all-powerful, so remember to take that frog with you. (Fully rely on God). He is able, for His power is for good.

Ponders of the Heart

Do you have a favorite make-believe superhero?

Does God's all-powerful nature scare you or comfort you?

Read Genesis 17:1, Psalm 91:1-2, and Revelation 4:8.

Prayers of the Heart

Dear Father,

Our Almighty God, we praise You. Help us know Your power is working in us and around us. What, Lord, do we need to fear if You are for us? Father, keep our minds focused on Your power and know that nothing is too hard for You. As I sit here praying to You, help me rest in Your love, wisdom, and power. In Jesus' name, amen.

June 13 ~ Our All-Knowing God

My middle child liked to push the rules in her teenage years. She would want to stay out past curfew, date boys who were trouble, and have friends who were too old for her. Tracie was a little hard to keep up with. One of her favorite tricks was to call after she was out and say, "Mom, can I spend the night with so-and-so?" I knew that was trouble, but occasionally I would say, "Okay." She knew that I knew she was up to something.

Even though Tracie liked to bend the rules, she always felt bad after she violated them. After a night out doing whatever it was she was doing, she would come home with a guilty look on her face. I returned a look that made her assume I knew what it was. Nine out of ten times, she would confess her transgression. What she did not know was I had no clue what she had been doing. I just knew it was something she knew better than to do. She thought I was all-knowing. I just knew my child.

Only One is all-knowing, and that is God. He has all knowledge because He is everywhere at the same time. God knows everything simultaneously and has the power to know the motives and the thoughts of every heart. He is completely aware of our deeds; we cannot hide from His knowledge.

God knows the plans of those who wish to use or abuse us, and He knows the danger we will face tomorrow. There is no heartbreak or confusion that will touch our lives that He is unaware of. Our past is not hidden from Him, and He knows how to use our past failures. God holds our past and future in His heart and works all things out for us with His master plan.

Because God is all-knowing, we cannot use tricks or manipulate Him. The God of all wisdom is for us. Like I did with Tracie, He will let us go our own way. He knows what lies ahead, and He will be there when we come home, seeking forgiveness and cleansing.

"'For I know the plans I have for you,' declares the Lord, 'plans to prosper you and not to harm you, plans to give you hope and a future. Then you will call on me and come and pray to me, and I will listen to you. You will seek me and find me when you seek me with all your heart'" (Jeremiah 29:11).

God sees the beginning to the end. We cannot change His sovereign will, so we can rest on the knowledge that He is always fighting for our good.

Ponders of the Heart

Do you go your own way, hoping God is not watching?

Do you realize when you go your own way, He is not only watching, but He is waiting for your return?

Read Job 37:16, Job 36:4, and Psalm 147:5.

Prayers of the Heart

Dear Father,

We need Your guidance. We are lost without You. Lord, we want to go and do the things You created us to be. But only if we surrender to You will we ever be able to have the strength and the wisdom to follow. Holy Spirit, come and fill us with Your power. You are our guide and protector, and You know our way home. We trust You; help us trust You more. You are our all-knowing God. We ask all this in Jesus' name, amen.

June 14 ~ God is Everywhere

"Where can I go from Your Spirit? Or where can I flee from Your presence? If I ascend into heaven, You are there; If I make my bed in hell, behold, You are there. If I take the wings of the morning, And dwell in the

uttermost parts of the sea, Even there Your hand shall lead me, And Your right hand shall hold me" (Psalm 139:7-10 NKJV).

Where does God live? Does He live in heaven, on earth, or does God live in churches? Where does He live? God is everywhere, and the theological term would be that God is omnipresent. He is near, close, and this nearness is universal. God is here with me as I am typing this devotional, and He is with you wherever that might be.

He is in Korea with our armed forces and in Birmingham. God is in all the rooms at hospice and at the same time present as we worship on Sunday morning. The Holy Spirit is at The Church of the Highlands, Oak Mountain Presbyterian, First Baptist, Liberty Baptist, and West Point Lake. He is everywhere. God is in our hearts and outside our hearts.

The Lord is present when a mother abuses her child and when people steal, rape, and murder. He is close to you when you are alone and when you're with your friends. God sees us at the movie theater and when we surf the web. He is present when people fight and make love. God is everywhere.

How comforting is that thought to you? When I am all alone in the middle of the night, and something goes bump, I am glad He is near. If I am praying for my son and his wife, I am thankful He is with them. When I am confused or afraid, my God is near me. The same is true when I throw a temper tantrum or yell at the dog. Right now, He is with me and with you.

Our past is in His hands, as well as our future. Our parents, grandparents, and dear friends who are in heaven are with Him right now. As He will be with our children and grandchildren once we are gone.

What would happen if God were not omnipresent? We would be like a fish with no water, or trying to walk with no muscles, talk without a brain. We would not, could not exist apart from God's presence. His presence is the essence of life, and apart from His essence, there is no life.

As the Psalmist proclaims, there is no place we can flee His presence.

"If I say, 'Surely the darkness will hide me and the light become night around me,' even the darkness will not be dark to you; the night will shine like the day for darkness is as light to you"' (Psalm. 139:11-12).

Ponders of the Heart

Do you have a difficult time remembering God is everywhere?

How different would your day-to-day be if you remembered He was with You?

Read Jeremiah 23:23-24 along with Psalm 139:7-18.

Prayers of the Heart

Dear Father,

You are with us in all we do and wherever we go. Father, that thought is too high for us to understand. Help us understand. You are near. Help us see and experience You everywhere. You are not a God confined to a certain building or in certain activities. You are with us all the time, and You are involved in every moment of our lives. We want always to seek You and be with our omnipresent Father. This we pray in Jesus' name, amen.

June 15 ~ Eternal God

"'I am the Alpha and the Omega, the Beginning and the End," says the Lord, who is and who was and who is to come, the Almighty" (Revelation 1:8 NKJV).

By the time Collier, our grandson, was one year old, we began teaching him numbers. We played a game called one, two, three. By the time he was at school age, I felt sure he would know how to count to at least ten. As smart as he was, it was much higher. Insights like these are the bragging rights of a grandmother.

Numbers are infinite. This means we could spend the rest of our lives counting, and there would still be more numbers to count. We could count forward with positive numbers or backward with negative numbers, but our counting would never end. That is an excellent picture of eternal life.

When time began, so did numbers. God said, "The evening and the morning were the first day." Genesis tells us the sun and the moon, as well as seasons, are used so we can mark time. We are trapped in time and space, so it is hard for us to understand many of God's attributes. They only make sense in view of His eternal presence.

The past, present, and future are known equally by Him because He is infinite. He is all-knowing and all-powerful. God is, was, and always will be.

Numbers will not matter one day. The sun and moon, along with the seasons, will end, but not so our eternal God. This eternal quality makes the Lord trustworthy. We can depend on His existence. I am very thankful and grateful that we serve the self-existent, self-sufficient, and infinite God. What overwhelms me is that Jesus came and gave His life, defeating death, and then returned to glory. Because of this, we who believe in the work and life of Jesus receive God's eternal life.

We were dead in our sin and in our spirit, but God, the Ancient of Days, offered us His life in exchange for our dead self. Our Jesus, who is everlasting, came and made His home in us, giving us the presence of His life, which is eternal. We will exchange this corruptible body for an incorruptible one.

God's work is perfect, and the thought of a new body is very intriguing to me. I am excited about my new makeover, and I can't wait to look in the mirror.

"Lift up your heads, O you gates! And be lifted up, you everlasting doors! And the King of glory shall come in" (Psalm 24:7 NKJV).

Ponders of the Heart

When did you receive the gift of eternal life?

Who was instrumental in bringing you to the Lord?

Do you need to share this good news with someone?

Read Isaiah 41:4, Revelation 22:13, John 14:23, and John 20:31.

Prayers of the Heart

Dear Ancient of Days,

You are the all-sufficient One and worthy of our praise. You are self-existent and infinite. We praise You for who You are, and we are amazed that You love us in Your greatness. Lord, You reach out to us and offer us eternity. You are beyond wonder and are more than we could hope or imagine. Our everlasting hope is in You. We pray that our praise honors You and gives You pleasure. In Jesus' name, amen.

June 16 ~ God is Holy

"Holy, Holy, Holy! Lord God Almighty! Early in the morning our song shall rise to Thee; Holy, Holy, Holy! Merciful and Mighty! God in Three Persons blessed Trinity!" Lyrics by Reginald Heber composed by John Bacchus Dykes in 1861

Who is your favorite person on earth? What is your most prized possession? In all the earth, where is your favorite place to go? If each of us answered these questions, our answers would be different. My favorite person is not your favorite person. Your most prized possession would not be mine. Our favorite places on earth would have special meaning to us.

If we took all our favorite people, our most prized possessions, and all our favorite places and rolled them all together, we could not begin to compare with the wonder of our God. God is beyond all; He is the prize of all prizes and is where peace, beauty, and rest abide. Our God is so high and lifted up that nothing in the universe compares with Him. The moral attribute that exalts Him is the attribute of holiness.

Holy comes from the root word meaning "to separate." God's essential character is so excellent and beyond our own that He is holy, holy, holy in comparison. God is so holy that we cannot come into His presence. His righteousness and beauty, power, and wonder would turn us to pure dust. Only by the gift of His grace is it possible for us to come, and we receive that gift by faith in Jesus Christ.

"and put on the new self, created to be like God in true righteousness and holiness" (Eph. 4:24).

When Isaiah came before the Lord, he cried out, "Woe is me, for I am undone!" When John saw the living Lord, he fell to the ground as if he were dead. When Moses wanted to see God's glory, God allowed him to see His back. The holiness of God creates such a chasm that only His holy Son can bridge the gap. We come into His presence only by His grace, the finished work of Jesus, and faith.

One day, I will see God's glory, but for now, I will look for Him in the beauty of nature, the face of a child, and the brightness of the sun.

Ponders of the Heart

Have you ever had an experience that left you unable to move or talk?

What do you think you will do when you see God face to face?

Read Exodus 33:18-23, Isaiah 6:1-5, and Revelation 1:12-18.

Prayers of the Heart

Dear Holy One,

There is nothing that compares to You. You are the sum total of good, beauty, righteousness, and power. Your holiness cannot be surpassed, and Your grace You give adds to the wonder of who You are. We praise You, Lord. Father, we adore You, and we come into Your presence by Your grace, and we worship our Holy, Holy, Holy God. In Jesus' name, we pray, amen.

June 17 ~ God is Righteous

My son-in-law, Ryan, got a ticket for parking in a no-parking zone. He told the park ranger he was not parking; he was just letting everyone out of the boat. The park ranger did not care; he gave him a ticket. Ryan decided to protest the ticket and went to court. The judge said, "How do you plead?" Ryan said, "Not guilty." The park ranger had a picture of the car parked by a no-parking sign. The judge said, "Is that your car?" Ryan said, "Yes". The judge said, "You're guilty."

At that point, the case was over. It did not matter what Ryan said, thought, or what we thought. The judge said, "Guilty," and that was it. He judged what was right and what was wrong.

When God is called righteous, that means He affirms what is right as opposed to what is wrong. There is no wrong in our God. He upholds perfectly that which He calls right. In God's righteousness, He has laid down moral laws, and He, our just judge, administers justice.

"Woe to those who call evil good and good evil, who put darkness for light and light for darkness, who put bitter for sweet and sweet for bitter" (Isa. 5:20).

God's righteousness is redemptive. He, by His grace, declares us not guilty on behalf of Jesus' sacrificial death for us.

"But now apart from the law the righteousness of God has been made known, to which the Law and the Prophets testify. This righteousness is given through faith in Jesus Christ to all who believe. There is no difference between Jew and Gentile, for all have sinned and fall short of the glory of God, and all are justified freely by his grace through the redemption that came by Christ Jesus" (Romans 3:21-24).

God gives us His Son's righteousness, and Jesus takes our sins to the cross. How is that fair? Jesus paid the penalty of death on the cross for us, and His righteousness is so pure that we are purified. This is known as the great exchange—His righteousness for our sinfulness.

Who wants fairness when we can experience God's grace? I will take His grace over what I deserve every time. How about you? My life has been full of His mercy. The goodness of God is ours because of Jesus. Thank You, Lord.

Ponders of the Heart

Are you thankful that God has not given us what we deserve?

Are there things you have done in this life that only grace could cover?

Read Isaiah 64:6, Romans 3:21-26, Romans 10:3-4, and Phil 3:9-11.

Prayers of the Heart

Dear Father,

I know the only right in me is You. I know the only one worthy to judge rightly is You. For You are the Righteous Judge, and I fall before You, thankful for Your grace and Your mercy. I pray with all my sisters and brothers in Jesus' name, amen.

June 18 ~ God is Love

"Love is patient, love is kind. It does not envy, it does not boast, it is not proud. It does not dishonor others, it is not self-seeking, it is not easily angered, it keeps no record of wrongs. Love does not delight in evil but rejoices with the truth. It always protects, always trusts, always hopes, always perseveres. Love never fails" (1 Corinthians 13:4-8).

The Bible is faithful to show us the depth and quality of love, but the Scripture also says God is love. That is more powerful than saying, "God loves". His Word tells us that the essence of love is found in Him. He is the standard, the source, and the fullness of what love is.

Agape is the Greek word for love. Herschel Hobbs, a faithful Southern Baptist leader and theologian, gives a definition of the word agape:

"as a self-giving love that relates to someone not on the basis of what the one loving will receive but for the purpose of meeting the needs of the one loved. Agape is an act of will rather than an emotional response."

God loves us because it is His nature. He offers His love not out of need, but it flows out of His being. Let us dissect the qualities of God's agape, beginning with the aspect of love being long-suffering.

What does it mean to suffer long? Could it mean to endure with patience? Do you know anyone through who God has manifested this quality? I think of some of you who have suffered for a long time. You have endured with great patience, and you still are.

We all know people who deal daily with pain and illness, and yet they stay cheerful. There are also people who are suffering, but they refuse to yield to the Lord. Yet we continue to pray for them and love them with perseverance. Some of you are dealing with questions and stresses with great resolve.

God has endured long with our sin-sick world. Not wishing that any should perish. He has endured long at our independence and our self-centered hearts as He slowly uses the circumstances of our lives to change us to the image of His Son.

Jesus showed the quality of long-suffering when He endured the shame and pain of the cross. Patiently, He continues to endure the sarcasm and the ridicule of this world. He waited patiently for us to come to Him, and He continues to wait for those we love to come to Him.

When I think about my own life and how stubborn I can be, my heart is overwhelmed with thankfulness. Why does He put up with me with such patience? It is His essence and nature. It is who He is.

It is God and His eternal substance that holds this world together. We can surrender our lives to Him, for He is the Author of love, wisdom, and goodness.

Ponders of the Heart

"So Jacob served seven years for Rachel, and they seemed only a few days to him because of the love he had for her" (Genesis 29:20 NKJV).

How long did God have to wait for you?

Do you know it was His love for you that made Him wait patiently?

Praise Him as you remember.

Read Genesis 29:15-30.

Prayers of the Heart

Dear Father,

Our hearts overflow with hope and praise as we think about the quality of Your love. We can all be stiff-necked people. We thank You for the years You waited for us to come to know You and the patient endurance You give us each today. The wonder that You draw us time and time again to Yourself even as we allow the same temptations to take us captive. Your goodness and love are beyond anything we could hope for, and yet You love us. In Jesus' name, we pray, amen.

June 19 ~ God is Kind

The dictionary defines kind as generous and warm-hearted in nature, and the synonyms are goodhearted, big-hearted, charitable, and generous. As I was thinking about kindness, it brought to my mind a very generous, kind, big-hearted act done at the Day Care Center at our church.

One of the ladies who worked for the Day Care Center had been out because of surgery. Her surgery was serious, and her recuperation time was lengthy. Because of her condition, she used all her sick days and vacation days.

After a month, this dear lady was sick and had to take more time off. She did not have sick days left. A co-worker secretly went to the director and asked if she could donate one of her own sick days to her.

That is, to me, a generous, warm-hearted, and charitable act of kindness. She had nothing to gain for herself, but she willingly gave up something that was valuable: paid time off.

What causes a heart to extend such kindness? The human heart, on occasion, can do charitable things and, on rare occasions, do them with no hidden motive. God's kindness flows out of His nature of love. He is always generous, warm-hearted, and charitable. That is the essence of the heart of God.

Have you got a problem? God is kind. Do you have a weakness? He is generous in His strength. Are you confused about what to do? God gives wisdom generously. Our God loves, and one of the ways He extends His love to us is by the kindness He shows.

If you have food to eat tonight, God provided that. The roof over your head was given to you by His generosity. Every good thing in our lives is God-initiated. God's warm-hearted nature was the power behind it all. God is love, and because of His great love, we are blessed.

Ponders of the Heart

What is the kindest act you have ever received?

Is there someone you know who could use kindness today?

Read Genesis 22:11-14 and John 1:29.

Prayers of the Heart

Dear Father,

Your kindness overwhelms me in the light of my stubborn pride. Your generous love humbles me in the depths of my heart. Father, I love You, and I thank You for Your love. Help me this very day to be a vessel You can use to extend Your loving kindness to someone. I praise You, Lord, and I pray in Jesus' name, amen.

June 20 ~ God is Never Envious

God is not envious; He is God. Romans 5:5 tells us that God pours His love into our hearts by the Holy Spirit. This is our clue to know we are not to be envious either.

I will have to confess to you that there was a time when jealousy crept into my life, and I envied a good friend.

My dear friend in the Lord is a wonderful teacher, and I was having feelings of envy. This is a confession to you and one I have made to the Lord and my friend. She is my sister in Christ. I hated these feelings because I loved her and yet was struggling with jealousy.

I kept bringing this back to the Lord and asking Him to root this out of my heart. I would think I had let go, but before I knew it, whack, it was back. The Lord kept telling me I had to confess this to my friend. He would not let me avoid this confession. When you go to someone to confess something like this, you must swallow your pride. I finally did, and at that moment, jealousy lost its hold on me.

The definition of envy is a resentful desire for another's possession or advantages. Oh, that makes me sick, but these feelings were there until I gave them to the Lord and allowed His love to fill my soul. I also needed to confess these feelings out loud. I realized that my pride was blocking what the Holy Spirit had poured into my heart.

If we focus on this world, we will experience dissatisfaction because the world cannot give us what we need. Discontent traps us in envy. God's love is never envious. He has given us His Spirit and placed His love in our hearts. We have all we need to free ourselves from jealousy. This is our hope. Satisfaction is found when we keep our eyes on Him.

Ponders of the Heart

Have you ever envied someone?

Did you deal with it in a way that freed you from the feeling?

If you have not dealt with this, today is a wonderful opportunity to do that.

Read 1 John 1:9 and Proverbs 28:13.

Prayers of the Heart

Dear Father,

We thank You for the cleansing power of confession. We praise You for the wonder of Your forgiveness and restoration. Thank You, Holy Spirit, for pouring the Father's love into our hearts. If anything is blocking that love, please show us so we can have this love running through our very souls. Lord, there is none like You. You are so good to Your children. In Jesus' name, we pray, amen.

June 21 ~ God is Not Boastful

King Xerxes was a powerful king with a controlling kingdom. The Bible says that he ruled over 127 provinces. In the third year of his reign, he gave a banquet for all the officials and nobles and the military leaders of Persia and Media. During the banquet, King Xerxes displayed the riches of his kingdom.

"There were couches of gold and silver on a mosaic pavement of porphyry, marble, mother-of-pearl and other costly stones. Wine was served in goblets of gold, each one different from the other, and the royal wine was abundant" (Esther 1:6-7).

No doubt he was putting on quite a show. People love to flaunt their stuff. On the seventh day of the banquet, King Xerxes was feeling quite good about his party and decided he would show off just a little bit more. He ordered his eunuchs who served him to fetch the queen with her royal crown.

Queen Vashti was very lovely, and I imagine so was the crown. The king's pride was dethroned when she refused the command. His good feelings turned to rage, and she was removed from her queenship. Not only that, but he sent men into the kingdom to fetch for him the most beautiful young virgins of the kingdom so he could choose a new queen. So much for love!

The queen was nothing more than a trophy for the king. She was just another way for him to flaunt himself, a notch in his belt. His love was boastful and prideful, and she decided she had had enough.

God's love is neither boastful nor proud. God does not flaunt His stuff, and I am sure His rule is far greater than 127 provinces, for He is the King of the universe and more. He cares for us, but not in a boastful, prideful way. His care is not because of how we look or what we can do but because of the nature of His love. We are of great worth to Him, but never to exploit us, for God is secure in His being.

Only those who are insecure will boast of what is theirs. Poor King Xerxes had so much, and yet, his much could not satisfy the insecurity inside. God's love has no restrictions attached, and it does not change with the wind.

What a gift His love is to us, and because of this gift, we can love others. It can be hard for us to surrender control to God, but the benefit is worth the struggle.

Ponders of the Heart

Have you ever exploited someone you said you loved?

Have you ever been loved that way?

Read Esther 1:1-2:18 and see the fallacy of human love in the heart of the powerful.

Prayers of the Heart

Dear Father,

We do not have to be beautiful for You to love us. How thankful we are that Your love is not according to our accomplishments. You have given us favor because You wanted to, and this is mind-boggling. We thank You as we bask in Your goodness. Fill us with the wonder of Your grace until it spills out on those around us. Let us boast in the wonder of Your great love. In Jesus' name, we pray, amen.

June 22 ~ God's Love is Not Proud

"Joseph, son of David," the angel said, "do not be afraid to take Mary as your wife. For the child within her was conceived by the Holy Spirit" (Matt. 1:20 NKJV).

Joseph was a righteous Jewish man who was waiting to marry when he heard the news that Mary was pregnant. Can you imagine how Joseph must have felt that day? "No, not my Mary?" How could that be true, and yet it was? The Bible says that because Joseph was a righteous man, he did not want to disgrace Mary, so he had in mind to divorce her secretly.

I can imagine there was some head shaking when they heard the news that Joseph was not divorcing her. The whole town would have the opinion that Mary had disgraced her family, Joseph's family, and herself. I must ask myself if that would be my mindset. I am sure Joseph heard comments against what he was doing. Yet, Joseph wanted to save Mary from any public shame.

His pride was not attached to his heart. His love wanted to protect, not retaliate. Joseph was a humble and loving man. I'm thankful that God chose such a man for Jesus' earthly father, and Mary was given a self-giving husband. A man who, even in the face of shame and public disgrace, would not place his pride above the good of someone he loved.

In this story, we see a glimpse of God's love for us. His love is not vengeful or full of prideful actions but is giving and full of concern for His beloved. He is the One who placed His very Son on this earth. His Son was ridiculed, beaten, and spit upon by sinful, ruthless people. It was His Son who was nailed on the cross for us.

Jesus suffered death so we could be free. The Son of God stayed on a cross that had no power to hold Him. Jesus was rich with mercy and grace. His love took public shame to spare us from eternal condemnation. God's love is neither proud nor boastful. Now, that is something we can boast about.

Ponders of the Heart

Have you or someone who loves you stood in the gap over public opinion?

As a Christian, are you standing in the gap between God's love and public opinion? How?

Read Matthew 1:18-25 and Philippians 2:5-8.

Prayers of the Heart

Dear Father,

The character of Your Son is that of humility. Father, if He, the King of kings and the Lord of lords, can humble Himself on our behalf, let that same attitude be in us. We pray for the manifestation and filling of the Spirit. May we walk in the Spirit and not in our flesh. Root out our foolish pride and fill our hearts with the wonder of Your love. In Jesus' name, amen.

June 23 ~ God is not Rude

"However, let each one of you love his wife as himself, and let the wife see that she respects her husband" (Ephesians 5:33 NKJV).

Sounds like Paul was sick of the way husbands treated their wives and wives their husbands. I would have to echo that complaint. It takes less effort to be on one another's side than vice versa. As married couples, we are to live our lives as a team.

There are people who marry the person of their dreams and then talk about them as if they were their worst nightmare. Why is that? We have an entire world to stand against; why not choose to stand with our man?

It is not just women who are quick to be disrespectful; men will get together and almost denounce the love they have for their wives in an attempt at machoism. Why do we treat the one we love so rudely? We share our lives with these spouses. We have families and buy houses and cars together. We are partners, and yet there are married couples who refuse to love and respect one other. God's love is not rude.

"What, then, shall we say in response to these things? If God is for us, who can be against us? He who did not spare his own Son, but gave him up for us all—how will he not also, along with him, graciously give us all things?" (Romans 8:31-32).

These verses goes on to ask who shall bring a charge against God's elect. I am sure during our lives; God could look at how we act and have a case against us. But He chooses to love us by His grace. This love and grace are the very power He uses to transform us.

If we extended such love to our spouses, children, and friends, I wonder if God would use this love and grace to help transform their lives. Not to mention ours. God's love is not rude. I want to remember that the next time I want to treat someone I love rudely. Father, manifest Your love, which is never rude, into our lives.

Ponders of the Heart

Read Romans 8:28-39.

Do the verses in Romans give you hope in this life?

Do these verses give you a sense of pride, or do they humble you?

Prayers of the Heart

Dear Father,

Thank You for the promise that nothing can separate us from Your love. Thank You, Father, that we are more than a conqueror because of Your grace. We know it was not our worthiness that made this possible. It was the worth of Your Son, our Savior. Fill us with the wonder of Your love. Manifest Your love into the relationships we hold so dear. Use our lives for Your glory. We pray in Jesus' name, amen.

June 24 ~ God is Not Self-seeking

My husband is a Civil War expert. He has memorized the Civil War battles and who the generals were in each battle, and details that I have a tough time listening to, much less remembering. I don't share his zeal for history.

He bought the movie, "Gettysburg," which is a four-hour epic about the Civil War. This movie is made up of battle after battle. In fact, I do not believe I saw one woman in the whole thing. Again, not something we share the same love for.

Bill has a favorite scene in the movie where a Northern soldier is questioning a Southern soldier about fighting for slavery. The Southern soldier is a poor farmer who owns no slaves and says to the Northern gentleman, "I'm not fighting for slaves; I'm fighting for my rights." The Northern soldier looks puzzled and says, "You're fighting for your rats?"

"No, no." says the Southern fellow, "My rights." Still not understanding the southern tongue, he says, "Your rats?"

How many fights have occurred over someone being right? Are you a person who cannot give up your rights, or are you married to or have children who insist on their way? What about at work or church? There are always people who are fighting for their rights.

1 Corinthians 13:5 tells us that God's love does not insist on its own rights, for it is not self-seeking.

In this world, most fights are over who is in control. We fight over money, politics, gender, police officers, children, and in-laws. You name it, and we will fight over it. The bottom line is we are fighting over our rights, and we can be as nasty as a rat about it. We can be dogmatic about telling others how to act, what to believe, and how they need to spend their time. We want to be independent of authority.

Usually, we do this to protect ourselves, our interests, and what we consider our rights. We are after what best serves us, even in love. Paul says that this is not how God loves. He is unselfish.

He does not need anything from us, but God is seeking our best and wants to care for and develop a close relationship with us. He pours His love into our hearts so we can feel and understand what true love is.

Loving someone with no hidden motives and no strings attached is a true miracle.

This is the kind of love that is offered to us through the Holy Spirit. We can appropriate this by faith in Jesus Christ. That simply means God has given us this love. A love that, by faith, we can give to others.

Oh, that God would prick our conscience when we are selfish and self-seeking. This mindset will leave us empty and keep our hearts in chains.

Ponders of the Heart

Who do you know that has selfless love?

Who in your life needs you to give them this kind of love?

Read Romans 5:5, 1 Corinthians 10:24, and Philippians 2:4-8.

Prayers of the Heart

Dear Father,

Thank You that Your love for us is free, and with Your love, we can love others the same way. Please protect us from the selfishness that often ruins relationships in our lives. Fill us with Your heart so we can give, give, and give without running dry. In Jesus' name, we pray, amen.

June 25 ~ God's Love is Not Touchy

You might think that growing up in Florida meant summer vacations at the beach. Not so. Our family much preferred the clear spring-fed lakes of Keystone Heights. We would spend two glorious weeks each summer soaking in the summer sun. I really soaked up the sun because I have fair skin, and these were the days before sunscreen. I thought each summer would be different. My skin would change, and I would come home with a golden tan.

Two days into the trip, I was so burned I could not stand the lake, the sheets on the bed, or anything touching my skin. The sun had, without my knowledge, reached down and burned my innocent skin until I had become a walking "ouch." You could say that my skin had become "angry" or touchy.

This is the picture of the word angered in the verse (1 Corinthians 13:5). God's love is not touchy, fretful, or resentful. It is not easily angered or provoked. Like human skin that has been burned by the sun, our hearts have been burned by human love or the lack thereof. We have all been hurt, abused, misunderstood, or rejected by others.

Hurt causes us to have sensitive, touchy, fretful, resentful, and misunderstood hearts. We guard ourselves, and we often snap when someone touches a tender place. God is not touchy, sensitive, or resentful. His love does not snap with anger when things are not said or done to His satisfaction.

These words are not to condemn us but to help us appropriate, by faith, the love God has poured into our hearts. When we are sensitive and touchy, we are hoping others will respond in such a way that it heals our souls and fills the void within. So, this love is more about us than caring about others.

Self-seeking love that is full of anger is a fretful heart looking for someone to heal its wounds and give them peace. But only God can do this. We put expectations on others that they cannot fulfill, and when they cannot, we are hurt even more. But when God offers us His love, and it fills the deep holes of our souls, we are free to give love without unrealistic expectations.

We do not have to walk controlled by our hurt and pain or offer our love just until someone touches a tender spot. We can apply a "Son" screen over our tender hearts and extend God's love to others.

Everyone longs to be loved, and we can be an example of Christ to a touchy world by loving the unlovable with Jesus' love.

Ponders of the Heart

Who do you seek love from that never satisfies?

Are you putting expectations on others that they can't do?

Read 1 John 3:1 and 1 John 4:7-18.

Remember, you cannot "do" love, but you can appropriate His love by faith.

Prayers of the Heart

Dear Father,

Lord, appropriate Your love in our hearts. Help us love others, even those who have hurt us. Help us to love those who can reach the tender, touchy, sensitive places of our souls. Allow Your love to flow through us to heal and encourage us. There is no greater love we can give than the love You have given to us. We pray this in Jesus' name, amen.

June 26 ~ God Keeps No Record of Wrong

God's love keeps no record of wrong is the way the NIV Bible reads: God's love has no Evil. Simply put, God forgives completely. He does not think back over your sin.

Chris asked, "Mom, if a person commits suicide, does that mean they go to hell?" I told him that a person is condemned because of unbelief. He said, "Mom, isn't God the only person who should say when you die?" I said, "Yes, He is, but Jesus paid the penalty for all our sins, and that would cover the sin of suicide." He said, "So you are saying that if a person believes in Jesus and takes their own life, they will not go to hell?" Bill gave the best answer. He said, "No, they put their family through hell."

We have a tough time understanding that Jesus Christ, God's Son, took our sins and the penalty of all our sins on Himself. In Chris' mind, you were only forgiven if you asked for forgiveness, and if you committed suicide, there would be no way you could ask for forgiveness. So, I said, "Chris, how many sins did you commit when Christ died on the cross?"

He came up with a bogus number, but I said, "Son, you were not alive when Christ died on the cross. You had not committed any sins. All your sins were in the future, and yet Christ died for all your sins, past, present, and future."

God's love keeps no record of wrong. He is not a God that is keeping score of your good acts or your terrible acts if your name is written in the Lamb's Book of Life. Jesus removed our sins, our evil, from us and placed His righteousness in us. God provided complete forgiveness.

That is powerful grace, and when the magnitude of that registers in a regenerated heart, the motivation to love God is powerful. We respond to Him, and He fills our hearts with love for Him and others. That is the mark of a child of God who is living in the reality of God's forgiving grace.

"For God so loved the world that He gave His only begotten Son, that whoever believes in Him should not perish but have everlasting life. For God did not send His Son into the world to condemn the world, but that the world through Him might be saved. He who believes in Him is not condemned; but he who does not believe is condemned already, because he has not believed in the name of the only begotten Son of God" (John 3:16-18 NKJV).

Salvation is not for those who act right but for those who believe in Jesus. Our faith in Jesus places us in the family, and God's love forgives us completely. Praise the Lord.

Ponders of the Heart

Do you agree that all your sins are forgiven, past, present, and future?

Do you live in this freedom with a desire to live a righteous life?

Read Romans 8:1-2 and Romans 12:1-2.

Prayers of the Heart

Dear Father,

What a wonderful promise that You keep no record of wrong. We realize that the penalty for our sins was paid for by Jesus. We are thankful, and we want to live and walk in the Spirit and not in the flesh. Lord, may we never take Your grace for granted. May our actions be motivated by deep love through the power and strength of the Holy Spirit. Help us remember the wonder of Your forgiveness, and may we extend the same grace to those who offend us. We pray this in Jesus' name, amen.

June 27 ~ God Rejoices in Truth

"The teachers of the law and the Pharisees brought in a woman caught in adultery. They made her stand before the group and said to Jesus, "Teacher, this woman was caught in the act of adultery. In the Law Moses commanded us to stone such women. Now what do you say?" They were using this question as a trap, in order to have a basis for accusing him" (John 8:3-6).

The teachers of the law and the Pharisees loved judging others. They liked nothing better than to catch someone sinning, and they especially wanted to trap Jesus. The failures of others gave them a prideful smirk of superiority. I can be such a Pharisee, so smug in my own self-righteousness. Judging others while wanting mercy for myself. This is not "the heart of God."

What did Jesus do in response to the Pharisees? He simply reminded them of their own sin and said that if they were without sin, then throw the first stone. They all left, sad that their self-righteous facade had been uncovered. Jesus, our perfect Savior, was left with the woman. He could have picked up a stone and hurled it at her, for Jesus is sinless. His love did not rejoice in her evil life but offered her forgiveness and a new life. He tells her,

"'Has no one condemned you?' 'No one, sir,' she said. 'Then neither do I condemn you,' Jesus declared. 'Go now and leave your life of sin'" (John 8:10-11).

Jesus does not rejoice in catching someone living a sinful life but rejoices when a person leaves a life of sin to follow Him. He rejoices when one turns to His truth that sets them free. We should be glad when others walk away from a sinful lifestyle and grieve, not judge when they do not.

In our self-righteousness, we can fall into gossiping or listening to gossip. I must check my heart when I have a tough time forgiving someone or giving up on them. We often use the failures of others to help us feel better about our own failures.

Again, these words are not to condemn us but to turn our hearts to the life Christ has placed in us. These words are to release us from the hold of our flesh and free us to walk in the power of the Spirit. We have been given such a great salvation and wonderful love dwells within our spirits. Oh, Lord, fill us until You flow freely into our lives and the lives of others.

Ponders of the Heart

Have you ever been secretly glad when another person was caught doing something wrong?

If the Pharisees had come to you with the woman caught in adultery, what would have been your response?

Read Philippians 2:1-4.

Ask our Lord to fill you with His love.

Prayers of the Heart

Dear Father,

What grace is ours through Jesus? Thank You; we can walk as children of light. Your love can fill us and satisfy our deep longing for love and worth. Thank You, that we can draw near to Your fountain of living water. Oh, Precious Father, fill our hearts so we rejoice in truth and hurt for those who are caught in a sinful lifestyle. We need Your wisdom and grace to live as Your children. In Jesus' name, amen.

June 28 ~ God Protects

Brennan Manning, a renowned author, understands the power of protective love. He is living because of such love. Brennan was the last name of a buddy in Vietnam who gave his very life for Mr. Manning. They were together in a foxhole when a grenade landed between them. His friend tossed the rest of a candy bar they were sharing as he rolled over on the grenade and gave his life to save his friend.

Later, Mr. Manning took his vows to be a priest, and it was customary to take on the name of a Saint. That particular year, the priests could choose a new name for themselves, and Mr. Manning dropped his first name and took the last name of his friend, Brennan. Every day, he is reminded of protective love, the love the New Kings James Bible says will bear all things. Yes, love bears all things, even to the point of death.

Jesus gave His life so we could have eternal life. This draws us to Jesus. His love gives eternal life, a new family and the Holy Spirit to live within our souls.

Brennan Manning's friend, who gave his life, is an example of God's protecting love. It is no wonder Brennan Manning filled his books with the message of God's amazing grace.

I have seen amazing acts of love from God in dealing with me and my family. I say amazing, gracious acts because we do not deserve His touch of love. He just gives us grace because of His nature.

There are so many things we can praise God for. But the greatest gift of all gifts is the gift of Jesus, and the great exchange is when He took our sins to the cross and rose from the grave to give us His righteousness.

Ponders of the Heart

How has God taught you about His grace?

Have you been humbled by His protection for you?

Read Hebrews 9:24-28, Hebrews 10:14, Hebrews 19-24, and 2 Cor. 5:16-17.

Like Mr. Manning's friend, Jesus rolled over our sins and gave His life for us.

Prayers of the Heart

Dear Father,

Your love for me is more than I can grasp. I constantly try to deserve it when I know there is nothing I did to cause You to love me and nothing I can do to cause You not to. Lord, You have protected me from myself and the condemnation of sin.

You give righteousness and forgiveness. You supply all our needs every day. There are no words to tell You how thankful we are. In Jesus' name, amen.

June 29 ~ Love Believes All Things

"And we know that all things work together for good to those who love God, to those who are called according to His purpose" (Romans 8:28 NKJV).

I like the way Paul puts it. He says, "And we know." What an emphatic statement. Paul, of course, is talking to believers when he says, "And we know." As believers, we should be able to rest on certain things. Knowing God is in control and He is working things out for our good is our resting place.

There is a Maytag commercial about washers that begins with a little boy going to school. All dressed up in a shirt and tie, he struts out of the school bus and is knocked into the bushes by a bully. He looks down at his pants, which have terrible grass stains. He brushes himself off and continues his day. Out of the corner of his eye, he sees little girls looking at him. He turns with a big smile to find out they are laughing at him. He looks down to discover a great big ink stain in his pocket.

His day continues to be a battle as he makes a D on a paper and gets food splashed all over him at lunch. By the end of his school day, he is no longer strutting. He finally gets home, throws his clothes in the washer, and the first words of the commercial are spoken, "If there is one thing that I have learned in life, it is that all things work out in the wash." Then you see this precious little boy strutting through the kitchen with his boots and undies on, knowing tomorrow is another day. You could say he believes all things.

God's presence helps us live with hope. His love in us keeps on loving when circumstances are falling apart. God's love keeps us trusting the One who gave His life for us. He has saved us from ourselves. Our Lord has placed something stronger than sin, death, and hopelessness in us. We have received His love, and a part of Him lives in us. This gives us a reason to hope and believe.

Paul said all things work together for good for those who love God and are called according to His purposes. If God is on His throne, we can continue to believe good is on its way. It is a done deal. It is possible for us to walk with this knowledge and deep conviction because God promises to work for our good. We can appropriate this promise by faith. Something is not over until He says it is over. God's love gives us the ability to continue to hope and believe all things.

Ponders of the Heart

Is there a circumstance you have been praying about for a long time?

What are you believing God for right now?

Read 2 Timothy 1:7-12.

Keep believing and resting in the wonderful truth that He is able.

Prayers of the Heart

Dear Father,

There are days when life kicks me down, and I feel like the little boy in the commercial, but You, Lord, keep Your promise that it will all work out in the end.

You see everything that happens to us, and You care. Every stain in our lives will be washed clean because of You. You are our hope and promise. We can start new and fresh each day knowing You are on our side and all is well with our souls. In Jesus' name, amen.

June 30 ~ God's Love Hopes

Now faith is confidence in what we hope for and assurance about what we do not see" (Hebrews 11:1).

I have a program on my computer where I keep track of the money we spend during the month and our income. This computer program allows me to put reoccurring bills and deposits, so they carry over from month to month. When I go to this program, I can see what deposits and bills are coming. You could say I hope a certain amount of income is coming, and I know for certain each month certain bills will come.

If I look ahead, knowing certain things affects what I do and how I feel today. Let's say I have 2000 dollars more income than expenses each month.

Then I can hope with a certain amount of conviction I will not bounce a check, but if I have 2000 dollars more expenses than income, I am sweating bullets each time I go to the store.

In our walk with the Lord, we can look to Scripture as our "life managing" program. Based on His Word and His ability to keep His Word, we can live our lives with faith and hope. Faith is based on a hope of certainty.

Hope is not wishful thinking but believing what we hope for is coming. Let me take a couple of verses in Romans 8 to explain.

"For those God foreknew he also predestined to be conformed to the image of his Son, that he might be the firstborn among many brothers and sisters. And those he predestined, he also called; those he called, he also justified; those he justified, he also glorified" (Romans 8:29-30).

God has predetermined to change us to the likeness of His Son. This is a hope, a promise to us, His children. Do you act like Jesus? Inwardly, God is at work in us, and this work He is doing is a promise that He will transform us. If I appropriate this truth by faith, it makes a tremendous difference in how I feel about myself and how I act. But mostly, it gives me hope that when I fail, God will keep His promises.

He also promises that He called me, and I am justified. My justification is based on His performance, not mine. Our hope in Christ is wonderful and magnificent. We who are in Christ are justified and made righteous.

But wait, the news doesn't stop there. He promises also to glorify us, which means we will have an eternal home in heaven. This is the promise of complete transformation. We are given hope for change because He has poured His love into our hearts. Paul tells us of this promise in Romans 5:5.

"And hope does not put us to shame, because God's love has been poured out into our hearts through the Holy Spirit, who has been given to us."

I am not saying that we will automatically be perfect. Believe me, this is a journey, and it takes a lifetime. God's promises are true, but it takes surrender and faith to ease the struggle that takes place in our human nature. But we can count on it all being worth the fight.

Ponders of the Heart

What promises do you find in these verses? Make a list so you will not forget them.

Which promise do you need God to help you believe and hope for?

Read Heb. 10:14, Heb. 13:5-8, Romans 8:29, and 2 Tim. 1:12.

Prayers of the Heart

Dear Father,

Lord, this month, we have been looking at Your attributes. You are more than we can grasp. As I think about Your sinless, perfect, and pure life that You poured out for us, I am speechless. There is nothing in this world that can compare.

The song "Nothing But The Blood" is running through my head. Only Your blood can wash us white as snow. You are our purity and our very hope in this sin-sick world. We worship You.

Father, how I pray for Your Spirit to move in our country, in our homes, and in Your church. We need a great revival that only You can bring. We stand before You with open hearts, asking for You to move in us. Give us vision, courage, love, and truth to make You known to our world.

In a world of uncertainty, we can hope all things for You are our confidence. Keep Your love active in us and Your voice in our ears. Lord, You are our refuge, our strength, and our help in times of trouble. We love You and thank You. Father, You are our very great reward. In Jesus' name, amen.

july

— " —

But you are a chosen people, a royal priesthood, a holy nation, God's special possession, that you may declare the praises of him who called you out of darkness into his wonderful light.

1 Peter 2:9

July 1 ~ God's Love Endures

I was driving home in a terrible rainstorm. Raindrops were coming down in huge sheets of water, making it impossible to see beyond my windshield. It was terrifying, and I wanted to pull over and cry. I kept going as I prayed the rain would stop. The interstate was full of slow-moving cars with people who probably felt like me.

The desire to survive kept me enduring the rain, fear, and danger. I pushed through the circumstance, feeling out of control but determined to persevere. I can be a headstrong person when necessary, and this was one of those times.

As I look back at driving and persevering through the storm, it reminds me of God's love. His love endures all things. When your parents die, God comforts you. If your spouse leaves you, His love never does. When you lose your job and can't pay your bills, God's enduring grace is with you.

The best example for me to grasp God's love is with the love I have for my children. When friends hurt or disappoint them, my arms are there to hug, and my ears to listen. If they are sick, I can make them chicken soup, and if they are lonely, they know the porch light is on. My love acts on their behalf through thick and thin. They are my children forever just like we are His.

If you turn from God's face because of disappointment, His love doesn't weaken. Jesus' love keeps coming like the waves in the ocean and keeps shining like the sun, day after day and year after year. Our Eternal God's love keeps on long after you take your last breath. His love endures evil, time, loss, tragedy, conflict, sorrow, life, and death.

Nothing in the world, or outside this world, will ever alter the enduring, non-weakening love of God.

We praise You, Father, our firm foundation.

Ponders of the Heart

Do you feel overwhelmed, over-burdened in life?

How important is it to know we are loved by God and His love endures forever?

Read John 15:11-17.

Prayers of the Heart

Dear Father,

Thank You for Your enduring, never weakening love for us. Lord, thank You we never walk a day without Your love. If there is one gift, one powerful gift we could give to others it would be Your love. A love that endures during trouble time and never gives up or weakens. Lord, You are more wonderful than words. In Jesus' name, amen.

July 2 ~ Love Never Fails

The digital camera invention was huge and the day I bought one you would have thought I discovered gold. They were so cool. You saw your pictures immediately and erased the bad ones just as fast. You could even download pictures onto your computer for safekeeping. It was very impressive. I know this sounds crazy to those of you who are young, but this was big. Technology is so far beyond that now, but at that time, it was remarkable.

Then and now, I have shoe boxes full of pictures. Some are awful. I need to go through them, organize the ones to keep and discard others. The problem is, before I can figure out what to do with them, technology changes. It is impossible to keep up.

My body has lasted over seventy years. It isn't obsolete, but it is getting there. My mind has spanned decades. All the changes I have seen, and changes my mind and body have experienced, would take hours to tell, so I'll just say things in this life fade, and become obsolete. This is the way of the world.

In the thirteenth chapter of the first letter to the Corinthians, Paul tells us the magnitude of what God calls love, and he ends by the emphatic statement, God's love, never fails. Technology will fail or fade and so will our wisdom. The organized church activities, our businesses, cars, and our bodies all will one day disappear or collapse. God goes on to say knowledge, prophecy, and tongues will pass away, but His love stays.

God holds us when everything we are holding drops us. This love will be with us when the sun and moon no longer shine. God will be our victory when all the success stories have ceased. His love never fails.

Do we believe this? God has placed in our hearts His love. This is never failing, fading love, and it will never be obsolete. It is the One remaining all-encompassing thing we need and have. Hallelujah. Praise to our God.

Ponders of the Heart

Has love ever disappointed you? How did you manage this disappointment?

Have you experienced for yourself God's love that never fails? Explain.

Read 1 Corinthians 13: 1-8.

Think over the distinct characteristics of God's precious love. Let these truths encourage you today.

Prayers of the Heart

Dear Father,

Your love is the greatest gift we can receive and the greatest gift we can give to another. Giving Your love is more powerful than wisdom and more lasting than silver or gold. Your love is the treasure of the ages from the Ancient of Days. Oh, Lord, thank You for loving us. In Jesus name, amen.

July 3 ~ A Noisy Gong

The Gong Show was a television show where people performed their talents. If the audience liked what they saw or heard, the people would continue until they finished and then receive a round of applause. But if you were terrible, or at least the audience thought you were, you would receive a loud gong, and you were finished. This was quite the ego buster.

In 1 Corinthians 13:1-3, Paul tells us without love we are nothing more than a noisy gong or a clanging cymbal.

"If I speak in the tongues of men or of angels, but do not have love, I am only a resounding gong or a clanging cymbal. If I have the gift of prophecy and can fathom all mysteries and all knowledge, and if I have a faith that can move mountains, but do not have love, I am nothing. If I give all I possess to the poor and give over my body to hardship that I may boast, but do not have love, I gain nothing."

God's measuring stick is love. If we know the Bible but lack love, we will be gonged. We can give all our possessions away to the poor or give our bodies to be burned but do not have God's love in our hearts, it is empty of true love. God will gong our efforts.

The Lord looks at the motives of our hearts, and we cannot fool Him. If what we do is about us showing off or being in charge, we are nothing but a loud, noisy cymbal.

Whatever I do on my own without God is powerless. I can do good things like feeding the poor or becoming a knowledgeable teacher for praise. If my motive is for personal praise, this is all I will have.

Only those things done with and through God's love will profit this world and the world to come. We have eternal love in us because it comes from God and out of our relationship with Jesus. His love continues forever, and it never dies.

I need this lesson. How often I can be enamored by what I know? My old flesh can try to be the in-house expert, but what people need to see, and feel is God's love pouring through me. God's kingdom is so different, and His ways are not our ways. How thankful I am for the gift of His Spirit. It is the gift that makes it possible for us to have love, wisdom, and purpose in His Kingdom.

Ponders of the Heart

How well is God's love flowing through you?

Do you know and depend on Jesus as you journey through life?

Read 1 Corinthians 13 and replace the word love for Jesus.

Prayers of the Heart

Dear Father,

 Help us. We do not want to be a gonging cymbal. We do not want to live a life stroking our ego. Lord, we want to journey through this life allowing Jesus to speak and love through us. The self-seeking life is empty and does not build Your Kingdom. We desire for You to work through us. Holy Spirit fill our lives with Your life. Pour Your love into us. Use every part of us for Your glory. In Jesus' name, amen.

July 4 ~ Celebrate

 Bill and I found ourselves alone on July 4th. Our children were in Jacksonville looking forward to celebrating the fourth with their cousins. At the time, we lived in Lagrange, Georgia, not far from West Point Lake. We decided it would be fun to watch the fireworks from the water.

 We jumped into his fishing boat and headed out to wait with the other nine million boats on the lake. What a pretty sight. It looked like a water city. Lights from the boats lined the shoreline, creating a warm friendly sight. In the background, you could hear the soft sound of music and voices. The atmosphere was full of fun and camaraderie.

The fireworks were beautiful, and I remember thinking how I wish the kids were here.

The wait was long, but as always, it seemed the fireworks were over before they started. The moment the fireworks ended, so did the peaceful camaraderie. It then turned into a race to the boat ramps.

Our boat was no match for the high-powered speed boats or the waves around us, but my Bill maneuvered our little fishing boat through the crowd. He had us safely docked and out of the water in no time. I can remember laughing at the confusion while feeling young and safe, while Bill understood the dangerous situation we were in.

We tried to join in the celebration one other time, but this time, a boat with no running lights came close to running us over. This was the end of us watching the fireworks on the water. What a shame. Fun can turn into a disaster when people want to be first.

Looking back on the situation. I am thankful my husband understood the danger we faced. He just naturally wants to protect me from danger even to the point he will refuse to take me someplace unsafe. He looks out for me. I am a blessed woman.

I have another protector, the One who gave me Bill. My Protector sees what is coming before it comes, and He knows how to protect me and guide me to my ultimate home.

We can remain confident in Jesus, our all-sufficient Protector. Oswald Chambers says it like this:

"If we have been learning to worship God and to place our trust in Him, the crisis will reveal that we can go to the point of breaking, yet without breaking our confidence in Him."

Life is dangerous and fun; the two can come together in a heartbeat, but praise the Lord, we don't have to live in fear or in hiding because we have the Protector, and He loves us. This is truly something to celebrate.

Ponders of the Heart

Do you live in fear or freedom?

Do you believe God will protect you? Why?

Read Galatians 5:1, Philippians 4:1, and Romans 8:15-28.

Prayers of the Heart

Dear Father,

We thank You for our country, and the freedom we enjoy. We are also thankful for the freedom we have in You. We celebrate Jesus and the freedom He bought for us. Thank You for the Holy Spirit Who intercedes on our behalf. The world is full of danger and fun. Help us live trusting in Your goodness and protection, never forgetting if we lose our lives in You, we will truly be living. In Jesus' name, amen.

July 5 ~ Despise

Playing Barbies is a game I despise. In case you missed my first statement, let me say again: I hate, despise, and loathe playing Barbies. So why do I play? It is because I love my granddaughter more than I hate playing Barbies.

I have been tortured by playing this game by my daughters and granddaughters for decades. All my girls have grown up enough; they don't play Barbies except Elizabeth, our youngest granddaughter.

Elizabeth likes me to play but wants to control the time. She controls which Barbie I am and what I am doing and saying. She is the boss of the game. This is just how her mother, Julie, played as a little girl. Both Julie and Elizabeth had to be my mouthpiece.

When I finally have all, I can stand, I will say, Elizabeth, since you know what you want the Barbies to say and do, you don't need me. I will just watch you.

She doesn't want that, so she promises she won't do it anymore, and that lasts maybe two minutes.

I still hate playing Barbies, but there I am, on the floor with my back killing me, saying what she tells me to say, so please allow me to say once more, I hate playing Barbies!

Love is a powerful motivation that will cause us to do things we don't want to do for the sake of others. There is no better example of this than Jesus giving His life on the cross for us. Hebrews 12:2 tells us:

"Fixing our eyes on Jesus, the pioneer and perfecter of faith. For the joy set before him he endured the cross, scorning its shame, and sat down at the right hand of the throne of God."

Jesus was devoted to God the Father and the plan of redemption. He did not want to endure the pain and suffering of the cross, but He looked past to the joy of our salvation. He was committed to our adoption as sons and daughters. There was no other choice if we were to become children of God. Only the precious pure blood of Jesus, shed on the cross, could defeat the sins of the world. It took a perfect sacrifice, and Jesus was born to be this for me and you.

Love is a powerful tool that will endure forever. 1 Peter 4:8 tells us:

"Above all, love each other deeply, because love covers over a multitude of sins."

Jesus is our perfect example of this love. His love covers a multitude of sins; in fact, Jesus' death and resurrection covers all our sins, past, present, and future. He paid it all for those who placed their faith in Him. What a gift! What a Savior.

Ponders of the Heart

What is something you do for those you love that you don't want to do?

How grateful are you that Christ paid the penalty for your sin?

Read Hebrews 12:1-3, Philippians 2:8-9, and 1 Peter 4:1-2

Prayers of the Heart

Dear Father,

Help me live loving You and others in my life. Lord, I want to see past myself and think of Your will. I long to live a life surrendered to You. Lord, I love You, and I am thankful for Your Word. Teach me, Holy Spirit. Give me ears to hear and a heart to trust You. In Jesus' name, amen.

July 6 ~ Inquiring Minds

Ryan, my son-in-law, is very inquisitive. He asked me, "Marilyn, why weren't there dinosaurs on the ark?" I didn't know the answer, so I said, "Ryan, I don't know. Maybe they were, or maybe they weren't. I don't know." He said, "I thought the fossils all came from the flood? And I thought the Bible said God brought all the animals to the ark?" I said, "Ryan, I just don't know. You will have to ask God when you get to heaven."

I don't know the answer to this question. Do you? I only know science must be judged by Scripture, not vice versa. God is our truth, and if science does not line up with what God says, the data is incomplete.

This simply tells me God has the last word, and at the end of the age, He will clear up any discrepancy between scientific data and His truth. I think God made us with inquisitive minds, some more than others. He gives us these minds not so much to give us answers to our questions but for us to seek Him. In seeking, we find something much more important than the answers. We find Him.

He wants us to have a relationship with Him. One that frees us to come with our questions and just spend time with Him.

I don't know if the dinosaurs were on the ark or not. I really don't care, but I do care about Ryan and my prayer for him is he will take his question all the way to the throne room of heaven.

When he sees God sitting on His throne, I doubt Ryan will care what the answer is to his question, but oh, what great fellowship he will have with his Father. It is true inquiring minds want to know but to know God satisfies all our inquiring.

Ponders of the Heart

Do you question the truth of the flood?

What would be your answer to Ryan's question?

Read Genesis 8:1-19.

Prayers of the Heart

Dear Father,

You called us into the ark of Jesus. The water may be turbulent, but we are safe in Him. The dinosaurs are extinct, wiped out, but, Father, more important are those who will be lost from You. Give us hearts to invite others into the ark of Jesus while we live our lives in thankful praise for Your provision. In Jesus' name, amen.

July 7 ~ God is Wisdom

"If any of you lacks wisdom, you should ask God, who gives generously to all without finding fault, and it will be given to you" (James 1:5).

I found a house I wanted. It is not new, but it is a great house. Some painting, hardwood floors, new carpet, and light fixtures, and you have a great house. I think we can buy it for a reasonable price, and it would be an excellent investment. But do we need it? Would this move be God's best for us? Does God even care about such things?

A wise person once said, "God's wisdom is revealed in His doing the best thing, in the best way, at the best time for the best purposes." Great insight. I, however, often get lost in circumstances, and I need a stopping place. God is my stopping place when it comes to wisdom. Let me quote from Neil T. Anderson:

"An old Chinese proverb tells of a young man who was raised in a peasant home with meager material possessions. One day, a stranger rode by his home leading several horses. He called out, 'If there is a young man in the household, I would like to give him a horse.' So, the young man received the most incredible gift someone in his economic status could possibly receive. What a great thing to have his own horse.

The next day as he was riding, he fell off the horse and broke his leg. Well, maybe owning a horse was not a good thing after all; maybe it is a bad thing. However, the following day some warlords came out of the hills and insisted the young man ride with them into war. The boy could not go because he had a broken leg. Suddenly, having a broken leg was a good thing.

The proverb continues and on, alternating between what appeared to be a good thing one day turning out to be a bad thing the next day. The problem is we really don't know what is good for us."

This sums it up perfectly. We don't know what is good for us, and often, what appears to be a curse is really a blessing. God is our foundation for living and the One who is bigger than the sum of our circumstances.

Only He is wise, and it is His wisdom we need. I'm thankful for His Word, which tells us to ask for wisdom, and He graciously gives it to us. If the wisdom does not come from Him then we find ourselves caught in a Chinese proverb. How many times I have found myself there, but with God's wisdom filling me, I can keep from traveling there.

Ponders of the Heart

What are some of the crazy things people believe?

What is going on in your life right now that you need God's wisdom?

Have you asked Him to give you wisdom over this issue?

Read 1 Corinthians 1:20-25 and Romans 16:27.

Prayers of the Heart

Dear Father,

Apart from Your grace, I am a fool. I don't want to be a fool except for You. I want to love You and rely on Your wisdom and not the foolishness of this world. You are my strength, refuge, and hope. I thank You that Your wisdom is all encompassing, and You freely give it to those who ask. I thank You and praise You for Your power, wisdom, love, and Your grace. In Jesus' name, amen.

July 8 ~ Prisons of the Heart

"Count of Monte Cristo" is a great movie. The movie tells an enormous tale, one you can think about for a long time. The main character was a man who was in prison literally, but sadder, so was his heart.

The movie begins with a young man who is full of innocence. He has childlike faith in people and life. You like him right off the bat, for in his innocence, he is also very brave and self-sacrificing.

With a turn of events, Edmund, who is the Count of Monte-Cristo, ends up in prison far from his home on an island where the conditions are barbaric and cruel. He, however, declares his trust in God and God's rescue that will soon come. You know the old saying, "God is never late, but He is rarely early." This man didn't believe it, for he gave up hope.

Edmund turned from faith and became a prisoner of his heart. He was caught in a web of hate and a desire for revenge as he turned cold toward God and men.

Every year, he would receive a beating from the overseer of the prison, but other than this, he was left to himself. Food was given to him through a trap door, and his bucket emptied the same way. No direct human contact other than the beatings. This continued year after year. His hope was gone. He lived energized only by his hate and his desire for revenge.

At this present time, I know no one in prison with metal bars, but I do know people who live in a prison of their heart. I see them all around me. Their eyes are guarded, and so are their smiles, for they have placed a cocoon around their souls to keep themselves from human contact. The lie is they can protect themselves from hurting. You know it is a lie, for in their eyes, the hurt is there, and the way they hold their mouth is far from a smile. They are trapped in sadness.

In some ways we are all caught in prisons. They take on different faces and the bars are not clear, but they are just the same there. What happens to us can take our freedom. This dilemma has been going on since the beginning, well, almost from the beginning of time.

"And the man and his wife were both naked and were not embarrassed or ashamed in each other's presence" (Genesis 2:25 Amplified).

There was a time when man was free in the presence of God and with his woman. But sin was crouching at the door, wanting to master them. Man turned from trusting God to trusting in a lie. The lie was the snare, and sin has held us captive ever since.

Edmund Dantes, in the movie "Count of Monte Cristo," heard the original lie from the evil one, "You can't trust God." Edmund Dantes imprisoned himself with the lie that there was no God. The rest of what happened in his heart was easy. Without God, hearts turn cold; they turn inward, and they live in a prison of lies, hurt, and deception. Oh, Lord, free us in You.

Ponders of the Heart

Have you had bitterness toward someone or bitterness because of something that happened to you?

With God's help, how do we deal with our bitterness?

Read Genesis 4:6-7, Galatians 5:1, and Philippians 4:1.

Prayers of the Heart

Dear Father,

How we love You. You are the One who sets the captives free. Father, we have experienced prison. We have felt isolation from You and from the truth. We have experienced believing a lie over the truth. God, we pray for ourselves and for all Your children. Set us free. By Your grace and in Your love. In Christ's name, amen.

July 9 ~ Freedom

Are we free? Yesterday, we talked about being in prison, the prison of sin. We become prisoners when sin lurks at our door and captures us, like Edmund Dantes in the movie "Count of Monte Cristo."

In the same movie, there was a priest in prison who had been there for eleven years when he popped into Edmund's life. I say popped in because the priest had been busy tunneling his way out of the prison. The problem was he had miscalculated and gone the wrong way. He ended up tunneling right into Edmund's cell. Edmund was scared as the stones beneath him began to move, and a head popped up in the middle of his cell.

The priest's response was priceless. He looked at Edmund, then at the prison cell, and began to laugh. He said, "I have gone the wrong way." He explained how long he had been there and how, day by day, he made his way to the wrong cell. Edmund could not believe his ears and asked, "How can you laugh?"

God was the priest's companion and this journey with God had taken him in a different direction. The Lord wanted to provide the priest with a new companion, and it was Edmund. Together, they could go the other way and, maybe, in another five and a half years, find their way to freedom. Edmund couldn't believe the priest's attitude. The priest was free in the Lord, and circumstances didn't hinder his freedom.

The priest in the movie does not make it out of the prison, but his heart was completely free. His dying words to Edmund were words of praise to God. When Edmund denounced faith in God by telling the old priest he didn't believe in God, the priest responded, "Ah, but He believes in you."

If you know the Son of God, you are free even if you don't know it or act like it. But we will never act free until we believe the truth that Jesus has set us free.

It is always a matter of faith. Do we believe God, or do we believe the lies of this age? Oh, to be so free that I could find myself in the wrong place at the wrong time and just laugh, turn around, and go in another direction. Believing God and not trusting in myself is freedom.

We can find ourselves on the wrong road, turning around in a circle, not knowing what to do. Our God is a prayer away. He has not given up on us, and He will lead us all the way to our heavenly home.

Ponders of the Heart

Have you ever met a totally free person? Are you a free person?

Christ's death made us free from what? List our freedom list.

Read John 8:31-36, Romans 6:5-7, Romans 7:6, Romans 8:1, and 1 Corinthians 15:55-58.

Prayers of the Heart

Dear Father,

By Your Spirit, plant the truth in our souls. Teach us to believe You. Help us appropriate these truths by faith. Set us free from the lies of this age so we might walk in the newness of life. We love You, and we want to live life with You. Lord, tomorrow, if we find ourselves in the wrong place, doing the wrong thing, help us let go, laugh, turn around, and go in the opposite direction. Father, You are the joy of our lives; be the joy in our living. In Jesus' name, amen.

July 10 ~ Bad Theology

On the night of our rehearsal dinner, I decided Bill did not love me. There is a picture of us sitting in his grandmother's bedroom, me in tears, and him trying to reason with me that I had lost my mind.

When I see this picture, I realize how my "stinking thinking" can fill my heart. This thinking comes from an insecure child who still lurks deep inside of me. I listen to her occasionally; in fact, I listen to her far too often.

One morning, I was sitting at the lake, thinking about a decision I had made. I feared what the Lord was going to do to me if it was the wrong decision. Then, very clearly, He quickened my spirit, and I was ashamed that this was my view of God.

I realized the insecure child who lives in my flesh was whispering in my ear. "God is just out to get you. You better not mess up. He is just waiting for you to fail so He can hit you over the head." This, my friend is an example of stinking thinking.

Our God, who gave His Son for us, is for us, not against us. He is interested in what we do and how we live our lives, but His motives are not to see us fail so He can whack us. We can be shallow and petty, but our God is not. He has created us for Himself, and He loves us.

I can picture God sitting beside me at the lake and saying, "Marilyn, how long do I need to be your God before you know my heart? How long before you trust My love for you? I am not out to get you. Don't you realize I gave my absolute best for you? Why would I want to punish you?"

My heart breaks when I realize I have been listening to this pitiful child in my flesh instead of listening to Him.

What lies do you listen to? The lies are so numerous we can't even begin to count them all. I pray God will reveal to us the lies we listen to, and by faith, we will yield to God's truth. Oh, Father, help us know Your heart toward us.

Ponders of the Heart

Do you believe the lie that tells you God loves all people, but He tolerates you?

Read Ephesians 1:15-2:10.

Maybe you listen to the lie that says God is not interested in the little things in your life, or you are too horrible for Him to love.

Prayers of the Heart

Dear Lord,

We yield to You not out of a motive of fear but out of the motive of great trust and thanksgiving. Lord, we don't understand Your unconditional love, but we come to receive it. Father, lavish Your love over us, in us, and through us. In Jesus' name, amen.

July 11 ~ Yielding

"Behold I stand at the door and knock. If anyone hears My voice and opens the door, I will come in to him and dine with him, and he with Me" (Rev. 3:20 NKJV).

I live in a two-story house. We entertain our company downstairs and, besides family, very few have ever been upstairs in my house.

When all the kids were home, having a two-story house was great because I could hide their messy rooms. The truth is, I could hide mine and Bill's messes also. We have places in our house that are open to just family. I don't know if we are unique in this or not. I know of homes where the entire home is open to me, and then there are homes of good friends, where I see very little of their houses.

Of course, you seeing my bedroom or me seeing yours is not the point, but I wonder if I do the same with my life. How private am I? Do I allow others to see the real me?

There are, of course, degrees of intimacy. Even Jesus had intimate friends. He had crowds of people He loved and ministered to: His family and the disciples. His apostles, Peter, James, and John, were His closest friends on earth. But His most important relationship was with God.

We do not need everyone to be our best buddy, but the million-dollar question is, does Jesus feel welcome in every part of our lives? I think that is the difference between deciding to ask Jesus into our hearts and yielding our hearts to Him. Then what about those whom God has given us to love and share our lives with?

I am not sure I am very relational. I have a tight circle called family. When Ryan became our son-in-law, I was amazed at how comfortable he felt coming in and out of our bedroom.

He would borrow this and that from Bill and end up at our mirror in the bathroom getting ready. You could tell he was comfortable in our entire house. I was a little uncomfortable about this, but I was glad he felt this way. God always knows what He is doing when He adds people to our families.

Ryan is part of our family, but for me, I needed help opening my entire heart to him and accepting him as a son. He was the first son-in-law, and without him knowing it, he taught me so much about giving my love to those my children bring home.

Since Ryan, we have added a daughter-in-law, Tonja, another son-in-law whose name is also Ryan, six grandchildren and a step-granddaughter and our most recent addition is a granddaughter-in-law. God has stretched our family and, in the process, stretched me.

Ponders of the Heart

Have you yielded your whole life to God?

Do you know of any part of your life you are holding back? Why?

Read Job 38:1-11.

Prayers of the Heart

Dear Father,

I admit my arrogance and my useless pride. You are the Lord of lords and the King of kings. I come to give you complete Lordship over my life. You allow me to be Yours. Let my heart so yield to You that our relationship is deep and intimate. May I never try to push You away. Father, let me breathe the sweet freedom of Your love. In Jesus' name, amen.

July 12 ~ Ancient of Days

My Bill tends to be habitual about things. He also does things with great fury. His routine is important to him. He has changed his routine now we are older, but He likes to do the same thing at the same time and, if possible, in the same place.

Years back, his routine included running every morning. He jumped out of bed, threw on his clothes, fixed himself a cup of coffee and was in his truck in ten minutes. He drove to the lake, ran for 30 minutes and was back home in the shower by 7:15 every morning.

Since I had more time in the morning, I would sometimes try to go with him. But because I was getting ready slower, he would be backing out of the driveway as I came out of the door. He wasn't very patient with me. But something, or should I say someone, came into our lives who changed his routine, our grandson.

When Collier was around, Bill got up a little slower. He had to have time for good morning hugs. Bill would run a little less, head to the office later, and he developed the patience of Job. Some might say, "Does he love Collier more than anyone else in his life?" He does love Collier, and Collier has stolen his heart, but I really think maturity has shown Bill the importance of children, especially grandchildren.

He understands children grow up before you know it, and you better take advantage of the day. This is a true statement because, as I write this today, Collier is in college, and we still slow our days down whenever we get the chance to be with him. This is also true whenever our other grandchildren come to visit. You could say they are all the apple of our eyes.

As I watched Tracie and Ryan, I realized they were blind to this truth. I remember when I was a young mom, the same was true. I was always trying to escape instead of drinking up the wonder of my children. Some things take time to learn.

This is also true in our spiritual lives. The greatest lesson I am slowly learning is relationships are far more important to God than activities. He wants me and not just for what I can do or what He can do through me. He really wants to enjoy my company as I enjoy His. I was walking the other day with nothing on my mind but praising Him. It was a great walk, full of satisfaction, peace and immensely overdue.

We are important to God. He does not try to escape us; He has an eternal clock with an eternal agenda. He watches us with joy as He works to teach us and have us mature right before His eyes. One name for God in the Bible is The Ancient of Days; I love this name, for it reminds me how powerful and faithful God was in the past, and He hasn't changed.

The patience and the love I saw Bill give to Collier is just a glimpse of the patience and love God has for His children. How I praise Him for His perfect fatherly love. Glory to His name.

Ponders of the Heart

Remember a time when you just enjoyed being with your family?

Do you remember a time when you and God just enjoyed being together?

Read Psalm 18:16-19, Psalm 37:3-4, and Psalm 37:23-24.

Prayers of the Heart

Dear Father,

    I want to love You with all my heart, strength and mind. I need You, it is true, but today I want to love You, not only because I need You, but I delight in Your presence. Lord, my Lord, I love You. In Jesus' name, amen.

July 13 ~ New Beginnings

    I have friends who are homeless. Well, what I mean is they sold their house, and they are building a new one, so right now they are without a house. They have packed up all their belongings and they have been staying with family. They are in limbo, but they seem to be doing well.

    Bill likes his routine, but what I didn't tell you is I like mine also. I like having my things in my house and have no desire to stay with family. I hold on to my routine tightly, even when those things are holding me hostage.

    What are you holding on to? God asks us to trust Him and let go. If Bill and I sold our house, would we be satisfied being in limbo? New beginnings can feel like limbo. If we find ourselves there, we need to be careful of the enemy. He hates us letting go of something that holds us hostage. He loves to keep us in bondage. But Christ said, "He came to set the captives free."

People are in bondage to things like houses, cars, clothes, etc.; other people find themselves in bondage to drugs, alcohol, and unholy relationships. They find themselves in bondage to what people think about them. The list goes on and on, but Christ came to set us free.

The first step is to recognize something or someone who has control over us. The second step is to call out to the Lord for victory over the bondage and for the strength to let go.

At this point, we might begin to think we are safe, but not so, for it is there the enemy begins to mess with our minds with doubt. "Did I do the right thing? Have I made a big mistake?" And before God gets us where He wants us to go, we have taken hold of something else or someone else, and we are back in bondage. Notice Satan speaks doubt to us in the first person.

What are we going to do? We can hold on to God, fix our eyes on Jesus, and trust Him with all our might. Faith is the harder road, but it is the right one. Faith must be grounded in truth, but truth without faith will not sustain us, just as faith without truth will deceive us.

Ponders of the Heart

Is there something you need to let go of but don't think you can?

Do you live a life of bondage or freedom?

Read Isaiah 61:1-3, Galatians 5:1, and Galatians 5:16-17.

Prayers of the Heart

Dear Father,

We want to hold on to You with all our might. We want to follow You, trust You and not hold on too tightly to the things of this world. Thank You for coming to set us free. We are no match for the evil one and his demons. Lord, build trust and truth in our hearts then we will walk in victory which You have won for us. We praise You, Lord, for Your wonderful love. In Jesus' name, amen.

July 14 ~ Seven Deadly Sins

"But as He who called you is holy, you also be holy in all your conduct, because it is written, 'Be holy, for I am holy'" (1 Peter 1:15-16 NKJV).

When my youngest daughter was in High School, she lacked confidence. She had joined the band at school but decided she wanted to quit. We did not think she should start something and then decide to quit.

How could we encourage her without shaming her? My husband has such a good way with our children, and I remember him marching on the sidewalk near where I worked, saying to her, "You cannot quit; you are a Collier, and Colliers don't quit." The point was to be faithful and loyal to your name and the name of your family.

We have been given the great privilege of being God's children. Our adoption is ours because of Jesus, and He has redeemed us from the penalty of sin. But I want more, don't you? I want to walk in freedom from the power and the influence of sin in my life. I want to honor God. Paul writes:

"Therefore do not let sin reign in your mortal body so that you obey its evil desires. Do not offer any part of yourself to sin as an instrument of wickedness, but rather offer yourselves to God as those who have been brought from death to life; and offer every part of yourself to him as an instrument of righteousness. For sin shall no longer be your master, because you are not under the law, but under grace" (Romans 6:12-14).

I don't know about you, but I need to do a self-examination, for the world has a way of creeping into my life. In my heart, I want nothing more than to walk in the freedom and the light of the Lord, but my deep heart desires can be swallowed up with earth-bound living.

Dante Alighieri, a Catholic layman of the 1300s, wrote a book called "The Divine Comedy." In this book, he named seven deadly sins. Deadly, in my opinion, because they will swallow up our lives into unholy living by drawing us away from fellowship with the Lord. The sins are lust, gluttony, greed, sloth, anger, envy, and pride.

In the next seven days we will be looking at each of these sins. This is not for condemnation but for the sake of living lives that are holy. God is holy, and we want to be like our Abba. Let's pray God will open our eyes to the bondage and destruction these sins can cause in the lives of His children.

Ponders of the Heart

Read Prov.15:27, Prov. 13:4, Prov. 14:30, Prov. 16: 18, and Gal. 5:19-26.

As you read these passages, which of these sins do you see in your life?

How have they affected your walk with the Lord and with others?

Prayers of the Heart

Dear Father,

We want to honor You as Your children. We are no match for this world. It can catch us so fast, and we are unaware of its hold. Lord, in these days ahead, show us clearly these deadly sins and how they have a hold on our lives. Cleanse us, and we will be clean. Heal us, and we will be healed. Lord, do Your work in us. In Jesus' name, amen.

July 15 ~ Lust

"When tempted, no one should say, "God is tempting me." For God cannot be tempted by evil, nor does he tempt anyone; but each person is tempted when they are dragged away by their own evil desire and enticed. Then, after desire has conceived, it gives birth to sin; and sin, when it is full-grown, gives birth to death" (James 1:13-15).

Desire is a synonym for lust. What do you desire? When lust or desire overpowers our self-control, we are in deep trouble.

Therefore, the Bible says that lust is one of the deadly sins. The idea is thinking beyond good sense: "I want it, I want it, I want it, and I will have it." It can be almost anything you want it to be.

Amnon was one of David's sons and is a good example of lust. Amnon had a half-sister whose name was Tamar. Amnon said he loved Tamar, but what he meant was his heart lust for her. Significant difference.

He pretended he was ill and asked David, his father, to send Tamar to take care of him. David agreed, and when Tamar came to fix Amnon food, he asked her to come sleep with him. She begged her half-brother not to force her to do such an evil thing, but his lust was greater than his control. The Bible tells us after he forced her to have sex with him, he hated her.

"Then Amnon hated her with intense hatred. In fact, he hated her more than he had loved her. Amnon said to her. 'Get up and get out!'" (2 Samuel 13:15).

Lust never satisfies. Now, Amnon lived with shame and hatred, and Tamar lived with disgrace, shame, and bitterness. An article I read about the deadly sins says it this way.

"Self-control and self-mastery prevent pleasure from killing the soul by suffocation." (www.rushman.org).

Amnon's lack of self-control had killed his soul as well as his sister's. This article goes on to say,

"Lust is the self-destructive drive for pleasure out of proportion to its worth."

Have you ever found this to be true? Often, the things I think I must have end up suffocating my life and never prove to supply the pleasure I thought.

Ponders of the Heart

Do you have something you desire so much you lust for it?

How does the Bible give us the way to live and not get captured by lust?

Read 2 Peter 1:3-9, 1 John 2:16-17 and 2 Timothy 1:7. Also read 1 John 2:16-17 and 2 Timothy 1:7.

Some translations say evil desires instead of lust.

Prayers of the Heart

Dear Father,

How we pray for victory over the lust of the flesh. So many sins begin with lust and the lack of self-control. Lord, give us control by Your Spirit. Save us from our old habits. Replace our old desires with a hunger for You. We are new in You, and You have given us all we need for godliness, and Your Spirit has given us self-control. Help us walk in victory over the power of sin. Father, we love You. In Jesus' name, amen.

July 16 ~ Greed

It has been said greed is getting your fair share and a bit more, while the antidote for greed is charity. Generosity is giving without expectation of something in return. We see a perfect example of greed being a deadly sin in Acts 5 with the story of Ananias and Sapphira.

The church had come together as a family. They were sharing food and possessions with one another with generous hearts. Barnabas sold land and gave the money to the church. This was truly an act of generosity.

Ananias and Sapphira wanted to sell land and give generously to the church, but the old "greed bug" bit them before the deed was done. They decided they would lie and keep back money for themselves. The result was God showed His displeasure by taking their lives.

How many of us would be dead right now if our greedy hearts were exposed? I would be dead as a doornail. Recently, I saw this firsthand and felt the seduction of greed. This was through the loss of a man's life that was built on money.

His relationships were formed and kept by his pocketbook. He was wealthy, and at his death, people wondered where this wealth would find its resting place. At his funeral, the topic was his money. The greed for more is very seductive.

Greed is the opposite of satisfaction and can kill the kindest soul. I'm reminded of the request in Proverbs for neither riches nor poverty.

"Keep falsehood and lies far from me; give me neither poverty nor riches, but give me only my daily bread. Otherwise, I may have too much and disown you and say, 'Who is the Lord?' Or I may become poor and steal and so dishonor the name of my God" (Proverbs 30:8-9).

Greed is truly a deadly sin in our culture today. Let Proverbs 30:8-9 be our prayer to God. I love the way the verse shows us the best way to manage wealth. This approach can only be ours if Christ has redeemed us and has placed a nature like His in us. Even after this, we can be seduced by greed.

Ponders of the Heart

What do you have that is more than you need?

If God has richly blessed your life, how can you share His blessings with others so you do not forget it was God who has blessed you?

Read Deuteronomy 8:10-18.

Prayers of the Heart

Dear Father,

Remove falsehood and lies far from Your children. Begin with me, dear Lord. Give me neither poverty nor riches. Feed me with the food allotted to me. I do not want my heart to grow cold toward You, my Lord. Father, give me enough to pay my bills so I will not be a bad witness. You are my provider and hope. Let my heart rest and delight in You and You alone. You, my peace and my joy, In Jesus' name, amen.

July 17 ~ Gluttony

When is it time to say, "enough." Do you know? Not knowing when to say when is the problem with gluttony. Most of us think when you say gluttony, you are talking about overeating. This is only partly right.

Gluttony is when the natural limits of something are abused. This could be shoes, clothes, entertainment, food, and drink. In fact, when the Bible speaks of gluttony, it usually refers to drunkenness. Gluttony is an easy sin to develop and a hard sin to break.

All sins are hard to break, for sin is natural for the natural man.

Years back, we began a health program called "Body for Life." In this program you had a cheat day each week. The rest of the week, you were to eat a balanced meal, but on your cheat day nothing was off limits. If you ever wanted to see gluttony in full swing all you would have had to do is show up at our house on cheat day. I have never eaten so many donuts in my life and have not eaten so many since. You would have thought we were starving to death. By the end of the day, I felt like a beached whale.

Gluttony is the excessive love of earthly goods and pleasure. Oh, that we would realize we were created for such a higher purpose. God does not want us to live for just the pleasures of this world, but He has given us His Spirit so we can have far more.

"For God has not given us a spirit of timidity, but a spirit of power, of love and of self-discipline" (2 Timothy 1:7 NKJV).

We can, by faith and His power, live our lives with balance. This includes the amount we eat, spend, and the amount we go. A life with balance and discipline gives us safety and freedom. Gluttony enslaves us to lesser things.

We no longer enslave ourselves to a cheat day where we become gluttonous maniacs, but we try to live with healthy eating habits. We splurge at times and over-splurge at other times, but by His Spirit, we can live lives of control. Where is your life out of balance? Remember the promise of God. You have been given His Spirit, and you can live a life of balance. Praise the Lord that He wants to sanctify every area of our lives. The key to the Christian life is a life of surrender.

Ponders of the Heart

Do you believe God is good and has a good plan for you?

Do you have a cheat day in your life? How are you cheating yourself by not surrendering to your Heavenly Father?

Read 2 Peter 1:3-9 and 1 Thessalonians 5:24.

Prayers of the Heart

Dear Father,

We bow before You. Keep our hearts steadfast on You. Let not the lesser pleasures of this life steal us away. We long to be free to love You with our hearts, minds, souls, and strength. You are our deepest desire and greatest delight. Father, let us eat up the wonders of Your love. In Jesus' name, amen.

July 18 ~ Sloth

What do you think when you hear the word sloth? I think of the word lazy. When I was a little girl, I asked my mom if I looked like my real father. She said, "No." She went on to say she watched my brother, Johnny, and me to see if we would be lazy like our father. Then she said, "But you are not."

The thought that I was lazy is a message Satan loves to play over in my mind. I have lived so many days of my life trying not to be lazy. A synonym for sloth is laziness, but sloth also could mean apathy, sluggishness, inactivity, and idleness.

Let me do some toe-stomping for a moment. Just remember, if I stomp your toes, I have already crushed mine. Do you have a zeal for the Lord, or have you become full of apathy and inactivity, or are you just idle? If you answer yes to these questions, then, like me, you are close to the deadly sin of sloth.

Zeal for the Lord is an energetic response to His heart and commands. Let us look at the commands of God and see if we have zeal or sloth toward them.

"And this is the command: to believe in the name of the Son, Jesus Christ, and to love one another as he commanded us" (1 John 3:23.)

"A new commandment I give you; Love one another. As I have loved you, so you must love one another" (John 13:34).

"Love must be sincere. Hate what is evil; cling to what is good. Be devoted to one another in brotherly love. Honor one another above yourselves. Never be lacking in zeal, but keep your spiritual fervor, serving the Lord. Be joyful in hope, patient in affliction, faithful in prayer. Share with God's people who are in need. Practice hospitality" (Romans 12:9-13).

And I thought I was safe because I never leave dirty dishes in the sink. Boy, was I wrong. Zeal for the Lord is our calling and our privilege. Passion for the Lord produces a lively living.

Ponders of the Heart

How do we battle spiritual fatigue?

What are some activities that might keep you in bondage? Your phones, T.V, or hobbies? I need to take a good look at my list.

Read Ephesians 5:15-21 and Hebrews 10:19-23.

Prayers of the Heart

Dear Father,

The sin of sloth makes us feel terrible. We do not want to be people who lack zeal for You or Your work. Precious Father, stir holy passion in our souls and give us zeal for You. Lord, place love in us for others, healthy love, wise, and holy love. We praise You, Father, for You are our passion. In Jesus' name, amen.

July 19 ~ Anger/Wrath

One summer, Julie was dealing with an infection just under the skin. This infection would cause what I would call a rising. She had to go to the doctor and have the rising lanced and take a round of antibiotics. As soon as she finished the antibiotics, she would develop another rising.

The infection would cause terrible discomfort. The procedure in the doctor's office would relieve the pressure and pain, but the procedure was painful.

Four rounds of antibiotics and a special wash, along with a special antibiotic wipe, things seemed to be under control. The doctor said the bacteria came through a break in the skin and caused the problem.

The infection made the area swell and the swelling restricted the blood from flowing freely and prevented the antibiotics from doing the job. This is the reason for the lancing. One doctor put it like this, "Once the area becomes inflamed and angry, the antibiotic cannot do its job."

Anger is a secondary emotion. In other words, there was another emotion that caused the anger. In the case of the body, it becomes inflamed and angry to protect itself, trying to isolate the infection. The same is true with us. We use our anger to protect. This method of protection is to keep others from knowing we are afraid, hurt, frustrated or out of control. It could be all the above. We are told in God's word to rid ourselves of all rage and wrath.

"Put to death, therefore, whatever belongs to your earthly nature; sexual immorality, impurity, lust, evil desires and greed, which is idolatry. Because of these, the wrath of God is coming. You used to walk in these ways, in the life you once lived. But now you must rid yourselves of all such things as these: anger, rage, malice, slander, and filthy language from your lips" (Colossians 3:5-8).

You say, "Great, but how"? To find the answer to how to rid ourselves of anger and receive the healing we need, we will need the Word of God. In the passages above, you see the word, therefore. This gives us a hint we need to see what is before, as Paul Harvey would say, "The rest of the story."

"Since, then, you have been raised with Christ, set your hearts on things above, where Christ is seated at the right hand of God. Set your minds on things above, not on earthly things. For you died and your life is hidden with Christ in God. When Christ, who is your life appears, then You also will appear with him in glory" (Colossians 3:1-4).

If our anger is a secondary emotion to fear, we must remember our lives are hidden with Christ in God. This makes us as safe as we can be. If our anger is because of hurt, Jesus is the Great Physician, and He can heal our hurt.

Our anger can come from frustration and feeling out of control. Jesus is our rest (Matthew 11:28). After all, control is an illusion. It is God who is in control, and we can trust Him.

Anger is a secondary emotion with first-degree burns. It destroys our peace and rest, it is a burning fire within us. Fury entraps us and licks us up like dry leaves in fire.

The outflow of our anger will destroy the relationships around us. It destroys trust, comfort, and confidence.m It robs us of intimacy. Our rage keeps us away from God and draws us into sin. If we are hidden with Christ in God, we are to lance this angry infection and rid our spiritual bodies of its poison. It is a deadly sin not only for us but for those we love.

"For you died and your life is hidden with Christ in God. When Christ, who is your life appears, then You also will appear with Him in glory. Put to death, therefore, whatever belongs to your earthly nature;" (Colossians 3:3-5).

Ponders of the Heart

Did you know anger was a secondary emotion?

How does that help you search for the primary reason for your anger?

Read Ephesians 4:26-32.

Prayers of the Heart

Dear Father,

Anger is such a powerful tool of the flesh and Satan. Lord, we do not belong to our flesh or Satan. We belong to You. We are Your children. Let us, Lord, walk and live in the freedom of Your Spirit.

Let us count ourselves dead to the ways of the world and our flesh. You died so we could be free. Lord, free us from the destructive emotion of anger. Put out the fire of rage in us by Your grace. In Jesus' name, amen.

July 20 ~ Envy

My mom would say she and I had a good relationship. I, on the other hand, never felt I pleased her. My sister-in-law, Gina, was one of my mom's favorite people. Mom would say, "Gina is so good to me." And she was.

Gina is one of the kindest people I know, and she was always kind to my mom. I was thankful for her kindness, but because I felt I never pleased my mother, I had times I was jealous.

What I just described is not envy because this sin goes a step further than wanting something more; it goes to the extreme. Envy resents the good others receive or might receive. I wished my mom and I had been closer. I wanted a relationship like the one Mom and Gina had, but because I loved them both, I was thankful for the relationship they enjoyed.

The opposite of envy is love, and I had too much love for both Mom and Gina for this sin to take over. Thank you, Lord. Unlike envy, love actively looks for the good of others for their sake. Envy seeks its own good above others and is closely related to pride. In fact, it is identical to pride.

When Bill's brother, Brooks, was a little boy, he saw another little boy with an ice cream cone. He asked his dad if he could have one. His dad told him no. I guess you could say Brooks was envious when the little boy came by with the ice cream cone. Brooks knocked it out of his hand and stomped on it.

We laugh, but I wonder if Brooks was just doing what some of us would like to do when this sin takes over our lives. Envy is a deadly sin that eats away at the fiber of satisfaction. Dissatisfaction can become a way of life. Looking at what others have and not being grateful for the blessing God has given us.

"For the rest, brethren, whatever is true, whatever is worthy of reverence and is honorable and seemly, whatever is just, whatever is pure, whatever is lovely and lovable, whatever is kind and winsome and gracious, if there is any virtue and excellence, if there is anything worthy of praise, think on and weigh and take account of these things (fix your minds on them). Practice what you have learned and received and heard and seen in me, and model your way of living on it, and the God of peace (of untroubled, undisturbed well-being) will be with you" (Philippians 4:8-9 Amplified).

What wonderful verses to break the door of envy and refocus us on the wonder of His grace.

Ponders of the Heart

Have you had or do you have an issue with envy?

How does God's Word help us refocus our heart away from this sin? Explain?

Read Philippians 3:7-21.

Prayers of the Heart

Dear Father,

We have all experienced the deadly sin of envy. Change us completely through and through. Let our hearts and minds reflect people who want to know You. People who realize the great gift is You. Refocus our eyes on You, the Author and the Finisher of our faith. Let our hearts rejoice in the gift of knowing You. Thank You for allowing us to be Your children. In Jesus' name, amen.

July 21 ~ The Father of Them All Pride

I was vacuuming the garage, and I asked myself, "Where did all those spider webs come from?" It was impossible to get all those sticky webs, no matter how hard I tried. The more I vacuumed, the more webs I saw. As I vacuumed one area, I saw a spider hurry to safety. The garage is better, but if there are spiders in my garage, there will be more spider webs.

What's a girl to do? I had a bug bomb, so I shut the garage and bombed it. I hope it helps.

As I was cleaning up the spider webs, I thought of the Father of all sins, pride. It is like those spider webs, entangling our lives and making them a sticky mess.

This thing called pride keeps us from recognizing our need for God. It keeps us from yielding to His authority in our lives and makes us think we can tell Him and others what to do. God has a way of cleaning us up by vacuuming our lives. He is not beyond knocking us from our self-made pedestal. Remember, pride comes before the fall.

"Pride goes before destruction, a haughty spirit before a fall" (Prov. 16:18).

God is constantly working to keep our hearts clean, but before we can take a deep breath of clean air, pride has crept back and woven another web of deception over us. This deadly sin can take on different manifestations. We have been looking at six of them.

The root cause of sin is pride. We know the villain who is responsible. His name is Satan, and we are victims by our human nature to his seduction. He is as creepy and crawly as a spider and weaves a web of destruction wherever he goes. His bait is our prideful nature, and he laughs when he catches us in this trap.

Pride was the sin of Satan and the fall of mankind, but God is the bomb. He can vacuum the mess and destroy the enemies faster than we can say, Daddy Longlegs.

There is the Day coming when Christ will return for His bride, and when we take flight with Him, there will be no more webs around us. Satan will be defeated, and pride-in-self will fall like a falling star. We will enter heaven clean before our Maker. Hallelujah and Praise the Lord. But until that Day, Lord, keep vacuuming our lives so we are clean.

Ponders of the Heart

Was there a time in your life when pride tripped you up?

How do we defend ourselves against this sin in our hearts?

Read Proverbs 8:13, Proverbs 13:10, and Proverbs 29:23.

Prayers of the Heart

Dear Father,

Pride destroys, turns our hearts cold, and sets us up for a fall. Lord, scoop us up with Your grace. Overcome our foolish hearts with praise for You and for Your greatness. Father, draw our hearts into Your presence and we will fall before You in awe of Your wonder and Your grace. In Jesus' name, amen.

July 22 ~ Be of Good Courage

"For we are God's workmanship, created in Christ Jesus for good works, which God prepared beforehand that we should walk in them" (Eph. 2:10 NKJV).

Rick Warren, in his book, "The Purpose Driven Life," says we get our English word, poem, from the Greek word for workmanship. Think about this for a moment. You are God's poem. You are a work of art designed uniquely for Him and His purposes. King David says:

For you created my inmost being; you knit me together in my mother's womb. I praise you because I am fearfully and wonderfully made; your works are wonderful, I know that full well. My frame was not hidden from you when I was made in the secret place, when I was woven together in the depths of the earth. Your eyes saw my unformed body; all the days ordained for me were written in your book before one of them came to be" (Psalm 139:13-16).

God knew what He was doing when He formed you, and He understands your design and your purpose. I have heard it said our Lord wastes nothing in our lives. So, whatever we face today or in our future, God is aware of it. We fear for our husbands, our children and friends when they are facing danger, trouble, or temptation.

If we belong to God, He knows our steps. God uses all kinds of things in our lives to teach us and to transform us. He uses circumstances, temptation, troubles, and beauty. His Word and His Spirit can teach us and help us avoid pitfalls.

Let's say you have just studied a lesson on deception, but you are unaware of the trickery that is about to happen in your life. It was not an accident you were given this information. God knows what lies ahead, and he wants to equip you before you face what is coming.

He is involved with the details of our lives. The big circumstances and the small ones. He uses things we learn in Bible studies to help us or others in our lives. In His love for us, He wants to prepare us before we face the problem.

We are not to walk in fear but walk fully aware of the knowledge God is giving us. The Lord gives us knowledge before He gives revelation. He wants to equip us for whatever we face in this life. We are to walk in the wisdom He gives us and remember that we are His poem.

Ponders of the Heart

Are you sometimes gripped with fear?

How do these passages encourage us to not be afraid?

Read Joshua 1:6-9.

Prayers of the Heart

Dear Father,

We are Your poems. Read us out loud so we can hear Your plans for us. Emphasize the words and tune of Your heart. Life has a way of taking the starch out of our souls. But You, Father, give life and energy. Give us awe and wonder. We want to live out what You have put in us. We want to be a blessing to Your Kingdom and every step of our lives to be driven by our love for You. In Jesus' name, amen.

July 23 ~ You are my Praise

"Heal me, Lord, and I will be healed; save me and I will be saved, for you are the one I praise" (Jeremiah 17:14).

"Billy, Billy." This is my cry in times of trouble, according to my children. Bill has long been and will continue to be my knight in shining armor. When Julie was a little girl, maybe two or three, we had a serious car accident. I ran a stop sign that was hidden by a big truck. A pick-up truck hit the left side of the car right behind the driver's door.

This sent the car spinning, and we hit a road sign on the other side. All the glass shattered, and the car was destroyed. Julie was in the back seat on the floorboard, and she was thrown from one side of the car to the other. This was before car seats for children. The craziest thing happened to me. I would not get out of the car. The police officer got into the car with me to take down my information, and he asked me if he could call someone for me. I asked him to call my husband.

Bill, my husband, was playing golf at the country club. They called the club and told Bill what had happened and sent him to me. When he arrived, I began to respond to the situation at hand. All my pent-up emotions came rushing out, and I finally got out of the car with Julie. I do not know if that is a symptom of shock, but my reaction to the situation was very strange.

I could not face what was happening until Bill came. Julie ended up having a broken collarbone, and I had minor bumps and bruises. When I look back at that day I am amazed at my reaction. His presence was my courage to face the accident.

God has used Bill more than anyone in my life to pry me out of "cocoon" living. My husband has often extended to me his courage and confidence in times of need. God has used him to heal deep insecurities in my life and save me from fearful living. But Bill is not my praise.

I now realize God is my source. God loaned Bill to me so I could receive healing from deep hurts and to help me develop into the person He made me to be. I praise the Lord for giving me Bill and using him in such a mighty way in my life. My husband is my best friend, and he is my earthly knight in shining armor, but God is my praise.

If God heals us, we will be healed, and if God saves us, we will be saved. We know of marriages that need healing and saving. There are people in our lives that are in deep trouble of heart and soul.

We can call out to God, believing that He can heal and save others. It might be we need to call out for ourselves. How we need to trust Him. We all need to open our hearts and receive all the healing and saving available to us. He is our praise. He is!

Ponders of the Heart

What healing do you need today?

What or who needs God's saving power?

Read Psalm 20 and Psalm 51.

Prayers of the Heart

Dear Father,

    You are our praise. Where would we be without You? How could we live one day apart from Your grace? We praise You and fall before You in humble awe. You are our help in times of trouble. You are our hope for all the days of this life and the ones to come. We bow before You with praise. In Jesus' name, amen.

July 24 ~ The Praise of His Glory

    During John Kennedy's administration as President, physical fitness was big in schools. We had to take physical fitness tests, which included pull-ups. I cannot remember how many pull-ups we had to do to pass, but for me, one was too many. I was sure there was a 450-pound weight tight to my legs when I tried to do a pull-up.

    They were the hardest thing for me to do. I could do sit-ups, run, jump and all kinds of exercises, but oh, those pull-ups.

    Sometimes life feels like a pull-up to me. Life can just be hard, overbearing, and just impossible. Relationships with people can feel the same way. I need help at times, don't you?

I can remember one time when I needed just one more pull-up to make the cut for fitness. With all my might, I tried, but I failed. I felt like a dejected loser. You might say I was cocky about my fitness, but my cockiness fell to humiliation. I really had a bigger problem than not being able to do pull-ups. The problem was pride. Placing my value on my ability to perform.

Bill had two boys who lived next door to him. Their names were George and Alan. They were both physically and mentally challenged. George spent his life in a wheelchair.

My Bill used to play basketball with George. He would spend hours shooting for George and then for himself. He also did the commentary on the game where Bill would include George in the success or the failures of the shots. George would never do a pull-up, sit-up or run the track, but he was important. Bill taught me this.

Years later I am sure I still cannot do a pull-up, but I try not to place my value on my performance. I still do it at times, but I know my value is in who I am not in what I do.

There is a King in my life. He is the King of kings, and He has made me His. He promises me that He is always with me and He will never leave me. This is more important to me than being able to do a pull-up. How silly, you might think. But where do you receive your worth? Do you pride yourself in your job, family, possessions, status, looks, or even your own self-righteousness? I am reminded of Paul's words when he said:

"Praise be to the God and Father of our Lord Jesus Christ, who has blessed us in the heavenly realms with every spiritual blessing in Christ. For he chose us in him before the creation of the world to be holy and blameless in his sight. In love he predestined us for adoption

to sonship through Jesus Christ, in accordance with his pleasure and will— to the praise of his glorious grace, which he has freely given us in the One he loves" (Ephesians 1:3-6).

Oh well, doing pull-ups is no longer important to me. I am loved.

Ponders of the Heart

Do you struggle with self-worth?

How does the Bible help us see the worth God places on us?

Read and ponder the verses above and add Ephesians 1:7-12. Believe Him.

Prayers of the Heart

Dear Lord,

You chose us. This truth is more wonderful than we can imagine. We belong to You. Your heaven is our home. Father, thank You for making our lives have purpose and thank You for making us Yours. Fill us with Your Spirit. We want to be witnesses for You in a dark sinful world.

Lord, give us love and grace, mercy, and forgiveness for those You place in our lives. We want to be vessels for You, so fill us up until we overflow. In Christ's name, amen.

July 25 ~ God and Father

There are wonderful Christian novels that speak to me through fictional lives.

One book I read was called "Eve's Daughters." The fictional character, whose name is Grace, grows up without knowing her father. She expresses the heart cry that lives in children who live without the knowledge, presence, or love of their father.

She feels she does not belong to anyone. The void lives so deep and wide that she searches for a father. In the book she asks a priest if they could pretend, he was her father, and it could be their secret. The priest tells her that would not be possible because he vowed to be a father to all those in his parish.

As I read those words, I was torn between the need for a child and the vow before God. How could pretending to be this child's father hurt? How could this secret break his vow? My heart ached for this little one, for I know the pain associated with not knowing your real father.

I had a stepfather that claimed me as his own, but I knew in my heart that I was not bone of his bone and flesh of his flesh. The wisdom of the priest began to occur to me through my own life. Even if he pretended it would not make it so. She would always know the truth. Pretending would not help it never does.

The priest being wise and loving helps Grace find her eternal Father. Grace's loss of an earthly father made her fertile ground for the One she needed most, God.

These words opened a floodgate in my soul. It is just like the Lord to open my eyes to how He uses the hard things in our lives to reach us. God is so personal and amazing. He used my absent father figure to prepare me to receive Him as my heavenly Father. What a glorious time of praise overtook me as He reminded me, I was His child, and I belonged to Him.

I am in awe of the unique and personal way God deals with each of us. It doesn't matter how unique we think our situation is; our Lord is so powerful and personal that He uses the failure of this world to draw us into His Arms. As this truth was revealed to me by His grace I was overwhelmed with tears. Tears are so hard for me, so when they come, they are sweet refreshments.

In the phrase, "Blessed be the God and Father of our Lord Jesus Christ" (Ephesians 1:3), the word blessed can also be translated as praised. The Greek word for blessed or praised in this verse is *Eulogetos*. The *tos* in the word means inherently worthy to be praised and ascribed only to God, for no one else is inherently worthy of praise. A touch of His presence, a revelation of His love, and a glimpse of His all-knowing power explode within us and outside us with praise.

Only God can be praised for being the Father of our Lord, Jesus Christ and only God can be praised for adopting us as His own. For those of you who, like me, never felt you belonged to someone can live with joy, and praise to God our Father. Out of His good pleasure He has given us lives that far outweigh our physical ones. Eternal life is ours through Jesus Christ.

Ponders of the Heart

What person or what part of life has failed you?

Do you sometimes feel you do not belong? God says you do.

Read Romans 8:12-17.

Prayers of the Heart

Dear Father,

We praise You and bless You. You are worthy of all praise, honor, and glory. Use all things in our lives for Your glory and our good. We want to thank You for being our God who deals with us so personally and perfectly. There are no words worthy to express our praise. We are so grateful You hear the words of our hearts. Oh, Lord, we love You. In Jesus' name, amen.

July 26 ~ Blessed

I wonder how hard it was for my stepdad to be my dad, especially when he had children of his own who needed and loved him? If they had their way, I'm sure they would have wanted their mom and dad to stay married and my brother and me out of the picture. Being a dad is hard enough of a job without adding the strain of being a stepdad for someone else's children. I was blessed beyond measure to have a stepdad like mine.

He came into our home and supported us with his love. My stepdad taught us to respect our home, our mother and to be diligent in all we did. He gave us room to grow and treated us with dignity.

He taught us many things, took the time to play with us and carted us all over the place.

We were like the Israelites, not always grateful. Like the children of God, we wanted things our way in our timing. The gift he gave us was himself. He loved us and treated us like his own.

When I think about how ungrateful I was at times, God reminds me I can still act ungrateful. He has given me all I need, but I cry out for more. His love is never ending and yet there are times I don't trust His love or His ways.

My earthly treasures are more than I could ever hope for, and yet I can be so ungrateful. There are times when I want to put Him in the closet for safekeeping until I need or want something.

I can react like a spoiled child when I don't get my way. In my flesh I want God to always say yes; but in my spirit, the longer I live I am grateful He loves me enough to give me what I need instead of what I want. He is a perfect heavenly Father.

What are some things we should never take for granted? He chose us before the foundation of the world. This is a good thing because it was before we had done anything wrong or right. He made us blameless and holy before Him by placing us in Christ and he predestined to adopt us as His children. Why? Because He wanted to.

My brother and I didn't choose our stepdad, but he chose us. We didn't choose God, but He chose us.

I pray that stepchildren will make room in their hearts for stepdads and love them. I also pray stepdads, by God's grace, be worthy of their love.

The prayer for myself is that I would fall before God, who has adopted me and love Him with all my heart and soul, for He is worthy of our praise, *Eulogetos*.

Ponders of the Heart

Have you been taking your salvation in Christ for granted?

Do you want to worship your Father right now?

Read Romans 8:12-15 and 2 Corinthians 6:18.

Prayers of the Heart

Dear Father,

We love You, and We thank You for the gift of sonship. Lord, out of Your kindness, You chose us, and out of Your grace, You gave us holiness through the life and ministry of Your Son. Keep our hearts open to You. Keep our mouths full of praise and wonder, and free us by Your Spirit so we can know You and live for You. In Jesus name, amen.

July 27 ~ Accepted

Tracie, my middle child, was in the ninth grade when we moved to Lagrange. She had to give up being a cheerleader because of the move and it was a long year before she could try out again. Like other girls, she practiced after school until the day of tryouts.

The day of tryouts was Saturday, and anyone could and watch. The excitement built as each girl did her best to make the team. As I sat there, so nervous for Tracie, hoping with all my heart she would make the team.

Each moment felt like years as they called the numbers of the girls who had made the squad. When they called Tracie's number, I was so excited. We laughed, smiled, and enjoyed the moment.

The sad part about tryouts is not all the girls made it.

I know the other side of tryouts. When I was going into the eleventh grade, I was a cheerleader through Junior High School and was an alternate for the varsity in tenth grade. Everyone said I would make it, and I really thought I would, but when the numbers were called, I was not one of them. It was a disappointing outcome, and I still remember how sad I was. For Tracie and for me these were defining moments. The moment was decided on our merit to be or not to be. She was to be, and I was not to be.

When God said we are accepted into His family. We are taken because of Christ's position, purity, holiness, and family status.

That is good news for the girl whose number was not called, and the girl whose number was called, because neither of could measure up to the standard of God. It took God Himself to secure our place and to keeps our place.

There is only one number that will make us part of the kingdom's team. That one number is Jesus, the One and Only. Praise the Lord, the pressure is off.

Ponders of the Heart

What is one disappointment in your life that stands out above the rest?

How does it compare with the acceptance you have in God's Kingdom?

Read Hebrews 10:14, Hebrews 10:10, and Hebrews 9:11-15.

Prayers of the Heart

Dear Sweet Jesus,

We Praise You, Jesus; we lift our voices in thanksgiving. We thank You, Father, for providing eternal life for us. Lord, our Lord, we offer thanksgiving and praise for Your acceptance of us through Your Son, Jesus, and it is in His name we pray, amen.

July 28 ~ I Will Not

The year Tracie, our daughter put Collier in Mother's morning out it just about killed her. Collier, who Bill called, "Mr. Friendly Boy," did not behave very friendly. He cried every time she left him. All her books told her that he is suffering from separation anxiety disorder, but not to worry; it is just a phase he is going through.

The "experts" said to make sure she kissed him when she left and tell him when she would be back. They told her to try to minimize the time she was away from him.

Tracie was thankful for the advice, but she hoped this phase would be a short one. She also said, "Mom, you never went through anything like this did you?" I replied, "Oh, no you just held on to my leg, screaming bloody murder if anyone else spoke to you."

Did you ever go through a spiritual anxiety separation disorder? I think I have been in one most of my life. I call out to the Lord and wonder if He hears me. The Amplified Bible has a verse for us if we ever felt this way.

"He (God) Himself has said, I will not in any way fail you nor give you up nor leave you without support. [I will] not, [I will] not, [I

will] not in any degree leave you helpless nor forsake nor let [you] down (relax My hold on you)! [(Assuredly not!] (Hebrews 13:5 Amplified Translation).

Don't you just love this verse? I will not, I will not, I will not. He will not. Can we ask for more assurance than this? Assuredly not.

I don't know what is going on in your life today, but the day I wrote these words they were peace for my soul. I pray these words have given you confidence today and a feeling of peace. A strong, loving, protective Father who would give His life before He would let you go.

Ponders of the Heart

Have you ever felt forgotten or lost?

Do you realize you have a Father in heaven that will never let you go? Praise Him for His everlasting arms.

Read Isaiah 43:1-13.

Prayers of the Heart

Dear Father,

I do suffer from separation anxiety disorder. I need you every moment of every hour. Help me walk by faith that you are here. Lord, You promise never to leave me alone, and I praise You for this truth and knowledge. Let me not just praise You for Your presence but help me enjoy You, hear Your truths and embrace them. Lord, I love You, and I am grateful You will never leave me. In Jesus' name, amen.

July 29 ~ Weakness

"My grace is sufficient for you, for my power is make perfect in weakness," Therefore I will boast all the more gladly about my weakness, so that Christ's power may rest on me. That is why, for Christ's sake, I delight in weaknesses, in insults, in hardships, in persecutions, in difficulties. For when I am weak, then I am strong" (2 Corinthians 12:9-10).

I found this to be so true in my life. God has allowed me to reach the end of my own strength and through my weakness, His power is released. The process of getting to the end of myself is painful, but the result of experiencing the power of God is spectacular.

Whenever I am dealing with people's lives as a wife, mother, friend, teacher, or counselor it is so important that I am resting in God's wisdom, His power, and not my own. I have never regretted resting in Him, but I have regretted it when I have depended on myself.

How many people have I hurt by human advice and directions. I wonder how many people I could have helped if only I had rested in the wisdom and power of God and not myself? How thankful I am that God wastes nothing, and He works things for good, but I don't want to be working against the One who gave me life.

Paul puts it this way:

"I can do all things through Christ that strengthens me" (Philippians 4:13 NKJV).

Jesus said,

"I am the vine, you are the branches. He who abides in Me, and I in him, bears much fruit; for without Me you can do nothing" (John 15:5 NKJV).

Such good news for us. We can depend on our Lord and remember He is faithful.

Ponders of the Heart

Do you have a control problem?

Have you experienced God stepping in and giving you His power at a time when you were weak?

Read John 15:1-7 and 2 Corinthians 3:4-6.

Prayers of the Heart

Father, God,

You are the wisdom, strength, and power we need to live as Your children. We do not have the strength or the wisdom to minister to this hurting world without Your Spirit. You are Savior. Help us surrender our control and ask for your grace and mercy to fill us with Your Holy Spirit. We want to serve You and help others find You. Father, let it be so. In Jesus' name, amen.

July 30 ~ Debauchery

Country music is something my husband listens to occasionally, so I guess I do too. We are often in the same car. The country song titled "The Drinking Bone" caught my attention. It seems Country music has a lot to say about drinking, divorce, sex, and partying. Sometimes, people think this is a fun way to live. It appears to me it is very destructive.

"Be very careful, then how you live- not as unwise but as wise, making the most of every opportunity, because the days are evil. Therefore do not be foolish, but understand what the Lord's will is. Do not get drunk with wine, which leads to debauchery. Instead be filled with the Spirit" (Eph. 5:15-18).

This is the definition of debauchery: Debauchery is wasteful living, led astray into excessive indulgence of pleasures, to lead away from virtue or excellence.

In other words, don't be drunk with wine, for "the drinking bone" can lead to a wasted life. My family has personally dealt with the results of "the drinking bone." It seems to be a generational sin that has plagued us. The Ephesian passages us to be wise in how we live. It also tells us to be filled with the Spirit of God. This is the prayer for my family, and I pray this also for yours.

Ponders of the Heart

Do you have a loved one whose life has been destroyed by alcohol?

What is God's will for His children?

Read Ephesians 5:15-21.

Prayers of the Heart

Dear Father,

You know the number of lives that have been cut short or wasted because of drinking and drugs. We see the results in the news media every single day. Lord, how we need Your Spirit. Forgive us for wasting so many hours of the life You have given us. Fill us with Your life and give us the power and the desire to live for You. In Jesus' name, amen.

July 31 ~ Prayer of Filling

"For this reason I bow my knees before the Father, from whom every family in heaven and on the earth is named. I pray that according to the wealth of his glory he may grant you to be strengthened with power through his Spirit in the inner man, that Christ may dwell in your hearts through faith, so that, by being rooted and grounded in love, you may be able to comprehend with all the saints what is the breadth and length and height and depth, and thus to know the love of Christ that surpasses knowledge, so that you may be filled up to all the fullness of God. Now to him who by the power that is working within us is able to do far beyond all that we ask or think to him be the glory in the church and in Christ Jesus to all generations, forever and ever. Amen" (Ephesians 3:14-21 NKJV).

Prayers of the Heart

Dear Lord,

We pray for one another. Our prayer is that You will grant us grace to know You and to be filled with Your Spirit. Father, we need Your help. We need revelation from You, and we need Your truth, grace, forgiveness, and Your mighty power. Your church has fallen into the ways of our culture. We have tried to be all the world wants us to be and be Yours.

Lord, it is not working, we are full of deception and problems. Our peace is gone, and we have lost our way. Reclaim Your people for Your glory. We need a fresh movement of Your Spirit. Help us know You, Lord. You can do more than we can even ask or imagine. We thank You. In Jesus' name, amen.

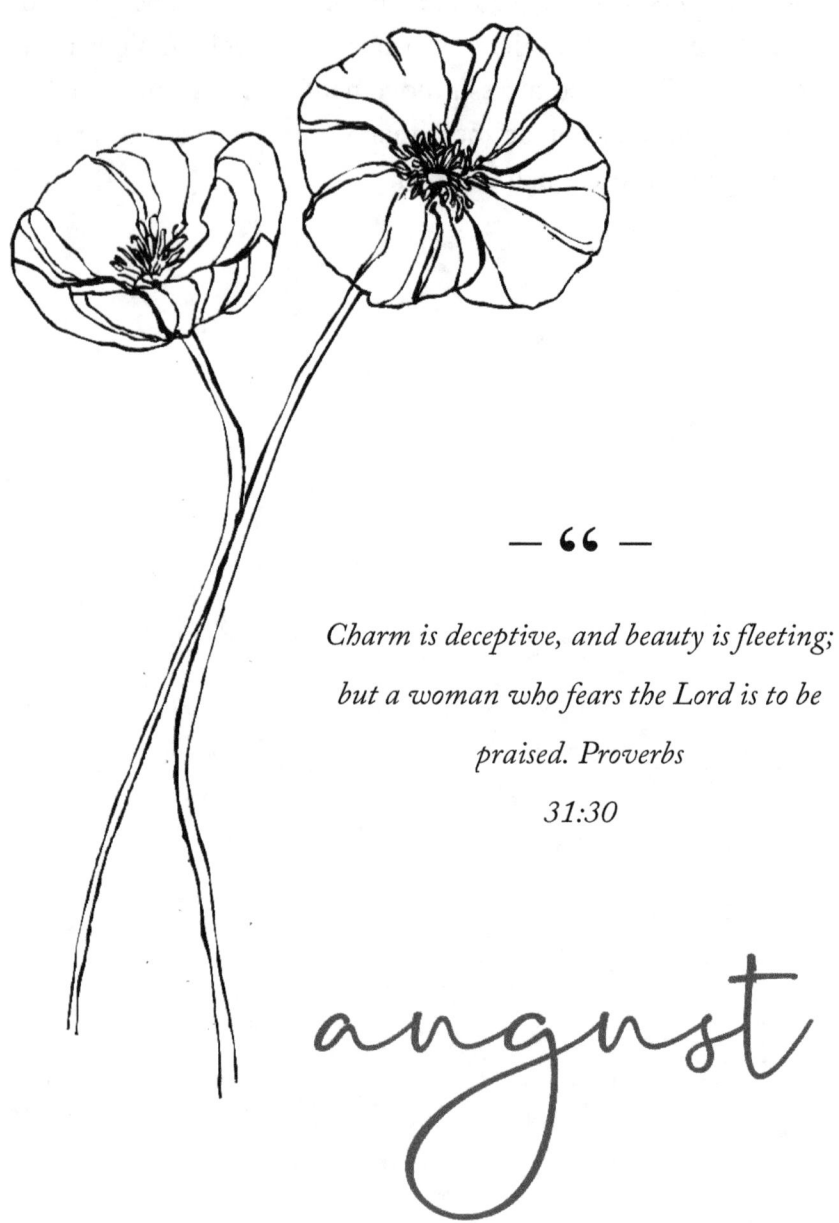

> *Charm is deceptive, and beauty is fleeting; but a woman who fears the Lord is to be praised. Proverbs 31:30*

august

August 1 ~ Female

My daughter asked if I had a cake mix. I told her yes, but no icing. Julie could not believe I would have one without the other. A cake mix plus icing is what makes a cake.

In Genesis chapter one, God tells us man was made in His image. The Hebrew word for man is Adam. This is the Hebrew word for humankind or human beings. So, when we are told God made man in His image, this verse includes females.

"So God created man in his own image, in the image of God he created him; male and female he created them" (Genesis 1:27).

God gives us a closer look at our creation in chapter two of Genesis. Adam was created by God, and Adam was the first man. God allowed him to name the animals and as Adam named them, he felt lonely. He could not find a suitable companion.

Our compassionate God caused Adam to fall into a deep sleep and took a rib from him to make a female counterpart. Does this mean that Adam lost part of who he was to Eve, creating two unique human beings? This is something to ponder.

Adam and Eve were blessed by God in chapter one, and He gave them an assignment.

"God blessed them and said to them. 'Be fruitful and increase in number, fill the earth and subdue it. Rule over the fish of the sea and the birds of the air and over every living creature that moves on the ground'" (Genesis 1:28).

The assignment God gave them was to be done together. You could say together they made a cake. One would be the cake mix while the other the icing. Both are equally necessary and important.

In chapter two, Adam uses a play on words when he says,

"This is bone of my bone and flesh of my flesh; she shall be called woman, for she was taken out of man" (Genesis 2:23).

The Hebrew word Adam used for woman was Issah, or female mate, and the Hebrew word *lys*, or male mate. God took one human being and made two counterparts out of the one so they could have someone to relate to, humanly speaking. Women are no less than men or no more, we are all uniquely human. We are made in the image of God and given an assignment from Him. Both males and females are needed to complete our roles.

Ponders of the Heart

Read 1 Corinthians 11:7-12.

Have you ever felt or made to feel you were not equal to men?

How does the Bible encourage you to be thankful you are a woman?

Prayers of the Heart

Dear Father,

I want to praise You for making me a woman. Lord, thank You for the women in my life who have been a blessing to me. I want to thank You for my grandmother, my mother, my daughters, granddaughters, and all the women of faith. Thank You for the ministry that is uniquely ours through our female make-up. Fill us with thankfulness as we live to please You. In Jesus' name, amen.

August 2 ~ Open Door and Open Heart

"Now Joshua the son of Nun sent out two men from Acacia Grove to spy secretly, saying, 'Go, view the land, especially Jericho.' So they went and came to the house of a harlot named Rahab and lodged there" (Joshua 2:1 NKJV).

Our first thought might be, or my first thought be, "Why are men sent out by God to spy the land staying in the house of a prostitute?" Could it have been because it was the only door open to these Israelites? They knew they would be welcomed, for harlots have what you might call an open-door policy.

Rahab was not just a harlot, she was an informed woman. She knew who they were and why they were there. The information she knew met an open heart, and this is a powerful combination in the hands of God.

She was a woman without a man to care for her, but this did not keep her from being a woman who cared for God's spies. She opened the doors of her house to these men as she opened her heart to their Lord. The trust and desire she had for the Lord was a great witness and comfort to the spies who were on a mission.

We see the way God used this woman to meet the needs of His men. She gave them shelter, protection, and escape. In return, she wanted God's people to show her His mercy.

This was a woman of action, faith, and willing to ask for mercy for herself and her family. I wonder if Rahab had tried to talk to God, or was she convinced a woman like herself was doomed to this life of sin? I am thankful she did not let her past decide her future.

Men had mistreated and shunned Rahab, yet God, in His mercy gave her a way out and she took it. She came out of her life of sin and joined the people of God. Rahab became part of the family of God. Adopted into the family of our Savior and recorded in the bloodline of Christ. Her opened door policy and open heart led her home.

As I read this story, I am thankful God shows us how He uses women mightily in His redemptive plan. We do have a wonderful place in His plan and His heart. You might say God has an open-door policy and an open heart for His creation. Let's be women who God can use. Women of action, faith, and willing to ask God for mercy. He is not only willing to use us, but this has been His plan from the beginning of time.

Ponders of the Heart

Do you believe He can use you?

What is something God is calling you to do for His glory?

Read Joshua 6:17, Hebrews 11:31, and Matthew 1:5.

Ask God to show you anything that is holding you back.

Prayers of the Heart

Dear Father,

Thank You for showing us by Your Word how women are included in Your plan. Thank You for Rahab's story. May it encourage us to be women of action, faith, and hope. Open our lives and the doors of our hearts to You and use us for Your glory. Lord, we love You. In Jesus' name, amen.

August 3 ~ Godly Wisdom and Courage

She was indeed a unique woman in a man's world, one who others came to for godly judgment. A prophetess and a woman of courage because when God spoke to her about war, she summoned Barak to raise an army to fight their enemies.

We might think Barak was a coward because when she told him to go and fight, he said he would go if she went with him. She agreed to go but told him a woman would take his glory for the death of Sisera, who was the commander of the enemy's army.

Deborah was her name, and you will find her story in Judges four and five. When she said a woman would take his glory, she was not talking about herself. It was Jael who would kill Sisera with a tent peg. She played a significant role which God called and equipped her for this time in history.

In her calling, Deborah was careful not to go beyond what God had called her to do. She went with Barak, instructed him on the strategy of the battle, but she was not a warrior. God had a job for Deborah and for Barak. She stayed focused on her mission by staying focused on God and instructed others to do the same.

I do not think Barak was a coward. He wanted Deborah there, for he realized God spoke to her, and he needed God's wisdom to win the war. She was filled with wisdom and courage. Never let someone keep you from God's call. He equips and uses His children who are willing to obey.

God can do what He likes, and He knows who is the best person for any job. But we also need to remember if He calls us to a place of leadership, He doesn't want us to step beyond our place. We are to stay focused on Him and help others do the same. John 15:5 tells us that apart from Him, we can do nothing.

Women with strong personalities are often made to feel there is something wrong with them, but God can use these women for His purposes.

Deborah was serving God by serving His people. She was not a woman trying to be a man. Devotion to God was her motive, and she wanted to give herself completely to His calling.

What a testimony for us. It is not likely we will be called to oversee a physical war, but we might be called to become prayer warriors for a spiritual one. We are part of His plan, but the victory is His. May our lives bring praise to His Holy name.

Ponders of the Heart

Has God ever given you clear directions in the war against sin?

Has God ever given you a word of encouragement or direction for someone?

Read Judges 4 and Hebrews 11:32-34.

Prayers of the Heart

Dear Father,

Thank You that our prayers have godly influence. Lord, teach us how to hear You, obey, and stay right where You put us. Help us move with You and not go beyond Your plan. Help us keep our focus. You are our God, and we are Your children. Father, keep us underneath Your wing of protection. Thank You, for women like

Deborah who can show us Your love for us and our value. In Jesus' name, amen.

August 4 ~ Sisters

Sisters come in varied sizes, styles, and personalities. My two girls are as different as night and day. Tracie is a very energetic, take-charge sort of girl. She loves sports, people, and taking naps. Julie, on the other hand, is quiet, full of wisdom, but a little passive aggressive. Even though Tracie is very vocal about what she thinks or feels, Julie is less verbal but more stubborn. Julie loves books and loves spending time with her family.

Tracie is sassy, and Julie is easygoing. Tracie is straightforward, our in-house fashion consultant, and a pushover if she hurts your feelings. Julie has an understanding ear, and she is the family's go-to girl for venting our woes. She is also the best aunt in the world to her siblings' children.

They have had a little trouble getting along. Sisters can be quite different. I know this by watching my girls and by God's Word.

"As Jesus and his disciples were on their way, he came to a village where a woman named Martha opened her home to him. She had a sister called Mary, who sat at the Lord's feet listening to what he said. But Martha was distracted by all the preparations that had to be made. She came to him and asked, 'Lord, don't you care that my sister has left me to do the work by myself? Tell her to help me!' 'Martha, Martha,' the Lord answered, 'you are worried and upset about many things, but few things are needed—or indeed only one. Mary has

chosen what is better, and it will not be taken away from her'" (Luke 10:38-42).

Jesus thought truth was more important than feelings. I wonder how well Martha took Jesus' rebuke about her excessive worry and "busyness?" Jesus was aware of the different personalities of Martha and Mary. He understood the quiet nature of one compared to the take-charge nature of the other. But personalities didn't take away the truth of what Jesus wanted for these sisters.

He wanted them to know and love Him as He loved them. Martha had the gift of hospitality, but this gift can throw you into a royal frenzy if you miss the presence of the Savior. Mary had a gift of sacrifice we see later in chapter 12 when she poured perfume at her Savior's feet.

"Here a dinner was given in Jesus' honor. Martha served, while Lazarus was among those reclining at the table with him. Then Mary took about a pint of pure nard, an expensive perfume; she poured it on Jesus' feet and wiped his feet with her hair. And the house was filled with the fragrance of the perfume" (John 12:2-3).

Martha is still serving while Mary uses her gift of sacrifice. Vastly different girls, sisters, who have come to know and love their Savior. I see different strengths and weaknesses in my girls, but both are special. Jesus, as well as their mother, wants them to appreciate their differences while they learn how to love one another and love God, who made them.

Ponders of the Heart

How different are the personalities in your family?

How can we learn to appreciate the different personalities and learn from them?

Read John 11:1-44.

Prayers of the Heart

Dear Father,

You make us so different. We have trouble with this, but You call us to work together and learn to appreciate our unique gifts and talents. Lord, help us value the people in our families. Today, I pray especially for all sisters. Help us see our family through Your eyes. Thank You for making us unique and for loving us. In Jesus' name, amen.

August 5 ~ Big Sisters or Little Mothers

Big sisters are usually on a mission of bossing little brothers. They really don't see it as bossing; they see it as being a co-mother. It comes out naturally. We can't help it. This instinct of mothering flows from us like cream from a pitcher.

When Randy, my little brother, came along, my mothering instincts kicked in. I was on a constant mission to watch out for him, partly because I wanted him safe and partly because I didn't want him to embarrass me.

Poor Randy had two mothers living under the same roof. I just wanted him safe, and I am not the only big sister who mothers their brothers.

Pharaoh was concerned about the vast population of the Israelites. He decided to have all the Hebrew boys killed at birth in order to slow down their growth. Moses was born during this time, and his parents saw he was a special child. They hid him as long as they could, but knew they had to let him go into God's hand. His mother made a little boat and laid it in the reeds of the riverbank.

Miriam, his big sister, was at the bank, "co-mothering" him by watching out for him. Pharaoh's daughter came to take a bath and discovered the baby. The Bible said she had compassion for him, and this was when Miriam stepped in to help.

"Then his sister asked Pharaoh's daughter, 'Shall I go and get one of the Hebrew women to nurse the baby for you? 'Yes, go,' she answered. So the girl went and got the baby's mother. Pharaoh's daughter said to her, 'Take this baby and nurse him for me, and I will pay you.' So the woman took the baby and nursed him. When the child grew older, she took him to Pharaoh's daughter and he became her son. She named him Moses, saying, 'I drew him out of the water'" (Exodus 2:7-10).

Excellent job, Miriam. You helped your little brother, and you helped your mother get her son back. I bet big sisters make great mothers unless, of course, they become smothering mothers. Always hiding in the bushes so they can see what is going on. Always making decisions for everyone. Watch out, big sisters; be sure you keep your helpful nature in God's control. Miriam had trouble later when she wasn't sure her little brother knew what he was doing.

She stepped out too far because her brother had become God's right-hand man. I guess Miriam was one of the reasons Moses spent 40 years on the back side of the desert. He needed to grow up. Big sisters, be good sisters but remember God intends for brothers to grow up and become men.

Ponders of the Heart

Read Numbers 12:1-16.

What lesson did you learn from the verses above?

How did Moses react to his sister and brother's criticism?

Prayers of the Heart

Dear Father,

We praise You for Your Word and how it reveals so much about us. I pray for family relationships today. You are Lord, not us. Help us seek Your wisdom and help us care for our families without becoming too big for our own good and theirs.

Father, families are under attack. We need Your love in us so we can love others. Protect us as we grow into the family of God. In Jesus' name, amen.

August 6 ~ Sister to Sister

The dictionary says a sister is a female offspring of one's parents or of one's father or mother. As we think about this definition, we can rejoice knowing if we are in Christ, then we are God's offspring. Therefore, we are sisters.

What does it mean to be an offspring of God? We will share family likenesses.

We received a new nature from our Heavenly Father, one that wants not worldly but spiritual things. Our perspective, purpose, and destiny change. Along with a desire to develop the same attitudes of Christ, our brother. Of course, this new family resemblance is "lived out" by fighting against our old way of living. We fight with faith and the power of the Holy Spirit. His job is to change us into the image of Jesus.

"Therefore if you have any encouragement from being united with Christ, if any comfort from his love, if any common sharing in the Spirit, if any tenderness and compassion, then make my joy complete by being like-minded, having the same love, being one in spirit and of one mind. Do nothing out of selfish ambition or vain conceit. Rather, in humility value others above yourselves, not looking to your own interests but each of you to the interests of the others" (Philippians 2:1-4).

What great verses to lead us into joyful, peaceful living with one another as sisters in Christ. We can rejoice with each other as we share the comfort of being loved by Christ and having the presence of His Spirit in us. We can come together as we let our new nature direct our minds and our hearts.

I love the part of the verse that reminds us not to be led astray by our selfish ambition and pride. But to celebrate His love and grace. For it was by grace, we were saved, and His grace will keep us. Therefore, we can look out for the interests of others. God has us covered. This chapter goes on with greater advice.

"Do everything without grumbling or arguing, so that you may become blameless and pure, "children of God without fault in a warped and crooked generation." Then you will shine among them like stars in the sky as you hold firmly to the word of life. And then I will be able to boast on the day of Christ that I did not run or labor in vain" (Philippians 2:14-16).

These verses I have marked in my Bible with a note to my children. This is my prayer for them because I know this is the secret to godly living.

A focus on Jesus unifies our differences and makes fellowship possible. God, our Father, wants His children to love and walk in fellowship with one another, just as I want this for my children. As we look at each other, I pray we will see our resemblance to Jesus and shine like the sun in our fallen world.

Ponders of the Heart

Do you have a sister or brother? How well do you get along?

How are we to treat one another as we ponder the verses below?

Read Philippians 2:5-11 and Philippians 3:8-11.

I am grateful Jesus shows us how to live and love one another.

Prayers of the Heart

Dear Precious Lord,

Help us hold on to Your Word. How we want to live in complete dependence on Your Spirit! Lord, may Your Words give us confidence in Your love and control so we can let go of selfishness and care about the interests of others. Thank You for giving us the desire to be like Your Son. Father, complete Your work in us. In Jesus' name, amen.

August 7 ~ Daughter-in-law

"Don't urge me to leave you or to turn back from you. Where you go I will go, and where you stay I will stay. Your people will be my people and your God my God" (Ruth 1:16).

Ruth was a gem when it came to loyalty and character. These qualities made her an exceptional daughter-in-law. When her husband died and her mother-in-law was left alone, Ruth decided to return to Israel with her. Ruth married her husband, his family and their God. I wonder how many marriages would still be intact today if other daughters-in-law learned from Ruth's story.

As a young bride, I had trouble with this. I was young, selfish, and often unsure about Bill's devotion to me. This lack of confidence caused me to be impatient as we grew together as husband and wife. I did not embrace and appreciate the gift of my husband's family.

After years of marriage, there were situations that helped open my eyes to my immaturity. My mother helped me with this. She understood that to love my husband meant to love his family. Once I was willing, the rest was easy.

I would consider my late mother-in-law as a dear friend and a sister in Christ. I am thankful she was part of my life and she felt the same way about me. The greatest thing we shared was our faith in Jesus, and the second greatest thing was our love for Bill.

Now that I am a mother-in-law, my desire is to be close to my daughter-in-law. I pray she feels loved and cherished. Our job is to respect and love one another and find our unity in our Savior, Jesus. The Lord puts people in our lives to love and to share life with them.

All these things are true if we trust Him. You might say, "You don't know my daughter-in-law." Or you might say, "You don't know my mother-in-law." Ah, but we can depend on the power of our Savior's love. He has loved us and poured His love into us so we can love others. Oh, that we would let His love flow into our families, even to our in-laws.

Ponders of the Heart

If you could ask Ruth a question, what would you ask her?

What about Naomi? Would you want tips on how to be a good mother-in-law?

Read Ruth 1 and 2.

Prayers of the Heart

Dear Father,

We are in awe of You. The more we know You, the more we want to know You. Lord, You work in our lives in so many ways. You have placed people in our lives to love, learn from, and grow with. We pray for humble, teachable spirits. We want to depend on You for direction and power to love those around us, especially those in our families. In Jesus' name, amen.

August 8 ~ Mothers

"And all those who heard it marveled at those things which were told them by the shepherds. But Mary kept all these things and pondered them in her heart" (Luke 2:18-19 NKJ).

The gallery app on my phone is full of memories with pictures that make my mind explode with special moments and melt my heart like marshmallows in hot chocolate. As I scroll through pictures of trips, birthday parties, weddings and pictures of faces that are no longer on this earth, I see my story.

I have a wall where each grandchild has a frame with their latest photo, and all the old photos are carefully stored behind the latest. On their birthdays, I take their frame down and hang each picture on the curtains around our eat-in kitchen. It is fun to see how they have grown and remember each stage.

This all began when my granddaughter, Bailey, turned sixteen. The other grandchildren wanted the same treatment, and being a grandmother who loves those kiddos, each grandchild has a picture gallery on their special day.

If it was possible, I would like to arrange the memories in my mind. One section would have facts I have learned over the years, facts about math, science, history, and common sense. I would have a file room full of Biblical facts I have studied and restudied during my years as a believer.

The next section will be about memories of experiences in my life. There would be childhood experiences. This room would be full of dust because I can't remember a lot about those days. I would need to spend time cleaning and sorting this part.

A very special room would be the experience of falling in love and dating Bill, our early years of marriage, and the long season of raising our children. In this room, I would sit on the floor of my mind and look at each moment, treasure some, regret others, and desire with all my heart to "do-over" some.

My memories can take me back in time, especially when someone shares a similar experience. It helps me know I am not alone and we share common stories.

When Collier, my first grandchild, was born, it reminded me of the day I became a mother. I looked around the hospital room and saw my three grown children. Faces of smiles, concern, and love.

There were my children, no signs of peanut butter on their faces. No wet pants, untied shoes, or sticky fingers, just three grown children who have stored boxes of memories already in my heart. Yes, mothers ponder the lives of their children.

Mary was a mother, just like all mothers. She was thinking of the days behind and the days ahead. These cherished moments she would ponder forever. She was storing memories and making room in her heart for more to come. Her Son, Jesus, would one day be her Savior. He would one day take away the sins of the world, and in the process, her heart would break.

Jesus' mother would hope, pray and love Him just like we love our children. Being a mother is wonderful, but can you imagine what it was like for Mary to be the mother of the Son of God?

Ponders of the Heart

What is your favorite memory as a child?

If you are a wife or mother, what is your favorite family memory?

Read Luke 2:15-20.

This would be a good time for us to pray for our children.

Prayers of the Heart

Dear Father,

We thank You that nothing can separate us from Your love. (Romans 8:38-39.) We pray, Your children, that we will live righteous lives and remember the price You paid for our salvation. Father, we praise You and pray that You shall supply all our needs according to Your riches in glory in Jesus Christ (Philippians 4:19). In Jesus' name, amen.

August 9 ~ Grandmothers

My good friend, Nancy, told me being a grandmother was wonderful. She showed pictures and told stories and even her email address, big mama, let you know everything she said, she lived. I watched Nancy, and in my heart, I kept waiting for the day I would join the Universal Club of Grandmothers.

As a young wife I was not sure I would like being a mother, but now I know it is a great joy. But still, what about being a grandmother? Would I love it and be good at it? I just didn't know.

Naomi came home a defeated woman. She was bitter, and she wanted the women of the town to call her Mara, which means bitter. Her life had not turned out the way she imagined. Naomi could not see past her pain and disappointment.

She had given up on God and on blessings coming her way. Naomi was in survival mode until her days of life ended. Her circumstances were not very promising, but her God was full of promises, and He was able to follow through. His ways were bigger, and His thoughts were higher than hers. He works like that in our lives.

"The women said to Naomi: 'Praise be to the Lord, who this day has not left you without a guardian-redeemer. May he become famous throughout Israel! He will renew your life and sustain you in your old age. For your daughter-in-law, who loves you and who is better to you than seven sons, has given him birth.' Then Naomi took the child in her arms and cared for him" (Ruth 4:14-17).

When Naomi became a grandmother, the grandmothers in Naomi's town didn't dare call her Mara. They knew what a blessing she had received, causing them to praise God. I imagine Naomi and her friends dancing in the street with tambourines, singing praise songs with faces full of joy as their skirts blew in the wind. He had given Naomi a grandson, and He would renew her desire to live.

He would be a delight and sustain her in her old age. There was even the thought he might be famous, and he was. He was the great-great-grandfather of King David, who was in the bloodline of our Lord. Naomi didn't know little Obed future, but he was enough to put a smile on her face and renew her purpose in life.

The second Collier was born, I became a loving grandma. I loved being one, and I am also good at it. Oh, but don't call me grandma; just call me GiGi. That's what Collier calls me, and when he calls me, I come.

As I delight in my role as grandmother, I pray for his future and pray he will be a man after God's own heart. My prayer for my grandson is God will draw him close. I hope to be a seed planter in his life, one who plants the knowledge and the love of God in his heart.

My work and desire as a grandmother have increased because I now have six grandchildren: four granddaughters and two grandsons. This is my chance to show them my love for God and His love for them. What a story I have to share, the story of Jesus.

If you are a grandmother, reevaluate your role in your grandchildren's lives. Be a seed planter for God in their tender souls. You might be a grandmother-in-waiting. Decide now to plant the love of Jesus in their lives. This is our chance for a "do-over" in the lives of our children's children.

What a gift God gives us in our old age: the gift of grandchildren. Bill says it is great to be a granddad, but I think being a grandmother is greater. Praise the Lord for the gift of being a woman.

Ponders of the Heart

Did your grandmother influence your life?

If you are a grandmother or will be one soon, how do you plan to plant seeds of faith in their hearts?

Read 2 Timothy 1:3-7.

Prayers of the Heart:

Dear Father,

I want to thank You for the gift of being a grandmother. I want to be a vessel to plant into the tender souls of my grandchildren, Your great love. Father, my prayer is my grandchildren will be Yours and they will love You with all their hearts. Fill me with Your Spirit, so I have influence that points them to You. In Jesus' name, amen.

August 10 ~ Widows

Some of the remarkable women I know are widows. I look at them, and I marvel at the joy, the peace, and the faith they have. I say remarkable because their Lord has been their joy, their peace, and He has been the object of their faith. These women are my heroes. They are the ones who have faced adversity and survived victoriously in the Lord.

I am sure they have bad days; they are on this journey called life, just like all of us, and yet I see the strength of the Lord in them. I encounter the depth of their dependency on God, and they show me how faithful Jesus is to His children.

We have widows in Scripture who show us deep commitment and character. The poor widow who puts in two mites (Luke 21:1-4) and Anna who recognized Jesus in the temple. (Luke 2:36-38).

"There was also a prophet, Anna, the daughter of Penuel, of the tribe of Asher. She was very old; she had lived with her husband seven years after her marriage, and then was a widow until she was eighty-

four. She never left the temple but worshiped night and day, fasting and praying" (Luke 2:36-37).

I'm not sure if the passage is telling us she was a widow for 84 years or she was 84 years old, I think, probably the latter, but regardless, she was a widow who was using her life to praise and seek the Lord. God is not blind to such faith or is it that such faith and dependence produce eternal perspective? She was prepared and available to recognize and know Jesus even before He said one word or did one miracle. She was in touch with the deep things of God.

She reminds me of some widows I know, women who have a thirst, hunger, and a lifestyle that is prepared to recognize and receive the things of God.

The generous widow in Luke 21 gave all she had because she knew all she had belonged to God, her provider.

"As Jesus looked up, he saw the rich putting their gifts into the temple treasury. He also saw a poor widow put in two very small copper coins. 'Truly I tell you,' he said, "this poor widow has put in more than all the others. All these people gave their gifts out of their wealth; but she out of her poverty put in all she had to live on'" (Luke 21:1-4).

These widows had learned God was all they needed, for God was all they had. This is a hard lesson for us, but to know the Lord with such confidence must be freeing and glorious.

Ponders of the Heart

Read Matthew 6:33, 1 Timothy 4:8, and Mark 4:3-8, 13-20.

What are the things we depend on instead of God?

What promises do you see in these verses that change who or what you depend on?

Prayers of the Heart

Dear Father,

We thank You for Your faithfulness and how You care for Your children. We want to walk in faith and not in sight. We want to know and believe that You are our provision and our very lives. Father, we thank You for the witnesses we have in Your Word and those in our lives. Lord, we love You. In Jesus' name, amen.

August 11 ~ Elizabeth

My mom is one of ten children, and she has four sisters. These ladies were special role models for me. If I were in trouble and needed refuge from the world, they would be there to help me, and my mom would trust them to do so.

We cannot be sure Elizabeth was Mary's aunt, but from Luke 1:36 we know she was a relative. The genealogy from Luke 3:23-28 is considered Mary's genealogy on her father's side. Since Elizabeth was a descendant of Aaron, Mary's relationship with Elizabeth would be on her mother's side.

If Elizabeth was Mary's mother's sister, it is reasonable to see why Mary would seek refuge there. She might have wanted to verify what the angel said about Elizabeth's pregnancy. But regardless, Mary knew she would be welcome.

I understood things about my aunts. First, they knew my mother and loved her, but they also knew she could be a pill to live with. They were special ladies because they loved me as their sister's child and were willing to be a go-between for Mom and me.

Can you imagine the conflict Mary's mother must have felt when she found out her daughter was pregnant, not married and claiming she was pregnant by the Holy Spirit? What a mighty role Elizabeth played in confirming for Mary the work of God in her life.

"When Elizabeth heard Mary's greeting, the baby leaped in her womb, and Elizabeth was filled with the Holy Spirit. In a loud voice she exclaimed: 'Blessed are you among women, and blessed is the child you will bear! But why am I so favored, that the mother of my Lord should come to me?'" (Luke 1:41-43).

"Wow! Thank you, Aunt Elizabeth. I needed confirmation, understanding and someone who believed me." Mary must have felt those feelings after Elizabeth's confirmation. Once someone understood, she felt free to express the praise that had been bottled up inside her.

If you are an aunt, what a blessed role you can have with your nieces and nephews. You can be a relative who understands what it is like to live with their mother or father. This special connection could be like the one we see with Elizabeth and Mary. God is good.

Ponders of the Heart

If you were in Mary's place, who would you confide in?

If you were Mary's mother, how do you think you would react to Mary's news?

Read Luke 1:39-56.

Mary, Joseph, and Mary's mother were people just like us. They had pressures, expectations, emotions, doubts, and fears.

Prayers of the Heart

Dear Father,

Your care is beyond what we can imagine. Your perfect plan is for our good and encouragement. Lord, help us be people who love and encourage others, especially those in our families. Help us allow You to use us as vessels of encouragement and support for others. Lord, use every role we have as women to bring You glory. Again, Lord, we proclaim we love You. In Jesus' name, amen.

August 12 ~ The Good, Bad, and Ugly

Which are you? I wish I could say I am good, but I can be all three. This reminds me of a nursery rhyme about a little girl who was very good except when she was horrid.

This would be a description of me. I can act good and sometimes horrible. I said act. This isn't who I am; it is just how I act. Thanks to Jesus, He has made me righteous.

Michal was the daughter of King Saul. She had saved David from her dad. King Saul must have thought how bad, while David must have thought how good. Later, Michal proved to be bad and somewhat ugly in her ability to understand her husband's heart for God.

In 2 Samuel, David is victorious in bringing the Ark of the Covenant back into the city of Jerusalem. This was a mountaintop experience for him. As David came into the city, his joy before the Lord caused him to dance in the streets in his ephod, which is a fancy name for underwear.

David's wife, Michal, watched from the window of the palace. She was not impressed. She felt such emotionalism brought shame to her and David's position as king. I can see her point, can't you? Well, we are wrong, for God was pleased by David's display of dancing and joy.

"Now as the ark of the Lord came into the City of David, Michal, Saul's daughter, looked through a window and saw King David leaping and whirling before the Lord; and she despised him in her heart" (2 Samuel 6:16 NKJV).

Notice in the passage above she is called Saul's daughter and not David's wife. Is it because she is acting like her father and not like David's wife? She is being driven by family pride instead of joy in the Lord. She despised David in her heart just like King Saul had. God allows her to know she has missed the mark:

"Then David returned to bless his household. And Michal the daughter of Saul came out to meet David, and said, 'How glorious was the king of Israel today, uncovering himself today in the eyes of the maids of his servants, as one of the base fellows shamelessly

uncovers himself!' So David said to Michal, 'It was before the Lord, who chose me instead of your father and all his house, to appoint me ruler over the people of the Lord, over Israel. Therefore I will play music before the Lord. And I will be even more undignified than this, and will be humble in my own sight. But as for the maidservants of whom you have spoken, by them I will be held in honor.' Therefore Michal the daughter of Saul had no children to the day of her death" (2 Sam. 6:20-23 NKJV).

No doubt pride makes us bad, and we act ugly. My husband has seen the worst of me. When I was a newly married woman, I threw our Sony television out the window because I did not want Bill to watch a boxing match. I was such a brat. Thinking I was right to do such a dumb thing. I have grown up, but still, there have been times I have rolled my eyes at him in frustration and stuck out my tongue when he made me mad.

There are other things I could confess, like how my mouth has gotten me in real trouble. But nothing I have ever done is more awful than when I judge him with a prideful heart.

What a warning to wives and husbands to not let our family pride or selfishness keep us from rejoicing in the Lord. Like David, we should not think too highly of ourselves. But dancing in the street in my underwear, I don't know. Maybe if the Spirit filled my soul.

Ponders of the Heart

Has pride kept you from praising the Lord with all your heart?

How do we find freedom to praise the Lord?

Read Proverbs 11:2, Philippians 2:1-4, and Philippians 4:4.

Prayers of the Heart

Dear Father,

We pray to be wives who rejoice in the Lord, especially when we see our husbands rejoicing. If only Michal had humbled herself and rejoiced with her husband, what a difference this would have made. She would have been known as David's wife and not King Saul's daughter. Lord, may our hearts always rejoice in You and recognize Your joy in others. In Jesus' name, amen.

August 13 ~ Good Wife, Bad Husband

"When Abigail went to Nabal, he was in the house holding a banquet like that of a king. He was in high spirits and very drunk. So she told him nothing at all until daybreak. Then in the morning, when Nabal was sober, his wife told him all these things, and his heart failed him and he became like a stone. About ten days later, the Lord struck Nabal and he died" (1Samuel 25:36-38).

It is very hard to find a good wife in the Bible. As wives we need Jesus in control of our hearts. Of course, this is true for all people. We might think we are superior to men. The Bible proves us wrong; we have all sinned and come short of the glory of God.

In our focus passage, Abigail was an exceptional wife, married to a very foolish man named Nabal. In fact, his name means fool, and he lived up to this description.

David sent men to Nabal, asking for bread, water, and meat. He claims ignorance of knowing who David was. He was not about to share with the newly elected king. Nabal's servants, knowing the danger he had placed them in, turned to Abigail, his wife.

She responded with wise actions and stopped David from getting revenge, saving the lives of her husband, his servants and herself. Then, with respect for her husband Abigail confessed her action. Nabal's heart hardened; instead of yielding and confessing his ignorance, he became like a stone.

I wonder how often Abigail had prayed for her husband and how, time after time, God gave him an opportunity to really look at his life. Yet, he turned in pride and refused to accept the responsibility for his own foolishness.

Abigail had done her part and God did the rest. She had been an instrument sent by God to turn David from revenge. David responded as a man who loved God. Abigail was also an instrument sent by God to Nabal to turn him from his prideful foolishness and he responded with a stone-cold heart. The result for him was a final judgment.

Nabal had been given a good, faithful, and wise wife. He was a wicked, foolish man and husband. God gives us chances to listen, but He will finally allow us to self-destruct. God honored Abigail by removing an unmovable husband and giving her a new one.

"Then David sent word to Abigail, asking her to become his wife. His servants went to Carmel and said to Abigail, 'David has sent us to you to take you to become his wife.' She bowed down with her face to the ground and said, 'I am your servant and am ready to serve you and wash the feet of my lord's servants'" (1 Samuel 25:39-41).

A good wife was found in the middle of a bad circumstance, yet she allowed God to use her, and she played a significant role in His work. Abigail lived in a time when a woman could not be single and survive, so when judgment fell on Nabal, God provided a new husband, King David.

Bad husbands don't excuse us to be bad wives. In fact, it may be the very soil God uses to transform us into women who depend on Him. As I place the desire to be a "good" wife on myself and on you, remember our goodness is found by the supernatural Spirit of the Lord working through us.

Ponders of the Heart

How does Abigail's life challenge you to depend on God?

How does Abigail's life show you God is faithful in hard circumstances?

Read 1 Samuel 25:1-44.

The verses above are a great story of God's protective love and provision for His child.

Prayers of the Heart

Dear Father,

I want to be a godly wife. One who loves, respects, and serves her husband. When my husband acts contrary to who he is, help me to be kind and loving. Lord, may my actions and my love spur my husband in his walk with You. You are my strength and my refuge. You are my provider and my protector.

Lord, may we take each special relationship You have placed in our lives and be faithful. Help us be living witnesses for You. In Jesus' name, amen.

August 14 ~ Beauty, Courage, and Prayers

"Go, gather together all the Jews who are in Susa, and fast for me. Do not eat or drink for three days, night or day. I and my attendants will fast as you do. When this is done, I will go to the king, even though it is against the law. And if I perish, I perish" (Esther 4:16).

How many arguments could be avoided if wives would fast and pray before speaking their minds to their husbands? Family decisions would have divine directions if we took the time to fast and pray with our husbands. It blows my mind to think how often I have missed opportunities in my life because I did not pray.

Prayer is the beginning of courage, wisdom and Christ-like living. I can't think of another place where prayer is more needed than in the relationships between husbands and wives.

As I listen to issues between spouses, I picture two little Boston Bulldogs pulling at different ends of a rope. They pull and tug until you think they are going to pull each other's teeth out. The best way to win a tug of war is to let go of the rope. When the tension is gone, the battle is over. The one who lets go is left standing, and the other one ends up on their bottom. Landing on our bottom hurts and has a way of humbling us.

I wish more wives or husbands would let go of their wills and seek the Lord in prayer. With the tension gone, the tug of war, or should I say the tug of will, God is free to bring about His plan and will. He will supply wisdom and understanding. Maybe we will be able to look at the situation with clearer eyes and laugh at ourselves.

Esther was a praying wife. She had won the king's heart with her external beauty, but it was her internal beauty that gave her the praying heart. She was asked to put her life on the line for her people, but before she risked it all, she needed to know her life, her plan, and her people were yielded to the will of God. She was a woman who was dependent on the Lord. She did not act on her own.

A woman of faith must also be a woman of prayer, for you cannot have one without the other. Esther realized this and before she went against the law of the day, she needed to know she surrendered to a higher law, the will of her God.

I have heard it said that, as women, our sinful nature is an independent spirit. We do not see this in Esther. She is not flippant about her plan, nor does she presume on the Lord. She prayerfully responds to the challenge before her with grace and beauty as she approaches her husband with honor and respect. She relied on God to deal with her husband's heart.

You might not be married to a king, but you can respect your husband as if he were. Who knows, he might just surprise you and begin to act with the character and courage of one, especially if you are giving your request to the Lord in prayer. Maybe if we acted more like queens, with quiet grace, our husbands might treat us more like one.

Reverence for the role of husband and respect for our roles as wives can make living together a life of mutual admiration. This is a choice we can make, and with this choice, everyone wins.

Ponders of the Heart

What burden do you have for the church? Have you prayed?

Are there things you need to talk over with your husband?

What do you need to learn from Queen Esther?

Read Esther 4:1-9:32. It is a great story; you will love it.

Prayers of the Heart

Dear Father,

As wives, help us respect our husbands. We come to pray for our marriages. Lord, help us pray and yield to You when it comes to our husbands. May we treat them with respect and love. We pray our words will be kind, wise, honest and loving. Lord, may we never forget what a privilege it is to be a wife and an honor to be Your child. Teach us to seek Your will and Your way, and counsel us in all areas of our lives. In Jesus' name, amen.

August 15 ~ Coming Home

The book, "Where Yesterday Lives," by Karen Kingsbury, is a story about five children coming home to bury their fifty-year-old father. These children had been close as children, but as adults, they had drifted from one another.

They had an event in their past that had affected each of them in different ways. The decisions made by each child and the effects these events had molded who they were and how they related to each other.

Traveling back home made them come face to face with who they had become. The funeral was a special day in the book. Sounds strange that I would say their father's funeral was special, but it was. They each had prepared a eulogy to express who their father was to them and what he had meant in their lives. It was through the eulogies that peace and reconciliation occurred. Ellen, the oldest child and the one I thought had the best relationship with her dad read her eulogy last.

In her eulogy, she expressed the insight she was given about her dad from her siblings. She did not know he was Amy's hero, or her brother told his deepest secrets to his dad as they played golf. Her view of her brother was he did not confide in anyone. Jane, her sister, endured a childhood trauma and felt her dad had not been there for her. No one was aware of this trauma. It was her dad's love and prayers that brought her brother, Marty, home.

She thanked her siblings for letting her see a fuller picture of their dad. It was like seeing him for the first time through their eyes. Her dad was able to love and support each child without being exclusive. He had loved and ministered to each of them just as he had to her. She wondered how she could have been so blind, so selfish.

As I reflected on this family's special day, I realized I could stray from my sisters and brothers in Christ. I can take an event and perceive or make wrong decisions about myself or others and God.

I need interdependent living, and independent living can take me off the narrow road of grace and love.

There is fullness of God I can only discover in the lives and hearts of others. We are unique people, and God deals with us uniquely. He is an individual God as well as a God with a large family. He loves us intimately, but not exclusively. He is visible in our lives and in the lives of His other children. We miss parts of God when we lose sight of Him in others.

"As a prisoner for the Lord, then, I urge you to live a life worthy of the calling you have received. Be completely humble and gentle; be patient, bearing with one another in love. Make every effort to keep the unity of the Spirit through the bond of peace. There is one body and one Spirit, just as you were called to one hope when you were called; one Lord, one faith, one baptism; one God and Father of all, who is over all and through all and in all" (Ephesians 4:1-6).

Ponders of the Heart

What is one important thing you have learned from other believers?

How well do you remember that God loves you intimately but not exclusively?

Read Ephesians 3:14-19.

Prayers of the Heart

Dear Father,

I love the fact that You know us through and through. Lord, we can only know a small part of You, so help us draw together so we can share what we know and our unique experiences with one another. You deal with us so intimately and You teach us through Your Spirit and through Your family. We can't wait to be with You and share together all You are and all You have done. In Jesus' name, amen.

August 16 ~ Plans

My daughter, Tracie, had big plans. She wanted to move far away from us to attend school. She was convinced distance from us meant freedom and boundless joy for her and thought maybe Alaska would be a good choice.

She was in the ninth or tenth grade at the time and had embraced the lie that we were her enemy, the killjoy of her life. There are children who feel this way about their parents. It is one of the great lies of this age.

We might laugh or shake our heads in amazement that she would feel this way, but if we were truthful, we could treat God the same way. In Psalm 2:1, David asks the question, "Why do the nations conspire against the Lord?" He also tells us in Psalm 2:3:

"Let us break their chains and throw off their shackles."

The nations plot against the rule of the Lord, and they want to be free from Him. Not only nations but also families and individuals.

Do we want to make our own plans and rules? We might say we do not want freedom from God, but our lives reveal something different. We are told God laughs at our plans and tells us He has confirmed His King, Jesus. There can be no other King. Like Tracie, in our immaturity, we can fail to recognize who the real enemy is. When we try to live our plans, we are rebelling against our biggest refuge, God. He is our wisdom, strength, and compassionate Lord.

God is not the killjoy of our lives; He is our joy and not our enemy. He is our great provider and protector. Jesus is worthy to be King. God established His King, and all plans contrary to this truth will fail. Thank goodness.

The Psalms warn the rulers of the earth and the kings of this world that they will bow down to Jesus. They are warned to yield to His sovereign rule.

"Kiss his son, or he will be angry and your way will lead to your destruction, for his wrath can flare up in a moment. Blessed are all who take refuge in him" (Psalm 2:12).

Tracie has learned her parents are her biggest supporters. We now live down the street from her, and she is thankful we are there. She is confident that we are on her side. What about us? Do we believe that God is for us and not against us?

Apart from God, life is meaningless. Our great enemy and our bondage come not from God but from the father of lies and the selfishness of our flesh. Thank goodness God is patient with us, but let us heed the warning in Psalm two and kiss the Son, taking refuge in Him.

Ponders of the Heart

When you were young, did you believe your parents were killjoys?

Do you know those who think God is a killjoy?

How can we help them?

Read Psalm 2:1-12.

Prayers of the Heart

Dear King Jesus,

We bow before You with praise and honor. You are our great refuge and our hope. Lord, we want to embrace Your plans, not ours, and we want to proclaim You as Sovereign King of our lives. Thank

You for the patience You show us in our immaturity. Thank You for Your great mercy and grace. Lord, we love You! In Jesus' name, amen.

August 17 ~ Foes

"Lord, how many are my foes! How many rise up against me! Many are saying of me, 'God will not deliver him'" (Psalm 3:1-2).

David had enemies and rivals who wanted to be king, but no foe could hurt worse than his own son. Absalom wanted his father's throne. As David's oldest son, people assumed he would one day be king, but David looked to God's will not his son's.

The betrayal of another person is hard, the betrayal of a friend is cruel, but that of a family member is devastating. This destruction comes in different degrees. It can be over words spoken in private and spoken in public. Deceitfulness can be done by a person, over a place or things. All betrayal hurts and destroys, but for David the biggest failure of all would be betraying God.

Absalom was blind to the authority in which David ruled. David's kingship was not his to give away, even to his son. His kingship was given to him by God, so it belonged to the King of kings, not to David. Absalom didn't care he was determined to take what he felt was rightfully his.

We are told in the Bible that Absalon was handsome and a leader. He had a palace and riches beyond compare and yet he wanted more. His betrayal and disloyalty to his father was soaked in his own selfish heart.

How often do we see this in our world? The more we have it seems the more we want. It makes me wonder, when is enough, enough?

God has blessed me more in my life than I could ever imagine, and yet I can get the "I wants" in a New York minute. So can my children and my grandchildren. In America, we forget too often we were to be one nation under God, blessed to be a blessing. We forget as believers; all we have in this world has been given to us by God and belongs to Him.

Absalom was unfaithfulness to God. He wanted to rule himself and others. As much as this betrayal grieved David, he stood steadfast knowing the crown was in God's hand not his.

As a parent, I want my children to be blessed, but there is only one King. My hope for myself and for those I love is to bow before our King Jesus with gratefulness and not to betray Him.

We all fail and make poor choices, and at times, we want to rule ourselves and others. I am aware of my own failures as a Christian and a parent. David must have felt he had failed his son. If you are a parent, you can relate to what he was feeling. I sure can.

David gave his wounded heart to God. His devotion to the Lord was stronger than any other loyalty in his life even to his own children. His heart was fully devoted to God. He had learned that God was ruler, and He had the final word.

Foes can come as close as family members. They can be the ones we have given our very best love, but we owe our deepest love and devotion to King Jesus, the Lord. This is a strong statement for us when we decide we want to control our own lives. Wasn't this the sin of Eve? Oh, what a lesson to learn from Eve and Absalom not to take our focus and heart away from God, but to be loyal to Him like King David was.

"I lie down and sleep; I wake again, because the Lord sustains me. I will not fear though tens of thousands assail me on every side" (Psalm 3:5-6).

Ponders of the Heart

Have you experienced pain from betrayal?

Do you know God can heal your pain and give you His peace?

Read Psalm 3.

Prayers of the Heart

Dear Father,

We can feel like David, surrounded by enemies. We have felt betrayed by those we love and have given so much to. You are our deliverer and peace. We long to rest in You. Take these burdens and fears for only You can sustain us in times of trials and troubles. We join with Christian parents everywhere and pray for our children and our children's children. Lord, give us contented hearts. We belong to You, King Jesus. In Jesus' name, amen.

August 18 ~ Safety

Hear me when I call, O God of my righteousness! You have relieved me in my distress; Have mercy on me, and hear my prayers" (Psalm 4:1 NKJV).

Bill and I played a game with our children and our grandchildren where we chased them, and they ran squealing into the other one's arms for safety. I usually chased them, and they usually ran to Bill for safety.

It was a game, but you would think they were in serious trouble the way they would run as fast as they could and squeal so loud. Safety came when they leaped into Bill's arms. If this wasn't a game and I really wanted to hurt them, they would be wise to run to him for safety. He is bigger and stronger than I am, and he could protect them.

David was a strong leader, the king of Israel. He had warriors, but he knew where his safety rested. His relationship with God is shown so clearly in the Psalms. He ran to God much like our children and grandchildren ran to Bill.

We read in the Psalms how David depended on the Lord, time and time again. He humbled himself knowing God would answer his prayers. He might have been king, but David's King was the Lord. God was his refuge, and his strength. He knew his righteousness was found in the Lord and when he cried for mercy God answered his call. He was David's deliverance.

David even marveled at the persistence of men to shame him, and he wondered at how peoples of the earth loved worthless things instead of loving the God of mercy and love. He knew the Lord loved him and could be trusted. This brought great joy into David's life and into his heart, even during great anguish.

"Fill my heart with joy when their grain and new wine abound. In peace I will lie down and sleep, for you alone, Lord, make me dwell in safety" (Psalm 4:7-8).

God is faithful to His own; there is safety in this truth. He is merciful and answers the prayers of His children; we find comfort in His faithfulness. We can cry out to the Lord, knowing He is a good Father that comes to the aid of His children. But we must wait for His perfect timing and trust that His ways are perfect. Oh, for us to trust and praise Him more.

Ponders of the Heart

Do you have a hard time understanding how people think?

Do you need to stop right now and give God praise for His mercy and love?

Read Psalm 4:1-8.

Prayers of the Heart

Dear Father,

Hear our call for help, we need Your mercy. There are times when it feels like the whole world is out to get us. In fact, the world is against Your children. Help us to lie down and rest knowing You not only are willing to help us, but You are also able. There is nothing too hard for You and You care about us. Lord, make our hearts glad and our lives sure. There is none like You. In Jesus' name, amen.

August 19 ~ Love Your Enemies

"You have heard that it was said, 'Love your neighbor and hate your enemy.' But I tell you, love your enemies and pray for those who persecute you, that you may be children of your Father in heaven. He

causes his sun to rise on the evil and the good, and sends rain on the righteous and the unrighteous. (Matt. 5:43-45).

Lord, it's impossible to love, pray, and do good to those who hate, use, and persecute me. If I do, they will destroy me. I must take care of myself, shouldn't I? All these thoughts come into my mind when I am in the middle of being hurt and used.

But I have seen God empower people to rise above what is humanly possible. I was talking to a young woman, let me call her Jane. She has shown me the power of God in her life. She was a victim of a woman who stole her husband, and now this woman shares time with her children. You would think this other person would be satisfied, but not so. She continues to persecute Jane. She even uses Jane's children.

As this young woman shared about a particular situation that had occurred, she was very insightful about what to do. Jane said she prayed for this woman because she believed she would be an influence on her children. She was more concerned about her children than the persecution she was experiencing. Jane told me she encouraged her children to love this stepmom because she was their dad's wife. Wow! This is not insightful; it is supernatural.

God has done a work in her heart. I do not believe she is naive; Jane knows this woman is her enemy. She feels the pain of her persecution, but she has been empowered by God to pray for one who hates her and spitefully tries to use her.

King David was also empowered by God to love his enemies and pray for them. These are the words of his heart toward his enemies:

"Be angry, and do not sin. Meditate within your heart on your bed, and be still. (Selah) Offer the sacrifices of righteousness, and put your trust in the LORD" (Psalm 4:4-5 NKJV).

When David told his enemies not to be angry the Hebrew word means to be disturbed, be afraid, be in awe of God's power and protection, but don't sin. Be still and let God reveal to you what you are doing and repent in your heart. Sacrifice or give yourself to acts of righteousness by placing your trust in the LORD.

David is praying for his enemies to repent, yield and trust God. He prays for those who hate him and are persecuting him. He is praying for them to come to know the Lord and be saved.

Again, I say, "This is impossible!" Is it? Only one who knows God and is allowing the Holy Spirit to fill his soul will be able to pray and respond to his enemy like this. Oh, the power and the wonder of the Holy Spirit in the life of a child of God.

David knew, Jane knows, that the best peace from persecution comes when their enemies come into fellowship with God.

Ponders of the Heart

Do you pray for those who try to hurt you?

Who do you need to pray for today with the power of the Spirit God has given you?

Read Colossians 3:1-11.

Prayers of the Heart

Dear Father,

You are my power to live beyond the old man. You are the reason we can rise above the mire of this world and love even our enemies. Lord, we pray You will give us passion to forgive those who hurt us, pray for those who persecute us, and to love others as You have loved us. We need Your Spirit to transform us into the person You redeemed us to be. In Jesus' name, amen.

August 20 ~ Seeking God in the Morning

What is the first thing you think in the morning? If you are like me, those thoughts can vary. Sometimes, I wake up thinking about the task before me, or that my back hurts. I always think, "I need coffee."

My favorite way to wake up is to sing a song of praise to the Lord. There are days Bill wakes me up, or I'm awakened by the clanging of the alarm clock. I wake up thinking, "No, not morning already."

I have concluded I really have little control over those first thoughts in the morning, but after I am awake, I have choices to make.

Max Lucado, in his book Grace for the Moment, says, "Because of Calvary, I'm free to choose. And so, I choose."

He says he chooses love, joy, peace, patience, kindness, goodness, faithfulness, gentleness, and self-control. He lists each choice and his reasoning for deciding these choices. Yet he knows he is only able to decide on the fruit of the Spirit because the Spirit dwells in him. He decides to love God and what God loves. Problems he faces in life, are an opportunity to experience God. I love this quote from his book:

"I am a spiritual being. After this body is dead, my spirit will soar. I refuse to let what will rot, rule the eternal."

It is such comfort to know that Christ has given us the freedom to decide. It is always easier for me to make good choices in the morning before the day tries to take my focus. In Psalm 5:3, David puts it this way:

"In the morning, Lord, you hear my voice; in the morning I lay my requests before you and wait expectantly."

I imagine there were days when David's first thought was on his task as king of Israel. He, like me and you, had little control over his first thought in the morning, but after that, He chose to seek his God.

Ponders of the Heart

What is the first thing you do in the morning?

What are the promises we can experience by seeking the Lord in the morning? Go ahead; make a list.

Read Colossians 3:1-11.

Prayers of the Heart

Dear Father,

How we seek You this day. We seek Your mercy and Your grace. Lord, we offer praise to You. Our joy is found in You. Help us direct our hearts toward You every day. We choose You. In Jesus' name, amen.

August 21 ~ The Heart of the Matter

"You are never a great man when you have more mind than heart." (Beauchene).

Why is it, after fifty-four-something years of marriage, he still makes my heart jump? This is a man whose dirty socks I wash, clean his bathroom, and wake up to his morning breath. How can it be he still creates such emotion in me?

It is a matter of the heart. We have a wonderful marriage because we have more heart toward one another than mind. I don't try to figure out why I love him so much; I just do.

Here is a quote on my wall that describes my thoughts about our marriage:

"Every love story is beautiful, but ours is my favorite."

The heart is where relationships are born and where they live. Most people think I am talking about feelings, and it is partly, but it is much more. Your heart involves your mind and your emotions. It is the real you. Here is a good way to discover your heart. What do you love? Go ahead and make a mental list. I will share mine with you.

I love the color of the ocean and the beauty of sunsets and sunrises. There is nothing like a good cup of hot coffee in the morning and long walks in the mountains. Deep conversations with my husband, my children and my grandchildren are wonderful. Because I hate messes, I adore clean sheets, clean clothes, and a clean house.

Little birds hopping around on my back porch are fun to watch. I also enjoy shopping with my girls. We talk, laugh, and have fun watching people in the mall. There are people who look like they just got out of bed, while others are dressed for success. It is fun just to spend time together.

I love to see Chris, my son, laugh, smile, and cut up. He is quite an entertainer.

We have been blessed with six grandchildren who are the joy of our lives. When Collier played baseball and football, Bill and I enjoyed every minute. He was fantastic. You should hear Reagan and Bailey, my two oldest granddaughters when they are together. They laugh, or should I say giggle. Their laughter makes me smile through and through. Taylor and Elizabeth can play for hours, and even though they make the biggest mess, I still love it. Clayton is our mystery boy. I am blown away by him. I think he might be a genius.

I love being with friends and talking about things that matter.

Each time my mother and I bonded, my heart melted. I loved her but my relationship with her at times was strained.

Hot baths are the best and listening to praise music. I crave Bible-based teaching and love to write. But above all else, I adore the Lord. Spending time with God and His Word is my favorite time in the morning.

This is my list of the things I love. Now, you know the real me.

The Bible speaks clearly about our hearts. We can receive a new heart from God in Christ, Halleluiah. We can ask for a cleansing when we fall into sin, and because we have an enemy who wants to destroy us, we must do all we can to guard our hearts.

"I will give you a new heart" (Ezekiel 36:26).

"Create in me a pure heart, O God" (Psalm 51:10).

"..., guard your heart, for everything you do flows from it" (Proverbs 4:23).

How do we protect our souls? With social media, television, and the world we live in, it is hard not to be influenced. Bill and I have turned off more than a few television programs as they promote morals that defy the Bible. I need to protect my eyes and ears, but I also want to protect my heart from bitterness toward others. I guess what I'm saying to you and to me is not to let our souls grow cold, for without a tender heart we are just bodies with a brain.

Ponders of the Heart

What is on your list of the things you love?

Share your list with someone and let them get to know the real you.

Read Ezekiel 36:25-27, 2 Cor. 5:16-17, and 2 Cor. 10:3-6.

Prayers of the Heart

Dear Father,

We thank and praise You for giving us new natures. Oh, how we needed one. We want to guard our new hearts. We don't want pride or fear or resentment to reside there. Father, we don't want to open our minds to evil thoughts that lead to evil actions. Cleanse our souls. Lord, out of these new natures we find a good life. We praise You. In Jesus' name, amen.

August 22 ~ Foggy

A thick fog covered the beach, but it did not keep me from taking a long walk along a path where others walk, run, and ride bikes. The fog created a covering of sorts, and I personally liked it. I wanted to be alone. For most of the walk, I was alone with my thoughts and out of the gaze of others.

When a person came along the path, they were visible to me and me to them for just a short period of time. I felt free to concentrate on my thoughts, questions, and dreams. God was with me in the fog, and our fellowship was sweet.

Sometimes, I would see someone walking toward me, but because of the fog, I questioned what I was seeing. "Is this a man or a woman? Are they walking, running, or riding a bike? Oh, this is a woman, no a man. He is walking his dog."

Again and again, I played my guessing game of who was coming. I felt safe, at peace, protected and free. Fog doesn't always affect me this way, but today it was a good feeling.

For the life of me I can't always figure out this thing called "life." I try to understand what is going on in my limited sight. All I know to do is to keep on walking and keep on communing with God.

I get frustrated at times and want to see what is coming. Trying to figure out if it is good or bad is a tiring job. I look with all my might. Listen with both ears, and think with all the brain power I have, but I just can't figure out life.

The fog is thick and only God has eyes to see through this fog. On the other hand, I sometimes rest without knowing. As Bill often reminds me, "It's not over until it is over!" I hang on to this and just keep moving. When I let God be God and trust Him, I can walk feeling safe, secure, protected and yes, even free. Isn't this something? God can see and I don't have to.

Do you have situations full of fog? Do you have some things you can't figure out? I sure do and do you know what? I think this is the way it is supposed to be. God wants us to let Him be our answer, peace, and our guide. When we do, He extends to us peace, protection, and freedom.

I know it is foggy, but let's run instead of walk. Let's laugh instead of fret. Sing instead of moan and keep leaning on God. Don't worry when the fog clears. He will be there. He will rejoice with us or wipe away the tears. Our God is forever on our side.

Ponders of the Heart

What is in your life you just can't figure out?

How can you keep walking in the confusion and not give up?

Read Genesis 18:14 and Jeremiah 32:17.

Prayers of the Heart

Dear Father,

You are the God of the impossible. You will make a way, and You know the way. When we hear Your voice help us obey and trust You. Lord, You are our Truth, Life, and our Way. We love and praise You. In Jesus' name, amen.

August 23 ~ Special Days

The first family began with Adam and Eve. Their first child was Cain, then Abel. After Abel's death, Shem was born.

The Bible records for us the heritage of families. I have read those names, skipped over some, but now I am beginning to understand why they are important. Family was the first institution ordained by God. The thread of families runs through history. One generation to the next generation and on and on they go.

The Israelites' understood the importance of family history. Women were devastated if they were childless. In Genesis we see the story of Sarah, Leah and Rebecca and the links they were willing to go in order to have children. They did not want their family line to end.

My husband has always had an interest in his family history. Me, not so much, but the older I get the more our family story is important. Bear with me while I explain the background of August 23rd for the Collier family.

Dick Collier, my father-in-law, was born on August 23. He married my mother-in-law years later, on this same August date. You could say he was a smart man because this was a sure-fire way for him never to forget their anniversary. These two events make this date special in the life of our family. But God was not through with this important date. No, not by a long shot. On August 23, 2002, Collier Alan Blair was born, our first grandchild and Dick and Betty's great-grandson. Collier's name honors our family.

I realize more and more that God cares about the details of our lives.

When you get older and look back over your life and the life of your family, you can get a small glimpse of eternity. Picture a vine with me. The vine runs along a path, around a rock, down to the riverbank, and up to a tree. Sometimes it wraps around the tree trunk and keeps on climbing until you have no idea where it stops. Often, the vine will split and climb to the right and left, covering the branches of the tree. This is a picture of our family heritage, and if you stretch your mind, it is a picture of eternity.

God has placed eternity in our hearts, and it all started with Adam and Eve.

"He has made everything beautiful in its time. He has also set eternity in the human heart; yet no one can fathom what God has done from beginning to end" (Ecclesiastes 3:11).

It is impossible to see all God has done, and yet His faithfulness is seen in creation. We see the sun come up and go down each day. The seasons and the beauty and size of the ocean point to our magnificent Lord. His eternal Hand is visible in nature, and He reveals Himself to us as He works in our lives and the lives of those we love.

I was there when Collier took his first breath, and now, he is a grown man about to get married. I hope to be there when he says, "I do." I wouldn't mind seeing a few great-grandchildren. However, if not, and God has called me home, I will see those who have gone before me and wait for those who will come later. Then, we will experience eternity together with our Lord. We will have the memories of our lives and hear stories from family members we have just met.

Our stories and genealogy will be joined to the whole family of God all the way back to Adam and Eve. These special days of eternity will be more wonderful than we can imagine.

Ponders of the Heart

Are you a history buff? How far have you traced your family tree?

Do you have a strong history of Christians in your family, or are you the first?

Who is in heaven you can't wait to meet?

Read John 14:1-4, Psalm 16:11, and Revelation 22:1-5

Prayers of the Heart

Dear Father,

Thank You for my life, my husband, children, and grandchildren. You have blessed me with sons-in-law, a daughter-in-law, and friends I love. I have never gone hungry or without a roof over my head. All these blessings and so much more I praise and thank You. But, Lord, the gift of heaven and being with You and Your children is more than I can imagine. Help me share Jesus with others while I am still on this earth, so Your house is overflowing with Your family tree. In Jesus' name, amen.

August 24 ~ Death

Death is a reality, but just because it is, doesn't mean it is a subject we deal with every day.

There are days though when the subject of death cannot be avoided. I had a day like this not long ago. I talked with a man who had recently lost his mother after her prolonged battle with a painful disease. The same day I talked with a man whose wife was fighting a painful disease and death was imminent. The pain both men felt grieved my soul.

I hurt for the pain and the suffering of both women, but I was grateful for the men in their lives who stood by them. It took me back to my dad's fight with cancer that took his life and the way his family rallied around him. We who loved him so much, felt his pain and we also felt helpless.

There is nothing harder than to watch someone you love die. In fact, some people cannot get past their grief to be with them. In the case of my dad, there were times I could not stand what I was seeing. I marveled at the strength my mom had during this time. God supplies grace when we need it.

The greatest love we can show is to be there to support and love those fighting their last battle, but there is a point where death must be faced alone. I think of Jesus and the death He faced. Those He loved watched at the foot of the cross, but it was Jesus who endured. Even His Father turned when all our sin was placed upon Him and the penalty of sin rested on His perfect soul.

I cannot begin to feel the pain my Heavenly Father endured at that moment, but through the experience of my own pain when my dad died, I can get a glimpse of His. The difference for the believer is death has lost its sting, says the Bible, because our sin was placed on Jesus.

The man who has just lost his mother said to me, "I don't think death is as bad for them as we think." I hope he is right.

"When the perishable has been clothed with the imperishable, and the mortal with immortality, then the saying that is written will come true: 'Death has been swallowed up in victory. Where, O death, is your victory? Where, O death, is your sting?'" (1 Cor. 15:54-55).

Victory is ours if we are in Christ and for those we love if they are Christians. Again, my thoughts go back to my dad, and how God reached down and saved him. He saved my dad right before he began his battle with cancer and death. If l live to be a hundred and fifty years old, I will never get over the wonder and grace of our Lord. Jesus took the sting of death and gave us the victory.

Ponders of the Heart

Do you know the Lord, and are you confident that you will be with Him in heaven?

Who do you know that needs salvation?

Don't give up. Keep praying.

Read 1 Corinthians 15:50-58.

Prayers of the Heart

Dear Father,

May our hearts be full of praise for You today. We will all face death and those we love will also, but You have taken its sting and given us victory. Father, there are no words we know to completely express our thankfulness. May the truth of these words give us comfort and praise. In Jesus' name, amen.

August 25 ~ Holy Air

My grandson had one of those air trampolines when he was little. I'm not sure if this is the right name for this toy, but it is the best way I know to describe it. It is like a covered trampoline which is inflated by an air pump. When it is full of air, Collier could jump on it like a trampoline. The air must be continually pumped into it, or it deflates.

Without air, it lays on the ground useless, but when you turn the air pump on, it begins to inflate. In just a matter of minutes, it was ready, and he could jump. The opposite is also true. When you turn the pump off, it deflates quickly. The air blowing into the toy is a must for it to be useful.

What a good illustration to show us our need for the Holy Spirit. God's Spirit is His breath in us who are in Christ. We desperately need His breath continually, for without it, we will deflate back to fleshly living.

I thought the toy should fill with air and then stay this way until we let the air out. The sound of the air pump irritated me, and I wanted to be able to turn it off without losing the air it provided. Most

Christians think the same way. They want the Holy Spirit to come and fill them, then let them go on their merry way, living victorious lives apart from His continual touch.

We do not have a plug in our souls to hold His Spirit. We do, however, have the availability of His constant presence and power.

I have days when I feel like a deflated toy, lying on the ground useless. This is when I am trying to live apart from the breath of God. Each moment His Spirit is blowing fresh wind of life, and we can receive His breath. We do not have to live without His life constantly and continually within us. What a wonderful privilege it is to belong to Jesus.

"Therefore He says: 'Awake, you who sleep, Arise from the dead, And Christ will give you light'" (Ephesians 5:14 NKJV).

In John Eldredge's book, Waking the Dead, he prays:

"My dear Lord, Jesus, I come to you now to be restored in you- to renew my place in you, my allegiance to you, and to receive from you all the grace and mercy I so desperately need this day. I honor you as my sovereign Lord, and I surrender every aspect of my life totally and completely to you. I give you my body as a living sacrifice; I give you my heart, soul, mind and strength; and I give you my spirit as well."

In this prayer we see a man deflated and receiving the breath of God's Spirit to prepare him for his day. I love how he prays for the very thing we all need. We need to receive grace, mercy each day to surrender every part of our lives to God. He knows what we need before we ask, but He wants us to come to Him and give our hearts to

Him each day. We need His continual filling as we move about our lives.

Ponders of the Heart

Do you feel overwhelmed by the commitment?

How do these verses below encourage you?

Read Romans 12:1, Luke 10:27, and 1 Corinthians 6:17.

Prayers of the Heart

Dear Father,

Fill our souls with the breath of Your Spirit. Lord, fill us continually, for apart from You, we are useless, deflated souls. Apart from Your life, we are vulnerable to the attack of Satan and his demons. Blow fresh wind into our souls so we can live abiding in and receiving all You have for us. Let all we do be for Your glory. In Jesus' name, amen.

August 26 ~ The Ditch

"Is there no balm in Gilead? Is there no physician there? Why then is there no healing for the wound of my people?" (Jeremiah 8:22)

Imagine you are walking down a dirt road when it begins to rain. The rain is making the road beneath your feet wet and slippery. All at once, you misstep, and down you go, sliding off the side of the road into a ditch.

On the way down, you receive scratches and bruises all over your arms, legs, and face. You twist your ankle and cut your knee. Pain covers your body as you hit hard. You lie still for a few minutes, wishing someone was there, someone to help. Instead, you are completely alone, and you feel assaulted and dejected. At this moment, all you know is pain.

As you gather your thoughts, you realize that home is a mile or so away. There in your home there are people who love and care about you, but they don't know what has happened. The thoughts and the knowledge of their love are like the warmth of the sun on a spring day. These people who have loved you are like a delicious meal for a starving man.

The knowledge of their love compels you to get up and, with painful effort, make your way back home. Slowly but surely, you limp home and open the door. The faces of those who love you turn toward the door. They have been waiting for you, anxious about your return, and when they see you and what they see registers, they rush to your side.

Before you know it, you have had a warm bath, been tenderly dressed in your most comfortable clothes, and healing ointment has been placed on your wounds. The dirt, the grime, and the blood are gone, and you sit before those who love you, beat-up, but clean.

If we had spiritual eyes and could see our hearts and souls, this would be a picture of the redeemed in this broken world. Our hearts have been assaulted, as well as our souls. We can, at times, find ourselves in the ditches of life, feeling dejected and alone. We can lose our spiritual insight.

When we are lying in this ditch, we forget the love and care we have experienced from people who love us. We are not even aware of God's love that gives us hope. We lay there in the ditches of life, completely deceived and discouraged, believing the lie that we are all alone.

Then our Savior calls us and beckons us home with cords of His love.

If you are in the ditch today, let this message draw you home. Hear His love calling. If you love someone who is in the ditch today, go get them and pull them out with the cords of His love. We all need His healing touch. Do not lay in the ditch. Even if it hurts, get up and come home. Do not believe lies. He loves you and wants to heal you. Come home!

Ponders of the Heart

Are you in a spiritual ditch today?

Do you know someone who is?

Read Isaiah 61:1-4 and verse 10.

Get out of the ditch and help others climb out with you.

Prayers of the Heart

Dear Father,

Our Healer, pour over us with Your healing blood. Jesus, we see the wounds You bore for us, and we see the wounds of those we love. We come to You, Jesus. You know our pain, and You have healing and restoration for us. Wash us, and we will be clean. Heal us, and we will be healed. Jesus, You have experienced this life, and You know how to minister to us. In Jesus' name, amen.

August 27 ~ Life after the Ditch

Imagine once more about our pretend ditch story. You have survived, and your healing is going quite well. It has been weeks, and as you heal, those who love you are slowly returning to their lives.

One morning, you wake up with a strange thought. Up until now, you have had only good, thankful feelings, but today, your thoughts are accusing. "Why didn't they come looking for me the minute it started to rain? God, You knew I was out there; why did You allow the rain? You knew the road was slippery, and I would be hurt! Why is everyone forgetting about me? Don't they know I still have pain in my leg?"

You hear these thoughts, and you wonder why you are in this frame of mind. You even feel a little guilty for thinking like this. After all, everyone was so nice. You also hear a faint voice, which reminds you of the love and concern everyone showed and how loved you felt. This faint voice is telling you not to allow these negative feelings to overtake you. There is a battle in your mind, and you don't know which thought is right.

Let's say these accusations seem more powerful, and you start developing quite an attitude; indignation wells up in you. You feel a comfort in your indignation, and you begin to really be mad. Before you know it, you have been transported back to the road, and the dirt under your feet is beginning to feel slippery again.

At this moment, you realize the enemy has been working in your mind. You begin to slip, and you see the ditch below you. You prepare yourself for a hard hit as you lift your eyes to heaven and yell, "Help!"

Right when you think the fall is inevitable, you find yourself being lifted up. You open your eyes, and you are being carried by an eagle high above the road and the ditch. I told you to imagine! He places you right at the door of your house and tells you to go inside.

As you turn to leave, you see the spirit of self-pity, doubt, and pride hanging around the threshold. You turn back to the eagle, and he says you must walk into the house of truth and safety alone. With faith, you walk into your home once more.

This is an illustration of the cunningness of our enemy. He plays with us primarily in our minds. He never gives up. Our flesh is weak, and our wounds are deep. The good news is Jesus is a yell away, really a whisper. To stand, we must know the truth. If we are to walk by faith, we must have faith. The enemy wants to trick us back to the ditches of life. He wants to keep us falling. If we don't wise up to his tricks, we will find ourselves buried once more in his mire.

Jesus wants to keep us from falling and heal our deep wounds. He wants to free us from all the pain our enemy has caused so we will be whole. The Lord uses our circumstances to strengthen our faith, while our enemy wants to use our situations to defeat and destroy us. Oh, that we would be children who listen to God's voice and fight the enemy's speaking in our minds.

Ponders of the Heart

What traps does Satan use in your life to trip you up?

How well are you using the armor of God to prepare for the battle?

Read 2 Corinthians 11:3 and Ephesians 6:10-18.

Prayers of the Heart

Dear Father,

 We are weak, but You are strong. We are vulnerable without Your armor and easily led astray. Humbly, we come to You confessing our need for Your mercy. We pray for Your wisdom to guide us, Your mercy to hold us, and Your power to protect us. Father, fill us with Your love and let us hear Your voice. We praise You for Your wonderful grace. In Jesus' name, amen.

August 28 ~ The Stronghold of Legalism

 In the movie "Just in Time," a young girl is learning to live without her mom, who was killed in a car accident. Her father is left alone to care for her. Because of his work, it is necessary that he has a live-in nanny. After trial and error, Faith comes to live with them to care for Lily.

 Faith is part of a large Italian family, and in one part of the movie, she takes Lily to play with her nephews. One of the nephews takes something from Lily, and she becomes furious. Her method of coping is hitting. When Faith corrects her and tells her to apologize, she refuses. She tells Faith, "You are not my mother, and I do not have to mind you!" Lily turns and runs away with Faith right behind her, calling her name. Lily sits down, pouting as Faith tries to get to the bottom of the young girl's pain.

While I was watching this scene unfold, I was thinking of what I would do. What would you do? Would your focus be Lily's pain or her disobedience? I found I was focused on Lily's disobedience. This is the stronghold of legalism.

Faith responds by telling Lily she knows she is not her mom, but would she tell her about her mother? Lily began to cry and told Faith that no one would let her talk about her mom. Faith held her and told her she could tell her anything. And this is grace. Faith touched the hurt in Lily's young heart with God's mercy and grace.

What is the difference between teaching and instructing our children and legalism? What is the difference between doing the right thing and legalism? It is motive.

If we are concerned about being right and being in control, there is no vision beyond a person's actions. Legalism is rooted in pride and not grounded in the grace we have received from our Lord. The letter of the law is legalism, while grace goes beyond written laws to the heart of the matter.

God looks at the heart. When we walk in His grace, we extend grace to others. Here is a quote that catches my heart each time I read it:

"It is better to have a heart without words than words without heart."

As the scene in the movie unfolded and I was able to see this lady touch a hurting child's heart, I saw the power grace has to heal. How often do I not give people the grace the Lord has given me? I turned to the Lord and asked Him to quicken my spirit to respond to others with the love He had poured into my heart. I know legalism is a part of my flesh, but praise to God; He has rescued me:

"O wretched man that I am! Who will deliver me from this body of death? I thank God-through Jesus Christ our Lord! So then, with the mind I myself serve the law of God, but with the flesh the law of sin" (Romans 7:24-25 NKJV).

The battle of the flesh will continue as long as we are alive in this world, but God has given us His Spirit and a new nature through Jesus Christ, our Lord.

Ponders of the Heart

Read 2 Corinthians 3:4-6, 1 Corinthians 10:23-24, Galatians 2:20-21, and 2 Corinthians 10- 3-5.

When you read these verses, do you see a stronghold of legalism in your life?

Who can we ask to break this stronghold and fill our hearts with grace?

Prayers of the Heart

Dear Father,

Break the chains of legalism over our hearts. You have given us grace over our sins, and we want to give grace to others in return. Lord, a moral man is a good thing, but being a child of Yours is much better. We want to live as Jesus lived, by mercy and grace. Let our motives and our love be grounded in Your magnificent grace. In Jesus' name, amen.

August 29 ~ Adventure

Most movies, television shows and videos incorporate adventure in the storyline. Writers know in the human heart, there is a desire for excitement. We often settle for watching it instead of living it; our hearts desire adventure, but we are also afraid of it.

Webster's Dictionary defines adventure as "an unusual or suspenseful experience, a hazardous undertaking. Synonyms would be risk or dare."

When Bill and I choose a movie, he wants adventure, and I want romance. At times, we find movies with both.

The other night, we watched a movie about white water rafting. Four men took a group of people on this adventure. One person that went along was a short, plump, middle-aged woman. She hated the cold water, she was afraid of the rapids, she hated using a port-a-potty, and camping was the pits.

I'm not sure why she went; the man who brought her wasn't sure why either, but once the trip began, there was no turning back. She was by no means the focused character, but I couldn't help but feel her pain. I hate cold water; I'm afraid of many things (hitting a rock in cold water would be one of them.) I like modern bathrooms, and camping is a lot of trouble.

She was stuck. She found herself in the middle of an exciting, suspenseful, hazardous undertaking. Something happened along the way; the group of people came together. They began to enjoy the adventure, the cold water, the rapids, the port-a-potty, and camping.

When the movie was over, Bill said, "I would like to do something like that!" I said, "I would not, but I need to." Fear, comfort, and apathy are not what makes life worth living.

On our trip to the Holy Land, I was baptized in the Jordan. The water was icy cold, and the further I walked, the more I wanted to stop and return to the shore. I was shaking, and my teeth were chattering. The water was freezing. After being plunged beneath the icy water and in dry clothes, I remember how energized and alive I felt. It was quite an adventure for me.

The sights and sounds of the Holy Land were exciting but a little scary. We were surrounded by Muslims, Jews, and Christians. There were soldiers with guns and angry voices everywhere. But I still sensed the presence of Jesus. I spent an entire night awake in Galilee as I imagined Jesus walking along the shore. I was overwhelmed by this trip. I am so thankful we went.

God wants His children to live an adventure with Him. This is the very reason we have an inborn desire for it. God is in control, so we can live free, trusting Him.

When we trust Him, we can experience a thrilling life with Him. Fear, comfort, and apathy will keep us on the shoreline and out of living. If you are like the short, plump, middle-aged woman in the movie and find yourself on an adventure God began, do not turn back because I bet before the trip is over, you will be throwing cold water, laughing through the rapids, and planting sweet-smelling flowers around the port-a-potty. Really, God wants us to connect and enjoy life with Him.

Ponders of the Heart

Are you ready for adventure or afraid of it?

Have you allowed God to take you on an adventure? If not, why?

Read Deut. 31:8, 2 Timothy 1:7, 1 John 4:18, Matt. 24:12, Rev. 3:16-16 and John 10:10.

Prayers of the Heart:

Dear Father,

Cast out all our fears and give us hearts that trust You. You did not give us a spirit of fear, nor did You give us a cold heart. You have given us a new heart and a new spirit. In You, we can experience abundant life. Oh, Lord, drench us in the river of life! In Jesus' name, amen.

August 30 ~ Pruning

I am a plant killer. I forget to take them inside when it is cold, and I forget to water them. When I lived in Florida, I didn't have to water them because it rained so much, and it didn't get very cold, so plants were fine outside. Maybe that is the reason I forget, or I am just bad with plants.

However, I have plants that have sentimental value. I don't want anything to happen to them; one is in my dining room. One day I was there and discovered the Peace Lily in the corner was in bad shape. The leaves were limp and brown. This is never a good sign.

After close inspection, I realized it needed pruning. I got the scissors and started cutting off dead stems and clearing the dead leaves away. I cut trimmed, and when I was through, the plant looked bare. After watering it and carrying the dead leaves and branches away, the Lily looked skimpy but better.

Days went by, and I wanted to check the plant. I hadn't looked at it in about a week and you know what I found? New growth! The Peace Lily looked healthier; there were new shoots coming out and life was appearing from what I thought was a dying plant.

"I am the true vine and my Father is the gardener. He cuts off every branch in me that bears no fruit, while every branch that does bear fruit he prunes so that it will be even more fruit" (John 15:1-2).

God prunes us and cuts away the dead and useless things in our lives so we can bear eternal fruit. When I take scissors to a plant, I often think about if I am hurting them. When I cut a half-green and half-brown leaf away, I wonder if I am being too hasty. I know when God prunes us it hurts, but He knows the outcome.

He knows when to cut and when to wait. God knows how much to cut and how much to save. The Father prunes so we can bear more fruit. God's pruning still hurts; it is not fun, but it is good.

Sin is like those brown leaves. These are areas of our lives we have not watered with God's Word. Sin grows, and it always produces death. God has given us His life, and because of His mercy, He cuts away things that hinder our growth.

"I am the vine, you are the branches. He who abides in Me, and I in him, bears much fruit; for without Me you can do nothing" (John 15:5 NKJV).

The pruning will always hurt, but it produces fruit for eternity.

Ponders of the Heart

Have you experienced the pruning of God in your life?

What was the outcome?

Read Romans 5:3-5 and James 1:2-4.

Prayers of the Heart

Dear Father,

    No trial is pleasant. No discipline is fun, but Father, Your perfect work can produce fruit for eternity. Lord, we don't know exactly what this means or how it will look, but we trust You to use Your pruning for Your glory and our good. You are the Hero of our story. We want to be a part of Your plan. Prune us and let new shoots of life spring forth. We want to abide in You. In Jesus' name, amen.

August 31 ~ Prayers of the Heart

May these words of my mouth and this meditation of my heart be pleasing in your sight, Lord, my Rock and my Redeemer" (Psalm 19:14).

Dear Father,

    We come to honor You as our sovereign Lord. Dear Jesus, we come to be restored and give You our hearts, souls, and minds. Jesus, cover them with Your blood and seal us for the day of Redemption by Your Holy Spirit.

We thank You for making us acceptable in Your sight by the work You have done for us on the cross. Lord, we come to worship and praise You. We come to enter Your Holy presence.

'Lift up your heads, O you gates! And be lifted up, you everlasting doors! And the King of glory shall come in. Who is this King of glory? The Lord strong and mighty, The Lord mighty in battle. Lift up your heads, O you gates! Lift up, you everlasting doors! And the King of glory shall come in. Who is this King of glory? The Lord of hosts, He is the King of glory" (Psalm 24:7-10 NKJV).

Dear Father,

We bow before You and crown You King of glory. We open the gates of our hearts and welcome You in. We want to be in Your presence forevermore. Jesus, You are our Everlasting Door into eternity, and we praise You. We enter Your holiness with praise, honor, and thanksgiving. We receive and accept all that is ours because of the love You have given us. Lord, help us praise, love and honor You.

You are worthy of our heart's devotion, our love, and our worship. We pray all of this in Your name, Lord Jesus, with all glory, honor, and thanks to You!

"Whom have I in heaven but You? And there is none upon earth that I desire besides You. My flesh and my heart fail; But God is the strength of my heart and my portion forever" (Psalm 73:25-26 NKJV).

How we praise You, Lord. In Jesus' name, amen.

september

— " —

Come to me, all you who are weary and burdened, and I will give you rest. Take my yoke upon you and learn from me, for I am gentle and humble in heart, and you will find rest for your souls.

Matthew 11:28-29

September 1 ~ Wrath vs. Love

"If momma ain't happy, then nobody's happy," says the bumper sticker. I don't know if this was true at your house, but it was at my house growing up.

I remember a Saturday morning when we went to visit my aunt. Mother told us not to ask for something to eat. I don't know why; maybe we were always begging for food. That day she said, "Don't ask." We did. She was not happy.

Johnny, my ever-so-wise brother, said, "Just go in and start watching television, and she will forget about spanking us." He was wrong. She remembered. We experienced the wrath of Mom. I am sure my children could tell stories that would match this one. Mom's rules were to be obeyed.

Our disobedience resulted in Mom's anger. It is good our mom loved us, or we would not have reached adulthood. I hope you laugh as you read this little flashback, but the truth is our holy God is serious about disobedience. His standards are perfection, and only Jesus lived up to those standards.

In his book, The Passion of Jesus Christ, John Piper gives 50 reasons why Jesus died on the cross. The first reason he gave was Jesus absorbed the wrath of God for us. People often ask the question, "Why did Jesus have to die such a horrible death?"

He took our sins upon Himself and absorbed the full wrath of God. Think about this for just a moment. When God, the All-Powerful One, is stirred to wrath over evil, it conjures up a powerful energy in my mind, more than a hurricane, an earthquake, or a tornado. The power is unfathomable, and God's holy wrath and power come against sin.

As John Piper says, "Since God is just, he does not sweep these crimes under the rug of the universe."

But because God loves us, His wrath was placed on His Son, Jesus. He became our substitute.

After seeing "The Passion of the Christ," a dear man in our church said," I wonder how many of those stripes He took for me?" I thought, "Every one of them." Christ's suffering was so we could be healed.

Some might say, "I have never done anything so wrong that Jesus deserved, or in fact, I deserve such punishment." We often measure one another by looking at each other. The standard is not set by us but by God, and His standard is perfection because His nature is entirely pure. All of us deserve God's wrath. Let me end by using John Piper's words.

"Let us not trifle with God or trivialize his love. We will never stand in awe of God's love until we reckon with the seriousness of our sin and the justice of his wrath against us. But when, by grace, we awaken to our unworthiness, then we may look at the suffering and death of Christ and say, 'In this is love, not that we have loved God but that he loved us and sent his Son to be the {wrath-absorbing} propitiation for our sins,'" (1 John 4:10).

What a glorious truth! We deserve wrath, but Jesus took our place, and by His grace, we are forgiven and justified before God. Praise Him.

Ponders of the Heart

Do you struggle with why Jesus had to die on the cross?

How would you explain the reason to a child?

Read Galatians 3:3, Romans 3:19-26 and 1 John 4:10.

Prayers of the Heart

Dear Father,

    We praise You for Jesus' provision. May our hearts be sensitive to Your wrath toward sin and Your love toward us while we were sinners. Lord, we can't fathom such love. Help us stand in awe of You. We bow down in thanksgiving and praise. Jesus, heal us with Your wounds. In Jesus' name, amen.

September 2 ~ Mom Understands

    The plan was set. We were moving. The year was 1971, and the arrangements were complete. I would transfer to the Bank in Tallahassee; Bill would transfer to Florida State and move our trailer to live on the property we had bought with Bill's brother. We were excited, especially during the weekend when we cleared the land.

    I didn't feel wonderful that day, but I was sure it was the tuna fish. We had waited a long time before we ate, and the tuna caused me to feel nauseous.

    Time would change this medical diagnosis to pregnancy. The excitement of the move would change to regret. I could still transfer my job, Bill could still change schools, but my mom wouldn't be there.

People might have said, "She is a real momma's girl." At that time in my life, they were right. My mother knew about being pregnant. She had been pregnant three times and understood what it was like to have a baby. I don't know if Bill understood how I felt, but he changed direction for me.

Pregnancy is a scary thing, and it is good to know someone who made it through. It gives you confidence. You surely don't get much reassurance from movies.

What does it mean when the Bible says Christ was made perfect in suffering? Now, the same verses tell us Christ was sinless, so He was already perfect. He was God's Son, for goodness' sake. So why does the passage say He was made perfect by His obedience to suffering? It wasn't to make Him perfect; it was so He could relate to our humanity without sin.

"though He was a Son, yet He learned obedience by the things which He suffered. And having been perfected, He became the author of eternal salvation to all who obey Him" (Hebrews 5:8-9 NKJV).

Christ relates to our suffering because he suffered and understands what we go through perfectly.

He lives to intercede for us, to God, which amazes me. When we feel alone, rejected, misunderstood, and suffer pain, Christ prays for us. He relates to our circumstances and our feelings. This was part of God's plan. He wanted us to know our Savior would understand the issues of our lives through the experiences He faced.

Just like I instinctively knew my mother would understand what it was like to be pregnant and give birth. God wants us to realize that Jesus knows what it is like to live in a fallen world, even to the point of suffering death. Our Jesus knows how to intercede from firsthand knowledge.

Christ can relate to what we face today. He understands, and He cares, as Max Lucado says in his book 'No Wonder They Call Him the Savior.'

Ponders of the Heart

What circumstances in your life are causing you pain?

Have you taken your heartache to Jesus?

Read Hebrews 2:10, Hebrews 5:8-9, Hebrews 7:25-28.

Prayers of the Heart

Dear Father,

You came to earth, and You know what it is like to be human. You know the rejection of loved ones. You understand temptation, trials, and pain. There is nothing we experience. You do not grasp. You are our perfect Savior and intercessor. Lord, how we praise You. In Jesus' name, amen.

September 3 ~ Talking with Dad

It was just an ordinary day, and I was ironing. I can't remember what was on my mind. I just remembered I had a strong urge to call my dad. There was a problem with this; he was on one side of life and I on another; my dad had been dead for five years.

Time hasn't changed the fact that I still miss him and wish he was here, but the Bible promises Dad is in a better place. But for now, death separates us and makes it impossible for me to talk or be with him.

On the front page of the paper was a picture of a man's face. He was a man of faith, and his wife was missing at the time of the photograph. He was taking part in a prayer vigil for her safe return. This was on Saturday, but on Sunday, her body was found in a shallow grave. His hope for her safe return was gone. He will be separated from her by death. He is on one side of life; she is on another. We all miss our loved ones and wish for more time with them. My heart breaks for the sadness we all experience on this side of life.

The reality is death separates. Each person either knows or will know the reality of this truth. Death is our enemy, for it separates us from the living. Even so, death separates us from God. The Bible puts it this way:

"For all have sinned and fall short of the glory of God" (Romans 3:23).

"For the wages of sin is death, but the gift of God is eternal life in Jesus Christ our Lord" (Romans 6:23).

We were born with a nature to sin, and therefore, we sin. Our sin has a wage, and it is death. The best definition of death is separation from life. God is the source and the essence of life. Therefore, death is separation from God. But the Bible says:

"The gift of God is eternal life in Christ Jesus our Lord " (Romans 6:23).

"When you were dead in your sins and in the uncircumcision of your flesh, God made you alive with Christ. He forgave us all our

sins, having canceled the charge of our legal indebtedness, which stood against us and condemned us; he has taken it away, nailing it to the cross" (Colossians 2:13-14).

It was Christ who took our wages for sin. He died on the cross because we were dead, separated from God by our sins. Therefore, by faith in Christ, we can be alive in Him, and our separation from God destroyed.

Death of those we love haunts us. We long for our separation to be over. The pain and parting are real. Our enemy is death, but eternal life is found in Jesus, who is our life-giver. We still suffer in this life, but we have hope.

The separation we endure will end for those who are in Christ Jesus. We will be fully restored to those we love and to the One who loves us and gave His life for us. Oh, that we would pray for those who don't have faith in Jesus will come to know Him.

Ponders of the Heart

Who are the people you are looking forward to seeing in heaven?

How does the Bible give you hope that we will see them again because of Jesus?

Read Romans 1:16-17 and 1 Peter 2:24.

Prayers of the Heart

Dear Father,

We thank You for the promise that we will see You and our loved ones. Father, thank You for the gift of knowing and walking in Your righteousness. We praise You for the gospel message that saved and gave us life. We pray we will not be ashamed of the gospel, but we will share this good news with others. Lord, use our lives for Your glory. In Jesus' name, amen.

September 4 ~ Confidence to Come Near

Field trips were part of my school years, and one of my favorites was Marineland. It was a place like Sea World but on a smaller scale. There were dolphins, sharks, and an underground aquarium tank, but no Shamu.

Naturally, when my children came along, we were drawn to Sea World, not too far down the road from Marineland. Sea World was fascinating to us. We loved the dolphin show and Shamu, and the skiing show was spectacular. But the thrilling event was entering the shark exhibit.

The first thing you saw was a three-dimensional movie in which you felt like sharks were swimming off the screen at you. Then the movie screen would lift, and right before your eyes were sharks swimming around in a giant aquarium.

The person up front would give you information about these creatures and lead you in a single file into an underground cylinder. Sharks would be all around you. It was like being in the ocean with them, but you were dry and safe.

Safety is the most critical part of the experience, for sharks are predators, and we represent food to them. I have no idea if we are tasty, but to a hungry shark, we will do. They do not eat you because they are mean; they eat you because eating you is consistent with their nature.

Therefore, to come into their presence without fear is arrogant, stupid, and not without cost. The glass cylinder provided the protection needed so we could enjoy the thrill of the sharks without the fear of being supper.

Our God is a holy, pure Deity, and evil cannot come into His presence without consequences. His holiness is a consuming fire, and all sin is consumed in His presence. Coming into His presence without fear is arrogant, stupid, and not without cost. We need a cylinder of protection to enjoy the thrill of knowing Him without the fear of being consumed. The Bible says:

"Therefore, brothers and sisters, since we have confidence to enter the Most Holy Place by the blood of Jesus, by a new and living way opened for us through the curtain, that is, his body, and since we have a great priest over the house of God, let us draw near to God with a sincere heart and with the full assurance that faith brings, having our hearts sprinkled to cleanse us from a guilty conscience and having our bodies washed with pure water. Let us hold unswervingly to the hope we profess, for he who promised is faithful" (Hebrews 10:19-23).

Our cylinder of protection is Jesus. We can come near to God in His sanctuary with Jesus and be completely protected. As I type those words, I tremble with fear and wonder. Our hope and confidence are not in ourselves, our righteousness nor our goodness, but in the work of Jesus and His complete worthiness to enter God's presence. We come cocooned in the righteousness of Jesus, covered in His purifying blood. We are safe, welcomed, and loved. God bids us to come.

Ponders of the Heart

Do you ever wonder what heaven will be like?

Who do you know that needs to experience God's total love and forgiveness?

Read Hebrews 10:11-25.

I love the promises in these verses, promises for you and for me. Let's claim each one today with all our hearts.

Prayers of the Heart

Dear Father,

We come with confidence that Jesus has given us access to You. Lord, we know it is by His worthiness we may know You and be in Your inner sanctuary. We can draw near to You and You have cleansed us by the blood of Jesus.

Father, our conscience is clean, and you bid us to come. Whatever hinders us from coming close to You, show us so we might turn away and enjoy a closer fellowship with You. In Jesus' name, amen.

September 5 ~ Weakness to Power

I woke up today with a headache and backache. What a way to start a beautiful day. I looked in the mirror, and I looked like a mess. My eyes were weak, my hair was a mess, and my skin looked wrinkly. Even when I was young, I had bad days, and as I grow older, it will get worse. Our physical bodies are frail, and our human nature is also fragile.

What about mentally? I could use help in this area. I do not understand many things. Is there any hope for us? We, of course, should do all we can to take care of our physical bodies. We need to feed them and exercise our bodies and minds, but even then, we will have weaknesses. 1 Corinthians 15 has incredible promises about our bodies:

"So will it be with the resurrection of the dead. The body that is sown is perishable, it is raised imperishable; it is sown in dishonor, it is raised in glory; it is sown in weakness, it is raised in power; it is sown a natural body, it is raised a spiritual body " (1 Corinthians 15:42-44).

"And just as we have borne the image of the earthly man, so shall we bear the image of the heavenly man" (1 Corinthians 15:49).

We are born with weakness. The Word weakness in Greek is asthenia, which means powerless, sick, and frail in body and soul. But we will rise from the dead in power.

Dynamis is the word power in Greek, from which the word dynamo comes. That's a pretty explosive picture. In heaven, we will not wake up with headaches or backaches, and I even get the idea we will be able to understand heavenly things. We will bear His likeness.

The word likeness is also a fantastic word in Greek. The Word is eikon, and part of the definition is that we will be a direct expression of something. If we are a direct expression of Jesus, we will have amazing insight. Today, I wonder about things I cannot understand. I find peace in knowing I know the One who does understand. I find great comfort in the fact that one day, I will bear His likeness.

We know people who struggle with weaknesses in their bodies; we grieve for their bodies and souls. Jesus is the passageway to hope. What we suffer today does not have to be true in the hereafter. The most critical issue of life is what we believe about Jesus, and the second critical issue is whether we are going to believe and walk in the hope we have in Him.

We were by nature perishable, dishonorable, and weak, but we will rise imperishable in glory and power. Our image will mirror Jesus. I do not know what we will look like, but wow.

Ponders of the Heart

Read 1 Corinthians 15:35-58.

What physical, mental, or emotional weakness are you suffering?

How do these passages encourage you? Take time to praise the Lord.

Prayers of the Heart

Dear Father,

I am thankful for this day of weakness because it reminds me to look to You. I look to You for the grace to live this day and hope for my future. Lord, I am fragile, but You are strong. I am limited, but You are limitless. I am dull in my thinking, but You are all-powerful. You are more merciful and gracious than I can know. Lord, I praise and thank You. In Jesus' name, amen.

September 6 ~ Wishing Your Life Away

My daughter, Tracie, and her husband, Ryan, were having a little trouble getting along one weekend; they both had their own agenda.

They had both experienced a hard week and were exhausted. Ryan wanted to ride his motorcycle to relieve stress. Tracie's agenda included a nap and time for Ryan to finish her" honey-do" list. In the heat of the moment, unfair comments were made, not to mention some hurt feelings.

It is safe to say we often focus on our own needs and hurt those we love. As for Tracie and Ryan, exhaustion had sent them on a quest to satisfy their "self." In wanting to serve their own needs, they had forgotten the blessing of their marriage and the blessing of being parents.

Tracie and Ryan's story is one we can all relate to because we have all been there. Selfishness is part of our human nature, and only God can tame this beast inch by inch. I know I will travel this road many times before I reach heaven.

Let me give you a little test. How would you answer this statement? Things would be better for me if I could _____. Go ahead and be honest. What would you put in the blank? Having an answer does not make you a terrible person; it makes you human. Your answer only becomes a problem when the statement becomes the focus of your life. Let me fill in the blanks with standard answers.

Things would be much better if I had more money, a bigger house, or a nicer car. My life would be easier if my husband picked up his dirty clothes, wiped off his feet, and if he was nicer to me. Life would go smoother if my children went to bed when I said, kept their rooms clean and did not sass me.

If only I had a boyfriend, someone to love and take care of me, this would make life wonderful. Things would be better if I had an important job, more time off, and a boss who appreciated me. The common focus of those statements is "me." When "self" becomes our focus, we have lost focus.

Our deepest satisfaction is found when we focus on God and His purposes and not on ourselves. When we do, we can enjoy life's blessings, knowing He is aware of our needs. If our lives become disjointed and exhausting, we can come to Him for meaning and rest. We are reminded in John 14:1:

"Do not let your hearts be troubled. You believe in God; believe also in me."

Ponders of the Heart

What troubles your heart today?

Has your focus been on your Savior or your troubles?

Read Philippians 4:6-9 and let your heart experience peace.

Prayers of the Heart

Dear Father,

Why do we let life rob us of living? Lord, if we have You, what else do we really need? You are our greatest need and our greatest delight. You made us, and you know our needs.

Lord, help us trust You to provide so we can live in peace. We pray for the grace to focus on You and let You have our worries. We pray for a simple life, a life of worship, and a focus on Your purposes. In Jesus' name, amen.

September 7 ~ Fear of the Deep

Life experiences have a way of holding us captive. The impact of such experiences can have positive or negative effects.

One such experience in the life of my mother was the trauma of almost drowning when she was a young woman. She was at the beach when a riptide carried her offshore. Her future husband and my father were able to pull her to safety. She was forever grateful for his rescue, but my mom never overcame her fear of water.

Her fear of water has kept her pretty close to shore. She has been unable to experience the joy of floating and relaxing in water over her head. Her fear kept her from ever enjoying swimming, riding in a boat, or watching all of us enjoy the water. I have always thought living in Florida and being afraid of water was such a shame. Fear is a strong emotion and can often keep us on the shore of life.

Maybe you can relate to a trauma in your own life where fear keeps you from enjoying what others do. The most painful traumas are those that involve relationships. How many of us have been hurt by trusting someone who lets us down? We can experience hurt from our parents, siblings, spouses, and friends.

The result of these traumas is that we hold back part of our hearts in hopes of protecting ourselves. We might even mistrust the Lord. We want to love and trust Him, but the fear of letting go and allowing Him to be our life preserver is hard. We are afraid of going into a deep relationship, so we hold on to the side, never enjoying the freedom of resting in His faithfulness.

We know the end of fear begins with faith in Him. As we work to trust the Lord with all our lives, we can slowly learn to move from the shore of living into the deep water of His grace. Our hearts long for this. We long to float and live rich lives that are far more than just surviving, yet fear is a strong deterrent. We can let go if we believe He will never let us go. We can trust in His Word.

"But now, thus says the Lord, who created you, O Jacob, and He who formed you, O Israel: 'Fear not, for I have redeemed you; I have called you by your name; You are Mine. When you pass through the waters, I will be with you; and through the rivers, they shall not overflow you. When you walk through the fire, you shall not be burned, Nor shall the flames scorch you. For I am the Lord your God, The Holy One of Israel, your Savior'" (Isaiah 43:1-3 NKJV).

Past hurts make it hard to trust God, but God does not hurt His own. Let your heart and soul drink up this truth, and with faith and not fear, let go of the shore and let His Hand hold you up in the deep. Don't worry; He is big enough to touch the bottom.

Ponders of the Heart

What fear are you in bondage?

What fear has you missing the life God has for you?

Read Isaiah 41:10, Romans 9:33, and finally Proverbs 3:5-6.

Prayers of the Heart

Dear Father,

You are our refuge and our strength. You are our hope and our safe haven. Precious Lord, help us trust Your good plans for us and Your care. Help us not live in fear but in faith. You are the keeper of our souls. Thank You for Your Word. Take us into the deep and hold us with Your mighty right Hand. In Jesus' name, amen.

September 8 ~ Footprints

Have you ever played a game at the beach where you try to follow someone's footprints?

I remember as a child with short legs reaching to step in the next footprint. It was a fun game but not always easy. The sand was so full of prints that it was hard to find where to place my foot next, and the next print was out of reach of my short legs. Jumping and stretching to reach the next step often made me fall into the sand, laughing hysterically.

My feet were made for stepping, but not in someone else's steps, or were they?

We are told to walk in the ways of Jesus, but if you are like me, that is easier said than done. I either need help finding His footprints, or His prints seem out of reach. I often jump and stretch, trying to reach His lofty standards, just to find myself flat on my back with failure and bruised knees.

It is not that I think my ways are better; well, maybe I do believe this sometimes. But His ways are out of my reach. I think I am following Him and find I have wandered after another. Walking in the steps of Jesus is not an easy business.

A more complicated game to play in life is self-sufficiency.

We are not made to walk alone. We are made to depend on Him. This is our confidence as we try to follow Jesus. He is there to encourage us, come get us when we stray, and even carry us, as the poem "Footprints" points out. Jesus is our leader and our rear guard. He is our path and our guide.

When we allow our lives to be in Him, Jesus will show His glory in our land. Read and listen to these words in Psalm 85:13:

"Righteousness goes before him and prepares the way for his steps."

Jesus is our righteousness and our pathway to success. Apart from His presence, we are without righteousness and a path to follow. He is the perfect combination of mercy and truth, righteousness and peace.

"Love and faithfulness meet together; righteousness and peace kiss each other" (Psalm 85:10).

What great promises we have in Jesus. He is our path maker. As we run along in life, trying to follow in His steps, He is right behind us, lifting us and guiding us to the next big step. We do not need to strain or try to break free from His hold. We need to depend on Him and feel the freedom of the stretch. Knowing if we fall, He will pick us up and even carry us all the way home. What a Savior.

Ponders of the Heart

What do you want to do today that seems too hard for you?

Can you remember something God did for you or through you in the past?

Read Psalms 85 and 86 with your whole heart and praise Him.

Prayers of the Heart

Dear Father,

You are our guide, our righteousness, and strength. We are needy and weak. We need You, Lord. We want to walk in Your ways. We fall, we lose our way, but You are our Savior. Lord, hold us close. Let Your glory dwell in our hearts so others will see Your mercy, righteousness, truth, and peace. Father, You are the Way, the Truth, and Life. We long to walk in Your ways. In Jesus' name, amen.

September 9 ~ Procrastinate

Are you a procrastinator? Do you have closets that need cleaning out or bills that need your attention? What about your attic? Bingo. That is what I am procrastinating about right now. I need to clean out the attic. It is terrible. We made a royal mess in there.

Wrapping paper and old books are everywhere in the attic, and I need to give those books away. If Bill and I left this world, my children would not be happy when they opened that door. Why do I not just go in there and clean it out? It would be hard work, and what if there were roaches? If I were a roach, I would not live in that mess. It is also hot in the attic.

Procrastinating will never get it done. I will go to bed tonight knowing the job is undone, or I will go to bed refusing to think about the attic. Either way, I will keep putting this job off until I decide one day to stop procrastinating and get the job done. I could wait and let my children take care of the attic once I am gone. I like that idea.

My problem with this thinking is if I procrastinate about one thing, will I do the same with other important things? The natural man loves to put other things before the things of God. Do you find this true? We put off praying, studying the Word for TV, and telling others about Jesus. We live regretting or denying our wasted lives.

What is the deal? Why do we do this? Are we afraid to live with purpose, life will get hot with conflict, or are we afraid the nasty roaches of this world will get us? The Bible warns about procrastination:

"Therefore, as the Holy Spirit says: 'Today, if you will hear His voice, do not harden your hearts as in the rebellion,'"(Hebrews 3:7-8 NKJV).

The Word also warns against letting our fears control us:

"For God has not given us a spirit of fear, but of power and of love and of a sound mind" (2 Timothy 1:7).

The first passage reminds us to be careful of our old rebellious natures and to live the new nature God has given us. We can live with obedient hearts and courage and not fear because of the wondrous work of Jesus, our Savior and Lord. Let us not procrastinate but get moving and believe.

Ponders of the Heart

Read 2 Peter 1:2-11.

Do you, like me, need help with your walk with the Lord?

After reading the verses above, are you ready to walk in your God-given identity?

Prayers of the Heart

Dear Father,

We want to know You progressively and more intimately. You have given us all we need for life and godliness through Your Son, Jesus. Show us how to partake of Your nature, to drink deeply until our souls are filled. When You reach for us, help us respond with tender, receiving, and believing hearts. Lord Jesus, You are our need and our immense joy. We praise You. In Jesus' name, amen.

September 10 ~ Shearing

We had a hairy dog, Tex. She was part Border Collie, and in the wintertime, she looked like a butterball. Her coat was so thick that in the summer, she would be miserable if we didn't have her groomed.

When she became so old and achy, I shaved her myself each spring. Now, this was quite the job. It took forever, and I was not a professional; everyone who saw my work agreed. She did look better or at least cooler when I clipped her, but she would have looked better if a professional had done the job.

That old dog trusted me, and she would lie there and let me cut away at her coat. She looked as if she was really enjoying the attention and the shave. I wished the results equaled her cooperation.

We have Christians running around looking a bit like our dog, a little shaggy. They have tried to shave off their old ways, and they act a little better, at least at church. They have removed some of their hairy outer layers, but "The Professional" has not done the work.

They tried the "do-it-yourself, try harder program" instead of depending on the Holy Spirit, "The Professional," to do His work through them.

How do we cooperate with the Holy Spirit? I only know by faith as we place ourselves in His care. Under His control, we can search His Word and learn about Him and His ways. As we sit still, He will shear off our old ways of thinking and doing and give us a clean shave and a fresh start.

Nothing is more beautiful than a Christian who the Holy Spirit has sheared. He is our Professional. Spiritual shearing is difficult work and takes time. The more we cooperate with the Holy Spirit, the easier the job is, and the results are authentic.

I wish I could rest in the care of my Lord as easily as my old dog rested in my hands. If I trusted Him as Tex trusted me, I could rest in His Hands, enjoy His attention, and be cool and comfortable in my new authentic robe. I also would have His beauty shining through. That would turn heads, build His kingdom, and bring Him glory.

The truth about this life is shearing is an ongoing process. The Holy Spirit will continually do this as long as we are in these old bodies, but some sweet day, we will receive our new bodies, and we will not be bothered again with our old hairy selves. Praise the Lord.

Ponders of the Heart

Are we living like the culture we live in, or living out of our new nature?

Is it time for us to stand up for the Kingdom of Life? How will you do this today?

Read Ephesians 4:17-24 and Ephesians 5:8-14.

Prayers of the Heart

Dear Father,

We can feel pleasure when You work in our lives. Help us cooperate with Your work. We want our new nature to be what others see. We long for the freedom faith brings and the freshness of Your Spirit blowing new life into us. Wash us, and we will be clean. Free us, and we will be free. Lord, help us not walk in the ways of this world. Work on, dear Lord, work on. In Jesus' name, amen.

September 11 ~ The Day the World Stopped Turning

"Where Were You When The World Stopped Turning That September Day?" It is the title of a song by Alan Jackson. Those of us who were around September 11, 2001, cannot look at this date without thinking about the tragedy of that day. For a long time, I could not think of that without tears collecting in my eyes; even now, years later, I still get a lump in my throat, as I remember.

The loss of life, the evil planning, and the deception of those who carried out this plan still baffles my imagination. I believed the lie that we live in a safe environment. This lie was uncovered the day my son was attacked by a friend.

This friend had been out of Chris' life for years, and something snapped in this boy's mind. What do you do with such assaults? What do you do when you are praying for protection and the one you are praying for ends up with three broken ribs, a close encounter of being choked to death, and the betrayal of a friend?

In God's mercy and grace, His answer to me was to rest in Him. He is all-knowing, He is God, and He knows what He is doing. His love never changes. Regardless of the circumstances, God loves me and my son. I don't feel those things, especially in the middle of the circumstance. I cannot see these assurances of God's care, but faith whispers these truths as I remember Bible verses which tells me to hold on and believe.

When we got the call from Chris that night, and we were two hours away, I began to say Bible verses over and over in my head. The passage didn't always fit the situation, but it was truth and light in a very dark circumstance. I asked God to please send Chris someone to be with him. I called everyone I knew to call but couldn't find anyone to help. But God heard my prayer.

Chris' neighbor across the street came over and found out what had happened and went to the hospital in search of my son. She stayed with him, brought him home from the hospital, and took him to get his medicine. She told Chris she would be his substitute mom until I got there.

Yes, she is a Christian. She and her husband had been in the mission field for years, and God has taught them to serve. She did not hang up her missionary shoes when she returned to the United States.

Her concern might be a little thing to people. It is so easy to get caught up looking at the assault, the hurt, the unfairness of the incident, and miss God's provision. Even be ungrateful. But life apart from God is not living. He is our only hope in hopeless situations. The Lord is there, but we can miss Him. This was hard for me. Really hard. I watched Chris suffer pain in the body and soul.

I wanted to yell, "Unfair!" And it was, but God provided one of His own to minister to my son. Her love warmed my heart during a very bleak night. I thank God for His provision through a loving neighbor. We all saw God's provision of love through others during the tragedy of 9/11, and our God will continue to give us hope until He closes this age and brings us all home, where we will live forever in His safe, secure environment.

Ponders of the Heart

What verses in God's Word encourages you in harmful circumstances?

Can you remember a time when God sent a believer to help you? Maybe an angel?

Read Isaiah 43:1-4 and Romans 8:31-32.

Prayers of the Heart

Dear Father,

Though we don't understand many things, we will hope in You. You are our refuge and strength. You are our wisdom and provider.

Without You, Lord, we have no life. You are the light in the tunnel of darkness. You are our hope and comfort in the bleakest of times. Thank You, Lord, we are never alone. You will hold us with Your mighty Hand. In Jesus' name, amen.

September 12 ~ Sin Eater

We look to others to do things for us. In our lifetime, we might want someone to meet our need for companionship, security, and love. We could even want others to be responsible for our happiness and protection. People can also look to others for joy and strength. But what the people in the book The Last Sin Eater wanted someone to do for them was weird.

In the nineteenth century, in England, the lowlands of Scotland, and the Welsh border district, it was common to have a person in the community who was paid to take the sins of the deceased. They were to take the consequences of the deceased's sin into the afterlife.

This crazy custom came over by immigrants to the United States and practiced in remote areas of the Appalachian Mountains.

Now, this sounds unbelievable to me. I was amazed at this custom. Can you imagine the shame and the horrible life of the sin eater, not to mention the sense of false hope for all the others? But then again, do we have sin eaters, substitutions for God's grace, in our lives?

We might not have someone stand at our grave eating bread and wine to symbolize their eating our sins, but do we play the sin-eating game with God? Placing blame on someone else for our attitudes, decisions, and lifestyle. "It is her fault I am miserable." Or "It is his fault I am so depressed I can't work or pay my bills. " We love to play the blame game, but isn't the blame game a form of someone else being our sin eater? What a terrible lie that brings no freedom, just excuses.

If we want freedom from the weight of sin, we need to look no further than Christ's provision.

"What can wash away my sin? Nothing but the blood of Jesus; What can make me whole again? Nothing but the blood of Jesus.

0 precious is the flow. That makes me white as snow. No other fount I know. Nothing but the blood of Jesus. (Nothing but the Blood, Robert Lowry).

There is only one Sin Eater. There is only one who can take our shame and guilt, giving us freedom and no excuses. His name is Jesus. The blame game cannot restore, cannot bring peace, but He can. What false hope cannot give, Jesus can. Praise His name.

Ponders of the Heart

Who are you depending on today to take away your sins?

Do you play the blame game, or are you taking your failures to Jesus?

Read Romans 5:8-11.

Prayers of the Heart

Dear Father,

Help us understand the gift of Your grace. Teach us let go of blame, resentment, and guilt as we hold on to You. Your truth will set us free and give us purpose and meaning. Father, we have much to learn about walking in the Spirit. We pray for Your patience and Your mercy over our lives. Open the eyes of our hearts so we can see and understand the lies that keep us in bondage. In Jesus' name, amen.

September 13 ~ The Twos

Are the twos terrible or terrific? If you ask a two-year-old's mother this question, she might reply, "Terrible." Exactly what happens to a child in their twos? "Collier, you want GiGi to help you with your shoes?" "No, Caljur, do it," is the reply. The experts say this is an important developmental stage that helps a child discover personal identity.

It is a natural development that follows the first stage of bonding. Healthy bonding prepares a child for the healthy second stage of identity. When either or both stages are hindered, people can spend the rest of their lives out of whack. I am definitely out of whack, as are my husband and children. At best, we are all dysfunctional.

How do I know? The fall made it impossible for us to do things exactly right. Our relationship with our heavenly Father has been damaged, and apart from Him, we cannot get it all right. The good news is He spends, patiently, I might add, the rest of our lives "functioning" our dysfunction. Praise His Grace.

Even though we can't fix ourselves, we can ask God to reveal our dysfunction and the root cause. The root is so deep we need supernatural help to uncover the truth. As He gives us our answer, our job is to give it right back to Him. He will then remind us He has nailed it to the cross, and we are to count ourselves dead to on this issue.

God is in the business of restoring our spirits to His Spirit. He restores our souls, which are where we have our minds, wills, and emotions. As we bond with Him, He heals and restores us. We then move out securely to be missionaries to our world.

With our hearts joined in Jesus and as we live out of our new identity, we are free to be who He made us to be, His children. This is a tricky balancing act, one He gets right every time.

Here are a few test questions:

Do you have trouble bonding with others?

Do you have trouble owning up to your problems and circumstances?

Do you understand blaming is not dealing with life?

Do you spend too much time isolated?

Do you spend too much time depending on others?

If you are anything like me, you said yes to some, if not most, of these questions. God is in the business of reconciliation.

Ponders of the Heart

Are you in your terrible twos or terrific twos spiritually?

Read Psalm 139:7-18 and Psalm 139:23-24.

Are you listening, learning from Your heavenly Father, and walking in your true identity? It is a tricky balancing act that you will always need Him for.

Prayers of the Heart

Dear Father,

Thank You for the patience You show us as You help us grow up in You. We sometimes act terrible, but we want to be terrific. Thank You that You are always with us. Thank You that our identity is in You, kept by You, now and always. Father, we will never get it all right but reveal the things hindering our growth. Uncover our dysfunction as You teach us to live out of Your provision. Thank You for Your love, work, and making us Yours. In Jesus' name, amen.

September 14 ~ A Higher Goal

West Wing was a successful TV series with a large cast and a broad storyline. The characters were ambitious, opinionated, outspoken, and energetic. Even though their views differed from mine, I still found the show interesting. What intrigued me was the way they spoke their minds with conviction and honesty.

This honesty often stepped on someone's toes. The toe stomping was usually done face to face, not behind someone's back. Even those on the same team were often in each other's faces in a verbal battle of wits and opinions. In the bantering, feelings were hurt, view debated, and tempers heated up.

The dialog was stimulating and heated. My mind struggled to keep up with the discussions, and I often wondered, "How do they talk so fast?" All this made the show fast-moving and entertaining, but that was not what intrigued me the most. What fascinated me the most was the way they forgave each other and remained true to the cause.

Their cause was the country of the United States of America. The characters have a higher goal than themselves, their opinions, and their feelings; this goal was the good of the country as they serve at the pleasure of the President.

Isn't this interesting? People could come together, disagree in method or mindset, and yet yield to achieve a higher cause—not only yield but be willing to forgive the verbal bantering with one another. They believed and trusted that each person was devoted to the cause, and this devotion demanded honesty above personal feelings. You could say they developed thick skin to personal feelings to be part of a team.

I think the church of Jesus Christ would do well to take notice. Listen to the words of Paul to the church in Philippi:

"Therefore if you have any encouragement from being united with Christ, if any comfort from his love, if any common sharing in the Spirit, if any tenderness and compassion, then make my joy complete by being like-minded, having the same love, being one in spirit and of one mind. Do nothing out of selfish ambition or vain conceit. Rather, in humility value others above yourselves, not looking to your own interests but each of you to the interests of the others" (Philippians 2:1-4).

I have much to learn about serving at the pleasure of Jesus Christ. What about you?

Ponders of the Heart

Has the corporate church lost our unity?

How can you be part of building unity and not a unity breaker?

Read Romans 12:9-21.

Prayers of the Heart

Dear Father,

Forgive us for living as if we are the only one that matters. Forgive our arrogance and unforgiving hearts. We stand forgiven because of Your grace and work. Thank You for the understanding You have given us but help us know we do not understand all we need to know. When we disagree with others, help us seek Your truth and pray for unity in Your church.

Father God, we serve at the pleasure of the King of kings and the Lord of lords. In Jesus' name, amen.

September 15 ~ Freedom

The gospel song, He Touched Me, rings out in my head when I think about our freedom in Christ. Steven Mansfield's book, The Faith of George W. Bush, tells us that President Bush's faith has given him freedom. He was a late bloomer who struggled to come into himself, and this struggle led him to God, peace, and freedom.

Does your faith in God give you freedom? Christ came to set the captives free. President Bush felt a heavy burden, and he felt a load of guilt and shame; when Jesus touched him, it gave him the freedom to become the man God wanted him to be.

He would be the first to admit that he was not perfect, but he is sure he is on the right road to freedom. He knows this because he belongs to Jesus and serves the audience of One, Christ. Freedom is the will of Jesus for those who belong to Him.

"The thief comes only to steal and kill and destroy; I have come that they may have life, and have it to the full" (John 10:10).

What has shackled you with life's burdens? If we are believers in Christ and still feel shackled and burdened, is it possible we need a new touch from Jesus? We need a fresh touch of faith, purpose, or healing. Whatever has us shackled and burdened, Jesus is our way to freedom.

This freedom is found depending on Him and who He has recreated us to be. Freedom is the fruit of trusting Him and believing Him. He does have a plan, we do have a purpose, and we do matter. He came to give us life. Jesus is the source of life and satisfaction; we can experience abundant life in Him.

John 10:10 begins with these words:

"The thief comes only to steal and kill and destroy."

The thief came to steal our lives, kill our zeal for living and destroy our joy. But Christ came to give us back our lives, our purpose.

Ponders of the Heart

How would you describe freedom in Christ?

How has Christ fulfilled John 10:10 in your life? If not, ask Jesus to set you free.

Read Luke 4:18-21.

Prayers of the Heart

Dear Father,

We will trust You today and wait on You. You tell us, Father, that those who wait, depending on you, will renew and exchange their strength for your strength. You tell us that we will mount up on wings, like eagles. We will run and not be weary; we will walk and not faint. This sounds like sweet freedom to us. Oh, how we praise You. In Jesus' name, amen.

September 16 ~ The Love of Life

Our family loves the water, maybe because our home state is Florida. When I say we love water, I feel like I need to explain. I can never remember a time when summer vacation did not include a trip to the lake or the ocean. During the summer, we spent time in the water.

My mother and dad had a pool, and from the time my youngest daughter, Julie, was old enough to walk, she wanted to be in the pool. Their pool didn't have steps, just ladders, and she would hold onto the ladder in the shallow water. She did this until she was able to swim.

We all love to swim and ski. Wakeboards and boat riding are still a part of our lives.

When we lived near West Point Lake in LaGrange, Georgia, Bill's fishing boat was one of his favorite pastimes. We dreamed of having a lake house, and we all enjoyed a trip to the ocean as often as possible. I have been on fishing boats and a cruise ship in the open seas. All those experiences add to my saying, " I love the water."

But I have my limits. I would be terrified to sail on the open sea, surf, or scuba dive. The fear of drowning or being eaten by a big fish keeps me from enjoying those adventures. With my love of water, I would enjoy those things, but fear keeps me planted near the shore. Fear, indeed, is a killjoy.

In John 14:27, Jesus tells us, *"Peace I leave with you; my peace I give you. I do not give to you as the world gives. Do not let your hearts be troubled and do not be afraid."*

Even as I confess my fears, I think God wanted our Christian lives to be an adventure. The Webster's Dictionary defines adventure as "an unusual or suspenseful experience." Life was supposed to be an extraordinary and exciting experience. The reason it is not, is because we are too busy staying close to shore.

We stay in the shallow end of life, holding on to the ladder. Some dare to venture out from their comfortable lives and go on a mission trip. We are quite satisfied with this little adventure as long as we can see the shore of our comfortable lives. Knowing we can get back there when we want. What does this tell us about our trust in God?

Please don't misunderstand what I am trying to say. We need to walk before we run. We need to learn to swim before we sail. We are to have boundaries of good sense, but do you think we are controlling our boundaries, or are they controlling us? God is not a God of fear. He is all-knowing and all-powerful. God's Word says it like this:

"For God has not given us a spirit of fear, but of power and of love and of a sound mind" (2 Timothy 1:7 NKJV).

Notice we are to be of sound mind. If you can't swim, hold on to the side until you learn. If you don't know how to sail, stay out of the water. And if a Great White shark is swimming around the boat, for goodness' sake, stay in the boat.

God has given us a mind so we can discern danger and help us make sound decisions. The more we know Him and His Word, the sharper our sound mind will direct us. But the same is true. If we ignore His truths and continue our own understanding, we can get into troubled waters in a heartbeat.

The Lord wants to direct our courage while He gives us power by knowing His voice and ways. We are to be motivated by love while using the sound mind of the Spirit as we discern His will, but we are not to be afraid of living. Are you living? If not, fall in love with life, the life He has given you, and live the great adventure.

Ponders of the Heart

Are you a person with fear that keeps you from living?

How does Psalm 27 encourage you to face your fear so you can have a great adventure with God?

Read Psalm 27.

Prayers of the Heart

Dear Father,

You are our light and salvation. You are our strength and courage. Oh, Father, help us live this great adventure called life. Living, trusting You, discerning Your will, and walking in Your ways. And, Lord, if the waves of life overtake us, we will call out Your name. We want You and will seek You all the days of our life. In Jesus' name, amen.

September 17 ~ Walking With God

My youngest daughter knows the concept of "walking with. " If I call Julie up and say, "Julie, you want to ride to the mall with me?" If she says yes, you know you have a good companion. She comes along. She doesn't come to boss you, tell you how to drive, and she doesn't come with her agenda other than to keep you company. This makes Julie "easy company."

She is not in a hurry and does not have a goal other than being with you. She is an example to me of what the Bible means when it says someone walked with God.

"Noah was a righteous man, blameless among the people of his time, and he walked faithfully with God" (Genesis 6:9).

I am concerned that God's children want God to walk with them instead of them walking with Him. We have our agenda. We know where we want to go, and we want Him to bless our goals. Do you think we have the cart before the horse?

The word walk in Hebrew is Halak, meaning to come along with it. It means to walk without any suggestion of a definite destination. How is it possible to walk with someone without us suggesting how we are to get there? If they know the destination and you are sure of their ability to get you there, then you can rest and enjoy the ride and the company.

This is the kind of child God is looking for—a child He can call up and say, "Marilyn, you want to walk through life with me?" And if I say yes, then I need to take Julie's good example and go where He wants me to go, knowing He knows how to get me there and what we are to accomplish. God just wants my company. He does not need help from me, although He will include me.

The Lord will use our trip to teach me, fill me with joy, and show me His ways. What a great trip. If only I could learn to be "easy company." Enoch is a great example of a man who walked with God.

"Enoch walked faithfully with God; then he was no more, because God took him away" (Genesis 5:24).

"By faith Enoch was taken from this life, so that he did not experience death: "He could not be found, because God had taken him away. For before he was taken, he was commended as one who pleased God" (Hebrews 11:5).

Oh, that we could be people of faith who walk with God, trusting His ways, and learn to be "easy company."

Ponders of the Heart

Who in your life would you say is "easy company"?

Are you walking with God, or are you about God walking with you?

Read Hebrews 11: 1-6.

Prayers of the Heart

Dear Father,

    How arrogant we can be to think we know the way or the agenda. We want to be about walking with You. You know the way and Your agenda is always best. We can walk with You all the way home. Let us follow You and enjoy being with You as we go. Father, thank You for Your patience and love. In Jesus' name, amen.

September 18 ~ Scoffers of Faith

"Above all, you must understand that in the last days scoffers will come, scoffing and following their own evil desires" (2 Peter 3:3).

    Who are the scoffers of our age? It's hard to tell unless they come jeering and openly discrediting our belief in Jesus. Who are they? The media as a whole and Hollywood would be two groups you could say are modern-day scoffers of "The Way."

    What is humorous is when the media is interviewing someone, and the person praises God or gives Him credit for the good done. The professional interviewers are stunned and at a loss for words. They don't expect God to come into the equation and would rather Him not.

The problem is theirs because they are the ones who asked the question. Maybe in their arrogance, they think they understand what makes us tick. To sell papers, they want certain answers. But occasionally, they meet a person of faith, and they are at a loss for what to do with their answers.

I was watching an interview with Linda Petty. She is Kyle Petty's wife, a Nascar hero. They have devoted themselves to a camp called Victory Junction. This is a special camp for children who are terminally ill. The media was singing the Petty's praises, but Linda was singing God's.

The interviewer tried desperately to get Linda to give glory to Kyle and the racing industry or make this a tribute to her son, Adam, who died in a plane crash. But Linda was firm in her standing. She was proud of the camp, proud that Kyle's name had been used for good, but she knew only God could give these children the hope they needed. She stood firm. The media didn't know what to say. God was glorified and I was blessed.

Linda understood it was not about her. It was about God, her Savior, her Hope for herself and these children. We need to realize scoffers will sneer at our faith.

They do not know or understand us. Our job is to be true to who we are and plant seeds that the Holy Spirit can use to open their eyes. I thank God for the strength He gives His own to speak out for our Savior.

"The Lord is not slow at keeping his promises, as some understand slowness. Instead he is patient with you, not wanting anyone to perish, but everyone to come to repentance" (2 Peter 3:9).

Don't you, like me, pray that Linda Petty's words brought a reporter or someone listening to repentance? Thank you, Mrs. Petty, for witnessing our hope in God.

Ponders of the Heart

Have you encountered a scoffer?

As we face the fact that scoffers are all around, how are you preparing yourself for the encounter?

Read 2 Peter 3:1-18.

Prayers of the Heart

Dear Father,

Holy and faithful Lord, we praise you. Let the words of our mouth and the praises of our hearts be for You. We live in a world that needs You, a world that is hurting for Your truth. Oh, Father, as long as we have breath, let us praise You and proclaim Your greatness. You alone are worthy of our praise. In Jesus' name, amen.

September 19 ~ Hiding from God

Playing hide-and-seek with a two-year-old is hilarious. When my grandchildren were little, they loved to play hide-and-seek. They would hide in places that I had just hidden.

Collier, our first grandchild, all the way down to Elizabeth, our youngest grandchild, as toddlers, would push me out of the way and jump in my hiding place. I would say, "I wonder where my grandson or granddaughter is?" They would call out, "You will never find me." I let the game continue, knowing, all along, their little hearts were beating fast as they waited patiently for me to open the closet door or peep under the bed and find them. Then, it was my turn, and we started all over again.

I knew there would be a time when the game would be more challenging. They would figure out not to hide in my hiding place, and if they did, I would find them. But for a time in each of their lives, I enjoyed the excitement I saw in their eyes and their little voices calling out with all their might, "You never will find me here."

Collier was especially funny when we hid together. I would say, "Collier, hold Gigi's hand, I'm scared," and he would take my hand and put it over his eyes. What is he thinking? This is the reasoning of a two-year-old. I laugh, but how ridiculous it must seem to God when we try to hide from Him, thinking if we cannot see Him, then He cannot see us.

"But Jonah ran away from the Lord and headed for Tarshish. He went down to Joppa, where he found a ship bound for that port. After paying the fare, he went aboard and sailed for Tarshish to flee from the Lord" (Jonah 1:3).

Jonah is one of the examples in the Scripture of what can happen when we hide from God. How ridiculous it was when Jonah boarded the ship and, in a sense, called out to God as they left port, "You won't find me here." We know the story: God found him, and Jonah found himself in the tummy of a big fish. Yuck.

Obedience is much better than disobedience. Jonah repented and obeyed God's instruction and went to Nineveh, but Jonah still had growing up to do. God was compassionate and patient with Jonah, as He is with us.

Have you ever hidden from God, running away from His call? I have, and I do not mind telling you it is a dark, lonely place. It stinks; it stinks just like the belly of a fish would. I am always thankful when he hears my cry and comes and rescues me. He knows I am sorry, and I call out to Him because I believe in Him. But He also knows I have more growing up to do. God is patient and thankfully loves us enough to never let us go.

Ponders of the Heart

Have you ever tried to hide from God?

Why do you think we do that?

Read Psalm 139.

Prayers of the Heart

Dear Father,

You search and know us. Thank You for the promise that we can never flee from Your presence. We are thankful You know what is best for us and have a plan for our lives. Father, show us our sins so we might repent and walk obediently. You are our joy and salvation. We are always in Your safe, secure sight. We love You, Lord. In Jesus' name, amen.

September 20 ~ The Vastness of God

Can't you just get lost in the title of this devotional, "The Vastness of God"? How can we even fathom His immensity? His mind is infinite, and ours are finite. He is our creator, and we are His creation.

We can't understand how powerful He is, yet He wants to reveal to us His love.

I am so thankful that He is beyond my capabilities, beyond comprehension, and yet intimate. He is full of wonder and calls us wondrously made. His Word is eternal, and in it are the keys to eternal life. We can never understand His vastness, yet we can get lost in the awe of our Lord.

If we stopped and pondered eternity more, we might develop patience. If we stopped and pondered His vastness, we might develop a deeper faith. And maybe if we pondered His love going on and on and on and on, we would experience more peace.

"Your throne, 0 God, is forever and ever; A scepter of righteousness is the scepter of Your kingdom" (Psalm 45:6 NKJV).

Considering His vastness, we can surrender our day with all our concerns. We do not know what tomorrow holds, but we can know the One who does.

Knowing God holds our days, months, and years can give us peace in facing life. God's love is deeper than the ocean. His wisdom is higher than the mountains, and He understands the complexities of our lives completely. He is more powerful than evil, and His rule is forever. Who can stand against us? His kingdom is controlled by righteousness. Praise You, Father.

Ponders of the Heart

What do you want to praise Him for today?

What do you need Him to help you with right now?

Read Psalm 104.

Prayers of the Heart

Dear Father,

You are our eternal Father and King. You will reign forever. How we praise You. You alone are worthy of all praise, honor, and glory. Praise the Father, praise the Son, and praise the Holy Spirit. Thank You for Your Word. Thank You for our salvation and Your unfailing love, which is ours forever. In Jesus' name, amen.

September 21 ~ Cooperating With God

"Collier, let Gigi change your diaper." "No, Gigi. Stop it." "Collier, you want to take a ride to the store?" "No." "Collier, please give me the stick." "No, leave me alone!" The battles with a two-year-old. Why can't they cooperate with us? Why does everything have to be a battle? I asked Collier that question, and he thought the word cooperate was hilarious. He laughed and laughed and laughed.

His mother had been trying to teach him to cooperate. I know because sometimes he would say, "Okay, Gigi," Those words were music to my ears. I also tried to teach him to cooperate and be nice. If he wanted something, I would say, "Collier, what do you say? What is the magic word?" He would say, "Please, Gigi." That worked every time.

One day, I had to finally get on to him, put him in the chair, and said, "Collier, don't you get up until you can be nice."

I walked past the chair, and he waved and said, "Hi, GiGi." From that moment on, I was done.

There were also those times when he would run to meet me, call me on the phone, and tell me he loved me. Then there were, and still are, those hugs and kisses that melt my heart.

Oh, with cooperation, I would give him the world if I could.

I wonder if God thinks like this about us. "Marilyn, let me change your life a little. It is a little stinky."

"No, God, leave me alone."

"Marilyn, you want to go with me and help me with this person?"

"No, I want to do what I want to do."

"Marilyn, you want to let go of that before it hurts you?"

"No, God, stop it."

I bet God has terrible twos in His family. Why can't we cooperate with Him? Why do we think everything needs to go our way?

When Collier got sleepy, why did he not want to go to sleep? Why is it that when I need to rest and let God work, I keep pushing to fix everything and everyone?

If I give Collier useful information like, "That will hurt you," why doesn't he listen? When God sets up boundaries in His Word, why do I step over the line or at least step on the line? Collier had an excuse; he was two. Saying no and being two go together. What is our excuse?

How can we cooperate with God? Paul puts it this way:

"Not that I have already obtained all this, or have already arrived at my goal, but I press on to take hold of that for which Christ Jesus took hold of me. Brothers and sisters, I do not consider myself yet to

have taken hold of it. But one thing I do: Forgetting what is behind and straining toward what is ahead, I press on toward the goal to win the prize for which God has called me heavenward in Christ Jesus" (Philippians 3:12-14).

Okay, let us try cooperating. Altogether, let's say, "Okay, God." Why don't you give Him a little wave and say Hi. It sure worked with me, and His love is much greater and His heart more tender. Go ahead and try it.

Ponders of the Heart

If God speaks, will you listen? He speaks to us in His Word.

If God leads, will you follow?

Read 2 Timothy 4:7-8 and 1 Corinthians 9:24-27.

Prayers of the Heart

Dear Father,

Your Word tells us that You are holding on to us. Hold on and we will hold on to You. Help us trust, believe, and walk with You. We want to be children who cooperate with all You want to do with us and for us. We need You, and we want to believe You will never let us go. Father, right now, we look to You and say, "Okay, Lord." In Jesus' name, amen.

September 22 ~ Eating from His Hands

"Give us today our daily bread" (Matthew 6:11).

A bird feeder was one of the treasures I received on Mother's Day. It was in the shape of two hands, and on the front, the words, "By His Hands, we are fed." I loved it and placed it on our deck so I could watch the birds and squirrels eat. Some people get upset when the squirrels eat out of a bird feeder, but I don't; it's fun to watch them. They are a hungry little bunch.

We have a whole crew in our backyard that regularly visits our hands. There are big, little, and different-colored ones, and one doesn't have a tail. Some will eat together, while others eat alone, and there are bullies who will not share.

I have one that is especially beautiful to me. This little squirrel is the color of chestnut and is small. He will crawl right up into the hands and eat while he keeps his eyes peeled for intruders. His fur is silky, and he has those innocent, gentle eyes. He has delicate little hands he uses to partake of the bird seed. The sight is beautiful to me. I see the handiwork of God in His creation.

There is the truth in the words, "By His Hands, we are fed." That is true for all of us. The Bible tells us that God is our provider. He provides certain things for the good and the evil, just like I provide birdseed for the birds and the squirrels, but I do not think this means He does not have His favorites.

When we come wanting to eat from His Hands, I know it pleases Him. I know that when we crawl into His hands to partake of His divine nature, He gives without reservation. When we search for wisdom among the morsels of His food, we find it. And when we search for truth in His Word, He opens our minds and allows us to eat and be satisfied.

Though I have found it entertaining to watch squirrels, birds are nobler creatures. They seem to wait for their turn, and when it is their turn, they can get their fill. Not so with squirrels. They run each other off, seldom share, and eat, eat, eat, and eat some more. Sometimes, I think they are pigs instead of squirrels.

This truth also describes us. We have those who are nobler. They wait for the Lord. They let what He gives them be enough, and they often share. Others of us are more like squirrels or, should I say, pigs. (Ouch.) We want and want and want. We run others off, and we do not want to share.

Thankfully, God can use everything and anything to teach us. We are not just created beings. We who are in Christ are recreated beings who can walk out of a more noble character. We can walk in the character of the Spirit, the Holy Spirit. God gave this new nature to us, and yet we must constantly beware of the old squirrel in all of us.

Ponders of the Heart

What are the benefits you see being in God's Hand?

Are you more like a squirrel or a bird?

Read Isaiah 62:3, Isaiah 49:15-16, and Isaiah 64:8.

Prayers of the Heart

Dear Father,

Hold us close in Your Hands and provide all we need. We want Your presence in our lives. Father, like little birds or squirrels, allow us to crawl into Your presence and be so close that Your Hands hold us. We want to recognize the wonder of Your protective, gentle, strong Hands holding our lives. In Jesus' name, amen.

September 23 ~ Mastering

"Sin crouches at your door; its desire is for you, but you must master it" (Genesis 4:7 NKJV).

Have you ever had fleas in your house? We experienced this, and the fleas were awful. It was a mystery how they got inside because our dog stayed outside. She was protected from fleas by some medicine the veterinarian gave us. But the fleas got into the house just the same.

They bit me in the kitchen, the den, my study, and even in the bed. When I took a bath, I would see a couple in my bath water.

We used a spray that promised to kill them, but we still fought to get rid of them. They are so tiny you can't see them, so you think they are gone until they bite you. They crouch at the door, just waiting for the opportunity to come inside.

The Word of God tells us that sin is like this. It crouches at our door, and its desire is to master us, rule over us, and eat us alive. Sin is like a flea: subtle and obscure. It appears small but carries with it a big bite. Sin's desire is to master us, but God tells us not to let it.

What little sin is biting at your heels? Does this sin find its way to you in the kitchen, the den, or even in your bed? What can we do about these pesky things? The first command is found in Romans

6:11, where Paul tells us to reckon ourselves dead to sin but alive to God in Christ Jesus our Lord.

Reckon me dead to sin. What exactly does that mean? When we reckon ourselves dead to sin, we are saying that sin has no power over us; it's a bluff. We are to know that sin has no place in our lives, no power in our lives except what we give it, and we are to stand firm against it and drive it out.

When I called the pest control man, I wanted him to show up with a mighty spray that would kill the fleas inside and out and the eggs. I wanted to be free from those annoying varmints when I went to bed. They had no place in my life. The same is true with sin.

My plan is to call out to God and ask Him to plunge me deep into His anti-sin spray. I don't want to save even one sin that will sneak up and bite me. As God's child, sin has no place in my heart, mind, and soul. I want to be free. We know the One who will gladly come to our defense if we call. Reckoning ourselves dead to sin and alive to God can be our first step in conquering sin's trickery over our lives.

Ponders of the Heart

What sin likes to bite at your heels?

What instructions does God's Word give us about mastering sin?

Read Genesis 4:6-8 and see what happens when we let sin master us. Also, read Romans 6:5-14.

Prayers of the Heart

Dear Father,

Sin nibbles away at our hearts and lives, wanting to master us. You are our true Master, and Jesus has made a way for us to live in freedom. Because of Jesus, we can have power over sin and live lives of purity. Please teach us how and give us the strength to believe and obey. We love You, Father. Thank You for Your grace. In Jesus' name, amen.

September 24 ~ Accumulation

"But seek first the kingdom of God and His righteousness, and all these things shall be added to you" (Matthew 6:33 NKJV).

How can a refrigerator collect so much stuff? What about a dresser drawer or a closet? I spent all morning cleaning out the refrigerator. There was enough salad dressing to open my own salad shop—not for days, mind you because there was only a small amount of dressing in most of those bottles.

I threw them out, cleaned and wiped out the refrigeration until what was left was usable or at least visible. Everywhere I look, I see an abundance of accumulation, and with the accumulation, I see myself spending my time keeping up with all this stuff.

It is a good feeling to clean out the refrigerator, as well as closets and dresser drawers, but what about our lives? There may be things we need to clean out. We may need to resign from several committees or let go of some TV shows. Our efforts of going and doing can take us away from resting and being.

Chasing this world has run us down, and we need to get out of the rat race before we become a rat. What are we looking for? God's kingdom. His righteousness. The Bible is not fuzzy about this; it says:

"Do not love the world or anything in the world. If anyone loves the world, love for the Father is not in them. For everything in the world—the lust of the flesh, the lust of the eyes, and the pride of life—comes not from the Father but from the world. The world and its desires pass away, but whoever does the will of God lives forever" (1 John 2:15-17).

Again, I ask the question: What are we looking for? Have our lives become a vast opportunity to accumulate the stuff? Let these words fall on your heart:

"See what great love the Father has lavished on us, that we should be called children of God! And that is what we are! The reason the world does not know us is that it did not know him. Dear friends, now we are children of God, and what we will be has not yet been made known. But we know that when Christ appears, we shall be like him, for we shall see him as he is. All who have this hope in him purify themselves, just as he is pure" (1 John 3:1-3).

These are great verses that motivate us to seek Kingdom living.

Ponders of the Heart

Does this verse give you a desire to be transformed?

What part of your life needs changing?

Have you asked God to change you?

Read Romans 12:2.

Prayers of the Heart

Dear Father,

Help us look around and see the number of earthly treasures we have accumulated. Lord, open our hearts and show us our priorities.

You are our portion and reward. We seek You, Your kingdom, and righteousness. Open the eyes of our hearts to Your heart. We love You, Lord, and we want to love You more. In Jesus' name, amen.

September 25 ~ Substitutions

"Dear children, keep yourselves from idols" (1 John 5:21).

Webster's Dictionary defines an idol as "an image or person regarded as an object of worship." I love the following definition: "Something visible but lacking substance."

In the above passage, John tells the readers to keep away from idols. He calls his readers little children. John is writing to believers who are children of God, and this tells me several things.

As children of God, we are in great danger of having an idol; in fact, it is a real possibility. I know I am guilty of this. I place worth on things that, in the eternal scheme of things, are worthless. They promise so much more than they could ever deliver. That is true of things, and it is true of people. This world gives them worth, but they lack real substance in God's kingdom.

Anything we allow to take the place of God will hold us captive and cause regret. We can easily end up empty and disappointed; that may be one reason John ended his letter by warning us to keep away from idols.

Some scholars believe these are the last words in the entire Word of God if you take the Bible in chronological order. Martyn Lloyd-Jones put it like this:

"The words of an old man are always worthy of respect and consideration; they are words that are based upon a long lifetime's experience. The last words of all people are important, but the last words of great people are of exceptional importance, and the last words of an Apostle of the Lord Jesus Christ are of supreme importance."

So how do we do this? How are we to guard ourselves against idols? Allow me to suggest a few:

- Remember the truth about ourselves. We are God's people, bought at the price of Christ's blood.
- Our true home is God's kingdom, and this world has fallen to the evil one. In other words, our lives have a higher calling, and we do not want to live for any of the substitutions this world offers.
- Even God's gifts are not to be worshiped. We are called to worship the creator, not the creation.
- Lastly, idols are temporary, and our God is eternal.

If we worship money, possessions, position, success, any person, children, or anything else in this life, we have placed our worship on something that is temporary.

There is only One worthy of our worship, and that is God. If we remember the truth about God and live in communion with Him, we can have victory over idols in our lives. This will protect us from sorrow and pain. Remember, little children, keep away from false living.

Ponders of the Heart

Read 1 Corinthians 7:23, 1 John 2:15-17, and Psalm 119:35-37.

Which of these verses speak the loudest to you?

What have you loved in this world that brought you sorrow and pain?

Let's believe these words God speaks over us and walk in obedience.

Prayers of the Heart

Dear Father,

You have made us Your own, and You paid dearly. Help keep our minds full of the truth of who we are and where we belong. Keep us looking up and abiding in the truth of Your Word. Lord, You have redeemed us from this world; let us see beyond the blue of the sky into our heavenly home. Draw our hearts to You and help us stay away from earthly idols. In Jesus' name, amen.

September 26 ~ The Loss of a Hero

"In the year that King Uzziah died, I saw the Lord sitting on a throne, high and lifted up, and the train of His robe filled the temple (Isaiah 6:1 NKJV).

King Uzziah was an admired king. He was a hero in the eyes of his people. The year he died, Isaiah saw the Lord. Often, our earthly heroes can skew our view of the Lord. Oswald Chambers, in "Utmost for His Highest," says it like this:

"Our soul's personal history with God is often an account of the death of our heroes."

When I look back over my life, I find this statement true, either by the death of one of my heroes or just by them moving out of my daily life. There is only one God, and our heroes may shine His light or speak His words, but they are only ambassadors. God will allow us to learn of Him through another, but in His perfect timing, He will lift the illusion so we can see Him face to face. How I praise Him for this.

Who are the heroes in your life? Are they still around, or are they gone? If they are gone, you can relate to the above statement by Oswald Chambers. Now, Oswald Chambers was probably many believers' hero, and when he died, they could become disheartened and give up or fall before God and experience Him in a way they never thought possible. Circumstances have a way of drawing us to God or refusing to see Him.

What a testimony of faith when Isaiah said? "I saw the Lord!" I have a friend right now who is in the middle of a heart-wrenching circumstance, and she is seeing God. She is more thankful, grateful, and full of love than me. If you knew her circumstances, you would say, "How can this be?" It can't be without a vision of God before you, high and lifted up. Oh, that we would see Him, rest in Him, and believe that no one is like Our God.

Ponders of the Heart

Who do you turn to when circumstances are hard?

Do you learn from your heroes of faith, or do you worship them?

Read Psalm 30.

Prayers of the Heart

Dear Father,

It is You we want to see. Let not even heroes of faith keep our eyes from Your face. You are our need and our salvation. Lord, let our eyes feast upon Your goodness. Let Your light shine in the dark places of our souls. Open our eyes to see You high and lifted up with the train of Your robe, filling our lives with Your glory. You are the Hero of Glory. In Jesus' name, amen.

September 27 ~ The Sum of All Fears

"Be strong and courageous. Do not be afraid; do not be discouraged, for the Lord your God will be with you wherever you go" (Joshua 1:9).

I recently read a story about a little boy who asked his mommy to stay with him during the night. There was a terrible thunderstorm outside, and he was afraid. His mother replied that she could not stay with him because she had to sleep in Daddy's room. After a moment of silence, the little boy replied with a shaky voice. "The big sissy."

Fear is an epidemic in our world. Here is a list of some phobias that might surprise you. There is peladophobia, the fear of baldness and bald people; Aerophobia, a fear of drafts; chaetophobia, the fear of hairy people; thalassophobia, a fear of the ocean or large bodies of water; odontophobia, the fear of teeth; and phobophobia, a fear of being afraid. The list can go on and on.

Even though these are extreme examples, fear is universal and has been a part of human existence since Adam told God in the garden that he hid because he was afraid. Here is a quote from Steve McVey in his newsletter, "The Grace Vine."

"Don't let your fears paralyze you. A sovereign God has ordained some things for you. His loving Son will accomplish them through you as you trust His supernatural Spirit to empower you. Do you feel afraid? Admit it and move on beyond it. Courage is not the absence of fear. Courage means that you act in faith despite your feeling of fear."

I needed to hear that; it would be a good quote for us all. We cannot conquer fear with self-confidence but walk through fear with faith and confidence. Believing that God is for us and not against us will give us the courage to stand when we want to run.

We can trust Him with our fears because He promises to always be with us, and God keeps His promises. His Word tells us He has plans for us, and those plans are good. We do not want to miss one thing He has planned. God is powerful, wise, and full of grace, and He will never forsake His children. He is our confidence, and we can run to Him for the help we need.

Ponders of the Heart

What is your biggest fear?

What can we do to face those fears?

Read Joshua 1:6-9 and Psalm 27:1

Prayers of the Heart

Dear Father,

Fear has often paralyzed us. You are our strength. Why do we let doubt reign in our hearts and minds? Father, give us the faith and courage to believe what You say. The faith to know You are faithful, and we can rest in Your mighty power and love. Thank You for the promises in Your Word that give us the courage to face today and all our tomorrows. In Jesus' name, amen.

September 28 ~ Social Disease

"And the Lord God said, 'It is not good that man should be alone'" (Gen. 2:18).

There is a modern-day social disease that is crippling our society, a disease that hinders meaningful relationships. It has us bound to silence, lies, fears, and loneliness. There are people who believe this is good. They think it is just an alternate lifestyle. People are born with these social differences, and we are to celebrate our advancements in understanding and providing help so they can be who they are.

The social disease I am talking about is isolation. Many people live in isolation. They do their banking over the internet, they work from home, their friends are in chat rooms or on a weekly television show, and they live lonely, isolated lives.

Isolation is a genuine problem. God said, "It is not good that man should be alone." We are relational people who need the input of God and others in our lives to grow in honesty and wholeness. Character is tested and perfected in our relationships.

I can become a hermit in a heartbeat. In fact, I have often longed for more alone time, but recently, I have found myself alone too much and feeling isolated. What I need, what we all need, are deep, meaningful relationships. We need each other, and through relationships, we can gain more knowledge of God.

The social disease of isolation is not only those who spend their time alone. It can be a disease that plagues us even in a crowd. We can live isolated lives where we play a part and hide who we are. As my husband often says, "Faking our way through life" by managing our misery.

How do we fight this social disease? How do we come out of the closet of hiding and join the living? As always, we must first confess our need to God and repent. Then, we must ask God to show us opportunities for meaningful relationships. When He does, we will need to turn off the television, get out of the chat rooms, put on our walking shoes, and join the club of relationships.

We might want to join a small group, take a class, go with a friend to volunteer to help with a meaningful project and join the living. Isolation can cause fatigue, or does it cause depression? Whichever it is, we need to rid ourselves of this social disease, for God was right; in fact, He is never wrong when He said, "It is not good for man to be alone."

Ponders of the Heart

Are you a social butterfly or an introvert?

Do you have deep personal relationships, or do you have a social disease of isolation?

Read Ephesians 4:17-5:2.

Prayers of the Heart

Dear Father,

We come to You today confessing our need for deep, lasting relationships, relationships that honor You and deepen our understanding of You. We want to be a shining light in a crooked world, not people hiding from life. Lord, help us see where You are guiding us and let us live with deep and meaningful relationships. In Jesus' name, amen.

September 29 ~ Toothless Lion

When my three children were young, we spent time with my older brother and his family. The cousins were close to the same age, and we enjoyed vacations together and keeping each other's children during the summer.

One summer, my brother's children, Jeff, Scott, and Missy, came for a visit. Scott, the middle child, was such a great kid. He was a helper, and you could always count on him to help however he could. He always had a smile on his face. I adored him.

I do, however, recall one time when I was not pleased with him. We lived in South Georgia at the time, and occasionally, small field mice would get into the house. I had a trap set, and one mouse met its end in the trap. Scott thought it would be so funny to chase me with this dead mouse.

"Scott, don't bring that thing close to me," I shouted, which was all the encouragement he needed to chase me. If you could have seen me that day, you would have thought a mountain lion was chasing me as I ran down the hall to my daughter's bedroom, slamming the door and locking it. I told Scott in no uncertain terms he would be in deep trouble if he didn't take the dead mouse out of my house and leave me alone. It was so out of character for him to torture me.

We laugh about it now, but at the time, I was terrified.

Here is the question. Why was I so afraid of a dead mouse? What in the world could a dead mouse do to hurt me? I overreacted.

I wish I could say I learned my lesson and no longer react in fear to things that cannot hurt me, but at times, I find myself reacting or, should I say, overreacting.

We are told in Scripture that nothing can separated from God's love, and He is for us. God is good, wise, strong, and will never leave us, but we run for fear at the sound of Satan, the toothless lion.

Satan is strong, but God is stronger. The Evil one is in this world, but Jesus has overcome the world. Satan prowls around like a roaring lion, looking for someone to devour by his lying nature, but God tells us to resist him and stand firm against him.

"And the God of all grace, who called you to his eternal glory in Christ, after you have suffered a little while, will himself restore you and make you strong, firm and steadfast" (1 Peter 5:10-11)

In Christ Jesus, we are more than conquerors. God is our provider, protector, and great reward. We need to stand firm in faith when Satan runs after us, when God is on our side.

Ponders of the Heart

What do you fear?

How can you depend on God and resist fear?

Read Romans 8:28-39 and 1 Peter 5:6-11.

Prayers of the Heart

Dear Father,

You tell us not to fear. We are safe in Your care, and still, we fear. Help us feel Your strength around us, and help us know in our hearts and minds that You have us. We are safe in Your Hands. Give us the courage to stand up against evil and hold on to what is true. We need You. Thank You for the promise that You are for us, not against us. We will win in the end. In Jesus' name, amen.

September 30 ~ Prayers of the Heart

"Whom have I in heaven but you? And earth has nothing I desire besides you. My flesh and my heart may fail, but God is the strength of my heart and my portion forever" (Psalm 73:25-26).

Dear Father,

How we humble ourselves in praise of Your greatness. How thankful we are that we know You. When we consider Your face, all else pales. You are our deepest need and desire. Father, how often we fail You, forget You, and even sin against You, but Your character of love is not based on our performance. It is central to the substance of who You are. Oh Lord, You alone are worthy of praise, honor, and glory.

"Your ways, God, are holy. What god is as great as our God? You are the God who performs miracles; you display your power among the peoples. With your mighty arm you redeemed your people, the descendants of Jacob and Joseph" (Psalm 77:13-15).

Dear Lord,

We honor You for Your wonders, Your miracles. You alone have redeemed us and called us Your own. Thank You that what is impossible with man is possible with You.

You are our Savior, the strength of our hearts, and our portion forever. Again, Lord, we praise You.

"It is good to praise the Lord and make music to your name, O Most High, proclaiming your love in the morning and your faithfulness at night" (Psalm 92:1-2).

Dear Father,

We praise You and sing to glorify Your name. You are the Most High God, and we love You. Thank You for Your faithfulness and Your presence in our lives. Father God, You are our story, and You are our song. We will praise You forever and ever. In Jesus' name, amen.

october

— 66 —

All Scripture is God-breathed and is useful for teaching, rebuking, correcting and training in righteousness, so that the servant of God may be thoroughly equipped for every good work.
2 Timothy 3:16-17

October 1 ~ Seasons of Change

"He made the moon to mark the seasons, and the sun knows when to go down" (Psalm 104:19).

Is there anything as refreshing in the South as the first cool snap of the year? Ah, fall. You sometimes think it will never come, but it comes every year. In fact, God uses the seasons to remind us of His faithfulness.

If we looked back on our lives with spiritual eyes, we would see how faithful He has been. Knowing He has been faithful to us in the past helps us face the unknown. Our future can be scary, but not if we frame it in His presence. He is always with His children what a wonderful assurance to face life.

How would you characterize the spiritual season of fall? I would say it is a time when maturity is changing the color of our lives. In our spiritual summer, we are growing with new life, and now, in the fall, our lives are deepening with the richness of God, who changes our very essence. We will continue to experience new growth for seasons to come and go, but spiritual fall is a special time of transformation, a time of enjoying the richness of His beauty as our lives are colored by Him.

There are distinct colors of fall, but the one I love the best is the rich color of red. It always reminds me of the blood Jesus shed for me. Oh, that we would wear the color red, which stands for redemption. Living as redeemed people, forgiven and in the right standing with God is our inheritance. The world notices because, by His blood, we are set apart from the world. Dear ones, we are to bear His color.

Ponders of the Heart

Read Colossians 3:12-17 and look at the colors of spiritual maturity.

What season are you experiencing in your spiritual life?

How would you describe those seasons?

Go ahead, use your imagination, and remember God is faithful in all the spiritual seasons of our lives.

Prayers of the Heart

Dear Father,

Thank You for showing us Your faithfulness each year with the seasons. They are there to remind us that You are our God of order and purpose. These seasons also reflect Your faithfulness in our spiritual lives. We are thankful for them. Help us wear the colors of transformation and maturity. We pray we might be brilliant colors of You in a dark, cold world. In Jesus' name, amen.

October 2 ~ Melting Away

"You were taught, with regard to your former way of life, to put off your old self, which is being corrupted by its deceitful desires; to be made new in the attitude of your minds; and to put on the new self, created to be like God in true righteousness and holiness" (Ephesians 4:22-24).

A summer of melting away some weight and seeing transformation would be a good description of the summer I watched my youngest daughter melt over 38 pounds. As each pound melted away, I saw the beauty of God's new creation appear.

Inside, Julie was and is a beautiful girl in Christ. She is a lovely, wise woman of God. Yet because of the society in which we live and the shame she placed on her weight, her beauty was hidden from the world.

I am amazed at my daughter. Her plan to lose weight included the ingredients of exercise. Each morning and every afternoon, she and I would meet and walk. As we walked, she and I would share our hearts with each other. I am telling you that God opened my eyes to the deep, rich beauty of Julie.

Her wisdom and interest made me feel like I was enrolled in college. This was a special time for me. Not only did I see her outward beauty being developed into what God created her to be, but I saw her inner beauty appearing. She was letting her light shine, and the light was radiant to her mother's soul. My daughter became my teacher and her mother her pupil.

This devotion was written as her weight was melting away. Oh, how I pray she will keep her eyes on the Author and Perfector of her faith as she continues to march toward freedom. You and I both know the snares along the way, but our God is faithful, and He has His plans for this young woman. She may falter, but He will always be there to keep up His excellent work in and through her life.

There are times when I would love to see into the future, and this is one of those times. I would love to see God's plan for Julie. You know He came to set the captives free. He is setting her free. I just pray that in her freedom, she will not lose sight of the One who gave Himself for her liberty.

The truth is the beauty of our spirits is often hidden by the coats of shame. It could be the shame of failure, rejection, or the shame of family heritage. The list is endless, and yet, as human beings, we all carry coats of shame.

When we became children of God, he took our coats and exchanged them with coats of righteousness. The big question is, are we still putting on coats of shame instead of dressing up in grace, mercy and righteousness? All I have to say to Julie is, go, girl, go all the way to freedom. And for all the rest of us, I pray that we will burn our coats of shame and let the beauty of Christ come shining through.

Ponders of the Heart

Read 2 Corinthians 5:17-21 and read Isaiah 61:1-3.

Are you still dealing with shame?

How do the verses above give you a fresh look at what Christ has done for you?

Prayers of the Heart

Dear Father,

You have created us to be the beauty of Christ because He has borne our shame. Father, how we praise You and worship You for Your great kindness and mercy. Help us walk, live, and be free in the freedom Christ has given us. In Jesus' name, amen.

October 3 ~ Boldness

"'Lord, if it's you,' Peter replied, 'tell me to come to you on the water.' 'Come,' he said. Then Peter got down out of the boat, walked on the water and came toward Jesus" (Matt. 14:28-29).

Don't you love Peter's boldness in the above verses? Right in the middle of the storm, when it was reasonable to be scared out of your wits, Peter wanted to get out of the boat and walk on the water to Jesus. He is either a man of great faith, a completely ridiculous person, or a man who loves Jesus, come rain or shine. I think he was the latter.

Who would be your choice of company? My choice would be my husband, Bill. Now, he can be picky for sure, but I would rather be with him come rain or come shine.

I am confident he would never lead me into trouble, and if we found ourselves there, he would always help me if he could. Peter knew Jesus was all he needed in the storms of life, even literal ones.

Peter's first question to Jesus was, "Is that You?" Peter knew that everything he had in his mind and heart was worthless if the figure on the water was not Jesus, but he also knew all things were possible if it was his Lord. Peter asked to be involved in this new thing, and Jesus told him to come on. I love it.

I wonder what the other disciples were thinking when Peter asked to come to Jesus on the water. They must have thought he had absolutely lost his mind. I wonder if anyone tried to stop him. Surely, Andrew, his brother, was ready to step in. Or maybe they were not worried because they thought Jesus was fixing to rebuke such foolishness.

Jesus did not rebuke Peter. He had a thrill to His voice when He told Peter to come on. Such faith, such an adventuresome spirit, must have pleased our Lord. After all, Jesus had just told them to be of good cheer and not to be afraid. Peter decided to obey, and while he was obeying, he asked to get out of the boat.

I am so jealous when I see Peter's boldness, and I wonder if I will ever be able to have, as Max Lucado says, "an ounce more devotion than fear." This is exactly what I want: more devotion to Jesus than fear. Oh, Lord, fill my heart with deep devotion.

I regret to say that I can be so careful not to hope for the impossible because I do not want to be wrong or disappointed. If I don't get over this attitude, which is nothing in this world but unbelief and pride, I doubt God will ever move beyond my comfort zone. After all, what pleases God is faith (Hebrews 11:6). Come, sweet Jesus, come to us and show us how to walk on the water.

Ponders of the Heart

When was the last time you asked God to do something bold in your life? Something only you can do with His help.

Do you really believe He can do anything and He is willing to answer our prayers?

Read Isaiah 43:10-13 and Isaiah 43:18-21.

Prayers of the Heart

Dear Father,

Some of us are always trying to save ourselves, while others are reckless. If we are fearful, let us have enough courage to ask if we can join You when You call. And if we are impulsive, help us make sure we are following You and not the wind. In Jesus' name, amen.

October 4 ~ Losing Focus

"But when he saw the wind, he was afraid and, beginning to sink, cried out, 'Lord, save me.' Immediately Jesus reached out his hand and caught him. 'You of little faith,' he said, 'why did you doubt?'" (Matthew 14:30-31).

At the time I write this, my son, Chris, is going through a tough time, a divorce. He can't fix the situation, but he is searching for answers about himself. With this desire to work on his life, he is seeing a counselor weekly.

He has been working hard with the counselor, and each session proves to be beneficial, but before he gets home each week, something happens. His car breaks down, or someone calls him to tell him news about his ex-wife. There seems to be a conspiracy over his life to discourage him each time he is encouraged.

Have you ever had a season like this? My son is having one right now, and if he is, then I am having one also. Once a mother, always a mother. There is a conspiracy over our lives, one that wants to discourage us and divert our attention to lesser things. This conspiracy wants us to lose our focus on Jesus and uses our circumstances to do it.

In Matthew's scripture, Peter goes from a faith hero to a faith zero when he takes his eyes off Jesus. Here, he is walking on the water heading toward Jesus when Peter sees the wind is boisterous, as the New King James puts it, and he is afraid and begins to sink. What a perfect picture of what happens to all of us when we lose our focus and the circumstances around us are all we can see. I can really relate to the feeling of sinking.

Have you ever sunk in your spirit? Has your stomach ever fallen as you think here it goes again? Do you ever find yourself in trouble with your boss, or in hot water with your husband? Hearing the news, your health is failing, your mother has fallen, your tire is flat, and so is your bank account? Circumstances can kick us in the teeth, and all we know to do is lose heart, or is this losing faith? We are so much like Peter.

Jesus is right there doing a new thing right before Peter's eyes, but he sees the boisterous wind and loses his focus.

I can learn from the situation because Peter knows what to do when he sinks. He calls out to Jesus to save him. I often fail to do this. My head would be under the water before I would cry out to the One who can save me. Peter calls out, and at once, Jesus saves him.

The Lord says to Peter what He would say to us. "O, you of little faith, why did you doubt?" What a hard-hitting question. It's one I need to think about for a long time, one we might all need to ponder.

Why do we not trust the One who died for us? Why do we not believe the One who redeemed us from eternal death and gave us eternal life? Why do we place circumstances above His power, love, and faithfulness? Again, I say these are questions I need to think about, ponder, and pray over. What about you?

Ponders of the Heart

Do you have a circumstance in your life that has taken your focus?

What can you do when you are in the middle of a trial?

Read Psalm 147:1-11 and take time to praise Him for His great attributes.

Prayers of the Heart

Dear Father,

You are our great provider and defender. Help our unbelief and our weakness. May we lean on You and keep our focus on You even when the circumstances have conspired to bring us down. We delight in Your unfailing love, and our hope is in You. In Jesus' name, amen.

October 5 ~ We Bow Down

"And when they climbed into the boat, the wind died down. Then those who were in the boat worshipped him, saying, 'Truly you are the Son of God (Matt. 14:32-33).

Have you ever had God move in your life and save your skin? If you have, like the disciples, you had no trouble worshipping.

When a man is pulled out of a raging sea, he is thankful. If a firefighter rescues a child, his parents bow down. When a son is found not guilty, the family gives praise to God. Mind you, not all bow down, but life has a way of humbling us. God often uses the elements of life to humble us so we can see more of Him.

This is what happened to the disciples in Matthew 14: 32. They were wet, scared to death by a storm, and what appeared to be a ghost was coming toward them. When they recognized it was Jesus and he stepped in the boat as the wind died down, they bowed down. The million-dollar question is, what does it take for us to bow down?

The disciples had seen miracles. In fact, they had just seen Jesus feed five thousand men. He had also turned water into wine, healed the sick, and given sight to the blind, but this was the first time they had bowed down.

See how patiently Jesus worked in the lives of His disciples? He uses everything in the lives of His children to help us see the Invisible One.

What does it take for us to see Jesus? Can we see Him in a sunrise, or do we take this for granted? What about in a child's face, in the blue of the sky, or does it take a fearful experience to stop us enough to reach for Him?

I hate to admit it, but I am more like the disciples than I care to admit. I want to change this. Do you? I do not want to take my Lord for granted. I want to experience Him in the warmth of the sun, the beauty of the sea, the green of the grass, and the majesty of the hills. In the depths of my heart, I want to see His power, beauty, and His majesty. Don't you?

We miss so much joy in life if we don't see Jesus. He is all around us and if we miss seeing Him and worshipping Him, we miss the most important thing in life. Worshipping Him because of our salvation is right but so is worshipping Him for the wonder around us every day. Oh, Lord, open our eyes so we will bow down.

Ponders of the Heart

When you pray, do you bow your head?

What about the posture of your heart when you pray?

Is your heart bowing before the Lord?

Read Psalm 46: 10 and Psalm 145:1-21.

Prayers of the Heart

Dear Father,

We want to praise You and see You more each day. Lord, we bow before Your goodness, majesty, power, and ways. You resist the proud, but You give grace to the humble. We want to be among the humble. Our King and Lord, we worship You. In Jesus' name, amen.

October 6 ~ The Walk of Faith

"having a form of godliness but denying its power " (2 Timothy 3:5).

It was a sunny Saturday afternoon, and we were all having a fun time water skiing. Betty, my mother-in-law, put up with our outings on the boat because she loved us. I am sure she had other things she wanted to do than be on a boat in the middle of the river. You see, Betty doesn't swim.

Brooks, her youngest, was getting ready to ski. He needed two skis instead of one, so Betty was going to slide another one to him. As she did, she slid right along with the ski. Here we are in the middle of the river and my mother-in-law went overboard. My father-in-law was going to take the time to take his shirt off before he went in after her.

He decided to throw her a life jacket which promptly hit her on the head. Just as she was coming up, Bill jumped in to save her and jumped right on top of her. She survived the rescue and soon was in the boat, but she could have made out better without our help. I didn't 'jump in on her, but I did question her actions. I said, "Betty, why did you do that?"

As I thought about Peter and his willingness to get out of the boat to walk with Jesus, I thought about the reaction of the body of Christ when one of us decides to walk by faith and not by sight. I think we try to rescue faith walkers much like we all tried to rescue Betty.

We throw lifejackets to faith walkers because we don't trust Jesus to keep them afloat. Christians can even offer man's solutions over God's direction and knock faith walkers in the head. We often question their call, and if they don't get back in the boat where they belong, we jump in and land on top of them.

Our thoughts might be if you can't swim, stay in the boat. Never taking into consideration it is not our ability God is after; it is our availability. He is the One with the ability.

In Second Timothy chapter three we are given a good descriptive look at the culture in the last days.

"But mark this: There will be terrible times in the last days. People will be lovers of themselves, lovers of money, boastful, proud, abusive, disobedient to their parents, ungrateful, unholy, without love, unforgiving, slanderous, without self-control, brutal, not lovers of the good, treacherous, rash, conceited, lovers of pleasure rather

than lovers of God— having a form of godliness but denying its power. Have nothing to do with such people" (2 Timothy 3:1-5).

Our culture has a form of godliness but denies the very power of God. I wonder if this is true of me and of you. How mighty is our God? How well do we believe He can do the impossible, even with us?

The warning is to be careful when you decide to get out of the boat and walk by faith and not by sight. It might be your friends in the boat who will cause you the most harm. Even if they think they are helping you.

We also need to be careful before we try to rescue others who feel a call to get out into the deep water of faith. We might not understand the walk of faith they are following. So, unless it goes against the Bible, don't hit them with your life jacket. God might be doing a new thing in their lives. And if you receive a call and decide to get out of the boat to walk by faith, remember someone might try to save you, so duck.

Ponders of the Heart

Have you ever taken a giant leap of faith?

Did someone try to talk you out of the leap?

How did you handle it?

Read Hebrews 11: 1,6, and Hebrews 11: 38-40.

Even those with the best intentions can get in the way of faith walking. We must depend on God, for He is the Lord.

Prayers of the Heart

Dear Father,

You alone are worthy of our lives, and You alone know the way we should walk. We want to listen to Your voice and be children who walk by faith. You are our guide. We do not want to be people who have a form of godliness but deny Your power. Speak to Your children and show us Your ways. We love You, Lord. In Jesus' name, amen.

October 7 ~ Godly Leaders Needed

"So Jehoshaphat reigned over Judah. He was thirty-five years old when he became king of Judah, and he reigned in Jerusalem twenty-five years. His mother's name was Azubah daughter of Shilhi. He followed the ways of his father Asa and did not stray from them; he did what was right in the eyes of the Lord. The high places, however, were not removed, and the people still had not set their hearts on the God of their ancestors" (2 Chronicles 20:31-33).

The Lord is incredible, and I love Him and depend on Him for my life. Even though I confess my love for Him, I feel there have been times that I was careless in leading others, especially my children, in the ways of the Lord.

There is a narrow line between leading and beating someone over the head with the law. The law kills, but grace gives life. My hope is God can make good out of my failures and successes.

In the Chronicles of the Kings of Israel and Judah, you will find good, bad, and careless kings. When the leadership was good, the people of God experienced a revival. If the leadership was ungodly, the people of God turned to other gods. But when the leadership was careless, the people of God remained comfortable in their sin. How important is diligent godly leadership? I would say, after studying Chronicles of the Kings, that diligent godly leadership is critical.

What about our country? We have an opportunity to elect our leaders every four years. What do we think is the most needed quality of leadership: intelligence, popularity, economic sense, or foreign policy? Do we realize the quality of leadership needed most is godliness and diligence?

What do I need as an American more than a stable economy, a mighty army, and lower taxes? I need a leader who has a heart tender toward God. We need a godly, diligent leader who will direct us back to our heritage: "One nation under God, indivisible, with liberty and justice for all."

When we say our pledge, we are saying we are unified, undividable, and inseparable as a nation under God. What a mighty proclamation of truth. We can only be those things when our leader diligently directs us in the ways of the Lord.

Our leader not only needs to know God personally, but he also needs to be a leader who is not ashamed of the gospel. Oh, that God would show us grace and help us choose a leader who, like the psalmist might say:

"I proclaim your saving acts in the great assembly; I do not seal my lips, Lord, as you know. I do not hide your righteousness in my heart; I speak of your faithfulness and your saving help. I do not conceal your love and your faithfulness from the great assembly" (Psalm 40:9-10.)

Ponders of the Heart

What do most people look for when choosing our leaders?

How do you think we have failed in our country?

Read 1 Timothy 2:1-2, Romans 13:1, and Jeremiah 29:7

How our country and our elected officials need our prayers.

Prayers of the Heart

Dear Father,

You created this great nation to proclaim Your name to the nations of the world. You gave our forefathers the wisdom to know that with You, we could face anything and stand united under Your care and Your protection. Forgive us for our arrogance and our departure. In Your mercy, send us a leader who will follow Your ways and not be ashamed of proclaiming the wonder of Your love. Forgive this nation and open our eyes to our need for You. In Jesus' name, amen.

October 8 ~ Weeds in the Garden

Cursed is the ground because of you; through painful toil you will eat food from it all the days of your life. It will produce thorns and thistles for you, and you will eat the plants of the field. By the sweat of your brow you will eat your food until you return to the ground, since from it you were taken; for dust you are and to dust you will return." (Genesis 3:17-19).

I have this great flower bed off the back deck. I failed "Green Thumb 101," so I am thankful this soil makes growing flowers easy. Do you know what else grows in good soil? You guessed it, weeds.

The flower bed flourishes with flowers and weeds. Because gardening is not my thing, I often let the weeding go and before you know it, they have taken over the garden. Every time I wished I had not waited so long.

The Bible tells us that weeds, and thistles are part of the curse of the fall. We will deal with them until the Lord comes again and brings with Him a new heaven and new earth. Another part of the curse that is like weeds is sin. Sin has a way of growing even in the life of God's children.

If you have rich soil in your soul, you are, in a sense, good soil for sin. Just like weeds want to take over our gardens, sin wants to take over our lives. God is the gardener. He begins by pulling the big weeds of sin out of our lives—sins like stealing, cheating, drunkenness, rage, cursing, killing, and adultery. He begins to remove these destructive behaviors from us and replace them with new desires.

New desires that want to serve Him and serve others. We might feel that our souls are in decent shape, but God is aware of the little weeds of sin that still need pulling up. Sins like greed, gossip, envy, self-righteousness, and contention.

My weed-pulling is not as particular as God's sin-pulling. I go get some pine chips and cover my little weeds up, but before I can say "Round-up," they are back again, bigger than ever. God doesn't cover up our little sins; He diligently keeps pulling them up until He gets the root of the problem.

I know that as long as I live under the curse, there will be weeds in my garden. The same is true for you. God knows that as long as we are in these earthly bodies, we will be prone to sin. I guess this means

I will keep on pulling weeds out of my garden, and God will keep pulling sin out of my life by its roots.

His purpose is to beautify what is His and keep those weeds of sin from covering up what He made us to be: a sweet fragrance of Jesus, the Rose of Sharon.

Ponders of the Heart

What trips you up the most? The big sins or the small sneaky ones.

Are you cooperating with God as He weeds your life?

Read Galatians 5:19-25 and look at the weeds of sin and the fruit of God.

Ask Him to keep on weeding the sin out and growing His sweet fruit in its place.

Prayers of the Heart

Dear Father,

Thank You, Lord, that You are diligently working in our lives to weed out any sin that wishes to overtake us. You have already made us Yours and purified our spirits within. Your desire for us is to be a light so others can see You. Lord, You are the Master Gardener, and we are blessed to be in Your Hands. We thank You and praise You, Lord. In Jesus' name, amen.

October 9 ~ Believing Jesus

"Jesus said to her, "I am the resurrection and the life. The one who believes in me will live, even though they die; and whoever lives by believing in me will never die. Do you believe this?" (John 11:25-26).

These words of Jesus hit me hard because sometimes when you are full of sorrow it is hard to believe. Martha's brother was dead, and she was full of grief. She knew Jesus was the healer, and He could have saved her brother if only He had been there.

I don't know how Martha knew Jesus was a great healer, but she knew. Maybe she saw Him heal a sick man or heard He did, but she believed. Her brother was dead, and Jesus could have prevented it.

We are told in this passage that Jesus stayed away two days after knowing Lazarus was sick. Martha didn't know this. If she had known, knowing Martha, her conversation with Jesus would have sounded a little different. Martha was famous for speaking her mind. Jesus' words to Martha were direct, and told her death was no problem for those who believed. Then He said to her, "Do you believe?" What was Martha's reply?

"'Yes, Lord,' she replied, 'I believe that you are the Messiah, the Son of God, who is to come into the world'" (John 11:26).

She said she believed He was the Son of God and He was the Anointed One, but she didn't say she believed He had power over death. Her belief system was telling her this was now an impossible situation.

This is what hit me—not her lack of belief but mine. My heart fell before Jesus, and I confessed that I was one of little faith. Oh, I believe

Jesus is the Son of God, that He is the Anointed One, and He has come into the world. But do I believe He can do the impossible?

How afraid are you to believe in miracles? I am terrified. I don't want to believe because what if Jesus doesn't do it or do I believe the things I ask are impossible for Him?

Jesus told Martha to have the stone rolled away. Lazarus's body had been in the tomb for four days. What do you suppose happens to a dead body after four days? Talk about an impossible situation. By all right this was one.

Jesus told Lazarus to come out, and he did, with his grave clothes wrapped around him. My point is if Jesus can do this, He can do anything. These words hit me hard. I do not want to be one of little faith, not just asking and believing Jesus for small things, safe things. He can do impossible things.

Have you stopped asking Jesus for salvation for a lost brother, physical healing for a friend, or emotional healing for your spouse? Oh my, let us not be people who give up our faith. Nothing is impossible for Jesus.

Ponders of the Heart

Do you have an impossible situation?

Have you given up hope that Jesus hears you?

Read John 11:21-44.

Jesus can do the impossible, but it is always in His way and His timing, which is perfect.

Prayers of the Heart

Dear Father,

We confess our unbelief. You can free us from it. We want to hear You, believe You, and walk all the days of our lives knowing You can do the impossible. Lord, we have some impossible situations in our lives. We put them into Your "possible " hands. We love You, Lord. We want to live believing You. In Jesus' name, amen.

October 10 ~ Hope Does Not Disappoint

"And hope does not put us to shame, because God's love has been poured out into our hearts through the Holy Spirit, who has been given to us" (Romans 5:5).

Seasons come and go because of God's faithfulness. Winter is cold, spring is warm, summer is hot, especially in the South, and fall is cool. Occasionally, the winter months might give way to a warm day, and with warm days comes the promise of spring.

This past summer, there were some cool weekends, and with them came the promise or hope of fall. On one of those weekends, I remember people saying, "This won't last." I thought, "Well, of course not. It is August. Summer is hot, and August is in the summer." But I loved the break and remembering the promise of fall.

There are always those who complain about the weather. I can be one of those, but when I do complain, I want my attention to turn to God's promises. One of my favorites is that one day, I will be with Him, and I will be like Him, finished with this old fleshly nature.

God has made me dead to sin and alive in Him. These great and wonderful promises are sure, not because of me, but because of His divine power to keep promises. He is the great promise Keeper, and I belong to Him.

I have times when I see little spiritual growth. I feel useless to Him and worthless. He then reminds me He has given me all I need for godly living: the Holy Spirit. By the power of the Holy Spirit, He is changing me. It is a slow process, but He has changed my heart. I can rest in His peace.

Oh, the work of our Lord in the lives of His children. He is faithful, and even in dry spells, He gives us hope. Listen to these verses in Romans and let them minister to your soul.

"Therefore, since we have been justified through faith, we have peace with God through our Lord Jesus Christ, through whom we have gained access by faith into this grace in which we now stand. And we boast in the hope of the glory of God" (Romans 5:1-2).

Just like we can rest in the heat of summer because we know fall is around the corner. We can rest knowing we have peace with God through our Lord Jesus Christ, and we have a future hope of glory, and this hope is also just around the corner.

Until then, let's enjoy days where one season gives way to the hope of another, and for goodness' sake, let's be partakers of our promises in Christ. We can stand firm in His faithfulness.

Ponders of the Heart

What do you put your hope in?

What are the things you are sure of?

Read Romans 5:1-8, Philippians 2:14-16, and 2 Peter 1:3-8.

Prayers of the Heart

Dear Father,

You are faithful, and we can be sure of Your promises. Lord, when our lives enter the "dog days" of living, we can put our hope in You and in Your promises. Thank You for Your Word, which sustains us and gives us hope. Thank You for the love You have poured into our hearts by the Holy Spirit. This love keeps us hopeful, like a cool day in summer. You are so good to us, and right now, we just want to praise You. In Jesus' name, amen.

October 11 ~ Repent

"Repent, then, and turn to God, so that your sins may be wiped out, that times of refreshing may come from the Lord" (Acts 3:19).

I can tell when one of my grandchildren is up to something they should not be doing. They become quiet and invisible. We have a bonus room in our house, and this is where the grandchildren often wander. If they become too quiet, we go check because we know things are not as they should be. If we call them and there is no answer, we go on high alert.

That was also true with my children, and to this day, it still is. When I don't hear from them, or they avoid me, I know something is up. In fact, aren't we all like this? Who do you hide from when you are up to something you know is wrong?

If you are like me, there are certain subjects you avoid with certain people. And when I have sinned, I don't always want to face the music, so I hide and try to become invisible and quiet.

When this happens, I go with my natural tendency, which is to hide from God, or I can remember what His Word says and repent. Repent seems like such a nasty word to the world, and if I am not careful, my old, shamed base identity will send me running, but what does God's Word say, and what does it promise?

First, repentance is the beginning of cleansing and the process of returning joy. Why joy? Joy because our fellowship with God is restored, and this brings great peace and comfort.

What does the Bible tell us about John the Baptist? He came before Jesus to prepare the way for Him. (Mark 1:2-3) Read how John prepared the way.

"And so John the Baptist appeared in the wilderness, preaching a baptism of repentance for the forgiveness of sins" (Mark 1:4).

When John came to prepare the way, his message was repentance.

This always precedes coming to Christ in a person's life. It is not just feeling sorry, but makes us surrender, stop hiding, and start facing. We in the Christian community say that sin in Greek means to miss the mark, but Jesus didn't speak in Greek, and the Greek language did not have a word equal to the Hebrew word sin, but sin in Hebrew was much more descriptive. To the Jews, sin was *awen*, which meant moral worthlessness or a painful burden. A derivative of *awen* was *awon* which meant to twist, pervert, or bend down.

Christ's attitude toward sin is more than missing the mark. John's ministry to prepare for the Lord was to call the Jews to repentance. A ministry that might be wise for us to rediscover. Deep regret and sorrow prepare us for His coming into our lives with refreshing freedom and rejuvenating joy.

The next time you hear your Lord say, "Where are you? " Stop hiding and start facing. Repent and turn to Him, and let Him have your sin so you can experience the rich refreshing of His wonderful presence. Nothing is worth losing His sweet presence.

Ponders of the Heart

What do you do when you are caught in a lie?

How have you experienced joy from repentance?

Read Matthew 3:1-17.

Let God show you anything He wishes you to repent from so you can draw near and be filled fully with His presence.

Prayers of the Heart

Dear Father,

We wish to be close to You, never hiding from You. Show us anything that is keeping us from drawing near to You. Father, help us confess our sins and get them into Your light. Refresh us and return to us the fullness of joy we find in being Your children. Lord, we love You. Thank You that we never need to hide from You. In Jesus' name, amen.

October 12 ~ Holiness

"But just as he who called you is holy, so be holy in all you do; for it is written: "Be holy, because I am holy" (1 Peter 1:15-16).

Under the stairs in the hall, there is a closet, and this is where we have our Christmas decorations. In one of the boxes, our Nativity scene is carefully packed away because the story behind the scene is precious to us.

When it is time to decorate the house for Christmas, the Nativity takes a prominent place in our home. Everyone who enters our home will see this holy scene, but the Nativity is not holy to all. For the Nativity scene to be holy, the eye of the beholder must recognize the holiness of the moment it stands for. In and of itself, the Nativity scene has no value.

1 Peter 1:15-16 declares we are to be holy in all our conduct for the Lord is holy.

In his book *Holiness, Truth, and the Presence of God*, Francis Frangipane provides a wonderful definition of holiness.

"While the word 'holiness' means 'to be set apart, separate, ' a possible interpretation of the Hebrew root word for 'holiness' is, 'to be bright; clean, new or fresh; untarnished. Holiness produces separation from sin, but mere separation from sin cannot produce our sanctification; holiness comes from the Presence of God. You may avoid 'touching what is unclean, ' but if you are not united through love to the Fatherhood of God, you will never know true holiness; all you will have is religion. Christ in us is our holiness, for as close as our relationship is with Him, to that degree we reflect His holiness."

Just as our Nativity scene reflects holiness in direct proportion to one's relationship with God, our holiness is in direct proportion to the presence of God in our lives. Our separation from sin is important, but separation from sin cannot produce holiness in us. Only God's holy presence does this. To be bright, clean, new, or fresh, untarnished is not to be full of religion but to be full of God.

Knowledge about God or God's rules will never make you or me holy, even if we follow them. Our knowledge must move to personal intimacies with the Lord. This personal intimacy with God will bring about our separation from sin, but more importantly, it will bring about the essence of God in and through our lives, which will be our holiness. This is the only way we can be holy, as He is holy.

Ponders of the Heart

How would you describe holiness?

Who do you know that has the essence of God shining through them?

Read Matthew 23.

Read Jesus' words carefully and ask the Lord to show you how to let go of religion and hold on to Him.

Prayers of the Heart

Dear Father,

We do not want religion; we want You. We don't want to practice a form of godliness and have no power. Lord, we want to be so full of Your presence that we shine with Your light, Your freshness, Your untarnished holiness. You alone are holy, so we pray and ask You to make us authentic. Whatever it takes, drench us in You. We want to be holy, for You are holy. In Jesus' name, amen.

October 13 ~ Defining Moments

"He replied, 'Whether he is a sinner or not, I don't know. One thing I do know. I was blind but now I see!'" (John 9:25).

This was a defining moment in the life of this man. He was blind, and Jesus gave him sight. Not everyone appreciated his sight, but he did. His life was changed in a moment. We know it did when we read the conversation he had with the Pharisees and Jesus.

He placed his faith in the Son of God. What a glorious day this was for him and for others who saw this wonderful miracle. Defining moments are like that, but we can get stuck there. God is the God of miracles. He, in His mercy, will give us defining moments that can change the course of our lives. But the Lord wants more for us as we continue this journey called life.

Being blind and then being able to see was a significant life-changing moment. When Jesus touches our lives, He changes everything. Becoming a believer is the most important moment in all our lives, but He wants more for us, as He did for the blind man.

Let's look at some defining moments in the life of a believer. We have already talked about one: salvation. After we are given spiritual sight, we can often see times before conversion, where, in hindsight, we see that God was drawing us to Him. He uses life events like marriage, births, and deaths as opportunities to experience His presence.

Revelation about God is a moving journey throughout our lives, or it should be. He has wonderful things to teach us about His love, mercy, and His ways. It is through these things we learn about Him and who we are as His children.

At the end of life, we will be able to see how all the pieces fit together into His perfect plan. But sometimes, people grab hold of a revelation, a defining moment, and hang there. They cannot move forward with God; they get stuck.

How sad to get stuck knowing something and miss walking on with God. I don't want to do that, thinking for a moment I know all there is to know about Him or His ways. Knowledge of God should not take us away from walking with Him. Defining moments do not define us; God does.

How about you? Knowledge of God is huge. We want this, but living in a relationship with Him offers us so much more. Revelations that change us are wonderful, but moving from revelation to revelation is much more significant. I thank the Lord for defining moments in my life. The good ones and the bad ones. God has more instore for us. He wants to keep us moving toward Him and home. Our defining moments are just pieces of all God wants to reveal to those He loves. I praise His continual work in our lives.

Ponders of the Heart

What are the defining moments in your life?

How have they changed how you think and feel?

Read John 1:35-39 and John 1: 40-51.

These disciples kept changing, learning, and experiencing God.

Prayers of the Heart

Dear Father,

How we thank You for every opportunity You have given us to see You and trust You. Sometimes, we see You clearly, and other times, we just need to trust. We have failed in this and other times we have succeeded, but Lord, You have always been there. Jesus, give us eyes to watch for You and hearts of praise and courage. Keep us moving until the day we see You face to face. In Jesus' name, amen.

October 14 ~ The Thrill of Victory and the Agony of Defeat

"Since, then, you have been raised with Christ, set your hearts on things above, where Christ is seated at the right hand of God. Set your minds on things above, not on earthly things. For you died, and your life is now hidden with Christ in God. When Christ who is your life, appears, then you also will appear with him in glory" (Colossians 3:1-4).

The dedication of the athletes in the Olympic Games is inspiring. I love to watch athletes from all over the world competing. I also find that my competitive nature is nasty.

When America loses, my competitive nature is out of control. I want nothing less than gold for America. You could say I am a sore loser and a bad winner. I always get so nervous for our athletes; in fact, at times, I hide my eyes or go into the other room. I just can't stand to see them lose or see their faces when they lose. Bill always says, "Marilyn, you will never know the thrill of victory if you can't stand the agony of defeat."

Maybe this is why I love God's Word so much. He promises us victory. We have won, will win, and someday, we will enjoy the complete thrill of victory in Him. But just like well-trained athletes, we must train ourselves by focusing on the right things.

We are told to set our hearts on things above, lofty, heavenly things, and not earthly things. Think of all that an Olympic athlete does to dedicate his life to training. I might think he is giving up too much. He might think at times the same thing, but if he keeps his focus, he will be faithful to his lofty goal to compete. The difference between Olympic athletes and those who are in Christ is those athletes could lose, but we are sure winners.

How do we know this? The Word of God tells us. We have died, and our lives are hidden in Christ. He is our victory; He has won the fight by defeating death, and He has purchased for us His righteousness. How I praise Him.

If I feel and experience the agony of defeat, it is usually because of one of two reasons: either I am focusing on the wrong goal, or I haven't finished the race, and it feels like failure. Our hope, thank goodness, is not in our success but in His success. We are truly more than conquerors in Jesus. One sweet day, we will stand up and take any gold crowns and lay them at His feet.

Ponders of the Heart

Have you ever felt the agony of defeat in your life?

Have you ever felt the thrill of victory?

Read 1 Corinthians 9:24-26, and 1 Corinthians 15:54-58

I am sure that I will never stand and take a gold medal in the Olympics or hear the National Anthem played for me, but one day because I belong to Jesus, I will see victory, and so will you.

Prayers of the Heart

Dear Jesus,

You are the victor of the game called life. You have won and given us victory in You. Lord, You have taken our shame and swallowed it up in victory. Thank You for our crown of glory, a crown that will never rust or fade, one kept for us in heaven. Jesus, help us keep our focus on things above, not things of this earth. Keep us focused on You, our Crown, and our Lives. In Jesus' name, amen.

October 15 ~ I Can Do It

"Come to Me, all you who labor and are heavy laden, and I will give you rest. Take my yoke upon you and learn of me, for I am gentle and lowly in heart, and you will find rest for your souls. For My yoke is easy and My burden is light" (Matthew 11:28-30).

Bill had a busy week. He had been under the gun at work and was feeling tired. We were planning a weekend trip to Birmingham. It was our grandson's birthday, and we were looking forward to a weekend of celebrating.

Our daughter, Tracie, also had a busy week. She wanted us to come Friday night and help her get ready for the birthday party. This was fine with me, but Bill needed to cut the grass. He planned to do this on Thursday after he got home from work.

I thought, "I can do that. I'll cut the front yard for him. Could I start the lawn mower?" I was willing to give it a try. I pulled the cord again and again, but no go. I went back into the house just to turn back around, determined to try it one more time. I said a quick prayer, jerked the rope, and the dead mower came to life. I thought, "Okay, here I go."

This was the highlight of the whole experience. In about fifteen minutes, I thought, "This is really hard, and it is hot out here." After forty-five minutes, I didn't think I was going to make it. Determined to finish the job, I kept going. Fifty minutes into the mowing, I was sure I was about to faint.

Slowing down and reserving my energy was my next plan of action as I told myself, "You can do this. You can. Just keep going." Finally, after an hour and fifteen minutes, I was finished.

Pushing the lawn mower back into the garage, I grabbed some water and sat down. After talking to myself about being a baby I made my way upstairs, got into the bathtub, and laid in the cold water for ten minutes. I was feeling my age and someone else's. I appreciated my husband immensely and hoped never to get the urge to mow the grass again. Mowing grass is not my thing.

I can clean our house from top to bottom. Trim the hedges, blow off the driveway, clean the back porch, and even wash my car, but please don't make me mow the grass again. There are a few things I want to leave to my men folks, mowing grass and cleaning fish.

Bill hadn't asked me to mow. If I had told him my plan to help him, he would have said, "No. I'll do it." But I wanted so badly to help, and I thought I was doing a good thing. He appreciated my sacrifice and knew I had the best intentions, but he didn't want me to do these kinds of chores. And I am in complete agreement with him on this. He is right.

In my Spiritual life, when I have found myself in the deepest trouble, way over my head, it has been when I have stepped in to help God with something He did not design me to do. The job might need to be done, but apart from His supernatural power and His calling, it is better, I have found, to leave God's business alone.

It is the same scenario. I get started with my plan to help God. I make progress and think, "I can do this. " Then, in just a little while, I begin to see I might be in over my head. Now, if God has called me, He will equip me. If he has called me to do something, I know the help is there, but if this is my idea, I am in deep trouble.

The truth is God doesn't need my help. He chooses to work through me on things of His choosing, not mine. He is gracious to me if my motives are pure, and He will let me down and place me in cool, refreshing water of rest. But if all my efforts were for my glory, He is faithful to teach me a good lesson, one that keeps me wishing I had never even heard of my plan much less tried to do it.

I'm thankful for many of my failures because, in them, I have learned some valuable lessons. 1. Don't ever try to mow grass. 2. Don't ever learn to clean fish. 3. Don't ever try to be God; there is only One, and I am not Him.

Ponders of the Heart

Have you ever found yourself in a job that was way too hard for you to do?

Have you ever said yes to a task God has not called you to do?

Read Job 42:7-9.

Prayers of the Heart

Dear Father,

We were created to love You and serve You, but only You know how this is to be done. Give us ears to hear You and not make up our own plans. You have plans for us and work to do through us. But Praise You, Father, that You do not need us; You just love us and want us. We will take this plan over ours any day. In Jesus' name, amen.

October 16 ~ Enjoying the Ride

"So do not fear, for I am with you; do not be dismayed, for I am your God. I will strengthen you and help you; I will uphold you with my righteous right hand" (Isaiah 41:10).

Hidden deep in a box of old pictures is a picture of me riding a roller coaster. This picture is worth a thousand words. I am scared to death. There is no denying it. I can, to this day, remember how it felt. I thought I was going to fall out of that thing and die right there at Six Flags.

That picture is followed up by another picture when my grandchildren got me to ride on a roller coaster at Disney. The face is the same, the fear is the same, and the promise is never to be talked into riding a roller coaster again.

Part of me, the smug part, thinks this is the prudent way to feel. Roller coasters are dangerous. The other part of me, the part that wants to be thrilled, thinks I wish I could overcome the fear and enjoy the ride.

Beside me in the first picture is Bill. If you think I looked scared, you should see his face. Whoa. He looks more terrified than I do. But he has ridden many roller coasters since. He not only has ridden them but has discovered the thrill of riding them. He has conquered his fear, and in conquering his fear, he can enjoy the ride. This makes me a little jealous, but don't tell him. Oh no, there is "Miss Smug" showing herself again.

If riding a roller coaster were the only place in my life where fear controlled me, I would be okay with it because they are not a top priority for me. But God tells me in His Word that I am not to live my life afraid. He promises to be with me with His strength and hold me with His powerful, righteous hand.

Isaiah 41:10 in the Amplified Bible adds,

"Do not look around you in terror and be dismayed for I am your God."

This verse tells us that He is our "I Am." We are to look to Him and not around in terror. Have you discovered this place of rest and confidence in the Lord, or do you, like me, have places of fear that control your life?

If you and I need faith in the promises of God. One way is to read His Word and trust those promises in the middle of our circumstances.

James tells us to be doers of the Word and not just hearers. Believing God is the only way to do what we hear.

I may never enjoy riding roller coasters, but my prayer for you and me is we will trust the Lord our God and enjoy the ride of life. I cannot say for one second that I have obtained this goal, but I am going to keep seeking and asking until my trust in God is stronger than any fear I face.

Ponders of the Heart

Do you struggle with fear and anxiety?

Have you had a fear that God has removed from your life?

Read Isaiah 41:9-20.

Did you see the number of times God says, "I will?" This is our very hope. He will, and we can trust Him.

Prayers of the Heart:

Dear Father,

Let Your Words rest deep in our souls. Let the confidence of our lives be rooted in You, in Your promises, and not in us, others, or our circumstances. Lord, there are circumstances that scare us, and we need Your help. Move in our souls and show us who we are, and we do not need to be afraid. Thank You for Your love and promises. Father, we will not fear, for You are our Lord. In Jesus' name, amen.

October 17 ~ Purity

"All who have this hope in him purify themselves, just as he is pure" (1 John 3:3).

The hope this verse is talking about is how God has lavished His love on us, and we are His children. The purification of oneself is not motivated by law but by love.

Is it possible to walk pure before the Lord, and if this is possible, what would be the benefit?

Purity is being uncontaminated, clean, and unpolluted. We are to be pure. What exactly does this mean to you? What does purity look like and how can we aspire to such a lofty goal?

In the Olympic Games, it is not unheard of for an athlete to be from one country and compete for another or for an athlete to train in one country while representing another. That is also true with coaches. Just imagine a person coming to America to train and being privileged to live in democracy and prosperity. If they are not careful, our country is bound to contaminate them with our way of life.

Think of a woman from Iraq coming here and experiencing freedom and respect as an equal to men and then returning home. While we might think, "Good for her." The influence of our country would be to her disadvantage after returning home. We are told we now belong to the kingdom of God, and just like an Olympic athlete, we are training in a foreign land, and if we are not careful, we will lose our devotion to His kingdom.

Our pollution comes from the environment around us. We become entrenched in the ways of the world. Instead of us having an influence, we are affected. Would this be God's desire for His children?

How do we keep our purity? The only way I know is by His power, so we find ourselves in need of close personal contact with God. When an athlete comes here to train, if the country they are representing is smart, they will send with their athlete companions, people who will remind them of who they are and what country they belong to.

God has given us the Holy Spirit to live in us to remind us who we are and Who we belong. He has also given us His Word so we can communicate with our Father. Purity pursued from love and relationship is much stronger than purity followed out of fear and law. This is why 1 John 3:3 reminds us that our hope is there because God has lavished us with love.

Ponders of the Heart

What areas of your life have you entangled?

Has God given you the ability to be an influencer for Him?

If not, why not ask Him to show you how you can be an influencer for His Kingdom?

Read 1 John 2:15-17 and 1 John 3:1-3.

Prayers of the Heart

Dear Father,

We come to You confessing we often forget who we are and Who we belong to. Quicken Your Spirit within us so we can remember. Lord, You are our hope and purity. Help us abide in You by Your Spirit. Open the eyes of our hearts so we can see You. Apart from You, we are doomed. In Jesus' name, amen.

October 18 ~ Is Purity Possible?

"And now these three remain: faith, hope and love. But the greatest of these is love" (1 Cor. 13:13).

Can God's children walk in purity and not be contaminated by this world? Faith is the door, hope is the door handle, and love is the motivation. This is what Paul says is the most excellent way.

There are not three easy steps to purity, nor are there three hard ones. Pureness is a gift from God that we must believe is ours. Walking in this truth is in direct proportion to the hope we place on the finished work of Jesus.

Behavior often reflects more of what people believe about themselves or God than what they say they believe. If I trust God has placed me into His family and given me a new nature and identity, my behavior will begin to reflect this truth. If I think I am rotten to the core or if I feel shameful, my actions will line up with this belief. Before I was in Christ, I was rotten to the core. Before I was placed in Him, all I knew was shame, but now God says I am a new creation.

Because you and I are in these old bodies, with the influence of the world, we will sometimes stumble and fall. But this is not God's desire for us. He wants us to believe we are who He has made us to be and walk in this hope. The proof of our walking in this truth is purified lives.

What in your life needs purifying? In other words, how are your actions showing that you don't believe God? It is so much more about believing than performing. If you believe who you are in Christ, it will change your behavior. Here are some questions to ask ourselves:

- Do we worry instead of praying? If so, do we not believe God answers prayers?
- Do we fix instead of waiting on God? Then, do we not believe God is able or willing to handle the situation?

I am trying to believe that God hears my prayers and knows the exact way to answer. Waiting for Him to move is an act of purifying me from self-protection and self-sufficiency. There are people, even Christians, who disagree with me. They believe God helps those who help themselves. I have never found this in the Bible. God's Word tells us that He helps those who depend on Him and call on Him in their time of need.

Your life might need to be purified from the lust for things. Things can quench our desire for God. If we believe that Jesus is our life (Colossians 3:4), we will seek Him. He will change the desires of our hearts, and we will find rest for our souls. Purification is a lifelong process. My prayer for us is that we are moving in a forward motion. I don't want to get stuck in muddy water. Yuck.

Ponders of the Heart

Do you struggle with purity in your life?

Do you feel stuck in past failures?

Do you need a refresher course on God's love?

Read 1 Corinthians 13.

Ask God to give you the faith, hope, and love to accept His grace for living. Thank Him and start living in hope.

Prayers of the Heart

Dear Father,

We know our lives need work, and we want to be all You created us to be. Not just in words but in life. Lord, show us Your faithfulness in such a way that we plant our lives deeper in hope, faith, and love. We are sorry we have fickle hearts. Our faith must be in You, not in our ability or performance. Show us Your glory. In Jesus' name, amen.

October 19 ~ The Benefit of Purity

"Spiritual perception is based upon purity of heart. What we see in life and how we see it is rooted in the soil of our inner thought-life. If we would experience clear and open vision concerning the Kingdom of God, a pure heart is most essential (Holiness Truth and The Presence of God by Francis Frangipane).

When I read the words above, I want to cry out to God and say, "Oh Lord, create in me a pure and steadfast spirit. "How I long for spiritual insight. But am I ready for my life to be plowed up and weeded for God's planting of purity? How sick am I of the pollution of this world, and how much do I want a better way? Am I trying to serve two masters?

When bacteria pollute our bodies, they go to work to isolate and destroy the infection. This is often a painful process.

When Julie, my youngest, had an abscessed tooth, the whole side of her face swelled until her eye was almost closed. The strange thing was that before the face swelled, her pain was excruciating. When we took her to our dentist, he said when the infection breaks through the bone and swells the face, the pain lessens.

The body was isolating the infection in hopes to rid the body of this impurity. She was out of pain, but her vision was impaired. It took the help of our dentist and an antibiotic to get rid of the infection.

We might be able to work on ourselves and isolate ourselves from unhealthy habits that cause us and others pain, but to be pure, we need the soil of our inner thought life purified. This work is beyond self-control. We need God's transforming power to purify us. If we try to go it alone, we will have little to no Spiritual discernment.

Our dentist did not call Julie on Saturday morning and ask her if he needed to meet her at his office. He waited for us to call him. God often waits until we are ready for His help and call out to Him with a sincere heart.

"Blessed are the pure of heart for they shall see God" (Matthew 5:8).

Ponders of the Heart

Do you want a pure heart, and what would it take to have one?

Have you prayed for God to transform you with His power?

Are you afraid?

Read Psalm 51:1-2 and Psalm 51:7-13.

Oh, that we would trust Him beyond our fear.

Prayers of the Heart

Dear Father,

Have mercy on us according to Your loving kindness, according to Your tender mercies. Wash us, Lord, and we will be clean. Take the inner thoughts of our lives and purify us with Your cleansing power. We want pure, faithful hearts so we might know, hear and obey You. We want what only You can do. Do it, Father, please, do it. In Jesus' name, amen.

October 20 ~ Garbage Man

"The next day John saw Jesus coming toward him and said, 'Look, the Lamb of God, who takes away the sin of the world!'" (John 1:29).

Monday is the morning my husband takes out the garbage. He carries the garbage can to the end of our driveway, but it is our garbage man who takes it away. I don't think I have ever thanked him. Not my husband, but the garbage man.

Being a garbage man is a thankless job, but what a mess we would have if there were none. I need to remember that and give him a wave of thanks.

Unappreciated jobs are a specialty for moms. We know about picking up after people one day just to pick up after them again the next. What about cleaning bathrooms and floors, washing clothes and dishes over and over and over? If you are a wife and mother, you are shaking your head in agreement. These are thankless jobs, but thank goodness someone does them.

We all have people who make our world a little cleaner. There are people who wash cars and clean office buildings and churches. We can hire workers to wash houses and driveways. If we are very industrious, we might do many things for ourselves, but if you look around, I bet you can find someone who helps you keep your world a little cleaner.

One of the reasons we own a cleaning service is because keeping my surroundings tidy has always been important to me.

But keeping my inside world pure is a tougher job. My thoughts and attitudes need to be adjusted more often than I want to admit. The influence of lies, assaulting me and the natural inclination of wrong thinking and doing is constantly knocking at the door of my mind. If I am not careful, this can lead to wrong actions.

I'm a dirty mess, but I have a Savior. A Redeemer who is my Garbage Man. He, the Holy Son of God, is washing me and cleansing me on a daily, hourly, minute-by-minute assignment. He has, and He will continue to take away and cleanse me from all my sins.

Do I take His ministry for granted as I do my garbage man? Do I think my once-a-week church attendance or tithe is enough gratitude for the work He does on my behalf? Or is my heart full of praise? Read the words of Max Lucado in his book '*Grace for the Moment.*'

"When you recognize God as Creator, you will admire him. When you recognize his wisdom, you will learn from him. When you discover his strength, you will rely on him. But only when he saves you will you worship him.

Christ has saved you and me from our garbage, our sins. He took it away and dumped it in the heavenly dumpster where the holy fire of heaven would burn it up. Jesus has cleansed us and made us pure. What a wonderful, merciful God we serve. Oh, my heart is ready to worship. Worship my King, who often wears the hat of my Garbage Man.

Ponders of the Heart

Have you ever thanked your garbage man?

What sin in your past brings you overwhelming joy because it is gone forever?

Read Hebrews 8:12, Colossians 1:14, and Romans 5:8-9.

Prayers of the Heart

Dear Father,

How we thank You for Your grace that has cleansed us and made us Yours. Oh, Father, we do not want to take You for granted. We want to live each day aware of Your work in our lives. We want to, as Peter says in 1 Peter 3:15, sanctify You in our hearts as Lord. In Jesus' name, amen.

October 21 ~ Redeemed

"Let the redeemed of the Lord tell their story—those he redeemed from the hand of the foe, those he gathered from the lands, from east and west, from north and south" (Psalm 107:2-3).

Our dog was a wanderer. The older he got, the more he wanted to wander. One day, he got out and was caught by the dog pound. We found out where he was and brought him home. It wasn't long before he escaped again, and, you guessed it, they caught him again. This time, we had to buy him back.

Our dog was old, not worth much, just a mutt, but we bought his freedom and his life. We paid good money to redeem a good-for-nothing dog that was worth a lot to us. I wish I could say our old dog learned his lesson, but he didn't. He wandered until his dying days.

This is a great picture of what Jesus has done for us. We are born with a wandering, adulterous heart. We often wander away from God and His protection, chasing after other things like an unfaithful spouse.

In His mercy, He comes for us so He can bring us home. We aren't worth much; we are naturally sinful and often shameful, but He buys our freedom with His life. God paid for us with the life of His Son. The precious pure blood of Jesus has redeemed us from His wrath and our sinfulness.

After washing us clean, he places us in His kingdom and dresses us in the righteous robe of Jesus. And what does He want from us? God wants our wandering hearts so we will stay safe in His care.

We are worthless people who are worth everything to Him. Let our wandering hearts be still and find our worth in being His child. One thing is sure; because He has redeemed us, we will never find ourselves on death row. He has given us life, and this life is in His Son. Jesus' sacrifice was once and completely sufficient. The price was enough to cover all our wandering. But the truth is there is no place like home.

Ponders of the Heart

Have you ever found yourself homesick and far away from home?

Are you grateful God will come after you when you wander from Him?

Read Psalm 49:15 and Titus 2:11-14.

Praise the Lord for redeeming you and ask Him to fill your heart with satisfaction.

Prayers of the Heart

Dear Father,

You have sought us and made us to be Yours. Thank You, accept our praise and thankfulness. Lord, forgive our wandering ways. Bring us home again and again, for apart from You, we have no home, life, or hope. You, Father, are our Master, King, and Lord, and we don't want to wander from You. Draw our hearts to You until we see You face to face. In Jesus' name, amen.

October 22 ~ Afterwards

"'But,' he said, "you cannot see my face, for no one may see me and live.' Then the Lord said, 'There is a place near me where you may stand on a rock. When my glory passes by, I will put you in a cleft in the rock and cover you with my hand until I have passed by. Then I will remove my hand and you will see my back; but my face must not be seen'" (Exodus 33:20-23).

Moses wanted to see God's glory. He needed to know God was with him, and with boldness, he asked to see His glory. The Lord was pleased, but He knew His fullness was too much for Moses. So, God agreed to hide Moses in the cleft of the rock, cover him with His Hand, and when He passed by, The Lord would remove His Hand and allow Moses to see His back. What an awesome picture of God's tenderness toward His own.

I love these verses, but in Hebrew, the word back is best understood as afterwards. This takes my breath away. I don't know why exactly, but it does. God is saying to Moses that he could see God's afterglow. I had to stop in my tracks when I read this and ask the Lord to give me a tangible picture that would help me imagine what this might mean.

My thoughts turned to sunsets. I thought back over the times Bill and I were at West Point Lake and the sun was setting over the water. It looks as if the sun is dipping into the water, and I can almost hear a sizzling sound.

We cannot look directly into the sun without it making our eyes water, hurt, and burn. If we were closer to the sun, it would burn us alive, but at sunset, when the light is dim, and the glow is soft, we can look with pleasure at the setting sun. The afterglow of sunset is magical.

This is my tangible picture of God's "afterwards." The weight of who God is is too much for us as human beings. He is Spirit, He is holy, and we live in tents of clay. But how it must please Him when we desire to look upon His face and see His glory.

Moses wanted to experience all that God was, but God knew Moses could only endure His afterglow. So, God, in His mercy, showed Moses all he could stand. I bet if we ask and if we believe,

He will do the same for us. Oh, the Word of God gives me such wonder I can hardly stand it.

Ponders of the Heart

Does it thrill you or frighten you to think of seeing God's glory?

What do you imagine it will be like in heaven when we see God on His throne?

Read Exodus 33.

Ask God to open your heart to His Word and let Him thrill you.

Prayers of the Heart

Dear Father,

What wonder You stir in us. How we long to see You face to face. Father, give us boldness to seek You above all things. Give us the courage to come and ask to know You. We do not want to be cold toward the things of the Spirit. We want to love, seek, know You, and experience all of You that we can endure. Lord, let us see Your afterwards. In Jesus' name, amen.

October 23 ~ Scarred

"After he said this, he showed them his hands and side. The disciples were overjoyed when they saw the Lord" (John 20:20).

My right arm is marked with a scar. It happened when I was six years old while catching minnows in a ditch. I even missed the first day of the first grade. The pain of the wound is gone; the memory of the accident is vague, but the scar after all these years is still there.

We all have scars of one kind or another. Some are visible, while others are painful and hidden in our souls. There are those who wear their scars like a badge of courage, while others cover them as if they were marks of shame. Some talk about them, and others hide them deep in their heart. But we are all marked with the scars of living in a sinful world, with sinful people and an enemy that is out to get us.

Jesus was no exception to this rule. He lived among us, suffered with us, and died to take away death, shame, and sin while giving us victory and a new life. He did all this, but He did not escape this world without scars, and we won't either.

Life is hard, and we are at war, but one sweet day, we will lay down this life and begin a new life in new bodies. Will we still carry the marks of our scars? I don't know. Your opinion is as good as mine. But I will have to say I think not. Only the scars of our Savior will be worthy of remembering. It is His wound that healed us and His life that defeated Satan. It will be His scars we can rejoice over.

"Surely he took up our pain and bore our suffering, yet we considered him punished by God, stricken by him, and afflicted. But he was pierced for our transgressions, he was crushed for our iniquities; the punishment that brought us peace was on him, and by his wounds we are healed" (Isaiah 53:4-5).

Ponders of the Heart

Do you have any scars?

Do you hide them, or are you proud of them?

What about the scars of your soul? Do these scars keep you in bondage?

Read Hebrews 12:1-3.

Prayers of the Heart

Dear Father,

We want to thank You for bearing our shame and sin. We want to thank You that by Your wounds, we are free and being healed. Lord, we know we are not worthy. Father, Your grace overwhelms us. You brought us life and hope. In Jesus' name, amen.

October 24 ~ Beautiful

"Let the king be enthralled by your beauty; honor him, for he is your lord" (Psalm 45:11).

Digital pictures give a bad picture taker like me grace. I take the picture, and then we all look at the results. What I find interesting is that everyone judges the picture according to how they think they look. If they look good, then the picture is good, but if they look bad, then we want a do-over.

The optional word here is "think." Usually, I am never completely satisfied with how I look. I can be critical of my appearance. So, when I read Bible verses that say God sees me and says I am beautiful, it is hard for me to believe. Do you have a tough time believing God sees you as beautiful?

Since the fall of man, we dare not believe God sees beauty in us. Because we are born with a sinful nature, and we live with shame. We are separated from God by our sin, and we know He cannot look on or be in the presence of sin. So how can the Psalmist say that the King desires our beauty?

The right answer to this question is Jesus. We know the right answer, so why do we struggle with this truth? Why do we refuse to see ourselves drenched, covered, and inputted with His beauty?

Old habits die hard, and so do old messages. We still believe the message of our shame, and the enemy wants us to stay in bondage. You say, "I still think and say some horrible things, and I do things I know are wrong. How can you say that God sees beauty in me?"

I assure you I know what you mean. We all struggle with the same questions. I am always looking to my performance instead of believing what God says about His redeemed, and I bet you do, too.

The crazy part of all this is if we believe what God says, I think we could then see victory over our thoughts, words, and actions—not all at once, but one step at a time, as we believe Him and not our old messages.

In the story of Cinderella, she is found by her prince. She goes from a girl covered with cinders to a princess in a palace. We all love this story because, in our souls, we all long for transformation. Our deepest longing is for our dreams to come true and our hearts to be transformed.

Cinderella's life was transformed, but what if she went to live in the palace with her Prince Charming, and she couldn't believe her good fortune?

So, every morning, she went down to the kitchen in the palace and cleaned out the cinders from the fireplace. She dressed in her old rags and served each person in the castle. She fed the animals and brought the prince his tea in bed. Bowing before him but never took her rightful place beside him.

She was refusing her transformation. This is what we do when we refuse to believe that God, in His grace, has transformed our hearts. He has given us a new identity, and now, because of Christ, He looks at us and sees our imputed beauty.

Oh, that we would praise Him and accept the gift of His grace by refusing the old messages and walking in the newness of believing Him. I want to start today. I think I will go and buy a pair of glass slippers so I can remind myself to be thankful and walk according to His transforming grace. Someday, there will be a family portrait of us, and we will see the beauty He sees. Oh, Lord, Your grace is amazing.

Ponders of the Heart

Do you have a tough time believing that God sees you as beautiful?

What old messages from Satan does he play over in your mind?

Read 2 Corinthians 3:16-18 and Psalm 16:3.

Celebrate the transformation that is ours in Christ.

Prayers of the Heart

Dear Father,

Just as we have a tough time looking at pictures and seeing our beauty, we have a hard time believing that by Your grace, You have transformed our hearts. Help us believe that You have made us new, and we now have good hearts. Help us refuse to listen to the old messages and walk in the light of Your Word. In Jesus' name, Amen.

October 25 ~ Mouse in the Closet

"but I see another law at work in me, waging war against the law of my mind and making me a prisoner of the law of sin at work within me" (Romans 7:23).

We have all heard it said that confession is good for the soul. Well, here I go. There is a mouse in my closet. I opened the closet door and there was stark evidence that a rodent had been there. Immediately, everything about my house felt dirty and invaded.

This is the second time a mouse has found its way into our house of sixteen years. The first time I saw one, no one believed me, but then they saw the little creature. It took me months not to look for more of those little guys. Now, just when I had comfortably settled into a sense of security, one is back.

I have one ear intently listening to the possibility of the trap going off. When it does, if it does, I will have to deal with it. I might just let Bill take care of it. The whole thing is very yucky to me.

I have this mouse in my closet, but I have another confession: there is a rat in my flesh. I thought it was gone. I have dealt with it before. The Lord has heard my confession, and I try to keep away from the situation. The old saying that if you ignore it, it will go away is not working.

In this case, if I ignore this issue instead of dealing with it, there will be a rat hiding in my heart, dirtying up and invading my soul. This rat is an attitude I have towards someone, and I don't want to feel the way I do about them. I relate to Paul's cry when he said:

"O wretched man that I am. Who will deliver me from this body of death?" (Romans 7:24).

I am hoping that by confessing this to you, this rat will vacate my soul. I want every sign that he has been there gone. I don't want this attitude in my soul. Just as I want my home on this earth to be clean, I want my heart to be pure and holy for Him. But I'm here to tell you I need help.

Thank goodness Paul gives me and you the answer.

"Thanks be to God, who delivers me through Jesus Christ our Lord!" (Romans 7:24-25).

Ponders of the Heart

Do you struggle with resentment toward someone?

Does your heart feel cluttered with unforgiveness?

Read Romans 7:24-8:6.

Ask God to kill the rat inside of you as I am asking the same for me.

Prayers of the Heart

Dear Father,

We do feel wretched. Lord, come and wash us, and we will be clean. We long to live, walk, and breathe by the Spirit and not by our flesh. Defeat this enemy in us. Kill those rats in our hearts and take all the evidence of them away. Create clean hearts and restore the right spirits within us. In Jesus' name, amen.

October 26 Plans of Life

"Many are the plans in a person's heart, but it is the Lord's purpose that prevails" (Proverbs 19:21).

The actor, Michael J. Fox, is a favorite of mine. His mannerisms and his looks remind me of my younger brother, Randy. When I watch a Michael Fox movie, it touches my heart and reminds me of home.

Mr. Fox played the part of a young surgeon in the movie *Doc Hollywood*. His plan was to move to Hollywood and become a plastic surgeon. He would be rich, underworked, and overpaid. Ah, the American dream.

His plan was set, but not in stone, because a pretty ambulance driver in the hick town of Grady ran his plan off the road. Instead of becoming a rich, famous plastic surgeon, he was fast becoming an M.D. in a small hick town he loved. His plan had run amuck.

Has this ever happened to you? My plans have run amuck many times, and I have a plan in my head right now. One that I have the urge to put into motion, but I don't want to fool myself anymore with lofty plans of my own. My desire is to be following the plan God has and to play the part He has designed just for me.

He often asks us to wait and be satisfied as we trust Him. All three of those things are hard, and without His grace, we could never make it. Waiting is hard. It is not natural for us to keep our heads occupied and not instigate our own plans while we listen to Him. Being satisfied while being ready to respond to Him is also tricky. But trusting is a minute-by-minute battle. This is where I find myself today.

Running life as a race instead of a journey is where most Americans find themselves day after day. We are so busy running the race we forget to breathe, smell the roses, and enjoy the sights and the sounds. When we can slow down, it seems wrong. We feel like we are running out of time because we are not running.

God promises to be the One with the plan. He is responsible for directing our steps, and if we stop, slow down, and listen, He will commune with us and direct us one step at a time.

Many people, even Christians, believe they don't have time to wait for God, listen to Him, or that He even directs their steps. They feel it is up to them and God has given them control over their destinies.

Shoot, I think this at times. If it wasn't what I believed, then I would walk in peace, patience, and confidence. There are days I am far from this.

The good news is that whether I know, believe, or accept it, God is in control of my life. It might not look or feel like it, but the Bible confirms He is.

"Lord, I know that people's lives are not their own; it is not for them to direct their steps" (Jeremiah 10:23).

Now, if you are a sure-footed fellow, this might rub you the wrong way, but if you are an insecure puppy like me, you find your peace in this truth. I might not know where I am going or where I am, but praise the Lord, He does. You might think, like me, you have run off the road and are stuck in the muck, but be patient; help is on its way.

Ponders of the Heart

Have you made plans that have failed?

Have you mapped out someone else's life just to be wrong?

Read Psalm 139:1-18.

Be at peace; God has the right plan for us and the ones we love. Pray that we will cooperate with Him.

Prayers of the Heart

Dear Father,

You know the plans You have for us—plans that are good, not for harm. We are trying to wait on You and not make our own plans. We are trying to trust and believe You. Please help us remember Your Words and hold them close to our hearts. In Jesus' name, amen.

October 27 ~ A Turtle's Existence

"There he went into a cave and spent the night. And the word of the Lord came to him: 'What are you doing here, Elijah?'" (1 Kings 19:9).

Turtles are sad-looking creatures to me. I don't know if they feel sad or weighed down, but they surely look like it. They creep along, carrying their houses on their backs. Whenever danger or even rest is needed, they stuff themselves inside themselves. What a lonely existence. I know because I have been known to take the turtle approach to living.

How about you, or do you know and love someone who approaches living like this? When we take counsel from ourselves, it can be not only lonely but also biased and blind. Mostly, we agree with ourselves, and it is hard to get perspective in our private world.

Have you ever looked closely at a turtle that has closed itself inside? There is not a crack anywhere. He is pulled in, and his skin has sealed him tighter than a zip lock bag. At least a zip lock bag has an opener on the outside. Not so with a turtle; he is there, and you aren't getting him out until he is ready to come. I don't know how to entice a turtle to come out, but God has a way of opening our shells with His light.

When He touches our hearts, the new ones He has given us, we will begin to unfold into the world. He feeds our hungry souls with His Word, and we begin to drift out from the shackles of hiding. If we walk in fellowship with other Christ followers, we can begin to share life with others and emerge out of our turtle shell living.

The devil is tricky, and he often works to keep us hidden. If he sees a crack in our shell, he will invite himself in. He works to convince us to stay safe inside. Stay away from God's Word and His people, and listen to him.

The good news is if Jesus is our Lord, then His Spirit is inside us. He is there gently prodding us along to come outside, leave our old man behind, and walk in freedom. We know it will be a lighter existence, but we are afraid without that outer shell, we will get hurt by falling rocks. We are right; we might, but God promises to be there and use even falling rocks for our good.

Now, to know all this and still live in my shell is crazy, shortsighted, and the act of being stubborn. I don't want to be like that, do you?

Okay, I'm ready to take off my shell. God has talked me into it, and I am thankful and a little afraid. But this time, when I take it off, I want to forget where I put it, so I cannot put it back on. This will be true freedom. Oh, Lord, help me and anyone else who is living tucked away in their turtle shell. Father, be patient with us, your "turtle girls." Now, that is a lie. We are not turtle girls; we are children of the King, and He is no turtle.

Ponders of the Heart

Are you living like a turtle girl?

Are you ready to trust the Lord and come out of hiding?

Read 1 Kings 19:1-18.

Even great people of God can run and hide, but God deals graciously with His own. This really encourages me. I hope it encourages you.

Prayers of the Heart:

Dear Father,

We do not want to be cave dwellers. We want to be Your light in a dark world. We want to live as Your children. Lord, free us from the shackles of self-imposed hiding. Help us have courage and be strong in You. Lord, we need You, and we love You. You are our hope and our confidence. In Jesus' name, amen.

October 28 ~ Death

"Where, O death is your victory? Where, O death is your sting?" (1 Corinthians 15:55).

Where were you when Kennedy was shot? On nine-eleven? Where were you when you heard your mother died or your grandmother? The list can go on, but the point is that the death of heroes and loved ones always makes an impression. It is a defining moment in life.

Death is not the only defining circumstance we face. There are more, like moving, sickness, loss of a job, loss of a home, injury, and natural disaster.

Life has many ups and downs, and things happen that shake our world apart. In these times, we see what we are made of and who we depend on. But I don't think many circumstances get our attention as much as death. The shock of death does have its sting, and it has victory, but after the shock, God's people are sustained by His presence.

God often uses these defining moments to reveal more of Who He is and call us to a deeper walk with Him.

If we resist Him during these moments, a hardening of our hearts will begin, and this makes it impossible to see or experience His grace. Does this last statement scare you? It does me, but I'm thankful. God's grace is there not only to sustain us but to move us from where we are to where He wants us to be. Moving is often slow and painful, but it is in the movement we regain strength, vision, and spiritual growth.

Are you in a defining moment in your life? Do you feel off-kilter? Take heart; this is not all bad. It is during these unsure times that we can be sure of Him and when we exercise faith in Him, He will show us His glory.

His glory is the manifestation of His holiness, and this has always been more than enough to get us through. In light of His glory, defining moments become Spiritual markers of growth that prepare us for our future home.

Death stings but is not the victor. Who is the victor? Christ Jesus our Lord.

Ponders of the Heart

How has God used situations in your life to draw you close to Him?

Does the promise that God is with you help you live today without fear?

Read Isaiah 6:1-4.

This was a defining moment for Isaiah, and God showed Isaiah His glory.

Prayers of the Heart

Dear Lord,

We need You every minute of every day, but never do we realize this more than in times of loss. Lord, nothing shakes our foundation like death, but at the core of who we are, there is You. How thankful we are that nothing will touch our lives without Your knowledge.

Nothing can take us from You. We can find strength and growth in Your presence. In Jesus' name, amen.

October 29 ~ Birthright

"Then Jacob gave Esau some bread and some lentil stew. He ate and drank and then got up and left. So Esau despised his birthright" (Genesis 25:34).

Esau pledged his birthright to his brother for the sake of his stomach. He was hungry and wanted something to eat. His brother wanted Esau's place in the family as the eldest son, and Esau gave it to him for a bowl of stew. So, the Bible said Esau despised his birthright.

It is easy for me to think how shortsighted Esau was, and no doubt he was, but the real question for us is, do we despise our birthright?

Let me use other words that might help us get more honest with ourselves. Do we take for granted the rights we have to be part of a family? Kids can take their parents for granted and all they do for them. Wives can take their husbands and children for granted. We can grumble about our home, car, or the amount of money and possessions we have.

Have you ever felt mistreated by your siblings? We can neglect our parents, children, husbands, and siblings for jobs, sports, or other hobbies. Are we nice, helpful, and courteous to everyone except those in our own family? When we treat the people and our responsibilities in the family with little regard, are we, in a sense, despising our birthright?

Esau got his stew, and Jacob got Esau's birthright. It would be like me giving away my house for a hotdog or my car for a brownie. If Esau would give away something so precious for a bowl of stew, the Bible concluded that it meant nothing to him, and when we show little regard for our family members, the same conclusion can be made about us. OUCH.

God has given us another birthright. He has made us His sons and His daughters. He has placed us in His family, and He has become our Father, provider, protector, and Lord.

How often do we despise the life we now have? When we grumble, we grumble against our Father. If we live and think like the world and show little regard for our Heavenly Father and His will, we are, in a sense, despising our birthright.

Does the world know we belong to the family of God? Would we give away our claim to heaven for a million dollars, a vacation house in the mountains, or the beach? If so, God might conclude that our eternal destiny is of little importance to us. He might conclude we despise our birthright. Oh, that it might never be that we take His grace, provision, and love for granted.

Ponders of the Heart

Those were tough questions. How did you do?

Did the questions cause you to stop and think about your actions toward your family?

What about your grumbling about your life?

Read Ephesians 4:1-6.

Prayers of the Heart

Dear Father,

Thank You for the life that You have given us. Belonging to You and being in Your family. What a wonderful blessing. Oh, Father, forgive us when we take Your grace for granted. Apart from You, we are lost, but with You, we have all we will ever need. Lord, we love You. In Jesus' name, amen.

October 30 ~ Evil

"You intended to harm me, but God intended it for good to accomplish what is now being done, the saving of many lives" (Genesis 50:20).

Joseph was a good man who was a little boastful about his dreams. Overall, he was a good person who had terrible things happen to him.

He was sold by his brothers into slavery, thrown into prison because he was accused of messing around with his boss's wife, and was forgotten by the cupbearer for two years after he interpreted a dream for him.

Joseph had a good heart, and when his brothers came searching for food in Egypt, he took them in instead of letting them starve. And when their father died, the brothers thought Joseph's kindness was about to end. He said to his brothers in Genesis 50:20 not to be afraid he would care for them and their families. You might think Joseph is a person who deserved God's blessing.

The Lord blessed Joseph, and He used the evil of his brothers for good. In Genesis, you also read about Joseph's father, Jacob. His story is different; Jacob did evil to others. He, as a young man, was a scoundrel. He cheated his brother, tricked and lied to his father, and cheated his uncle. That was, of course, before his uncle had a chance to cheat him. But God blessed Jacob.

How do we make sense of this? God took Jacob's wicked ways and used them for good. It seems right that Joseph was blessed. We think he deserved blessings, but Jacob deserved to be thrown on the backside of the desert and forgotten. He was a selfish, conniving, manipulating, ungrateful son, but God was working in Jacob's life for good.

I can't understand this. Can you? I wrestle with God over things like this, and when I am finished, I am reminded that God's Word is not so much about good and bad behavior. The Bible leaves nothing out. Human beings are sinful, and apart from God's grace, we would self-destruct. The Bible shows us God's power and grace over our sinfulness. This is the only way to read and understand Scripture.

God's love and plans are beyond our plans and behavior. In this life, we will face good times and hard times, but God is still in control.

Do our decisions have consequences? You bet they do. We can hurt ourselves and the people we love with the decisions we make.

When I look back over some things I have said and done, I have regret and sorrow, but as God's child, I have hope. How grateful I am that He is bigger, stronger, and wiser than my mistakes and successes. He is working things out with grace and mercy for our good.

We are His children because of our hope in Jesus and new birth, not because of our behavior. It is our loss and deep regret when we go our own way. My prayer is that we will seek the Lord and submit to His will.

God uses our lives for His eternal plan. Let's cooperate and trust Him with the outcome. This is our hope.

Ponders of the Heart

Do you consider yourself a good person or a bad person?

How has your attitude about yourself kept you in bondage?

Read Genesis 32:22-30

Rejoice over our merciful God.

Prayers of the Heart

Dear Father,

Thank You that our names are in the Book of Life. You have written them there with the permanent ink of Jesus' blood. This is where our hope lies. Not in our goodness but in Your purity and Your gift of the cross. Lord, we have Jacobs in our families; we pray for them. Show them Your face and give them a new identity in You. In Jesus' name, amen.

October 31 ~ Prayers of the Heart

"Because of the Lord's great love we are not consumed, for his compassions never fail. They are new every morning; great is your faithfulness. I say to myself, "The Lord is my portion; therefore I will wait for him"' (Lamentations 3:22-24).

Dear Father,

We praise You for Your great compassion, which never fails. We thank You for new mercies every morning. You are our portion and our very great reward. There is none like You. Your mercy and compassion fill our souls with hope and hunger for You.

Lord, may we never take Your love for granted. May we never despise our birthright in Jesus. Take our lives and use them for good. Take our hearts and turn them into a filling of Your living water. Oh, how we need You, Lord. How we need to walk and live overflowing with Your Spirit. We are Your people and Your children. Teach us Your ways and fill us with Your love.

"Since, then, you have been raised with Christ, set your hearts on things above, where Christ is, seated at the right hand of God. Set your minds on things above, not on earthly things. For you died, and your life is now hidden with Christ in God. When Christ, who is your life, appears, then you also will appear with him in glory" (Colossians 3:1-4).

Dear Father,

We thank You that we belong to Christ. We have a heavenly kingdom. Lord, help us focus on the things above. Help us reckon ourselves dead to sin and alive to You. We are hidden in Your Son. Thank You. One day, we will appear with Him in glory, but until then, help us keep our eyes on You. We praise You, Father. In Jesus' name, amen.

"Let the peace of Christ rule in your hearts, since as members of one body you were called to peace. And be thankful" (Colossians 3:15.).

november

— " —

God made him who had no sin to be sin for us, so that in him we might become the righteousness of God.

2 Corinthians 5:21

November 1 ~ Niche

Dreams are so interesting. They can be funny, scary, but always interesting.

I have crazy dreams. Once, I dreamed I wanted a pair of expensive shoes, ones that were too expensive for me, so I would try to get a part-time job at the shoe store. Not selling shoes but keeping their financial books.

In my dream the boss and his wife had gone on vacation, and a friend was working at the shoe store by herself. She was getting busy, so I asked her if she needed my help. My plan was to help her, get the part-time job and the shoes I wanted. In my dream I was scheming for my own purpose.

She was thankful, so I asked a customer if she needed help. She showed me the shoe and the size she wanted. In my conversation with her, she asked me if I recognized her. I didn't but told her that her voice sounded familiar. She seemed to know me and was glad to see me.

Off I went to find her shoes, but I couldn't. Looking around the back room I found a box I thought was right, but there were no shoes in it. I continued to look and found the right shoe box, but the shoes inside were wrong. Determined, I continued to look. By the time I came out of the back room, the shoe store was full of people, and the lady who wanted the shoes I was looking for had gotten mad and left.

It was clear that the shoe business wasn't for me. When I woke up, I told Bill about my dream. He laughed at me and said, "You were looking for your niche, but the shoe business was not it." Am I still looking for my niche? Is that what this dream was all about? As I said, dreams are interesting.

I am reading a book about a girl who has a burning desire to paint. She feels alive when she puts paint on the canvas. She concludes this must be how people who play musical instruments or care for orphaned children feel.

She had discovered her passion, and I went to bed thinking about my own desire for living. What is your passion? Are you still trying to find your niche? I think we all find ourselves there occasionally. We know in our souls that life is more heart than mind, but it doesn't seem like it. Life can feel empty, but life with passion is alive and exciting.

When life seems to dry up, I know who I need. Like the Psalmist, I hear the Lord say,

"My heart says of you, 'Seek his face!' Your face, Lord, I will seek'" (Psalm 27:8).

When life loses heart, we have lost our focus on the One who gives life. Our niche and purpose are found in knowing and serving the Lord. If we try to find our purpose in anything else, we might look and look, but our box will come up empty.

Ponders of the Heart

Do you have crazy dreams?

What would you say is your niche in life?

Have you found your purpose in the Lord?

Read Matthew 6:33, John 10:10, Colossians 3:1-3, and John 14:6.

Prayers of the Heart

Dear Father,

Your face we will seek. This is our deepest need and desire. Help us find our niche in You. You created us, and in You, we find our purpose for living. Forgive us when we go searching for other reasons for this life. When we do, we have empty lives. You are our hope and our salvation. In Jesus' name, amen.

November 2 ~ Truth

"Then you will know the truth, and the truth will set you free" (John 8:32).

'"Your mama was crazy, Mary Swan, a raving lunatic, that Shelia Middleton." Herbert butted in. He started to laugh with this awful, drunken cackle. Everyone stopped talking and stared. He had fairly shouted it.

What is a girl to do with such information? Mary Swan knew in her soul there was a dark secret about her mother. Miss Abigail's words kept rolling around and around in her head, "The truth will make you free." There are some truths better left alone, some said, but somehow Mary Swan knew she needed to come out of the fog and learn the truth about her mom and the truth about her life. She just wasn't sure she could handle it or if she wanted to."

The Swan House by Elizabeth Musser tells the story of a young girl named Mary Swan whose life unravels at the death of her mother. The unraveling leaves her in a web of lies and illusions. Would the truth set her free? She wasn't sure; she even doubted it; in reality, the truth just seemed to hurt. But in the unraveling, she discovers a richer, deeper life, one that God wanted her to have. One she would have missed if she hadn't been willing to come out of the fog of lies and find the truth.

What about us? What is life about? Do we even have a clue? It wasn't Miss Abigail who came up with the words, "The truth will set you free." It was Jesus.

He not only said the truth will set you free, but He is the truth.

Are we willing to come out of the fog of lies and illusions to walk in His freedom? What will the cost be, and will the cost be worth the changes made in our lives?

Christ came to set the captives free, and our job is to come to Him and walk in His freedom. Too often, we choose to be comfortable managing our misery, but Christ wants us to walk in freedom and truth.

You say, "Okay, Lord, I'm ready. But don't let it hurt. " Have you ever walked from a dark room outside into the noonday sun? The shock on your eyes hurts, but this is only until your eyes adjust. When we learn to walk in truth with Jesus, we will have adjustment, but it is true: freedom is the deep call of our souls. Let the fog roll away, Lord, and set us on fire with Your truth.

Ponders of the Heart

Do you feel you are in bondage to lies and illusions?

Do you know that Christ has set you free?

Read John 8:31-36 and Isaiah 61:1-3.

Ask God to open the eyes of your heart to your slavery and thank the Lord that He is the truth, and He came to set you free.

Prayers of the Heart

Dear Father,

We know there are illusions and lies in our lives. Some we have carefully created, and others are there because we have listened to them. But Father, you came to set us free. Help us, Lord. Give us Your strength and courage. In Jesus' name, amen.

November 3 ~ Warfare

"For our struggle is not against flesh and blood, but against the rulers, against the authorities, against the powers of this dark world and against the spiritual forces of evil in the heavenly realms" (Ephesians 6:12).

When your pet has been with you for sixteen years, they are part of the family. Our dog, Tex, was struggling with cancer. She had four surgeries in less than two years. She had a type of cancer that continued to produce masses in her chest and her elbow, and the last one was on her shoulder. The last time I picked her up, I thought to myself, "We cannot continue to put this dog through the ordeal of surgery."

She didn't have a clue as to what was happening to her. I said to her, "Tex, old girl, you have cancer that will continue to pop up. The only way to keep you alive is to keep putting you through these surgeries. You tell me when you have had enough."

Of course, this was impossible; she just didn't understand who the enemy was cancer. I'm afraid she began to think it was me. If you could have seen her big brown eyes looking up at me with a mixture of pain and sadness, you would understand how badly I felt for her.

Like our old dog, there are many things that happen to us in life we just don't understand why. We try to fight in our own strength, but we don't have the right armor.

We can be minding our own business, not messing with anyone, and wham, we get blindsided.

The phone rings, and you find out your mother is sick, your child has had an accident, you have lost your job; the list is endless.

Life doesn't always make sense, and we don't understand why so many bad things happen. My son, Chris, has a battle going on around him all the time. If one thing goes well, then two will go bad. His life has been one struggle after another, which affects my life immensely.

How can we understand and battle the struggles of life? We have an enemy who is at war with us. How do we prepare for these battles?

God's Word clearly says we are in a combat unit, but we often forget who our enemy is and how to prepare for the fight.

"Put on the full armor of God, so that you can take your stand against the devil's schemes" (Ephesians 6:11).

God tells us to suit up for war. He knows the schemes of the evil one and the fight that is before us. We need to listen to His warning and be ready. Our fight is not against flesh and blood. It isn't a fight against your neighbor, your boss, a co-worker, your children, or spouse. But it is against an enemy that will use all the people in your life to get to you.

What exactly is his evil plan? We will discuss that tomorrow.

Today, remember we are at war, and the enemy is the evil one. He is our foe, so suit up but stand firm. We are not alone in the fight.

Ponders of the Heart

What are you struggling with in your life?

Do you know who you are fighting with and who is on your side?

Read Ephesians 6:10-18 and I Peter 5:8-11.

Let God's Word wake us up so we can fight the good fight.

Prayers of the Heart

Dear Father,

Life is a war. Sometimes it is just a little cut here and a little injury there, but overall, we feel we are bleeding. Wake us up to realize that we are in Your army, and we need to suit up daily in the armor You have provided. You are our greatest reality, and our greatest need. Come and rescue Your people from this unseen enemy. In Jesus' name, amen.

November 4 ~ Life

"Above all else, guard your heart, for it is the wellspring of life" (Prov. 4:23 NKJV).

The web page of the American Heart Association has a quiz you can take to see how well you are taking care of your heart. We all know the importance of a healthy heart, however are we making a conscious decision to care for it?

In the quiz, they ask you if you know the warning signs of a heart attack and stroke; they ask you how often you exercise, do you smoke, what your diet is, how tall you are, and how much you weigh.

From the information gathered they also ask you about your family and medical history. The quiz results showed if a lifestyle changes were needed.

The findings showed I need to eat less salt and learn the warning signs of a heart attack and stroke. My body mass was normal, and my exercise plan was good. But even with all that, the web page warns that heart disease is the number one killer of women in the United States. Wow! This should tell us how important it is to care for our hearts.

I have a dear friend who has been told for years to lose weight, lay off salt, and exercise. His family history of heart disease is off the chart, and he needed to heed the warnings. Like many of us, he did not listen until the doctor told him that his heart was only working at 15% capacity. From the words of the American Heart Association, "Often people wait too long."

Proverbs give us a warning about guarding our heart, for it is the wellspring of life. Even though the heart muscle is the wellspring of physical life, this is not the heart the Bible is talking about. The Proverb warns us that someone is after controlling our souls. Take the warning seriously that the enemy is after our lives. He knows we will never be all God wants us to be if he can wound, stifle, and mangle our hearts. Again, let me remind you that we are at war and the enemy is the ruler of darkness.

This explains his evil plan and why life can seem so hard, everything from painting your house to washing your dog. The enemy will use anything just to discourage us. Discouragement in our hearts is where it all begins.

His plan is to keep attacking us year after year, month after month, until our hearts are working at a 15% capacity. Spiritual heart disease is the number one killer of Christian participation. We can go to our heavenly Father in prayer and ask Him to restore us to full capacity. In His Word, He gives us hope.

"I will give you a new heart and put a new spirit in you; I will remove from you your heart of stone and give you a heart of flesh" (Ezekiel 36:26).

Ponders of the Heart

Who or what does the enemy use to wound and stifle your heart?

Do you know who your enemy is and who is on your side?

Read Acts 5:3-4 and Philippians 4:6-7.

We see what happens to one man who doesn't guard his heart and God's desire for us to take an active role in guarding them.

Prayers of the Heart

Dear Father,

You have given us a new heart so we can love You with all our souls. How we long for You, and for Your protection. Lord, You have given us Your life in our hearts. Teach us to heed Your warnings and to take seriously the threat of the enemy. We are no match for him, but You are. Help us, teach us to listen, and Father, protect us with Your mighty arm. In Jesus' name, amen.

November 5 ~ Muttley

Our little dog was brown and black with a short, curly tail. He was just a mutt with no pedigree, but this didn't matter to us. We wanted to make sure his name elevated his identity, so we gave him what we considered a distinguished name: J. Muttley Dog.

Even with our best efforts, Muttley had identity issues. It wasn't because he was a mutt; it was because he acted like a cat. One day, he wanted to bark and chase a car, and the next day, he was jumping up on my husband's MG Miget and climbing around on it like a cat.

Muttley just could not decide who he was. One day, he wanted to be a cat, and the next day a dog. When he jumped up on the car, acting like a cat, it was funny until the day he fell off and broke his leg. I told Muttley this is what happens when you act like someone you're not.

Identity is a big issue for us all. We are born with a shame-based identity, and corrupt messages come our way.

When we come to Christ and receive salvation, we are told that we become a new creation.

"Therefore, if anyone is in Christ, the new creation has come: The old has gone, the new is here!" (2 Corinthians 5:17).

This verse is true, and I believe it, but I can act like the old me in a New York minute. I hate it when I do, but these old patterns and reactions follow me around like a lost mange dog.

"The acts of the flesh are obvious: sexual immorality, impurity and debauchery; idolatry and witchcraft; hatred, discord, jealousy, fits of rage, selfish ambition, dissensions, factions and envy; drunkenness, orgies, and the like. I warn you, as I did before, that those who live like this will not inherit the kingdom of God" (Galatians 5:19-21).

The longer we walk in the flesh and the more these patterns have a chance to develop, the more we must fight their presence. The world and Satan are on the side of our fallen nature. Thank goodness for God's grace, Jesus' provision, and the patience of our heavenly Father.

The Bible gives us hope for a better life:

"But the fruit of the Spirit is love, joy, peace, forbearance, kindness, goodness, faithfulness, gentleness and self-control. Against such things there is no law" (Galatians 5:22-23).

God loves His children, and when we decide to walk in our fallen nature instead of in the Spirit, we are in for a fall. He doesn't even have to say what I said to Muttley; God knows we know.

Our redeemed hearts are broken because our new nature does not agree with our actions. So, what do we do? We run back to the Lord, and He picks us up and tells us to sin no more. The worst thing we can do is hide from His presence. We cannot fight the old nature apart from His strength.

We will fail and sin, but Jesus died for all our sins. We are righteous in His righteous robes. So, we run to the Father, repent, and start over again.

Ponders of the Heart

Do you have a reaction or a behavior you hate?

Do you sometimes feel like a failure as a Christian?

Read Romans 7:21-25, Romans 8:1-4, and Romans 8: 29-33.

Prayers of the Heart

Dear Father,

We want to live out of the new person You made us to be. Lord, when we don't do this, it grieves our souls. All we can do is come to You and ask for Your power to change us. We are desperate for You. Help us know who we are in You. Come close, Lord, and let us feel Your life in us. In Jesus' name, amen.

November 6 ~ The Heart Matters

"Do not quench the Spirit" (1 Thessalonians 5:19).

In the 1998 movie, "You've Got Mail," Kathleen Kelly, played by Meg Ryan, and Joe Fox, played by Tom Hanks, fall in love over the internet. They know each other by the words of their hearts but not by face.

They share their deepest thoughts and feelings with one another, but they don't know their names, addresses, or where they work. I found this intriguing. The things we place so much importance on for our identity are hidden while the depth of the heart is revealed.

They get to know each other with no strings attached. They decide to meet. They set up a meeting place where Joe Fox, unbeknown to Kathleen Kelly, finds out her identity. Kathleen Kelly is the small bookstore owner whom Joe Fox has run out of business. In the world of "getting ahead," these two hate each other, but in the "no strings attached" world of the internet, they have fallen in love.

Oh, boy. What is Joe Fox to do? His first reaction is to call the whole thing off, but he is enchanted by the email girl and doesn't want to let her go. He devises a plan to win the girl of his dreams. He keeps his identity as an "email dream boy" to himself as he pursues Kathleen Kelly as Joe Fox.

His hope was she could love Joe Fox if he revealed himself to her with honesty like he did when he was on the internet with her.

At first, she wants nothing to do with this man who has ruined her life, but in time, she can't resist his charms. While he becomes a part of her day-to-day life, he continues to be her secret email confidante.

Finally, the time comes for "email boy" to meet "email girl". How will Kathleen Kelly react when she finds out her "email dream man " and Joe Fox are the same? Could there be a more romantic moment? All she could possibly ask for happened. Kathleen Kelly now knows and cares for Joe Fox, who is also her mystery man. Joe Fox loves both Kathleen Kelly and his email girl.

The deepest need and desire of our souls is to be known and loved for who we are. This is where the mind meets emotion, and emotion meets will. It is there that a person finds freedom and harmony. As wonderful as human relationships can be, they cannot reach the fullness we long for. This freedom to be fully known and loved can only be found when we are in the right relationship with God.

He gives us right standing with Him through faith in Jesus Christ. This eternal life is in our hearts and is what the enemy wants to steal from us. The enemy doesn't want us to know the love we long for and the acceptance we desire are ours in Christ. Once we belong to Jesus by faith, our spirits are alive. We are fully loved and fully accepted by God. No strings attached. Don't let the enemy steal away the truth. Come and meet the love of your life. He is completely satisfied with you.

Ponders of the Heart

Do you have a tough time believing God is satisfied with you?

Do you struggle with the promise of God's Word that Jesus has paid the price for all your sins?

Read Jeremiah 31:31-33, Ezekiel 36:26-27, and Romans 8:1-2.

Celebrate the new heart God has given you. Celebrate that He has made you completely acceptable. This is what being in Christ means.

Prayers of the Heart

Dear Father,

You have given us new life and new hearts. You have made us clean before You. We have full redemption. Praise You. Lord, help us believe You today when we mess up and when the enemy tells us that Your love and acceptance of us is impossible. Father, again, thank You for loving us completely and forever. Thank You for Jesus and the sacrifice He made on our behalf. We love You, our Lord and God. In Jesus' name, amen.

November 7 ~ Clean Heart

"The Lord does not look at the things people look at. People look at the outward appearance, but the Lord looks at the heart" (1 Samuel 16:7).

Reality shows have become so popular. I am not a huge fan, but I heard of one called "Is your house really clean?" I never saw the show, but the idea is that people come and check your house to see if it is clean.

Our family owns a cleaning service, but there is not a chance I would allow the reality show people to come into my house.

All houses have dirt, dust, and grime. Dust is under beds and on the tops of refrigerators. Dirt behind the stove, under the washing machine, and grime are in homes across America. Most homes have closets and cabinets that need cleaning. The list could go on and on.

My house is cleaner than most, but a white glove inspection would not be something I would want broadcast on national television. If a group of people looked deep enough, they would find dirt.

The Bible tells us that God looks beyond the surface of our lives and sees the very core of our being. What would God see if He looked deep within our souls? This question can be very unsettling because we have a fallen nature and a scheming enemy.

Let's turn the table on me for a moment. What would God see if He looked into my soul? If He looked into my soul in 1967, He would have seen a desperately wicked heart. But if He looked today, He sees a new heart—one where He lives. A heart that is sealed by the Holy Spirit.

I don't always act like a new person. On the surface, I might appear at times less than He has made me, but the inside of my heart is new, with a deep desire for Him. You see, His Son redeemed me. Jesus, His Son, paid the price so I could have a heart transplant, one that was fashioned by God. Yours too, if you are a Christ-bearer. This gift from God changes us from the inside out.

A big mess is made when a family moves, and all they own are put in boxes. After the move, the unpacking begins. They will unpack boxes and set up their kitchen. Boxes of kitchen dishes, glasses, pots, and pans are neatly put away in the cabinets, and for a little while, those cabinets will be clean, straight, and dirt-free. The rest of the house might be cluttered, but the cabinets will be clean.

If they locked up the cabinets, they would stay that way. This is what the Holy Spirit does for us after we get our new heart. He locks it up, and no filth of the world can reach us. We have been made clean. Let the Inspector come in. He will not look at the mess on the floor of your life; He is just interested in the cabinet of your heart. If His Holy Spirit has moved in, then you are clean.

Renounce the lies of the evil one and walk in the power of the Holy Spirit inside you. Believe what God has done for you, and if you believe Him, you will begin to pick up the muck around you and live your life as His child.

The enemy of our new hearts continues to bring up the past by replaying it in our minds, but God tells us that if the Son has set you free, you are free indeed.

Ponders of the Heart

Do you struggle with feeling unworthy?

Does the enemy keep you in bondage over past sins?

Read Psalm 86:11-12 and Ezekiel 36:26-27

Ask God to give you an undivided heart and help you to live by the power of the Holy Spirit that lives in You.

Prayers of the Heart

Dear Father,

It is so hard for us to believe we have new hearts. In the depths of our souls, we want to walk in fellowship with You. We long to live out our lives praising You and telling others about Your love.

We often listen to lies and fall under the weight of condemnation. Help us believe You and be thankful that You have sealed us for the day of redemption. In Jesus' name, amen.

November 8 ~ Fresh Faith

"Then Jesus said to the centurion, 'Go! Let it be done just as you believed it would.' And his servant was healed at that moment'" (Matthew 8:13).

The account in Matthew eight reminds us that Jesus is pleased with those who understand who He is and put their faith in Him.

The centurion in the story believed Jesus had power over diseases. He recognized this power was from above. The Bible says Jesus was astonished and told His followers He had not seen such faith in all of Israel.

This must have stopped the disciples in their tracks. They had faith in Jesus. They had left their homes, families, and jobs to follow Him, and here He was telling them their faith in Him did not match that of a Roman centurion. I wonder how the disciples' conversation went that night around the campfire.

I have a friend who is always telling me about a group of ladies she works with who have fresh faith. She tells me if God's Word says do this or don't do that, they stand on what He says. My friend is blown away by their fresh faith, and she cannot say enough about these ladies. She tells me that it encourages her to be more faithful.

I don't know these women, but I know my friend. I trust her and her judgment. Still, I can be a little skeptical when others start talking about fresh faith. People have disappointed me by talking farther than they walk.

Honestly, I could say the same about myself. This journey of faith is a bumpy road, and we often fail. I am reminded it isn't our faith that saves us, but the One we place our faith in. Jesus can do anything, but He works in our lives in direct proportion to how strongly we believe Him and surrender to Him.

It is time to give our hearts completely to Jesus and take Him at His Word. Believing He is all-powerful and is not against us. We need to know He is willing to save, provide, and transform us. Believing Him is the same thing as trusting Him.

How did a Roman centurion develop trust in Jesus? God, in His mercy, reached out to the centurion, and the man believed God. He understood if he, a Roman centurion, could give orders to his men and they would obey when he wasn't present, surely this man of God who could cure diseases, had the power to give an order and have it carried out.

God's grace is amazing, and in His mercy, He reaches out to people who have tender, willing hearts to believe. God is always looking for those who have fresh faith.

As I read this account in Matthew eight and remembered the women my friend told me about, I cried out to the Lord to fill me with fresh faith. There is nothing stale about the power of our God. He is the same today as He was then, and I could almost hear Him say, "As you believe Me, child, so I will do." Oh, Lord, I believe. Help my unbelief.

Ponders of the Heart

Do you have trouble believing that God can give you fresh faith?

Are you ready to cry out to God and ask Him to fan the flame of faith in your heart?

Read Matthew 8:5-13.

Prayers of the Heart

Dear Father,

You are worthy of praise, honor, and glory. You are worthy of our whole hearts. Fill us with faith to believe in Who You are and what You can do. Help us use our faith to unleash Your great power from heaven. We are desperate for You, Your presence, and Your power. We don't want our hearts to grow cold, full of bitterness and doubt.

Father, pour fresh faith in us so we will walk believing You and encouraging others to do the same. In Jesus' name, amen.

Nov 9 ~ Rejection

"Lord, if you are willing, you can make me clean" (Matthew 8:2).

Nothing in life is more painful or more common than rejection. We have all experienced this pain, but for some, they are continually marked by it. Some feel rejected by parents or spouses. Others feel unwanted because of their physical appearance or their mental capabilities. Some are rejected because of their race or gender.

Rejection is a common condition for humanity in some form or fashion, but just because it is common does not mean it isn't devastating. There are those who react to this painful experience with bitterness, and others react with self-loathing, but we all react.

I have watched people going through divorce struggle with self-worth, but when my son went through his divorce, the damage and the reality of rejection became close to my heart. He had lost so much weight that his clothes were hanging on him. His whole life was a struggle, but the impact hit me the hardest when my daughter told me of a conversation she had with my son.

He had come to visit her, and she had decided to take him shopping. My daughter is a "clothes-aholic." He was in the car, and they were pulling into the parking lot of the store. He turned to her and asked, "Do I look like a piece of crap?" Her heart broke as she realized the way he was feeling, and my heart broke to think he ever felt this way about himself.

Rejection had taken its toll on my son. In truth, he is a handsome guy. He is smart, relational, and has a good sense of humor. But truth can appear like a lie in the face of rejection.

The gospel of Matthew tells the story of Jesus meeting a man with leprosy. The man came to Jesus and knelt before Him, asking Jesus to heal him. The leper felt sure Jesus could heal him, but he wasn't sure He would be willing.

How many times had the Leper called out, "unclean, unclean," until he began to believe this was true? He hoped Jesus would have mercy and heal him. But he felt unworthy of this grace.

I wonder how many people are stuck in lies today. "I know Jesus could help me, but I don't deserve His help. I am just a miserable person." This breaks my heart. There are people who have let others decide their worth. They have let the common experience of rejection decide who they are.

What a lie. Only God can decide our worth, and He wants to give us the worth of His Son. How? By forgiving our sins, giving us a new spirit, and a new identity in Jesus. I hate the pain we cause one another and the destruction of shame.

God hates the pain and the destruction so much that He sent Jesus to take it away and make us clean. Look at Jesus' reaction to the leper.

"Jesus reached out his hand and touched the man, 'I am willing, he said. 'Be clean.' Immediately he was cleansed of his leprosy" (Matthew 8:3.)

Ponders of the Heart

What rejection have you suffered that has wounded you deeply?

How has your relationship with Jesus healed your wound?

Read John 8: 1-11.

See how Jesus responds and restores a woman caught in adultery. He does not reject those who come to Him. Jesus always remembered to love the person and hate the sin.

Prayers of the Heart

Dear Father,

We want to love the things You love and hate the things You hate. We often get so caught up in hating the things that we begin to hate the people and not the sin. Father, pour into our hearts Your love for people. You are our Healer and Redeemer. It is You that makes us clean.

Father, help us never forget You hate sin, but You never hate us. In Jesus' name, amen.

Nov 10 ~ Amnesia

"For you were once darkness, but now you are light in the Lord. Live as children of light (for the fruit of light consists in all goodness, righteousness and truth) and find out what pleases the Lord" (Ephesians 5:8-10).

One Tuesday Morning is a fictional Christian novel about September 11, 2001. Eric is a Christian man who has turned away from God at the birth of his stillborn daughter. He blames God because He could have prevented the death, and blames himself because he couldn't afford the best medical care for his wife.

He decides in his heart that the well-being of his family is his responsibility, so he works to become successful. He forgets God and his family as he accomplishes worldly success.

On September 11th, Eric is on the 64th floor in the south tower of the World Trade Center. Miraculously, he survives. He is found underneath a fire truck at ground zero with a broken ankle, some burns, and a serious head injury.

He is found and thought to be Jake Bryan, a firefighter from FDNY Station 57. Jake's wife is called and told that her husband has survived. Eric wakes up with no clue of who he is but is told he is Jake Bryan, who has a wife, a daughter named Sierra and is a firefighter. He doesn't know if this is right, but he has no other choice than to believe it because he cannot remember who he is. At this point, Eric enters life as Jake Bryan.

Eric was a man driven by self; Jake was a man driven by his love for God and family. Jake has left behind instruction books, his Bible, and his journal. Eric is like a clean sheet of paper, and Jake's life is being written on Eric's heart. Will Eric accept his new identity or reject it?

When we were born, we were like clean sheets of paper. Our history began, and every day, a little more was written in the recesses of our minds. Our brain records memories, both long-term and short-term ones. These memories have a lot to do with who we are and who we think we are. What if all those memories were lost? Gone like they never happened; this would be a scary thing for sure. I have great memories, and I am sure you do too, but we also have bad ones, and these are the ones the evil one uses to keep us from understanding our new identity in Christ.

Here are some of the memories used against me. "I bet if these people knew my past, they would not think highly of me." "I can't do this, and I'm not smart. Everyone is smarter than I am. I have just faked my way all these years. I don't even have a college degree." Even as I confess this on paper, I feel inadequate. Notice my accusations are in the first person. This is how the enemy works. He doesn't want us to know that God has made us clean, and we belong to Him.

I wish I could choose what to forget and what to remember, but I can't. I guess we need to enroll in the school of "God's child" and allow Him to transform us into the very thing He saved us to be. Let's be good students and let Him rewrite our history to His glory and our good.

Ponders of the Heart

What lies has the enemy played over in your mind?

Have you asked the Lord to help you believe who He says you are and Who you belong to?

Read Ephesians 4:17-24.

Ask the Lord to rewrite your history as I ask Him to rewrite mine.

Prayers of the Heart

Dear Father,

We are new creatures in Christ, children of Your kingdom. Lord, transform our attitudes and actions to match our newness. Help us take off the old self by rejecting those old attitudes and old habits, and put on our new coat of righteousness of Jesus. Thank You for rewriting our history in the annals of Your books kept safe in heaven. In Jesus' name, amen.

Nov 11 ~ Mothers and Grandmothers

"Then Naomi took the child in her arms and cared for him" (Ruth 4:16).

I have had the pleasure of being a grandmother for 21-plus years. I am blessed with grandchildren ranging in age from 7 to 21. It has been a "grand" time. They have filled my life with joy and fun, love, hugs, and purpose. I would not trade this season of life for anything.

When they were little, and even now that they are older, if I know they are coming, I get busy doing everything that needs to be done. Why? Because when grandchildren come, I can't seem to get anything done except be with them.

I don't know how that happened. After all, I was a mother of three children. They lived with me, and I took care of them and managed to do other things. I cleaned our bathrooms for the twenty-six years I had children at home, cooked and washed clothes. It was a rare thing for me to watch television, which wasn't a bad thing. I seldom took a nap, and I was busy every minute of every day.

When the grandchildren were little, if they were outside, so was I. If they colored, I colored. When they slept, I slept. If they played, I played. This is the difference between being a mother and a grandmother. A mother can multitask, and a grandmother can only "grandchild task."

What a wonderful thing to know someone loves you so much that you are right there with them, paying them complete attention. Mothers love their children, but they have to love their children while they multitask. It is the way things are. Both roles are such a gift from God.

Our God can be both our Father and our grandfather. He can be busy with the world and still give us undivided attention. He can look after the people in the Middle East and still be with us when we sleep, eat, and play. God can listen to our prayers and the prayers of people in Russia. His ears are completely attentive, and nothing goes on without His knowledge and His presence.

When I think about the relationships that are so precious in my life, I am thankful, but I need God more. He is the one who fulfills my very soul.

I hope my life is a gift to others, but I cannot be or do for them what they need most. God is their need. He is life, and without Him, we are not really living. He is our Father, Husband, Friend, Grandfather, and Confidant.

I am thankful for all the people who play a major or a minor role in my life, but thanks be to God. He not only takes up the slack for them, but He also takes supremacy over them. Oh, how He is worthy to be praised.

Ponders of the Heart

Who do you depend on in life?

Who depends on you?

Do you realize God is your greatest need?

Read Hosea 11:1-4 and Micah 7:18-19.

Let's praise Him together.

Prayers of the Heart

Dear Father,

    Thank You for never being too busy for us. Thank You that we are Your delight and Your treasure. Oh, Lord, this is too wonderful to believe, and yet we treasure the truth of Your love. Every ounce of it. Your love for us and Your presence with us do not diminish Your love for others. You, Lord, are more wonderful and powerful than we will ever be able to understand. In Jesus' name, amen.

November 12 ~ The Vastness of the Deep

    Picture a marina. Do you see the boats tied next to each other down a long dock? Sailboats, fishing boats, big boats, small boats; maybe you see a few yachts. You might picture a small fishing town on the ocean, or a marina beside a river or a lake. We have all seen them, boats tied for protection and availability.

    They float day after day, sometimes months or years, just floating on the water under their hull. If boats had feelings (work with me here), I wonder if they become comfortable tied to the dock or if boats yearn for an outing in the deep.

If I were a boat and I had feelings, I would probably yearn for the deep but fear it. I would probably look every day for my owner, hoping he would come so I could venture from the shore and fear when he came. (If I were a boat and if I had feelings.)

What about you? If you were a boat, would you want to stay comfortably anchored to the dock, or would you be ready to sail into the deep? What kind of feelings would you have? A boat is made to do more than float tied to a dock. A boat is made to travel over water.

We aren't boats; we are people made in the image of God. Made to reflect the glory of God as we venture out into the depths of His wisdom, strength, and love.

Every time I have the privilege to be a vessel He can use, I see myself as a boat tied to a dock with limited sailing ability. I forget the potential beyond my port, or recognize that God's power is available to me. The Holy Spirit's presence is with me, but I do not know the vastness of the presence and power that is mine to enjoy. I can sail out into the unlimitedness of God.

Let me give you an example. In days from now, I will be leading a prayer retreat for ladies. My mind has been busy planning what to say, how to say it, and using all my ability to get ready. This kind of thinking is like being tied to the dock. God knows exactly what He wants to be said, and all His ability is available to me.

I need to lean on His unlimited power and trust that He will help me. He wants me to go beyond the shores of my knowledge, wittiness, or oratory. God wants me to let Him use me to reflect Who He is. We were created to show His glory in mighty ways. He wants to do incredible things through us.

He is coming to untie us and let us travel in the depths of power, reflecting His glory as we go. Let's not be afraid of the deep. We were created for it, just like a boat was created for water. Let's ride.

Ponders of the Heart

Do you long to be used by God for His glory?

But do you tremble at the thought of what that might be?

Read Psalm 131: 1-3

Our hope in the Lord, now and forevermore.

Prayers of the Heart

Dear Father,

Let our fears wash away from our hearts. Help us depend on Your sufficiency. You are the wisdom and courage we need. There is none like You. Lord, You will provide Your glory, the way, and how, and we will provide the vessels. You are Who we need, and You are our deepest desire. Help us allow all that You are to reflect through us so we can bring You praise. In Jesus' name, amen.

November 13 ~ The Heart of Prayer

Years ago, we lived in a small town in Georgia. Visiting family in Jacksonville during that time made me thankful I lived in a small town. The traffic was horrendous, for sure, but it was the fear factor that amazed me. Precautions were taken constantly. People had security systems in their houses and cars.

When we visited my mother, we were issued keys and security alarm passwords. If you go out of the house, you better have them, or else you will not get back in. Doors, front and back, are always locked; cars are locked in garages as well, and alarm systems are put on when you leave the house. I was always afraid to get up in the middle of the night for fear I would set off an alarm.

Getting the paper on the driveway in the morning was like going through a checklist at NASA before opening the door. I might be exaggerating just a tad, but the difference in my lifestyle and theirs was amazing to me.

Now that I live in Birmingham, I am more cautious. We lock our doors at night, and the car is locked in the garage, but my car isn't locked. Our security alarm is not in service, but I feel at ease when the sun goes down. A knock on the door does not lead me to panic, and a walk to the mailbox does not make me fear for my life. Fear is one way to live, but not the best.

What about your prayer life? What is the motivation behind it? Is it fear? Fear over your circumstances, over your children, spouse, or your mother; what drives your prayer life? If it is fear that drives you to your Heavenly Father, this is one way to pray and have a relationship with God, but not the best way.

The heart of prayer is far greater than our fears. You might say I have no idea of the circumstances you face, and you are right, but God wants more than our fretful cries; He wants our whole hearts. He wants us to walk with Him in our joys, in our day-to-day, as well as in our fears.

A love relationship is at the heart of prayer, not just our worries.

We know prayer is significant. Prayer does not open the locked door of heaven, but is the doorknob to open an unlocked door to the throne room of heaven.

We are welcomed, even beckoned to come. What keeps us at bay? Why do we enter only when danger assaults us and those we love? Could it be the lack of a love relationship with our Heavenly Father?

We can have religious practices, but this is different from knowing and loving our heavenly Father. The enemy wants us to believe we are so unlovable that we dare not draw too close to God. We think that the door of heaven is locked to us, and we need a special password to get in. If we go in without the correct posture, we will set off an alarm in heaven.

The bottom line is we need more than fear attached to our prayer life; we need freedom. Freedom to come and go into His presence, knowing Jesus has made the pathway safe, and we need no keys or passwords.

No knocking is necessary; all we need to do is turn the knob and enter into His presence. We will find His heart open to us, for God delights in His own. He wants to walk with us through all of life. Let's go in and enjoy His constant companionship. Freedom and love are the gateways to the heart of prayer.

Ponders of the Heart

How is your prayer life?

Do you struggle with knowing God loves you and wants to be with you?

Read Psalm 37:1-9 and Psalm 100.

Open your heart to His love for you and the freedom to know and love Him. Let Him call you into His presence for a time of praise.

Prayers of the Heart

Dear Father,

We want to rejoice in Your love for us. You have given us the freedom to live and to know You through Jesus. We can come to You and rejoice, as well as ask for Your help and safety. We want more than fear to motivate our relationship with You. We want to have a deep, abiding connection with You. Fill our hearts with confidence that You want and welcome us every day and every moment of our lives. In Jesus' name, amen.

November 14 ~ God Spoke

"In the past God spoke to our ancestors through the prophets at many times and in various ways, but in these last days he has spoken to us by his Son, whom he appointed heir of all things, and through whom also he made the universe" (Hebrews 1:1-2).

As parents, we know it is our responsibility to teach our children about life. This starts with teaching them to talk, walk, eat, and sleep through the night. We then move on to teaching them to use the potty, dress themselves, and tie their shoes. The teaching goes on and on through their years until they reach adulthood. Oh, but wait, I do not think it stops there.

When my oldest son was preparing to leave home and go to college, I became obsessed with teaching him all the things I thought he would need to know. Before he left, he was exhausted, and so was I. Our days were filled with warnings and reminding him of things he already knew. It was important to me that he was prepared, and I felt it was my job to give him a complete course on life. My motives were good, but the task was impossible.

God has spoken throughout history. He instructs with words of love and warning. When God spoke, His message was to point people to His Son, Jesus. Finally, the Word of Life came to life and walked among us. (John 1:14) Jesus is the living Word from heaven.

Even though I drove Chris crazy trying to give him a life course in 40 days, I did give him vital information. My mothering stepped up a notch, and even if he didn't appreciate my obsession at the time, he now wishes he had paid a little more attention to his mom.

God has spoken to us with words of life, sent the Word of life to us to save us and teach us. We know Jesus, but if you are like me, you wish you had listened better. We still have so much more to discover about Him and how we are to live.

When I was young, I thought that by now I would have more figured out. Now that I am older, I realize I know very little.

The day we get to heaven, we will discover and see amazing things. We will see our Lord and Savior, Jesus, but I think it will take eternity to see and know what God wants to reveal to us about who

He is. We will become alive with wonder like little children. This will be when true life begins. There will be no lazy students but pupils who love our teacher and His instruction.

My prayer is that God will open our eyes to His wonder. I want truth where there is error, wonder where there is apathy, and revelation where there is ignorance. Our heavenly Father has spoken in the past and continues to speak to His children. Thank You, Lord.

Ponders of the Heart

What is something your parents tried to teach you, but you did not listen to?

What is something you tried to teach your children that they failed to follow?

Read Psalm 25:4-5, Psalm 119:12-16, and Isaiah 2:2-4.

Lord, give us Your eyes to see, ears to hear, and a heart to trust and obey.

Prayers of the Heart

Dear Father,

This thing called life is beyond us. We need You to teach us. Sometimes we think we know so much, and other times we realize we know so little. Lord, Your wisdom is complete. You are the Alpha and Omega of knowledge. Give us hearts of wonder, thirst for You, and open our ears and eyes so we can know and obey You. Thank You for Jesus. In Jesus' name, amen.

November 15 ~ Weakness

"My grace is sufficient for you, for my power is made perfect in weakness" (2 Corinthians 12:9).

The last time I went to youth camp, I tried to prove my youthfulness. What a mistake. I skied, played volleyball, stayed up late, got up early, and tried to climb "the wall."

The wall was 15 to 20 feet tall, and my task was to climb to the top. It was hard. Most of the youth couldn't do it. If I recall correctly, Tracie, my very athletic daughter, couldn't do it. What made me think I could? It was too hard for me. The closer you got to the top, the more distance there was between the places to put your hands and feet. I am not quite 4 feet, 11 inches. I finally fell in defeat.

I am so grateful for the safety precautions taken. There was a harness around everyone's waist and a rope attached to the harness. There was also someone on the ground who had the end of the rope that was attached to your waist.

The one on the ground holding the end of your rope could break your fall; in fact, they could pull the rope tight and give you a boost if they felt sorry for you. In my case, he felt sorry for me. He probably was thinking, "What is this woman doing?" I fell, and he caught me.

Tomorrow, I will be doing something that is beyond me. I am counting on my safety harness to catch me, and God's grace. In my weakness, He promises to be powerful. In my insufficiency, He promises to be sufficient. This time, as I approach this "wall", I am not approaching it thinking I can, but knowing God's got me and I can count on Him.

The truth is, I need the Lord every day. Tomorrow, I know I need Him 100%, but there are times when I think I need Him maybe 75% or 50%. In my arrogance, I can believe I've got the day covered. The truth is, I need the Lord 100% all the time.

This does not mean we lie in bed and expect God to live our lives for us. No, He wants us to do life together. He holds us and strengthens us to do what He has called us to do.

Lord, forgive me for thinking tomorrow is impossible without You and forgetting that it is also true today.

I need Him every moment of my life, and He promises to be with me. The truth is I need Him, but living a life wanting to be with Him is a life worth living.

Ponders of the Hearts

When do you know you need the Lord 100%?

Was there a time you tried to live life on your own?

How did that work out?

Read Ephesians 6:10-18 and suit up.

Prayers of the Heart

Dear Father,

We confess we need You 100% of the time. In our weakness, You are strong, and Your grace is our sufficiency. Lord, pour the blood of Jesus over us again so we will be clean from any self-sufficiency. We can do all things with You, but nothing of eternal value without You. Your grace is what we need constantly. Thank You for You are willing to give us Your life. In Jesus' name, amen.

November 16 ~ Thanksgiving

"It is good to praise the Lord and make music to your name, O Most High, proclaiming your love in the morning and your faithfulness at night," (Psalm 92:1-2).

As we celebrate Thanksgiving this month, I want to take the time to be thankful to our God. In the days ahead, I will use the word Thanksgiving as an acrostic for thankfulness.

T- for Trials- Don't let me lose you on the first word.

H-for Heaven

A-for Assurance

N-for Near

K-for Kindness

S-for Salvation

G-for Grace

I-for In Christ

V-for Victory

I-for Intimate

N-for Never

G-for Giving

Thanksgiving is a special time of the year for many people. I know it is one of my top two holidays. The tradition of Thanksgiving has changed over the years, but each season of life has been a wonderful time for our family.

When my husband's parents and my mom were alive, we would go to Florida. It was a priority because our family in Florida made our coming importance. Every year, we all look forward to four days of celebrating Thanksgiving. Over the years, we would have eight to twelve going.

The girls stayed with my mom, and the boys stayed with Bill's mom and dad. We girls would eat, shop, and go to the movies and the zoo. The guys played golf, watched football, and played cards.

After our parents passed away, it was harder to go to Florida. We still have families there, but it is not the same.

Thanksgiving traditions are still a part of the Collier family. But instead of being responsible for a sweet potato casserole, I now feel the weight of the whole Thanksgiving meal. I don't mind. I think my dressing is much superior to my mother-in-law's and my mother's. Some of my family members will not agree with this statement, but it is those who have not tasted my dressing. Sorry, Mom and Betty.

I really do miss the tradition of going to Florida because I love and enjoy our extended family.

We all have a human family, and some are closer than others, but God has blessed us with more. He has given us a heavenly family, one which He is the Father, and we are His children.

How thankful I am to be in God's family and to know that Calvary made this possible. The cross of Calvary and Jesus's death made our redemption a reality. So, this year, as we move toward Thanksgiving, I will try to quicken our souls with the gift of being in His family and having such a loving Father. Join me as we give thanks to the Lord.

"Through Jesus, therefore, let us continually offer to God a sacrifice of praise—the fruit of lips that openly profess his name" (Hebrews 13:15).

Ponders of the Heart

What are your Thanksgiving traditions?

How have they changed over the years?

What are you most thankful for today?

Read Psalm 100 and then sing a song of praise to God.

Prayers of the Heart

Dear Father,

How we want to open our mouths and give You praise. Lord, we want to have an attitude of thanksgiving in our hearts that overflows into the world around us. You are worthy of all praise. We thank You for Your grace to us. In Jesus' name, amen.

November 17 ~ Thankful for Trials

"Consider it pure joy, my brothers and sisters, whenever you face trials of many kinds, because you know that the testing of your faith produces perseverance. Let perseverance finish its work so that you may be mature and complete, not lacking anything" (James 1:2-4).

The definition of trial, according to Webster's Dictionary, is pain or anguish caused by a difficult situation or condition that tests patience or endurance.

When I look at this definition and when I look at the above verse, I ask myself, what are the trials I have faced in life?

What about you? What kind of trials have you faced? My range from parenting to the loss of my dad to cancer, with many degrees and variations of trials in between. I am sure you could say the same.

Life is made up of situations and conditions. They seem to come into our lives daily. Some trials hit hard and left us dazed and overwhelmed, like the day my brother called and said Dad had cancer. Then there are those trials that hit your conscience and pull at your hope. Children you fear have drug problems, aging parents, health problems, loss of memory, or relationships.

Count it all joy. Does God's Word really say that we are to count these trials with joy? How can we, or why in the world should we?

The passage in James tells us that trials test our faith and produce patience. This patience has a perfect work that matures us. What does this mean? I have faith, and if it is trials that produce patience, I'm not sure I want patience.

What do we want? Deep inside us lives a new heart—one Christ gave us when we became His. In this new heart beats a desire that is worth everything. This desire is to know God and Jesus Christ, whom He has sent. In fact, John 17:3 calls this eternal life.

Human life has a way of robbing our souls of our eternal purposes. Trials have a way of returning us to our roots, the depth of our longings. This new heart wants to know God and Jesus. Trials shake our souls and humble us. Then we run to God, we seek Him and pray to Him, and find He is there. This is pure joy, and it is worth everything.

I don't like trials that cause me to hurt. It is hard to think that anything good comes from pain. But we have something the world does not have. We have Jesus, and knowing Him and staying close to Him is our goal. He uses many things to keep us close, and that includes trials.

So, count the trials with joy, knowing these trials give us the opportunity to know God and Jesus Christ. Trials come to all people everywhere, but for those of us who are in Christ, we have hope, security, and a God who will see us through until we see Him face to face. What a perfect day this will be.

Ponders of the Heart

What has been the hardest trial of your life?

How did God work through the trial?

Read 2 Corinthians 4:16-18.

Our God is faithful, and He is with us through it all!

Prayers of the Heart

Dear Father,

We come to You so often to find relief from the pain of this life. We come to You so we will not lose heart over things that are wrong and people who are hurting. Lord, we don't always go away with an answer or a promise, but when we meet You, really meet You, we leave with hope. Lord, use trials of life to keep our eyes on You. In Jesus' name, amen.

November 18 ~ Thankful for Heaven

"No longer will there be any curse. The throne of God and of the Lamb will be in the city, and his servants will serve him. They will see his face, and his name will be on their foreheads. There will be no more night. They will not need the light of a lamp or the light of the sun, for the Lord God will give them light. And they will reign for ever and ever." (Revelation 22:3-5).

Do you ever feel like a duck out of water? I surely do. There are occasions when I can be in a room with people I know and love and feel alone. It is the curse of living in this fallen world.

Sometimes, it doesn't take much to take the wind out of my sails. A comment is made that pushes my button, and I react and spend the rest of the time wondering why I responded that way. Or I get dressed to go to a gathering, and I feel underdressed or overdressed. I find a corner, just waiting for the first opportunity to escape. Do you relate? We all battle these feelings.

Do you ever feel like life is an uphill climb, and you are in a wheelchair climbing it? I surely do. You try hard to manage your money, and everything in the house breaks down at once. You do the project; you call who you were supposed to call, and your boss doesn't agree with your method. You fail, he rails, and you feel stupid, abused, and defeated.

Your husband is miles away emotionally. When you try to talk to him, he tells you to get off his back. You feel like you have fallen off the boat without a life jacket. These are just examples of what can happen when living on planet Earth.

Do you ever feel like God is missing in action? You pray, hoping for an answer, but you feel like your prayers are hitting the ceiling and bouncing back with a note attached that says, "I'm busy." I do. Even in my heart, I know this is not true, and the words I am hearing in my head did not come from God but from my enemy.

Nevertheless, I feel this way sometimes. We can pray for our children, and instead of things getting better, they get worse. We can be accused of being religious fanatics by someone we try to share our faith with. The very person we are concerned about tells us to keep our narrow opinions to ourselves. You feel betrayed and crazy for even caring.

What about the folks you forgive over and over, just to have them keep doing the same thing to you? Why is life so difficult?

It is difficult because we live in a fallen world with fallen people. Folks, this is not heaven, and it will never be.

Peace in the Middle East. Come on. It will never be, not until there is a new heaven and a new earth. Be thankful this life is not all there is. This is just a temporary assignment. Heaven is coming and is sure. We are kingdom people. I give thanks to the Lord for His Kingdom that is to come. I am thankful for the promise of heaven.

We need to get through those tough times by remembering this is not heaven, but there are glimpses of it here on earth.

The beauty of a rainbow, the laughter of a child, the ocean, the vastness of mountains, and the love of your spouse. Praise and worship on Sunday can stir the deepest hope for tomorrow and joy for today. God makes sure we have wonderful times here on earth as He prepares us for the streets of gold. We need to believe in His goodness and keep our eyes focused on the things above when things get tough.

Ponders of the Heart

Are you going through a tough time right now?

What is something you can do to help you remember God's faithfulness?

Read Revelations 21.

Set your eyes on glory, but remember all the blessings God has blessed you with here on earth. Take time to be thankful.

Prayers of the Heart:

Dear Father,

We praise You for making us Yours and giving us hope and a future. We praise You, Lord, that this life can be good or hard, but this is not all there is. We have a glorious future, one given by Your grace. We look forward to when we will see You face to face, and Your name will be written on our forehead. Praise to our King. In Jesus 'name, amen.

November 19 ~ Thankful for Assurance

"He who has the Son has life; he who does not have the Son of God does not have life. These things I have written to you who believe in the name of the Son of God, that you may know that you have eternal life" (1 John 5:12-13 NKJV).

When I think my son's long wait for a wife is over and happiness is on its way, divorce happens. I feel a sense of peace when one of my children has financial security, and then her husband is given a two-month notice. Just when I think my husband is coming out of depression, it hits him again. When I finally think I will have a day to myself, the phone rings. Assurance in this life is rare indeed.

Sure, I love you, but… I want to help you, but... What in life can we be certain of? Not much, that is for sure. Is it any wonder we find it hard to believe that our salvation is secure? If it were up to you or to me, our salvation would be on shaky ground, but it is not based on us; it is based on Him, the Son of God. Wow. This is good news. News to be thankful for.

Blessed assurance, Jesus is mine

Oh, what a foretaste of glory divine

Heir of salvation, purchase of God

Born of His Spirit, washed in His blood

This is my story, this is my song

Praising my Savior all the day long

This is my story, this is my song

Praising my Savior all the day long

(Blessed Assurance, by Fanny J. Crosby)

Blessed Assurance was written by Fanny Crosby, an American writer and poet who wrote over 9,000 hymns during her lifetime. She became ill as an infant and lost her eyesight due to the treatment of a man claiming to be a doctor. Her father died months later, and her mother became the only means of support.

Fanny was raised by her grandmother, who gave her special insight into nature and the things of God. Her grandmother took the time to describe everything around her in detail, and she had her memorize the four Gospels, Proverbs, Ruth, the Song of Solomon, and many of the Psalms.

Even though her songs were written in the dark, she was so full of God's light that her songs reflect joy, hope, and full assurance in the Lord. In a world full of uncertain things, we can have full assurance that salvation is ours through Jesus Christ. This is a blessed assurance: Jesus is ours.

Ponders of the Heart

Have you ever been sure of something and been wrong?

Do you rest in the fact that Jesus has given you His righteousness?

In all of life's uncertainty, are you sure of your home in heaven?

Read 2 Corinthians 3:17-4:6.

Praise the Lord for His blessed assurance has come to us in our darkness and given us the light of His glory.

Prayers of the Heart

Dear Father,

You are the source of our lives and the One Who keeps us. Lord, nothing can take us out of Your Hands. You provide Jesus, and You have given us new and pure lives. We are Yours. Give us Spiritual eyes to see and help us walk in Your light. We praise You for the blessed assurance that is ours. In Jesus' name, amen.

November 20 ~ Thankful for the Nearness of God

"The Lord is near to all who call upon him, to all who call on him in truth" (Psalm 145:18).

When we had just one grandchild, I wrote this devotional.

We have a pack-in-play at our house that Collier never used. We had a room with twin beds that Collier never slept in. He preferred sleeping with Gaggie and GiGi. He wanted to lay his head right next to mine.

He snuggles so close that I feel like I have a little heating pad on my back. The first few nights, it felt strange with him so close to me, but in no time, I would get used to that little fellow being there, and I loved every moment of it.

There would come a day when he would be too big to sleep in our bed, but we might have other grandchildren who would enjoy a sleepover.

When he goes home, it is time to readjust. We readjusted the rooms and put away all his and Gaggie's toys. The special dishes he uses, and his sippy cups, are stored for another day. But the hardest readjustment comes at bedtime when I don't have his little head sharing my pillow. Oh, how I love the nearness of Collier, and how I miss him when he goes home. He has to go, but his presence is always near to my heart. Bill and I spend hours remembering his words and the funny things he does.

We are thankful for the special times we have had with Collier and glad he spends a lot of time with us. Years have gone by, and God has blessed us with five more grandchildren. At times when they were little, they would snuggle close to me in bed, but none of them spent as much time sleeping with GiGi and Gaggie as Collier did as a little guy.

What a gift grandchildren are, but the gift of all gifts is the promise of God being near to us. Paul puts it like this:

"God did this so that men would seek him and perhaps reach out for him and find him, though he is not far from each one of us" (Acts 17:27).

"Draw near to God, and He will draw near to you" (James 4:8 NKJV).

There is not a moment when God is not near me. He hears my cries, sees my pain, and He cares. I don't walk alone, and neither do you. God is always with us, and He listens to us. God is willing to guide, protect, and give us wisdom.

He is near, and I am thankful for His presence. In this room where I am typing, He is here. At night, when I sleep, He is near. In the car and in the store, I have a Father who comes with me, and His being with me does not keep Him from being with you. What a wonderful companion we have.

What a friend. What a gift of nearness. How thankful we should be for the nearness of our God.

Ponders of the Heart

When do you feel closest to God?

How can we readjust our lives to know Him more?

Read Psalm 34:15-19 and Psalm 47:10-11.

Rest, rejoice, and thank God for His nearness.

Prayers of the Heart

Dear Father,

We humble ourselves before You and praise You for seeing, hearing, knowing us, and being near. We are thankful that not one minute of one day do we face alone. You are but a cry away. Quicken our hearts and minds so we will remember. Let Your wonder and truth strengthen our hearts and purify our ways. In Jesus' name, amen.

November 21 ~ Thankful for Kindness

"But the fruit of the Spirit is love, joy, peace, forbearance, kindness, goodness, faithfulness, gentleness, self-control" (Galatians 5:22-23).

My grandmother had a welcoming face. You just knew she was glad to see you. When she rubbed your head or scratched your back, you knew she didn't mind. She was kind, not because she had to do those things, but it was just her nature. Her kindness made you want to be kind right back. She had what I would call a disposition of kindness.

The word in the above verse is the word *Chrestotes* in Greek. The word is descriptive of one's disposition and does not necessarily entail acts of goodness, as does the word *agathosyne*, which is active kindness. When a person has a disposition of kindness, they do many kind acts, but isn't it interesting that there is a kindness that goes beyond good deeds to a person's temperament?

The kindness I am talking about is a fruit formed by the Spirit of God in a person, a fruit that cannot be generated by the natural man. I have experienced this fruit in God's children, as they show kindness to children, the elderly and the poor.

I have also experienced these fruits: flowers at the door with a card that says, "I love you." The flowers were beautiful, and the thought was great, but the words on the card were motivated by a disposition of kindness.

God's nature is one of kindness. He loves us not because He has to, but because it is His nature. I am thankful for His heart of compassion. A disposition toward us that made Him choose to give us redemption, a spirit that goes beyond our behavior to our deepest need.

His disposition allowed Him to give us what we did not deserve or what we could never earn: His grace. It is this fruit the Holy Spirit wants to produce in us, the fruit of kindness flowing out of our lives to a hurting world.

I am thankful God can generate kindness in us, and Lord, we are anxious for this fruit to become ripe and ready for picking. We thank You for the fruit that goes beyond good deeds to disposition.

Ponders of the Heart

How have you seen and experienced the fruit of the Spirit?

In your life, who do you know has the disposition of kindness?

Read Galatians 5:19-23.

Ask God's Spirit to produce His disposition in you.

Prayers of the Heart

Dear Father,

Thank You for Your kindness toward us. While we were sinners, You died for us. Lord, You didn't have to do such a thing. We didn't deserve Your grace. It was out of kindness You gave Your Son. Father, produce Your fruit in us. We want to be children who are fully alive in You. We want our lives to give You glory. In Jesus' name, amen.

November 22 ~ Thankful for Salvation

What or whom do you need saving from? Some people need to be saved from an addiction, like drugs, alcohol, pornography, or materialism. Others need to be saved from selfishness, like Ebenezer Scrooge. Hansel and Gretel needed to be saved from the wicked witch and their wicked stepmother. Sleeping Beauty needed to be saved from the witch's curse by a love's kiss, and the Beast in Beauty and the Beast needed to be saved from a spell by someone loving him.

We are all in need of rescue, and somewhere deep inside, we know it. In this fallen world we get confused about what we need rescuing from, but we all need saving.

There are those who think they need to be rescued from their jobs when what they need is to be saved from self-imposed misery. Other people think they need to be freed from their spouses when what they need is to be rescued from their self-centeredness.

Some believe their weight is the problem, their mother, bank account, or their children. We all look to people or circumstances when we fail to see the spiritual battle all around us. The fallen world is at war against us, and we need to be rescued.

No wonder we love movies with heroes who save the weak, the good, and the needy. We like to think of ourselves as heroes, but the truth is we are damsels in distress. Our need is beyond our ability to overcome. We need a savior.

Jesus came to save us. He came to be our Savior. We have three enemies: a fallen world, the evil one, and our own fallen nature. Christ has overcome the world. (John 16:33) Jesus has defeated Satan. (I John 4:4) And in Christ, we have died to our old fallen nature and have been given a new heart. (Romans 6:11-14)

Christ has done all these things for us while we were enemies, dead in our sins, and while we were unable to help ourselves. Jesus has rescued us from eternal death and given us eternal life. Lord, open our eyes of thanksgiving for Your wonderful salvation.

"For I am not ashamed of the gospel, because it is the power of God that brings salvation to everyone who believes: first to the Jew, then to the Gentile. For in the gospel the righteousness of God is revealed—a righteousness that is by faith from first to last, just as it is written: 'The righteous will live by faith'" (Romans 1:16-17).

Ponders of the Heart

Where were you, and who were you with when you first believed the gospel?

Who needs to hear your story?

Read John 16:33, 1 John 4:4, and Romans 6:11-14.

Thank the Lord with worship and praise for His great salvation.

Prayers of the Heart

Dear Father,

Every day, help us realize our great need for You. We want to live our lives in awe and wonder because of our salvation. We do not want to live one day without grateful hearts. Open our mouths to share our story with a broken world. It is by Your grace and faith that we are Yours. Lord, give us Your wisdom over this foolish world. In Jesus' name, amen.

November 23 ~ Thankful for Grace

"For it is by grace you have been saved, through faith—and this is not from yourselves, it is the gift of God—not by works, so that no one can boast" (Ephesians 2:8-9).

I do not know anyone who received a transplant, like a liver, heart, or kidney. However, I have wondered about the emotions they go through.

If a person were on death row and suddenly given a pardon, they would feel relief and be overwhelmed with joy. If they were guilty of the crime, they might feel undeserving, but I bet they would still kick up their heels and run out of the cell the moment the door opened.

This could be the same emotions a person receiving a transplant could experience. After all, they just were given a chance to live and not die. However, someone died to give them this new hope. Here is another thought, who can they thank? They could not thank the person who gave them the organ; that person is dead. I guess they could thank the doctor or the family of the deceased, or they thank God for grace.

After Jesus raised Lazarus from the dead, Mary, Martha, and Lazarus gave a dinner in Jesus' honor. Martha served, and Lazarus reclined at the table with Jesus. Mary took a bottle of costly perfume and poured it on His feet and wiped His feet with her hair. They each thank the Lord in their own unique way.

If the wage of sin is death, we are on death row or waiting for a heart transplant. Our spirits are dead because of sin, and our destiny is the grave. But God offers us grace that is greater than our sin.

What is your biggest sin? If you asked me this question, I would have three or four that would come to my mind. Two of them would shock you and agree they are big ones. The others, you might say, were mistakes, but for me, they are biggies.

If we asked God what our greatest sins were, would His answer be the same as ours? God would say our greatest sins were obeying our sinful nature, and we all need a heart transplant.

From the foundation of the world, God knew we would need grace, and He provided it through His Son. Jesus was not born of man, but of God. Therefore, He did not have a sinful nature, but He had the same choice to sin as Adam. He just didn't. This is where God's grace comes in. By His grace, He offers us redemption.

Jesus lived a sinless life, and when He died on the cross, He defeated death. He rose from the grave and offered all who would believe a transplant: His goodness and purity for our fallen, sinful nature. We receive new life in Him. When He came out of the grave, we by faith, can come out with Him with a new nature, destiny, and a new family. God's grace is greater than all our sins.

I wonder if those who receive transplants are thankful for a while, but as their lives go on, do they forget to be grateful? Do they begin to take life for granted? The answer is different for different people, but my question to us today is, how grateful are we for God's amazing grace?

Are we mindful of His mercy, which has cleansed us from all our sins and given us new, eternal, transformed lives?

Ponders of the Heart

What are ways we can show God our thankfulness?

Do you have a favorite worship song you sing to the Lord?

Read Ephesians 1:7-8 and 2 Corinthians 5:21-6:1.

Prayers of the Heart:

Dear Father,

We have or will feel the pain of losing someone we love to death. The pain of being separated from those we love is hard, but because of Your great grace, those of us who believe in Jesus have hope. We have hope of seeing our loved ones again and the hope of seeing Your face. Death will not defeat us because You have won the victory. In Jesus 'name, amen.

November 24 ~ Thankful for being in Christ

"Noah was a righteous man, blameless among the people of his time, and he walked faithfully with God" (Genesis 6:9).

God was completely grieved over mankind's evil heart. He was so saddened He decided to destroy all creatures He had made. But Noah was a righteous man who walked with God. He listened to God's instructions to build an ark and obeyed. As he built the ark, he preached to the people with words and deeds, but they would not listen.

My husband and I took a trip to Kentucky to see the replica of the ark. I remember it being very foggy that day, and I could barely see the outline of the ark in the distance. However, as we came closer and the fog lifted, I was overwhelmed by how massive it was. Bill and I just stood there staring at this enormous boat.

This reproduction of the ark was built with modern-day equipment, but some of it was built by the Amish. This is so cool because they would have first-hand knowledge of what it was like to build an ark in Noah's day.

Can you imagine working on the ark every day for years? Noah had vision and instructions, but how did he get his sons to the task at hand? Noah had his hands full.

We are told in the Bible that Noah listened to God and obeyed Him. But what if when the ark was completed, he led the animals in and took his family inside, but he did not go into the ark? When it started to rain, and Noah was not in the ark, what would have happened to him? He would have died with the rest of humanity.

Even though he walked with God, Noah needed more to save him from the flood. He would not be able to survive God's wrath. The flood was God's judgment.

We struggle with judgment, but when you read the story carefully, God was patient until He wasn't. He had a man preaching to them and preparing them for what was coming. They had time to take God seriously, but they refused to come to Him and enter His protection.

In the Christian world, we often talk about accepting Jesus as our Savior. We tell people we must ask Christ to come into our hearts and be our Savior. God's Word tells us that Christ lives in His people, but more importantly, we must live in Him. The Bible talks more about being in Christ than Christ being in us. Noah knew that to be safe from the wrath of God, he had to enter the ark.

Christ is our ark. He provides us with safety from God's wrath. We will never have to experience God's fury because we are safe in the ark of Christ. I hope this is not new news to you, but if it is, I hope it is good news. Ephesians chapter one is filled with statements about the importance of being in Christ and the wonder of this position.

- Verse 3: who has blessed us in the heavenly realms with every spiritual blessing in Christ.

- Verse 4: For he chose us in him before the creation of the world.

- Verse 7: In him, we have redemption.

- Verse 11. In him, we were also chosen.

- Verse 13. And you also were included in Christ.

- Verse 13. Having believed, you were marked in him.

Being in Christ is our protection and our hope. We enter Christ by faith; it is God who shuts the door and seals us, just as God shut the door of the ark after Noah entered (Genesis 7:16).

I remember when I came to the door of the ark—a replica of the door God would have shut to protect Noah, his family, and the animals. I was overcome with emotions as I stood there. God has provided our salvation through Jesus, and once we open our hearts to this gift, He puts us in the heart of Jesus and shuts the door. What God shuts, no man can open. We can surely find reason to be thankful and praise God for being in Christ!

Ponders of the Heart

Do you get weary at the things you do over and over?

Do you sometimes feel you are at the end of your rope?

Read Ephesians 1:1-23.

Be encouraged that we are so blessed to be in Christ.

Prayers of the Heart

Dear Father,

When we feel alone, help us remember we are in You. It is hard to believe You are with us because we feel so unworthy instead of remembering Your great mercy. Lord, it is because of You that we are safe. We praise You, and we thank You for being sealed in Your family. In Jesus' name, amen.

November 25 ~ Thankful for Victory

"But thanks be to God. He gives us the victory through our Lord Jesus Christ" (1 Cor. 15:57).

November is the end of high school football. If your team is still playing in November, it has made it to the playoffs.

When my daughter Tracie was a senior, she cheered for her high school football team, which was in the state playoffs. What an exciting time that was. We went to every game with our dearest friends and had the time of our lives.

We laughed, shouted, and cheered with all our might at every game. So did the cheerleaders and the band. And when the team won, oh my, you would have thought we had conquered the world. In my friend's excitement one night, she almost knocked me off the bleachers.

When we left to go home after the game we didn't take any prize money, receive any trophies or a new car. The victory was really the football team; they just let us share in the excitement. Likewise, the win over sin and death was really Christ's victory. He is the one who played the game and won, not us.

If I watch a movie and the bad guy loses, and the good guy wins, I am happy. I am always on the good guy's side.

In the battle against sin and the fallen world, Jesus is the good guy, our hero, and Savior. Satan is the bad guy, the evil one, and the destroyer. But our Jesus wins. He has defeated sin, Satan, and death.

But this isn't the end of the story. Christ does more than win. He does more than take the victory. Jesus takes the win for us. He played the game for us, and through Him, we can experience the joy and the result of victory. We become the winners, the champs, and part of His team.

Football teams have first, second, and maybe even third strings. They have injured players, players who don't play, and players who do. When the team is victorious, they are all champions. When Christ won, we won. When Christ beat Satan, we beat Satan. When Jesus defeated death, we defeated death. Victory is ours in Jesus Christ.

"No, in all these things we are more than conquerors through him who loved us" (Romans 8:37).

Ponders of the Heart

Do you feel like a loser or a winner? We often experienced both.

How are you a winner in Jesus?

Read Romans 8:37-39 and 1 Corinthians 15:50-58.

Praise Jesus for the victory that is ours in Him.

Prayers of the Heart

Dear Father,

How we thank You for victory in Jesus. You have made us winners, and we are grateful. Lord, we have failed in so many important things, but You have taken all our failures and all our losses and made us a champion in Him. Thank You, Father, that our victory is not found in our abilities but in His. Oh, the wonder of Your mercy and grace toward Your children. In Jesus' name, amen.

November 26 ~ Thankful for Intimacy

"And this is eternal life, that they might know You, the only true God and Jesus Christ whom You have sent" (John 17:3 NKJV).

My husband, Bill, and I have lived together so long that we can almost read each other's minds. I can start a sentence, and he can finish it for me. This drives our children crazy. Bill and I are very thankful for this closeness because, to be truthful, our minds get stuck in neutral sometimes.

If he begins to tell me about someone and forgets their name, I can recall their name for him. When I forget my point in the middle of talking, he can finish my thought. It is a wonderful thing to have someone who can fill in the blanks for you when your memory takes a vacation.

In simple terms, you could say Bill and I know each other. Knowing someone to the degree that you can perceive, recognize, and understand their thoughts is really knowing them. We are intimate friends and companions.

Among the things I'm thankful for in this life, knowing Bill is at the top of my list. His companionship and friendship mean more to me than words could ever express. Without him, I would feel lost, and with Bill, I feel at home. He is the most important person in my life. He is my earthly king and husband. I adore him and love him. He is mine, and I am his.

God gave him to me, and every day of my life, I will be thankful for our relationship of intimacy.

The Lord knew I needed a man like him in my life. I didn't know how to be close to others, and it was hard for me to let people really know me. Then I married Bill, and he helped me relax and be myself. I felt accepted and loved by him even when I felt I did not deserve or measure up. It is through our relationship (mine and Bill's) that I have learned a little about loving God and embracing God's love for me.

So, I came today to praise my heavenly Father for giving me a husband who has taught me so much about love and closeness. This has helped me with how I relate to God and how to accept His love and acceptance of me.

Even with much left to learn, I have gleaned enough to be thankful. God has, in effect, said to us, come to Me, and know Me. I will let you become acquainted with Me and to a degree, understand Me. He also has said He knows, loves, and understands us better than we know ourselves.

When we have trouble putting our feelings into words, God understands. In His love, He helps us recall His teaching so we can walk in truth and light. As our loving Father, we feel the freedom to admit our failures to Him without fear and He also rejoices with us in our successes. The Lord listens to our hearts, feels our pain, and comforts us with the comfort of heaven.

I am thankful for the closeness I know and the intimacy that is to come. What a wonderful blessing to know that Jesus is mine and yours at the same time. He is our dearest confidant. Praise our God and Father, who knows us and allows us to come close to Him.

Ponders of the Heart

Who is your best earthly friend?

How intimate is your relationship with God?

Read John 15:1-11.

God desires for us to have a personal relationship with His Son.

Prayers of the Heart

Dear Father,

How do we thank You for allowing us to know You? Your grace and love overwhelm us. Thank You, Lord, for all You have done to make us Yours and to allow us to draw close to You. We want to know You more. We want to see You in everything and love others. We praise You, Father. In Jesus' name, amen.

November 27 ~ Thankful for Never

"No one will be able to stand against you all the days of your life. As I was with Moses, so I will be with you; I will never leave you nor forsake you" (Joshua 1:5).

Never, is somewhat like the word no. We often think of these words as negative words. We might say or hear someone else say, "No, I will never forgive you, or No, I will never believe you or trust you again."

People might say never as a promise and then break that promise. A parent or a spouse promises they will never leave you, and they do.

Others promise to be faithful, and they aren't. These failed promises create hurt and distrust in a person's soul.

It would be impossible, even stupid, to be thankful for the word never in these cases, but Jesus makes some wonderful promises with the word never, and these are the words I am thankful for. Let's look at some of those promises together.

"And Jesus said to them, 'I am the bread of life. He who comes to Me shall never hunger, and he who believe in Me shall never thirst" (John 6:35 NKJV).

"Jesus said to her, 'I am the resurrection and the life. The one who believes in me will live, even though they die; 26 and whoever lives by believing in me will never die. Do you believe this?'" (John 11:25-26.)

"Love never fails" (1 Corinthians 13:8).

"Keep your lives free from the love of money and be content with what you have, because God has said, 'Never will I leave you; never will I forsake you.'" (Hebrews 13:5).

" For prophecy never had its origin in the human will, but prophets, though human, spoke from God as they were carried along by the Holy Spirit" (2 Peter 1:21).

These are a few "nevers" I am thankful. If I come to Him for filling, I will *never* be hungry or thirsty in my soul. In Him, I have eternal life, and His love *never* fails. Jesus will *never* leave me. I can count on these promises because His words of promise did not come from man but from His heart, and He is faithful.

I spoke a word of witness to two ladies who came to my door. They stand for another religion. One that depends more on what they do than what God has already done. I pray for them. I pray that the words I spoke to them were words of life.

Oh, I pray they saw Jesus and not me. He will never fail them, but I will. How I pray His "never" in their lives and in ours.

Ponders of the Heart

What was a promise someone made to you that they broke?

How did you deal with the hurt?

Read Joshua 1:9

Take time today to thank the Lord for His promise to never leave us.

Prayers of the Heart

Dear Father,

We praise You for Your promises. How thankful to know You will never leave us. You are our security in this life and the one to come. It is Your power that keeps us. Lord, mend our hearts from the hurt others have caused as we look to You for our lives. In Jesus' name, amen.

November 28 ~ Thankful for Giving

"His divine power has given us everything we need for a godly life through our knowledge of him who called us by his own glory and goodness" (2 Peter 1:3.)

Looking back over my life, I realize it has been surrounded by givers. My mother started this ministry when I was a little baby. She was my caretaker. She fed, changed, and washed me and my clothes. I am alive today because she loved and cared for me.

Since then, my mother has continued to provide for me in so many ways. She gave her love to me from the very beginning of my life, and she continued to love me to the end of hers.

Givers are a blessing, and God has a way of sending them at the right moment. If you are reading this devotional, it is because God sent a precious friend in my life who walked with me through the process of editing and publishing this book. I didn't have a clue how to do this task, but I am blessed she was placed in my life. She is a giving person.

I have been blessed with people who have encouraged, instructed, and given me purpose. Hopefully, I have done the same for others.

For each "giver" that has come our way, we are and should be thankful, but all the giving in the world cannot begin to match what God has given to us through Christ Jesus, our Lord.

In the verse quoted above, we are told that God has, by His power, given us all we need for life and godliness. We needed life because we were dead in our sins, and He has given us a new nature so we can live godly lives. Think about what a wonderful gift this is.

Through Jesus and the power of the Holy Spirit, we can live godly lives. We will sin and fall into sin, but we do not have to be sin dwellers. We can walk in the Spirit and live godly lives. Why? Because Jesus is the ultimate Giver.

Jesus has given us His victory and righteousness so we might live righteous, victorious lives. He lived, died, and rose again to do for us what we could not do for ourselves. We have a share in heaven because Jesus has shared His inheritance with us.

Like Jesus, I want to give His love to those around me, encouraging and guiding them out of His great compassion and truth. He is the ultimate Giver, and I long to be filled with His heart. Holy Spirit, fill our souls with Your life so You flow out of us.

Ponders of the Heart

Who is someone who has blessed you with their giving?

Do you see yourself as someone who is generous to others?

Colossians 2:13-15 and Romans 5:8-11.

Rejoice over the remarkable things Christ has given to His own.

Prayers of the Heart

Dear Father,

We thank You for all the gifts of life and godliness You have given us. Lord, help us to understand and stand firm in the life that is ours in Jesus. We thank You for all the wonder of Your plan. We want to walk, giving out what You have placed in us. Help us to count our blessings each day. In Jesus' name, amen.

November 29 ~ Toothache

My tooth was hurting and the pain started yesterday. I didn't wait, I called the dentist immediately. My fear was I would have to have a root canal, and the cost is expensive.

The toothache seems so unfair to me. I go to the dentist twice a year, brush twice a day, and floss every day. If a person does all this, then they should not have to have a root canal, right? Right!

When I got in to see the dentist, I asked his assistant if this pain meant I would have to have a root canal. She said not necessarily, but I could tell she was hedging. So, when Dr. Martin came in, I started on him. I said, "Dr. Martin, it just started hurting yesterday. Does this mean a root canal?"

He looked at the X-rays and really couldn't see what was going on. He tapped on several teeth, put cold on them, and then used a technical machine to tell the pulse of the root of each tooth in question. He just couldn't tell what caused my pain. He said the best thing to do was to wait until we could tell where the pain was coming from. So here I sit, just waiting for severe pain to attack me so he can do a root canal on one of my teeth.

There is an outside chance it is my wisdom tooth, which he would pull. I'm not crazy about that idea either. In fact, the truth is, I need all the wisdom I can get. A little dentist humor to lighten my mood.

This whole ordeal reminds me of my sin patterns. We all have them. We have lies, strongholds, and old patterns of living that cause us to act and react to situations in certain ways. In other words, there are root causes to what we do and why we do them. The root cause can be a hurt, a situation, or an old perception.

In our society, we want to take care of the behavior and often leave the root cause decaying away. Christ came to take care of the root cause and free us from it, which will take care of the behavior. I guess you could say He wants to do a root canal on us.

When Christ wants to deal with the root of our sins, we often start counting the cost and not the benefit. That is exactly what I was doing with the dentist today. He humored me because he wasn't sure, but pain cometh in the morning.

The difference between my dentist and Jesus is my dentist practices dentistry, but Christ is sure of His diagnosis. It is painful to have a root canal. The shot itself isn't pleasant, but aren't we glad something can be done to relieve the infection? Letting Christ get to the root of our sin and destroy it so we can be healed is more than something good. It is miraculous.

Ponders of the Heart

Do you react to something in a certain way and do not understand why? There is a root cause.

Do you live with someone who doesn't understand why they act the way they do? There is a root cause.

Read Matthew 4:23-24 and John 15:1-5.

Let us bring ourselves and those we love to Jesus so He can destroy the root cause of our sin that keeps us in bondage.

Prayers of the Heart

Dear Father,

Take the diseased, rotten roots of our old lives and set us free from their hold on us.

Lord, these roots have caused enough pain in our lives. We long to abide in Your vine and live on the richness of Your sap. Father, pull down every stronghold that holds us captive until all the roots of our lives are found only in You. In Jesus' name, amen.

November 30 ~ Prayers from the Heart

"I love you, Lord, my strength. The Lord is my rock, my fortress and my deliverer; my God is my rock, in whom I take refuge, my shield and the horn of my salvation, my stronghold" (Psalm 18: 1-2).

Dear Father,

How we love You, Lord. Teach us to love You more. We want to love You with our mouths, lives, and hearts. You are our shield, and we need Your protection even against our own failures. Jesus, You are our salvation, and we are thankful that our salvation is secure in Your hands and not in ours. You alone are worthy of our praise and our lives.

We bow down before Your throne and worship You.

"He reached down from on high and took hold of me; he drew me out of the deep waters" (Psalm 18:16).

You did reach down from heaven and rescued Your people, and You have hold of us. Thank You for being our God, Father, and King.

"He brought me out into a spacious place; he rescued me because he delighted in me" (Psalm 18:19).

Lord, You delight in us. This statement from Your Word encourages us and overwhelms us. Only by Your mercy could You love and delight in us. Help us experience joy because of Your grace, how we pray that our love for You will delight and bring You joy.

"You, O Lord, keep my lamp burning; my God turns my darkness into light" (Psalm 18:28).

Lord, You are our light. We love You and praise You. In Jesus' name, amen.

december

— 66 —

For to us a child is born, to us a son is given, and the government will be on his shoulders. And he will be called Wonderful Counselor, Mighty God, Everlasting Father, Prince of Peace.

Isaiah 9:6

December 1 ~ Rabbi

"Turning around, Jesus saw them following and asked, 'What do you want?' They said, "Rabbi"(which means "Teacher"), "where are you staying?"' (John 1:38).

If you were appearing on the Television show "Who Wants to be a Millionaire," who would you choose to be your lifeline? People who were experts on different subjects, or would you choose people who are jack-of-all-trades when it comes to knowledge?

What if you knew the questions would be about God's kingdom, who would be your lifeline? Would it be your pastor, your Bible teacher, or the Pope?

Television shows like Jeopardy make you realize that even some of the most intelligent people in our society know little about the Bible and much less about the Lord. I am ignorant about so many things in this world that I cringe just thinking about appearing on shows like "Who Wants to be a Millionaire: " or "Jeopardy, " but this fear is nothing if I had to appear before the Judgment Seat of God without a lifeline.

Jesus begins to work in our lives as a "Rabbi" or teacher. He opens our eyes to the things of God. Jesus is our lifeline into His kingdom. Even though He begins as our teacher, He is so much more. Without Him, we have no hope of eternal life. Jesus is the source of life. He is the sustainer of life, and the Door into life. When we come to Him, He will lead us all the way to our eternal home.

There is so much we don't understand about His ways and His kingdom, but He will teach us if we seek Him as our lifeline.

Unlike "Who Wants to be a Millionaire", He does not come to help us just once, but every time we call. The depth of His wisdom is beyond our ability to ask the question or know the answer. Jesus knows the question and the answer before the question is in our minds.

Let's seek Him while He is near, praying that our eyes will be open to His instructions, and we will be among those who wish not to be millionaires in this world but to share in the riches of His Kingdom.

Lord, we long to know You and learn from You.

Ponders of the Heart

How well are you seeking Jesus as your lifeline?

Do you realize He longs to be your wisdom and your strength?

Read Isaiah 55:1-3.

Prayers of the Heart

Dear Father,

We come to You, seeking Your ways, Your heart, and Your face. Lord, we hunger and thirst for You. Only in You will we find the satisfaction our hearts long for. Keep our hearts and minds focused on You. Make our way straight. You are our Teacher and giver of life. We wish to live all our days under Your grace. In Jesus' name, amen.

December 2 ~ Bring Them to Jesus

"Cast all your anxiety on him because he cares for you" (1 Peter 5:7).

Do you know anyone who is paralyzed? Not just physically, but emotionally, mentally, or spiritually? In the ninth chapter of Matthew, friends of a paralyzed man brought him to Jesus to be healed. The man could not come on his own; he was paralyzed. Did he want to come? We don't know, but we do know his friends were bringing him to Jesus.

"Some men brought to him a paralyzed man, lying on a mat. When Jesus saw their faith, he said to the man, 'Take heart, son; your sins are forgiven'" (Matthew 9:2).

The faith of the paralyzed man's friends moved Jesus to compassion. Jesus notices our faith when we bring others to Him, who, for this reason or that, can't come to Him.

Hebrews 1:6 reminds us that God is pleased with faith and rewards those who seek Him. These guys brought their friend to Jesus, and He rewarded them by healing him.

Then Jesus said to the man,

"Take heart, son; your sins are forgiven" (Matthew 9:2).

Wait a minute. He was paralyzed, and Jesus was talking about forgiving sins. What was that all about? Commentaries explain that Jesus was considering the scribes who were present, but I wonder what the paralyzed man thought.

Has guilt over something paralyzed your mind and emotions? You find yourself stuck in limbo. You don't know what to do. In fact, you feel there is nothing you can do, so you give up. Satan is the author of guilt and hopelessness. These feelings are when we have left God out of the picture. If we belong to Jesus, He will not leave us there.

The paralyzed man might very well be under the weight of guilt or hopelessness. The enemy sets the bait in his mind, and he swallows the lie, hook, line, and sinker. He gives up. In order for Jesus to heal him on the inside as well as the outside, he needs to believe his sins were forgiven.

I love the fact that Jesus called him son, and He told him to be of good cheer. You could also translate this to say take courage. The amplified Bible says:

"Take courage, son; your sins are forgiven and the penalty remitted" (Matthew 9:2).

The freedom of being forgiven destroys paralyzed emotions, heals the paralyzed mind, and, in this case, gives health to a paralyzed body. Why, because spiritual health is given with forgiveness of sins and the penalty of those sins paid in full.

I have felt paralyzed in my life and this story gives me such hope. Jesus wants to heal us. He is our physical, emotional, and spiritual healer. We can always come to Him for our healing. But it does not stop with us. This story shows us we can bring those we love to Jesus for healing. We can bring them to Him even if they have given up hope and see no way out. You might ask how?

My first thought is in prayer. Picture in your mind bringing a person to the throne room of heaven and laying them at the foot of Jesus. He will be moved by your love and faith.

We can also bring others to Jesus by sharing God's Words and loving them. This world is so full of hate and discouragement. We can show the world and those we love a better way. Our world is starved for gentleness and care. Jesus is moved by our love for others and our faith in Him.

Ponders of the Heart

Are you someone who is stuck in hopelessness and guilt?

Do you feel there is no way out?

Do you have a friend you need to bring to Jesus?

Read Matthew 9:1-8.

I'm thankful neither the paralyzed man nor his friends acted like the religious leaders. I am also thankful that Jesus was moved by compassion for the man and his friends and was not deterred by the thought of the religious elite. There is much to ponder in these verses.

Prayers of the Heart

Dear Lord,

We have dear ones who have been stuck for so long. They are paralyzed with their finances, and unhealthy habits. They just don't see a way out, but they don't seem willing to come to You. We bring them to You. We are thankful that nothing is too hard for You. In Jesus' name, amen.

December 3 ~ Sickness of Sin

I have been sick for days with an illness it might be the flu, an upper respiratory infection, or one doctor called it "a sickness." I believe he was the most honest of all. What he was saying was, you are sick, all right, but I don't have a clue what it is.

Soon, this will be over, but for now, I just want to crawl into a hole with a box of tissues and Tylenol and sleep. Of course, one of the worst parts of what I have is I can't sleep. Nothing I try makes me feel better. My eyes, nose, and throat are red, and if I could see my eardrums, they would be red too. The good news is this will pass. My sickness is not terminal.

There is, however, a sickness that is terminal, and it comes from our sin nature. You and I were born with this deadly disease. Romans 6 tells us that the wages of sin is death. This means our sickness is terminal. We live our lives with this, and we feel terrible. Our behavior is bad, our thoughts are corrupt, and rest is impossible.

Each day, we get up, determined to do better, but we can't. We are trapped in this disease of sin. This is the bad news. The good news is God has provided a cure for our terminal illness of the soul through the life, death, and resurrected life of Jesus.

"God made him who had no sin to be sin for us, so that in him we might become the righteousness of God" (2 Corinthians 5:21).

Some might say we escape death, but Romans 6 tells us we don't escape it, but we died in Christ, so we will be raised to new life in Him.

"Or don't you know that all of us who were baptized into Christ Jesus were baptized into his death? We were therefore buried with

him through baptism into death in order that, just as Christ was raised from the dead through the glory of the Father, we too may live a new life" (Romans 6:3-4).

Why is this important for you and me? It is because we need to get rid of our terminal disease and receive a new nature, one given to us by God.

Like me, you have discovered you cannot fix yourself. You and I need a "start over," and this is what God gives us through faith in Jesus. He gives us an alive spirit born from above.

Ponders of the Heart

Is there a part of your life that needs a do-over?

What area of your life is God working on?

Read Romans 6:1-11.

Oh, how gracious our God is to us. How I praise Him.

Prayers of the Heart

Dear Lord,

How we praise You. In You, there is wholeness and life, and without You, there is only the disease of sin and death. Lord, we want to thank You that sickness in our bodies can remind us of the eternal sickness apart from Your grace. Thank You for Jesus, whose death is our death and whose life is our life. What a wonderful God we serve. We praise You. In Jesus' name, amen.

December 4 ~ Pandora's Box

The internet is full of valuable information, but you need to be aware that not all the information is good. One afternoon, I was looking online for a good deal for my son when an offer to save money on the item popped up. You guessed it, I was suckered in.

Before my good sense caught up with my brain, I was filling out a survey that linked me to nine different interest groups. I entered my email address and phone number. The phone did not stop ringing, nor did the emails stop coming for days. I opened the modern-day Pandora's Box. If I could have a do-over day, this would be a day I would rewind my stupidity and then erase the whole thing.

Usually, I am careful about my computer. I mainly use it for what I am doing right now, writing. I felt invaded by the internet world, and I opened the door and invited them in. I am reminded of Paul's words in Ephesians when he said,

"Be very careful, then, how you live—not as unwise but as wise," (Ephesians 5:15).

If only I had thought of those words before I foolishly went into cyberspace with my identity in hand. I can't rewind the day, but I have blocked the email addresses and phone numbers. In time, they will get the message. My only hope is that I outlive their beastly appetite for fresh, foolish flesh. Paul goes on to say,

"Be very careful, then how you live—not as unwise but as wise, making the most of every opportunity, because the days are evil" (Ephesians 5:15-16).

If you would allow me to put this verse in modern terms, terms I can understand. They would say, "Marilyn, think before you act. Think with the brain God has given you."

This is a small thing, but I hope it teaches me a big lesson. I want to find the information I want and need, but I do not want to give the whole internet world access to me.

These days are evil, and we must be wise as serpents and gentle as doves. That is why this passage continues with these words:

"Do not get drunk on wine, which leads to debauchery. Instead, be filled with the Spirit" (Ephesians 5:18).

Again, if you would allow me to modernize these words, they would say, "Don't be taken away with dull thinking, thinking like a drunk man. In fact, don't be under the influence of alcohol. It will dull your thinking, but be filled with the Spirit, and your thinking will be full of wisdom."

Even in this broken world, we can be wise if we allow the Holy Spirit to fill our minds with His wisdom. Remember, think before you click.

Ponders of the Heart

How do you protect yourself from the internet's seduction?

What about other worldly traps we find ourselves in?

Read again Ephesians 5:15-18, Col. 4:5, and I Corinthians 2:10-16.

God has given us the ability to live beyond the traps of this world.

Prayers of the Heart

Dear Father,

We thank You for Your Holy Spirit and our need of Him. We confess we need Your wisdom to lead and guide us. Thank You, Lord, that when You made us Yours, You placed Your Spirit in us and filled us with eternal life. Help us remember this and live for You. In Jesus' name, amen.

December 5 ~ Life and Messes

"Yet you, Lord, are our Father. We are the clay, you are the potter; we are all the work of your hand" (Isaiah 64:8).

Three new gallons of paint are sitting in our garage. There are three new rollers and a new trim tool. It embarrasses me to say, but they have been sitting there for a month. I just can't make up my mind to paint.

These are my excuses. I have been busy, but I knew that when I bought the paint. The real reason I haven't painted is that I will have to tear up the room. The furniture will be moved, curtains taken down and washed, the floors covered, baseboards taped, and after painting, everything will need to be put back.

If this last paragraph makes you tired, you understand why I haven't started the job. The thought of tearing up a perfectly tidy room to paint has stopped me.

The job I really don't mind. In fact, I enjoy painting. It is fun to turn on music, turn off the normal tasks of the day, and paint. I just don't like tearing up the room and putting it back together. Painting causes me to second-guess myself about the color I picked, but mostly, I don't like messes or change. My grandchildren know this about me, and so does God.

You might agree with me if you hate messes and change. But that is not true with our Lord. If He were here, He would be singing and painting as I pound away on this keyboard. How do I know this? He is in the business of making messes of our self-sufficient lives and changing them.

Jesus comes into our lives ready to work. He knows what needs to change, and He will be glad to do this for us. To the world, we might look like a mess, but He has a finished vision in mind. Our Jesus knows the plans and the beauty He wants to bestow on our lives. He is more than willing to roll up His sleeves and get to work.

Where I don't want to move the couch and look at the dusty baseboards, He comes to clean up my dusty life.

If I started to paint the den right now, it would take me the rest of the day. It might take me two days. The thought of Bill coming home with a disaster in the house would make me try to hurry. But when it comes to my life, Christ is not in a hurry. Time restraints never make Him hurry. If I am out of whack for a day, a week, or for years, it does not deter Him from the task at hand. His work is deliberate, beautiful, and perfect.

I am in a state of being remodeled right now. My life seems unusable and unorganized. The Lord has turned me upside down. I don't like the upheaval, and not sure how I will look when He is done.

Will my family even like me? I guess I will have to wait and see if they like His work. Wait, doesn't the Word say He is making me look like Him? (Romans 8:29) That sounds exciting to me, a major improvement. The work is His, the mess is mine, but the finished project will be well worth the work and the wait. If only I could be as sure about our den.

Ponders of the Heart

How is your life right now?

Has God been showing you some changes you need to make?

Read 2 Corinthians 3:18 and Hebrews 12:1-2.

Wherever we find ourselves today, let us rejoice in the knowledge that Christ will finish His work in us.

Prayers of the Heart

Dear Father,

Life can be such a mess. We need You so. Lord, we place the outcome of our lives in Your Hands. Stay close; help us feel Your presence. Help us trust You and the outcome. We come to You today, thanking You for the hope Your Word gives us and the faith that You are true to Your Word. Father, we praise You. In Jesus' name, amen.

December 6 ~ Feasting

"Just as the living Father sent me and I live because of the Father, so the one who feeds on me will live because of me" (John 6:57).

December is a month of get-togethers with delicious food. Companies have Christmas parties for their employees, and Sunday school classes have Christmas fellowships, and both make sure they have tasty food. Family dinners also highlight this special season.

Our family is no exception. For the last few years, we have had our traditional Christmas dinner on Christmas Eve, and on Christmas Day, we get together for breakfast. As the main cook, I liked this because it keeps me out of the kitchen.

Christmas Eve, while everyone heads to the mall, I do my main cooking. My husband is a last-minute shopper, and our kids like to go with him without my watchful eye. They all know he is easy prey to their "I want" sickness, which they have developed over years of Christmas Eve shopping with good old dad.

I stay home and get everything ready just the way I like it. With Christmas music blasting, I set the table with Christmas dishes and cook all their favorite food while I pick up the house, so everything is ready when they come in. With the table set and the aroma of the food filling the house, I get to serve those I love with the absolute best I have to offer. They are always gracious with praise over the table and food as we feast together.

Even with my best effort at preparing a delicious meal and their best effort to eat as much as they can, by the next day, we are ready to eat again.

Our physical hunger has a way of returning. We are well acquainted with our physical appetite, but do we realize we have a spiritual one as well?

Jesus knows of our physical needs as well as our spiritual ones. He knows our spiritual hunger can only be satisfied by feasting on Him.

Even as I type these words, it is easy for me to understand how His followers could misunderstand His words. He was talking about a hunger that even my best turkey and dressing can't touch. People try to satisfy the appetite of the soul with food and many other things, but this emptiness can only be satisfied with Jesus. Feasting on Him is where life becomes living, and satisfaction is born.

This December, I want to remember to serve Jesus whenever I can. Serve the warmth of His love, the richness of His peace, the satisfaction of His fellowship, and the full-body aroma of His redemption.

I want to set my table with special stories of His faithfulness and His gracious beauty. Enjoying a delicious Christmas dinner is wonderful, but if Jesus is the main entree, our hungry souls will be filled and satisfied.

Ponders of the Heart

Does the busyness of Christmas steal your time and heart away?

What can we do to make sure we don't miss Christ this Christmas?

Read John 6:41-68.

Jesus calls us to turn on our spiritual hunger and feast on Him.

Prayers of the Heart

Dear Jesus,

No one can satisfy like You. In You, we find peace, satisfaction, and rest for our hungry souls. Lord, this December, help us feast on Your words of life and help us serve You to others. In Jesus' name, amen.

December 7 ~ Approval

"No one can serve two masters. Either he will hate the one and love the other, or you will be devoted to the one and despise the other. You cannot serve both God and money" (Matthew 6:24).

We are all guilty of wanting to be liked. I want people to like me. The problem comes if I change who I am so they will like me. What drives us to be pleasers? It is probably rooted in shame-based identity. I'm not sure, but whatever causes us to become people-pleasers will drive us crazy, that I'm sure of.

Divided loyalty is a challenging thing. Working women and men must balance loyalty between their families and their jobs. Then there is the balancing act between husbands and parents, husbands and children, children and other children, and grandchildren and other grandchildren. The list can go on and on.

When our loyalties are divided, life is hard. But when we try to live in this world, pleasing those around us while still pleasing God, we have entered an impossible situation. If we allow our lives to be driven by the approval of others, we will end up on the dead-end street called exhaustion.

I am in my seventies, and I still get caught up in trying to please others. Expectations of friends, family, church, and spouses can control our lives. The opinions of others can also control our thoughts and actions.

This leads to a life in motion with a loss of identity and meaning. Without God's purpose in control, my life becomes trivial and pointless. Our God is faithful. He lets us hang ourselves. We get so strung out we call for help, and He helps us.

My sweet daughter, Tracie, has the hardest time saying "No," but she will learn or will keel over one day. I am afraid she moves in so many directions that she forgets where she is going. This doesn't surprise me; she comes from a long line of people who cannot say no.

God's design is that we live our lives to the audience of One. We were created for Him, and if we live with this in mind, we find peace.

Our Father has a perfect purpose for our lives. He has the plan, the purpose and has given us the equipment needed to carry out those purposes. Our job is to stay close and available to Him.

God is not a screamer. He is a whisperer, and we must be able to hear His Voice. I get into trouble when I lose focus on Him and focus on the noise around me.

If we lose our way and live outside His plan, we might as well play pin-the-tail on the donkey with our lives. You know the problem with this game—people are blindfolded.

Ponders of the Heart

Do you have too much chaos in your life?

Have you lost your focus on God?

Read Deuteronomy 6:4-5 and offer your hearts fresh and new to God and turn from the voices that compete with Him.

Prayers of the Heart

Dear Father,

We love You, and we want You to have our hearts. Oh, Father, forgive us for listening to those voices that compete for our love and loyalty. You are our greatest joy and greatest treasure. Lord, we love You. Help us love You more. In Jesus' name, we pray, amen.

December 8 ~ Mary's Joy

"My soul magnifies the Lord, and my spirit has rejoiced in God my Savior. For He has regarded the lowly state of His maidservant; For behold henceforth all generations will call me blessed" (Luke 1:47-48 NKJV).

Children signified God's blessings to Jewish women, and Mary's child represented God's richest blessing: His own Son. She must have been overcome with joy and wonder. She realized her unworthiness, yet all generations would call her blessed.

If you are a mother, there was a day when you received the news that you were going to have a baby. For many of us, this was a special day, but for others, this day was not on our timetable.

We all wondered about our ability to care for a baby, and our reactions were as different as we were. With each of my children, I had a different reaction, but when my child began to move within me, so did my heart. I loved those children before they were born, and to this day, they own my deepest love. Children are a joy and blessing, but they cost us our hearts as Jesus did Mary's.

With each of my children, the day the doctor confirmed I was expecting, it was not a surprise because my morning sickness had confirmed my condition. Even in sickness, the prospect of being a mom was exciting.

I found myself in the stores looking at little socks and shoes. I marveled at tiny clothes and baby furniture. All our plans were in light of when our baby would arrive, and in many ways, my children still control my calendar. Yes, being a mother is joyful, demanding, and sometimes a difficult blessing. But this blessing is for life.

Mary's praise is the praise of a mother's heart, but this Child would also be her Savior, and ours. Her Child was born to die for our sins.

Mary knew the Messiah's mission, but she did not know the method. She knew her people's oppression, but she did not know the depth of this oppression. The enemy was greater than Rome; it was Satan, and the evil one would be after her Son. She did not know that victory would come in death and that victory would appear after what looked like defeat. All she felt at this moment was praise.

In God's wisdom, we cannot see the future. He wants us to live one day at a time, depending on Him. We might not see into the future, but we can know the One who does. We can trust His wisdom and His power over our lives. So, like Mary, we can rejoice in today's blessings, knowing we are safely in His care.

Today, if you are a mom, thank the Lord for this blessing and pray that God will use your children for His glory. Don't let circumstances in your children's lives keep away your joy. Keep your knees on the ground in prayer and your eyes toward the heavens.

Our hope and our joy are ultimately in the One who was Mary's song of praise, our Jesus.

Ponders of the Heart

What worries you today?

What keeps you awake at night?

Read Luke 1:39-56.

Turn from worry to praise for Jesus; our Redeemer is near.

Prayers of the Heart

Dear Father,

Thank You for Your provision, Jesus. Oh, Lord, our need is great, and Your provision is enough. Thank You that we have been washed, sanctified, and adopted into Your family. Lord, we thank You for our children and pray their lives will bring You honor and glory. We pray they will love You with all their hearts and souls for now and forevermore. In Jesus' name, amen.

December 9 ~ Mary's Suffering

"When Jesus saw his mother there, and the disciple whom he loved standing nearby, he said to her, 'Woman, here is your son,' and to the disciple, 'Here is your mother.' From that time on, this disciple took her into his home'" (John 19:26-27).

It is not uncommon for a mother to suffer her child's pain. In a real sense, labor pains are just the beginning of the aching a mother will endure. The physical pain of labor is hard, but in most cases, it is not as difficult as the emotional aching we endure with our children.

One Sunday afternoon, Chris, my son, took a nasty fall on a wakeboard, breaking his ankle. After emergency surgery, I watched helplessly as he endured excruciating pain that I would have gladly suffered for him.

My daughter, Tracie, told me about a struggle she was having. My heart tore to pieces as I listened to her. I felt the lump in my throat and the tears in my eyes as if this situation had happened to me.

When we see wrong attitudes in our children, we grieve. When we see them heading for trouble, we fear for them. Like Mary, we ponder the things our children say and do and the circumstances in their lives deep in our hearts. Our lives connect to their lives on an intensely personal level.

I saw my children enter this world, and I held them in my arms within minutes of their first breath. It doesn't matter how old they are; they hold my heart in their hands. If they suffer, I suffer! If they rejoice, I rejoice! If they succeed, I succeed! If they died, part of my heart would die with them.

Mary was there when Jesus took His first breath, and she heard His first cry. She held Him in her arms, and she cared for Him as He grew into a man. When Jesus fell, she bandaged His knee, and when He laughed, she laughed right along with Him. Mary identified with Jesus on a very personal level, even if many things about Him remained a mystery.

During the birth of Jesus, Mary suffered labor pains, but the agony she endured as He breathed His last breath crushed her heart.

Could Mary's labor pains have prepared her for the cross? I doubt anything could have prepared her for the agony she felt that day.

Jesus, in His compassion, gave Mary a new son and John a new mother, knowing in time, they could help and love one another. Jesus knows our pain in life. He knows our suffering, and He cares.

Ponders of the Heart

Can you recall a time when your heart broke for another?

Can you recall a circumstance that was unfair to someone you love?

How did you feel? Angry, sad, deep pain?

Read Hebrews 4:14-16.

Take your heart to God in prayer.

Prayers of the Heart

Dear Father,

    Children help us know You as Father. The love we feel for them helps us understand the love You have for us. Thank You for You see our pain and our suffering. You know the pain of loving someone and having them suffer. You see the big picture. You know the reason for it all, and yet You sympathize with our pain. Father, help us look to You and not lean on our own understanding of things. Help us love even if it hurts. In Jesus' name, amen.

December 10 ~ Jerusalem

"Jerusalem, Jerusalem, you who kill the prophets and stone those sent to you, how often I have longed to gather your children together,

as a hen gathers her chicks under her wings, and you were not willing" (Matthew 23:37).

It was New Year's Eve, and I felt at peace. Jesus surrounded me with His presence in the Garden Tomb. I felt His closeness, and as my heart remembered His sacrifice for me, I was overcome with the knowledge of His love.

We had the privilege of having the Lord's Supper in the Garden Tomb, which was overwhelming for me. Tears of thankfulness and joy ran down my cheeks as I felt humble and so unworthy yet grateful.

I didn't want to leave this haven of His presence. I didn't want His closeness to depart, but the others wanted to go back into the old city. They wanted to experience the drama of the crowds. We certainly did. As we were going in, the crowds were coming out, millions of Muslims traveling home after a day of fasting and worshipping Muhammad, while thousands of Jews moved from the Wailing Wall to their homes.

It must have been like when Jesus traveled to Jerusalem during the Jewish Passover. The marketplace was hopping, with salesmen marketing their goods, people rushing, and throngs of people making their way back home.

My heart was still reeling from the experience in the Garden Tomb. My eyes were full of love. They had to be, for my heart was overflowing. We had spent several hours there, but these people had spent all day there. Where was their joy? Why did they look at me with such anger and distaste? How had they missed Jesus? His presence was there. I felt it.

Oh, some businessmen were busy, but mostly, I encountered angry, miserable, and preoccupied worshippers. How could this be? The absence of Jesus is the absence of grace and joy.

Did Jesus experience what I did, people who worshipped rules and laws and missed grace and therefore missed peace? I thought about their loss, and I wanted to open their eyes to their absence of joy. I wanted them to see Jesus and experience His love, grace, and peace, but I was afraid of them.

When Jesus approached them, He spoke words of compassion and truth. He told them of His love and His desire, but He also knew the coldness of their hearts.

Oh, that we would be people who are willing to let Him protect, comfort and give us words to comfort others. Jesus, I know of no better place to be than under the wing of Your care.

Ponders of the Heart

Where have you encountered religious people without joy?

Have you allowed these people to keep you away from Jesus?

Has their lack of love kept you from loving them?

Read Matthew 23:31-39.

Jesus has a heart for the lost. Ask Him for a heart of compassion and love for the lost and not fear.

Prayers of the Heart

Dear Jesus,

How You want to bring us peace and comfort. How You want to draw us under the wing of Your love. Help us experience Your care, protection, and peace. Lord, as we do, we ask You to send others to us so we can tell them about You. Give us love, courage, and transforming words. Let our hearts cry for the souls of lost people. We want a heart like Yours. In Jesus' name, amen.

December 11 ~ Independent Spirit, the Heart of Rebellion

We are all born with a heart of rebellion. I saw this in my children, grandchildren, and, most importantly, in me.

My husband and I believe we were born to be grandparents. Never has anything captured our hearts like our grandchildren. But in a heartbeat, their independent spirits can cause a bit of rebellion in their actions.

There are so many "yeses" in our house to make each of them feel welcome and loved, but there are a few rules. When they were younger, they were simple things like don't pour water on the floor in the bathroom and no hitting. Now that they are older, they know I do not like messes, and even though we have a pool, our house is not a beach house. They know I do not want them prancing around in our house with wet feet and no sitting on the furniture wearing a wet bathing suit.

Clayton, my youngest grandson, is a chip-eater, and he loves to leave his chip bowls everywhere. He knows how I feel about this, but I find his chip bowls under the bed, behind the couch, and in all kinds of hiding places. He knows they do not go there, but his rebellious spirit gets the best of him at times.

I find candy wrappers stuffed in vases or under throw pillows. This is crazy, and I don't think it is just the grandchildren who do these things. My grown children are also culprits.

Our family is no exception. We all want to rule our own lives. Our independent spirit is the very heart of our sinful nature. We want to do what we want to do, and we do not want limits put on our lives. There seems to be little respect for authority and restrictions in our world today. I see this same attitude in me. But this is wrong!

Jesus said in Matthew 16:24-26:

"Then Jesus said to his disciples, 'Whoever wants to be my disciple must deny themselves and take up their cross and follow me. For whoever wants to save their life will lose it, but whoever loses their life for me will find it. What good will it be for someone to gain the whole world, yet forfeit their soul? Or what can anyone give in exchange for their soul?'"

We are told that in order to follow Jesus, we must deny ourselves. This is often a misunderstood concept. What does it mean to deny yourself? Is denying yourself the same thing as self-denial? Neal Anderson, in his book *"The Bondage Breaker"*, says,

"Every student, athlete, and cult member practices self-denial, restricting themselves from substances and activities that keep them from reaching goals. But the ultimate purpose of that kind of self-

denial is self-promotion: to receive the top grade, to break a record, to achieve status and recognition. To deny ourselves is to deny self-rule. Dying to self is the primary battle of life."

Ouch. Self-rule is a sin. It destroys our lives and the lives of others, but primarily, it keeps us from allowing God to rule us. In conclusion, self-rule is the heart of rebellion and the number one obstacle to living the life Jesus is offering us.

When we try to live independent from God's rule and rule our own lives, it is rebellion against God. Until we deny ourselves, we will never be at peace with God, and we will never be free. We were not created to function independently of God, nor were our souls designed to function as masters. Denying ourselves is vital to spiritual freedom.

Ponders of the Heart

What in your life are you trying to control that is really controlling you? Your job? Your marriage? Your time? Your children? Your life?

Read Psalm 131. Rest in His rule and praise Him for His sufficiency in your life.

Prayers of the Heart

Dear Father,

How we want to trust You with our lives. We want You to rule over us and say no to our craziness. Lord, we need Your vision and Your wisdom governing over us. You are the King, and we are Your servants. Lord, help us know You. In Jesus' name, amen.

December 12 ~ Mary's Humility

"Then Mary said, Behold the maidservant of the Lord. Let it be to me according to your word. And the angel departed from her" (Luke 1:38 NKJV).

In the above verse, Mary accepted the will of the Lord and, by faith, the power of the Holy Spirit over her body. I don't think that at this moment she thought about all she would have to endure, how difficult it would be for others to understand. She was just willing to trust God.

This is a perfect picture of what Jesus meant when He said we must deny ourselves to follow Him. Joseph also had to deny his doubts and fears, but believe that Mary was indeed pregnant by the Holy Spirit. Believing and accepting God's rule over our lives is the walk of faith.

My faith walk has failed me at times. This happens when I choose to listen to myself instead of believing God. This has robbed me of God's best. My fear was that I would fail, and God would not come through for me. I was afraid to believe.

As I confess my failures, I praise Him for His mercy and how patient He has been with me. Thankfully, He is still working in my life. I want to deny myself and obey. My desire is to trust and be blessed by His rule over me, but I still have many fears. In Matthew 16, Jesus tells us that we must deny ourselves, take up our cross, and follow Him. Paul tells us in Galatians 2:20:

"I have been crucified with Christ and I no longer live, but Christ lives in me. The life I now live in the body, I live by faith in the Son of God, who loved me and gave himself for me."

The cross we pick up daily is His cross, which provides forgiveness for what we have done and deliverance from what we were.

Let this truth encourage you as it encourages me. When we pick up His cross daily, we are taking on what His cross provides. We are given forgiveness for our failures, our sins, and our unbelief. His cross provides for us deliverance from our old nature.

Oh, the mercy of our Lord. To pick up my cross daily means I am acknowledging every day that I belong to Him; this is my ultimate security and yours. By faith, we can begin to trust Him with every area of our lives. We can walk knowing we aren't responsible for ruling but for following. Oh, Lord, rule over us, I pray.

Ponders of the Heart

Do you allow God to rule over every area of your life?

What areas are you not letting God have control of?

Read Psalm 118:1-9.

Lay down striving and pick up His cross of forgiveness and deliverance. How thankful I am for His mercy.

Prayers of the Heart

Dear Lord,

We can be afraid of many things. Protect us. We often fail to listen to You because of our fears. Be our courage. You promise never to let go of us. Help us hold on to You.

Father, we thank You and praise You for the cross. Help us acknowledge every day we are Yours. Lord, Your mercy does endure forever. In Jesus' name, amen.

December 13 ~ Following Jesus

"To this you were called, because Christ suffered for you, leaving you an example, that you should follow in his steps" (1 Peter 2:21).

Have you ever tried following someone's footprints in the sand or the snow? I can remember playing this game as a child. It was fun to leap from one footprint to the next, trying not to fall flat on my face.

As short as I am as an adult, you can imagine how short my legs were as a child. Following an adult's footprint in the sand was fun, but I usually fell after two or three steps. The stride of their feet was too much for me.

1 Peter 2:21, taken out of context, can make me believe that I am capable of following Jesus' footprints. Verse 22 describes how He walked in His life.

"He committed no sin, and no deceit was found in his mouth" (1 Peter 2:22).

Now, wait a minute. I might as well give up now because I know I will fall short of these steps. Could it be that this verse, like the passage in Matthew 16:24-26, is talking about submission to His leadership, not our managing ourselves with self-effort? We cannot be like Jesus, but we can submit to Him and let Jesus be in us and live through us. We were never designed to function independently of God. Only when we are dependent on Him can we follow in His steps.

Let me illustrate this way. Let's suppose my dad made the footprints in the sand that I was trying to follow. He wanted me to be successful, and he was tired of seeing me eat dirt. So, in his love for me and his desire for me to achieve success, he took my hands, and as I jumped from one footprint to the next, he was there to carry me safely in the air as I reached for the next step.

With his strong arms lifting me up and flying me through the air, I would make it every time. His stride between the footprints was perfect for him, and I was able to reach the unreachable goal.

Isn't this what Jesus did for us? The unreachable goal was sinlessness and sonship. This step was beyond my stride and yours. The next step was to take our sins on His own body by way of the cross, suffering death for our sins. This is one I am thankful I didn't have to take. How about you?

Then, He made provision so we could live not in sin but in righteousness. This we do by faith. We can leap forward, reaching the goal because our Abba Father is carrying us from one footprint to the next. Our success is not in our efforts but in His. We make it because He is carrying us from step to step.

So, if we recap the last few days of devotionals, it all begins and ends with faith. In faith, I deny myself, leaning on His rule over mine. Next, in faith, I take up His cross daily by acknowledging that because of the cross, I have forgiveness of sin and deliverance from who I was. Finally, I follow Him, believing that He is carrying me from faith to faith by His Spirit to live in His righteousness and not in my sin.

Truly, His Word purifies our souls: By His stripes, we are healed.

Ponders of the Heart

Are you still living in a shameful identity?

Are you trying to live the Christian life by your own effort?

If you are, how are you doing with that?

Read Matthew 16:24-27 and I Peter 2:21-25.

Now let Him take your small hand in His and leap to the next step He has for you. And be free from the bondage of your own efforts without Jesus.

Prayers of the Heart

Dear Father,

We submit to Your authority and Your control. Take us step by step so our lives will bring You glory, and our lives will be free. We cannot follow You unless You are helping us. You are our righteousness and strength. Lord, we praise You. In Jesus' name, amen.

December 14 ~ Feeding on God's Faithfulness

"Trust in the Lord and do good; dwell in the land and enjoy safe pasture" (Psalm 37:3).

Psalm 37 offers us great instructions from the Lord on how to live. In verse three, we are told to trust in the Lord and feed on God's faithfulness. What exactly does feed on the Lord's faithfulness mean to you?

In my physical life, my body gets hungry, and when this happens, I need to eat. But sometimes, I get lazy, and I will settle for chips or crackers instead of taking the time to eat healthy food. When I do, my body suffers. I started seeing extra pounds creeping on my body, as well as a lack of muscle tone and energy.

Healthy food is necessary for healthy, strong bodies. Our spiritual life, which is far more important, needs feeding. What are you feeding yourself today, spiritually speaking?

In my reading today, God challenged me to feed on His faithfulness. How can I do this? As I thought through that, I began to remember the many times God has been faithful to me. I began to think about the beautiful sunrises and sunsets I have seen and the many springs, summers, falls, and winters I have experienced in my lifetime. That was just my appetizer as I reflected on God's faithfulness.

As I sit at my desk, the sun is coming through the window, and after five days of rain, my soul is feasting on its brightness. Do I stop to reflect that the sun is just a reminder of God's faithfulness? Just last night, my youngest daughter, Julie, asked me if I knew of anyone building an ark. I replied, "No, and there is no need because God has promised He would not flood the earth again. " We can trust His promises and feed on this truth.

Christmas is around the corner, and Christ is certainly the main course of God's faithfulness. God promised Satan that Eve's Seed would bruise his head. He promised Abraham that his Seed would bless the entire world, and through our Lord and Savior, Jesus Christ, we see God's faithfulness. We can linger over God's truth through Christ and never gain a pound of physical weight but be heavy in faith.

I wish this were true about the cinnamon roll I just ate.

Ponders of the Heart

How have you been taking care of your physical body?

How are you doing in taking care of your spiritual body?

What are the promises you hold tightly to?

Read Psalm 37: 1-11 and I Peter 2:1-3.

He has set a feast before you in His Word.

Prayers of the Heart

Dear Father,

We want to praise You for Your goodness. Let us see and realize Your wonder. Father, we don't want to miss You. We want to see You in our lives. See You when circumstances are good and praise You. We want to see You when circumstances are hard and praise You. Lord, open our eyes to Your presence. In Jesus' name, amen.

December 15 ~ Maturity of Soul

"Because Joseph her husband was faithful to the law, and yet[a] did not want to expose her to public disgrace, he had in mind to divorce her quietly" (Matthew 1:19).

Ego is an interesting word. Part of the definition is self-love. Oh, I understand that attitude, and you might too. Ego can drive us right over the rights of others. Isn't it refreshing when you see someone who is more concerned about the other guy than himself?

It is true ego can drive us over the rights of others, but how often do you see someone give up the right to be right?

Joseph might think he had just cause to stand in judgment of Mary. All outward appearances looked as if Mary had been unfaithful to him. He decided in his heart to take the high road. I can't help but think about the fiancé in the movie The Runaway Bride; he must have been so embarrassed, so hurt over the whole incident, but somehow, he decided to stand by her. Most people thought He was crazy.

Joseph was a righteous man, the Bible says, and it was because of his righteousness he had in mind to divorce Mary quietly. Now, isn't that interesting?

Some would argue that a righteous man would stand in the middle of the temple and shout accusations and judgment against this unfaithful traitor. Jewish law was not easy on such conduct, and after all, doesn't a man need to save face? Apparently, God, who is the One who judges, prefers grace and calls Joseph righteous for having a merciful heart for Mary.

Our flesh wants to prove a point, but the spirit wants to yield to a higher standard. We often think about the people we love and ourselves. My mom was famous for making me look at the big picture. I didn't want to understand the other person. I just wanted to strike out at anyone who hurt me. This is the old way, but God's way is different. Reacting in mercy and kindness, forgiveness, and gentleness takes spiritual maturity.

Amen, to the one who takes the high road, the one who is not ruled by ego. The wrath of God fell on the shoulders of my Savior for me, and when I think of that, I can let go of my hurt into God's faithful Hands. Because of Jesus I bear my sin no more. Why should I think it would be helpful to publicly disgrace another? Joseph, a righteous man, thought, no. He thought of Mary over his own ego.

Ponders of the Heart

Who do you know that has an overbearing ego?

How do you react when someone hurts you? With anger, revenge, or patience?

Read 2 Corinthians 1:3-7 and Philippians 2:1-11.

Prayers of the Heart

Dear Father,

There are things in our lives that if the world were shown, we would die of embarrassment. But because of Your grace, You have taken our sins and failures, and we carry them no more. Father, we praise You and thank You. Help us to remember this so we will not be driven by our ego. Fill our hearts with thanksgiving and mercy. Thank You, Holy Father. In Jesus' name, amen.

December 16 ~ Crisis of faith

"Joseph son of David, do not be afraid to take Mary home as your wife, because what is conceived in her is from the Holy Spirit" (Matthew 1:20.)

"Did I just hear right? My parents, our friends, and the priest will not believe me. I don't believe me." Could this be the thoughts Joseph had when he woke from his dream?

I have had dreams that seemed so real, but when I woke up, I dismissed them as just a dream. He could blame it on the meal he had the night before or what he wanted to be real because he loved and cared for Mary. Joseph found himself in a crisis of faith.

What would you say if your son told you his fiancée was pregnant by the Holy Spirit? What would your son's fiancée's parents say? Remember, Joseph and Mary were real people who lived in real families. They had peer pressure just like you and me and walking by faith and not by sight can create a crisis.

Does this fact encourage you? It does me. It encourages me because it helps me remember that faith is not seeing everything laid out before me. Hebrews 11: 1 says it best:

"Now faith is confidence in what we hope for and assurance about what we do not see."

Could it be that Joseph was a man who knew what the prophet Isaiah had written about the coming Messiah?

"Therefore the Lord himself will give you a sign: The virgin will conceive and give birth to a son, and will call him Immanuel" (Isaiah 7:14).

There is enough evidence to believe God's Word, but Joseph had the choice to reason away the wonder of God. How many times have I done just that? How about you? We might know the Bible and what it says, but does it have influence in what we think, say, and do? Knowing the Word of God for the sake of knowledge will never transform our actions. It will not change us unless His Word is our belief system.

Joseph was a man who used the Word of God and the meeting with the angel in his dream to overcome his crisis of faith. He would still endure those who thought he was wrong, but he was going to trust God. He believed, and his faith led him to an encounter with the power, love, and grace of God in the face of Jesus.

Ponders of the Heart

Have you ever walked through a crisis of faith?

How did you get through, and what was the outcome?

Read Matthew 1:18-25.

Ask the Lord to give you the faith to believe His Words beyond human reason.

Prayers of the Heart

Dear Father,

The heavens speak of Your wonder and Your glory. Why do we have such a tough time believing You are a God of wonders? Father, You work with power and out of Your love for us. Circumcise our hearts so we will love You and believe You. Help us win the crisis of faith and bring You glory. In Jesus' name, amen.

December 17 ~ Yesterday, Today and Tomorrow

Each of our lives is filled with memories, some good and some not so good, but nevertheless, we all have memories stored in our minds and hearts.

One way we capture memories is with photos. Our house is full of family pictures. I have pictures of my three children as babies and now as grown-up children with kids of their own.

Have you ever looked at an old picture and found yourself feeling the emotion you felt that day? I have cried, laughed, or just found my heart full of love as I look at the faces in pictures. Music can also bring back strong emotions as well as movies. I still cannot watch the movie *Titanic*. It brings back the emotions of my dad's death.

Bill and I have notes we wrote to one another when we were in high school. Those can really bring back some good but somewhat embarrassing memories.

Memories are wonderful, but we cannot live in the past. We can learn from events and happenings in our past; we can even treasure them, but we still need a purpose, a desire, and a hope for tomorrow. Looking forward to a trip, a wedding, or a birth—these are the things that will get you up in the morning or wake you up in the middle of the night, with you thinking, planning, and sometimes worrying about the details.

Our family just experienced the wedding of our oldest grandchild, Collier. We have so many memories of the wedding, and soon, my walls will be full of pictures to keep this memory alive. But life does not stop even with a wonderful memory like this.

We are now planning a cruise to Alaska, which has been on my bucket list for a long time. The trip is a year away, but before you know it, it will become a memory. This is life on planet Earth.

What about today? We can get lost in the past or anxious about the future and miss today. What are we to be about at this moment?

My purpose right now is to finish this devotional, and hopefully, you are enjoying it. But what else does God have planned?

Jesus is important in our past, present, and future. In fact, He is not only important; He is absolutely the most important person in history and in our lives. If we miss Jesus in our past, ignore Him in our present, and miss Him in our future, we have missed the essence of life.

Christ's followers and even those who don't know Jesus celebrate Christmas and Easter, but those celebrations have special meaning to those who know the Lord. We read, sing, and watch shows like The Chosen to remember who He was and what He has done.

We ponder how He came to earth as a baby, was born of a virgin, and lived a perfect life—a life only He could live. The cross reminds us of the price He paid for our souls. He died and conquered death so we might have eternal life in Him. The gift of salvation is ours by grace through faith. We then become children of God through Him.

Jesus' yesterday is our reality, so we can live today and have the promise of life tomorrow. We have the promise of heaven because of Jesus' past life on earth.

Our hope is planted in His finished work and our future with God is kept for us by Christ in heaven.

Most Christians have a good understanding of Jesus' life here on earth and a hope to be with Him in the future, but how does this relate to our daily lives? What is our focus on as we live today?

The Bible tells us that Christ came to set us free, give us abundant life, and give us His peace. But He also tells us to go and make disciples in His name. I don't want to miss out on the abundant life by missing the plans He has for me today.

As we remember what Jesus did for us on the cross and what our future holds because of His sacrifice, let us fill our days with purpose for His Kingdom and glory.

I am reminded that eternal life must take priority over temporal life. Help us, dear Lord!

Ponders of the Heart

What is one memory that makes you smile every time you think about it?

Do you know God holds your future?

What is God's plan for you today?

Read Jeremiah 29:11, Philippians 3:14, and Colossians 3: 1-4.

Prayers of the Heart

Dear Father,

Thank you for all You have done for us in the past and the hope we all have for a future in heaven. You have given us life, eternal life. Thank You, but we do not want to miss what You have for us today.

Help us hear Your voice and give us wisdom, strength, courage, and faith to follow. Your love is what we want. You are our life, and we love You. In Jesus' name, amen.

December 18 ~ Relief in Flight

"So Joseph also went up from the town of Nazareth in Galilee to Judea, to Bethlehem the town of David, because he belonged to the house and line of David. He went there to register with Mary, who was pledged to be married to him and was expecting a child" (Luke 2:4-5).

Was the trip hard? You bet! Was it costly and inconvenient? Absolutely! Was Mary relieved? I wonder?

Mary was about to give birth, but I do wonder if, for Mary, the trip was worth all the trouble just to be away from the stares and the gossip in Nazareth. What about Joseph; was he thankful for a reason to flee from the small-town busybodies to an area where no one knew who they were?

Then again, how many of Joseph's relatives had to travel the same road? There is no mention of others in the Bible. Were there others, but no support, no contact with the couple? Did Mary and Joseph know that right around the corner were Uncle Jacob and Aunt Esther, but they were not welcome to join them? What hurt and misunderstanding did this chosen couple have to endure?

Fleeting busybodies can bring relief but only hope and faith in God can bring peace and forgiveness. We can try to run from our feelings, but just like the disarray in my closet, it is still there.

I'm sure Mary and Joseph had times when the false judgment of others pierced their souls. As they traveled to Bethlehem and night came, Joseph and Mary must have been at the end of their rope. After the couple found a place to rest their heads, I wondered about their quiet whispers. Did they have hope and joy? Was Joseph an encourager? Was he one of those rare men who were able to speak words of hope into the soul of young Mary?

I like to see Mary and Joseph in their humanity and enter their story. Thinking about their trials and their troubles. It helps me look at my own story with hope. God is our hope. He is with us, and He has the perfect plan.

God's Word tells us the facts of what happened, but living through the emotions Mary and Joseph felt is not. They were not God, and they had limited vision, just like us. We go through trials, and Christians are often misunderstood. If we live our faith, people in this fallen world will think we are strange.

We can take comfort in the fact that Mary and Joseph made it, and so will we, not because of our faith or wisdom but because the One who chose us to stand is holding us up with His Mighty Right Hand. He has a plan, and He will see us through.

Ponders of the Heart

Are there people you know that think you are strange because of your faith?

Do you struggle with this world we live in and the mindset of some people?

Read Philippians 4:5-7 and Romans 9:33.

Find your hope in God.

Prayers of the Heart

Dear Father,

Thank you for giving us hope when others give us shame and grief because they do not understand us. Father, You give us peace when we turn to You and not the world for purpose. Help us keep our souls resting in Your love and in Your strength. You are our eternal hope, and our victory is in You. In Jesus' name, amen.

December 19 ~ Accepting No from God

"And he said, 'While the child was alive, I fasted and wept; for I said, 'Who can tell whether the Lord will be gracious to me, that the child may live? 'But now he is dead; why should I fast? Can I bring him back again? I shall go to him, but he shall not return to me" (2 Samuel 12:22-23 NKJV).

I am in the middle of trying to accept a no from God. Not just one, but several. I'm not sure the answer to this will always be no, but for now, this seems to be the answer. I am not the only person I know in this situation. God can answer our prayers but sometimes chooses to say "No."

In the song "Unanswered Prayers," Garth Brooks sings a lyric says he sometimes thanks God for unanswered prayers. I'm trying to believe that one day, I will thank God that He said no to my prayer, but I must admit my heart wants a different answer.

I do want His best for me and my family, and if no is what is best then I want to accept His answer over mine. God can see my tomorrows and protect me from big mistakes. He knows how to use my disappointments to grow me into the child He wants me to become.

David, a man after God's own heart, knew how to accept God's will over his own. How could the death of David's son be God's will? Why was this necessary in his life? I don't know. David didn't know, but he accepted it. David asked for his son to be spared. He asked, fasted, and he asked some more, but when the death angel came and took his son he rose up and worshipped. He knew the secret of accepting God's will and trusting in His eternal purposes.

The faith David had that he would see his son again comforted him. He knew he would face death and when he did, he would be reunited with his son. I'm sure he felt the pain of losing a child. Probably a loss he never got over, but his loss was lined with the silver lining of hope.

"So David arose from the ground, washed and anointed himself, and changed his clothes; and he went into the house of the Lord and worshiped" (2 Samuel 12:20 NKJV).

"Then David comforted Bathsheba his wife, and went in to her and lay with her. So she bore a son, and he called his name Solomon" (2 Samuel 12:24 NKJV).

By accepting, David was able to worship and give comfort to his wife. And the Lord gave them a son to comfort them. God's no, always have a yes attached. I am trying to remember that today and hold on to it. If you are in the middle of trying to accept a no from God, remember the story of David and keep your eyes toward heaven so you can receive His yes.

Ponders of the Heart:

Has God ever said no to one of your prayers?

How did you react to His no?

Did you experience a better Yes? If not hold on with faith for His yes.

Read 2 Samuel 12:13-25.

Prayers of the Heart

Dear Lord,

You know the plans you have for us, plans to give us hope and a future. Lord, help us to keep praying and keep asking, but when it is not Your will, we thank You for Your no. We want to live under Your plan and Your protection. You are the Sovereign Lord and only You know the right answer to our prayers. Father, lead our minds and our hearts for Your glory. In Jesus' name, amen.

December 20 ~ Dreaming of a White Christmas

"'Come now, and let us reason together,' Says the Lord, 'Though your sins are like scarlet, They shall be as white as snow; Though they are red like crimson, They shall be as wool'" (Isaiah 1:18 NKJV).

Dreaming of a white Christmas in Alabama is just that, dreaming. It has been a while since I have seen a white Christmas.

I could count on one hand the number of times I have seen one, but oh, how I can dream. The winter ground is so revealing, so stark and snow covers it all. I love to look out of the window and see everything covered in snow, the grass, the sidewalk, the road and all the ditches. It is such a beautiful sight.

Picture with me the reddest red bird you have ever seen perched on a tree branch covered with snow. Ah, what beauty. Picture the junkyard so deep in snow that not one broken-down, wrecked car can be seen. This is one way to cover up piles of junk. Snow has a way of covering up the ugliest terrain with a look of purity.

Is it no wonder that in our hearts Christmas is the perfect time for snow, Christmas which signifies to us a perfect baby boy born, who would become our Savior. A baby that would cover our lives with His purity. Our crimson-red sin, covered by the purity of His blood and making our souls as white as snow.

The hope of Christmas is more than dreaming of snow, it is God's promise of redemption from the stain of sin. The promise of new life and new hope with the purity of Jesus living within us. The physical beauty of snow is just a foreshadow of the hope that lives in the hearts of God's children. As Christmas approaches, I will continue to dream of a white Christmas and if it just so happens, I get one, I will remember the purity that is mine and yours because of Jesus who makes our sins as white as snow. Oh, how I praise Him.

Ponders of the Heart

Have you ever had a white Christmas?

What are the sins Jesus has made white as snow? If you say all of them, you are right!

Read Psalm 51:7-13

Take time to praise the Lord for what He has done for you in your life.

Prayers of the Heart

Dear Father,

Though sins were like crimson, You have made them white as snow. Though our hearts were filled with the stain of sin, You have cleaned it with the purity of Your Son. We thank You for the pure, white snow from heaven that came to us in Jesus. We pray, Father, that Your purity will fall into the hearts of us this Christmas and You will be praised. In Jesus' name, amen.

December 21 ~ Is God in or Christmas?

"The fool has said in his heart, 'There is no God" (Psalm 53:1).

How many people, even children of God, are celebrating this Christmas as a fool? How foolish are the fools of this world? I remind myself of this truth as the clock is ticking toward Christmas day. Will my heart be full of Jesus or full of foolhardiness?

My trunk is full of presents and many packages lie under our tree. The fridge is packed with food and all my favorite recipes I have searched out, so I'll be ready to create, what I hope to be, our best Christmas meal. The housecleaning has begun, the decorations are in place and the promise of family coming is right around the corner. We have a full schedule of joy, and wonder for the children, both the big and small ones. The anticipation of Christmas day in our hearts.

The joy of giving and the joy of receiving are just days away, but have we forgotten the reason for it all?

What a wonderful gift God has given and what a joy it is to receive the gift of all gifts, our Lord and Savior, Jesus. Oh, the wise parent and grandparent who is able to take the real wonder of Christmas and give it as a gift to the next generation.

The problem is not how we celebrate Christmas but our failure to use how we celebrate as a bridge to help others see the gift God has given to us by the birth of His Son. Many hearts are open to Jesus during this special season. Some hearts are open because of childlike wonder, and other hearts are open because they are broken. Both need Jesus.

There are people in our sphere of influence whose eyes have been blinded by the god of this age. During this season, let our prayer be that God would shine light into their hearts so they might see His glory in the face of Jesus. Let us also pray that His light will not be dim in us, but will radiate so brightly the world will see His love.

Ponders of the Heart

Will your Christmas be full of Jesus or full of foolishness?

How can we use our celebration of Christmas to open our eyes to the real wonder of the season?

Read 2 Corinthians 3: 5-6

Praise God for pouring His love into our hearts.

Prayers of the Heart

Dear Father,

How foolish we are at times. Our desire is to have hearts that are full of Jesus. We want to celebrate Christmas with such wonder and joy. We want to be wise and use our celebration as a praise to You and do it in such a way that Your love and light shine into the hearts of others. Do not let the riches of this world blind us to the richness that is found only in You. Father, we love You, for Your love is beyond measure. In Jesus' name, amen.

December 22 ~ Jehovah-Jireh, The Lord will Provide

"So Abraham called that place The Lord Will Provide. And to this day it is said, 'On the mountain of the Lord it will be provided'" (Genesis 22:14).

My husband received a notice from the IRS saying he was to appear in tax court. The IRS was taking him to court over an issue we thought had been resolved. It was taxes on the sale of real estate property on which they were showing a profit, and we were showing a loss. The proper documents had been sent showing our loss, but they wanted Bill to appear in court.

The day he was to appear, he wasn't sure he was going. That morning, I received a call from an IRS attorney explaining the absolute necessity for him to be there. If he did not show up the taxes would be levied against us.

When my husband walked into court, he could not believe what he had walked into. He was appearing before our government with no attorney, and he thought jail was his next stop. The most amazing thing happened.

A man walked up to my husband and asked him if he was Mr. Collier. Bill told him he was, and this man introduced himself as the IRS attorney. Bill showed him his documentation, and the attorney said he thought this was a mistake, and that was the reason he called our home that morning. He then told him not to worry; he would help him.

When court began, Bill said he couldn't believe the way the judge was treating people. He was sure things would not go well for him. When his name was called, he was petrified, but thanks be to God, the attorney was true to his word, and he proceeded to defend Bill. The case was dropped.

He couldn't believe it, and when he told me, I couldn't believe it either. The very power that was taking us to court was the very authority that defended us. The only thing Bill could say was God had shown him mercy and provided help. It was one of the experiences in our lives that we will never forget, especially my husband. God provided. We still don't know why or how, but we are very, very thankful.

Our Lord's grace is amazing, and never before and never again was His grace more amazing than when He sent His Son to earth to be our Savior. God, for the most part, slipped into our world in a quiet fashion. He came as a baby through the body of a young virgin. There was no grand entrance, but His entrance was significant, and the provision was complete.

The very One who had condemned us because of our sin is the very One who came to save us. The One we condemned and crucified is the very One who sits in heaven, interceding on our behalf.

Grace, God's grace is amazing, and He is Jehovah-Jireh, our provider. How humble my heart feels as I think about His provision of Jesus. Sometimes I question myself and wonder how I came to know my Lord, only to quickly realize it was the provision of God's grace. There are so many blessings that have come to us only by His grace. God is Our provider. Oh, how I praise Him.

Ponders of the Heart

How has God come to your aid in a difficult circumstance?

How are you preparing your heart this Christmas for the gift of Jesus?

Read Genesis 22:1-14.

God provides for his children through our Lord, Jesus.

Prayers of the Heart

Dear Father,

Thank You for the evidence in our lives of Your love and provision. You provide for us a way home through Your Son, Jesus. How can we say thank You for such a gift of Your grace? How, Lord? We bow before You in praise and thanksgiving. May our praise bring You glory, and our lives reflect our gratefulness. In Jesus' name, amen.

December 23 ~ Christmas Puppy

My youngest child, Julie, wanted a puppy for Christmas. At the time, our lives were too busy to have a puppy. I had a full-time job and three children to care for, and my husband, Bill, was not crazy about having a dog again, much less a puppy. So, in the wisdom of good parenting, we decided not to get Julie a puppy.

Christmas Eve is when Bill kicks into gear to do his shopping. He goes into panic mode, asking me what I have gotten the kids and if it is enough. I am a planner, and by Christmas Eve, I am not interested in shopping. I am done!

This Christmas, however, we both folded and decided to find a puppy for Julie. Tracie, my middle child, and Chris, my oldest, along with Bill, headed to a town near us to find a puppy. What they discovered was we had waited too late. There were no puppies to be found. Poor Julie, she was going to be disappointed. Christmas was ruined.

That evening, we continued our Christmas Eve tradition. I made lasagna, and it baked while we attended the Christmas Eve service at our church. After the service, our plan was to unwrap our new Christmas pajamas, hurry to put them on and enjoy our Christmas Eve dinner, all comfy and ready for Christmas morning. Returning home we had a surprise as we turned into our driveway.

There in the driveway was a bundle of white fur. A little puppy. The kids were overjoyed, especially Julie. Bill looked at me, and I looked at him. We had a Christmas miracle. Everyone played and enjoyed the puppy that night; he was such a cutie. He was not house-trained, which was not fun for me, but you cannot complain when a miracle comes your way.

The following morning, Christmas was a hit. Everyone was happy with Santa, and the puppy loved romping through the wrapping paper and the boxes.

That afternoon, there was a knock at the door, and there stood a young man who had the weight of the world on his shoulders. He looked up at me with the saddest, defeated look on his face. He said," Have you seen a white furry puppy?"

I wish I could describe the transformation that took place when I told him the puppy was here. I do not remember seeing a face change so quickly. He was beaming at my news. Immediately, my thoughts went to Julie, and I wondered if she would be devastated. But I could not get over the joy on this young man's face.

I invited him in and gave him our Christmas puppy. Julie took it well, and we still had a wonderful story about our Christmas miracle.

This makes me think about the transformations I have seen when an unbelieving person comes to faith. Defeated eyes become shining reflections of the Spirit and those who once had no hope are filled with joy. There is nothing like it. The gift of giving the puppy back was gratifying, but to be a part of giving Jesus to someone is life-changing.

"For God, who said, 'Let light shine out of darkness,' made his light shine in our hearts to give us the light of the knowledge of the glory of God in the face of Christ" (2 Corinthians 4:6).

When I think of what we have in our hearts to give and the change this gift can bring, I wonder what holds us back at times from sharing the wonderful gift of Christ with others.

Ponders of the Heart

Who do you know that has been transformed by the gospel?

Has God placed a person on your heart who needs to come out of darkness into his light?

Read 2 Corinthians 5:14-18.

Prayers of the Heart

Dear Father,

Help us see the darkness in the eyes of others and help us speak light into their souls. Lord, life is hard, but there is hope and joy with You. Father, God, we need you. In Jesus' name, amen.

December 24 ~ Groaning with Hope

"We know that the whole creation has been groaning as in the pains of childbirth right up to the present time" (Romans 8:22).

As a mother, I can relate to the groaning and pains of childbirth. I remember my groaning, but I was not without hope. The first time it was scary, and I wasn't sure of what to expect. I didn't enjoy the pain, but the joy of motherhood was worth it.

With my second child, the birth pains were there, but my hope was stronger, and the third time, the labor was longer; the pain was stronger but not as strong as my hope. The hope of a newborn baby conceived out of love. This is how I made it through the long 24 hours of childbirth. If you have had a baby, you can relate.

Mary, the mother of Jesus, can also relate. We are not told of her pain in childbirth, but we are told of her persevering hope and joy.

"But Mary treasured up all these things and pondered them in her heart" (Luke 2:19).

Mary relived, pondered, and treasured the birth of her Son, just like we do after the pain of childbirth has subsided. I can just imagine her looking into the face of her baby and being awestruck with wonder and joy. Is there anything more precious than a baby fast asleep as you look into their sweet little faces? Mary, the mother of Jesus, held him, and He held her heart.

Life is painful. You know it is true. We groan for relief, but we who are in Christ groan with hope. The god of this age is after us, wanting us to live in the lie that he has won the battles over us. But we live in the assurance of hope that we are victorious in life because of Jesus.

I thank God for the Spirit within us, who testifies with our spirits that a better day is coming. We are not slaves to fear or slaves to sin; we are children of God, and He has won the war for us.

All of this reminds me to keep my eyes on Jesus, my heart turned toward my heavenly home, and my confidence in His victory for me.

It also reminds me that laboring in hope brings about new life in the Spirit. Labor on children of the King.

Ponders of the Heart

What battle are you fighting today in your life?

What do you do to keep hope for a better day alive?

Read 2 Corinthians 4:7-12.

Don't give up, persevere with hope in our Lord.

Prayers of the Heart

Dear Lord,

Life is hard and painful at times. Help us remember we have hope, reminding us that we are not alone. You use even our pain for our benefit. Help us keep our eyes on You and our hearts open to Your Spirit. Father, You are our help, hope, and glory. We praise You, Lord. In Jesus' name, amen

December 25 ~ Expecting God to Speak

"But when the fullness of time had come, God sent forth His Son, born of a woman, born under the law, to redeem those who were under the law, that we might receive the adoption as sons" (Galatians 4:4-5 NKJV).

Expecting is a word we use to say that a woman is going to have a baby. As I write this devotion, my middle child, my eldest daughter, is expecting her second child and our third grandchild. She is expecting, and so are we.

I type these words with a smile on my face. Being a grandmother is a wonderful thing, and the anticipation I feel as I think about this new baby coming has me smiling from ear to ear.

At just the right time, our new addition will arrive, and if the Lord is willing, my husband, Bill, and I will be right there. We will be excited and nervous at the same time. What seems to be a long way away will be here before we know it.

My daughter, Tracie, will suffer the most with this pregnancy, or maybe it will be Ryan, her husband. Heaven knows Tracie's hormones are doing jumping jacks in her system. At any rate, the waiting is hard for all of us, but especially for Tracie.

The bad news, which I will not remind her of, is that it will get harder before it gets better. Those last days before giving birth and the next few days after giving birth are grueling.

As we celebrate Christmas today, we can think about the first Christmas celebration. Mary's time had come, and the Bible tells us that it was in the fullness of time. I am sure Mary would tell us that she felt the full impact of this timing.

The Bible says that God sent forth His Son, born of a woman. We know this woman was Mary. God sent His Son, and Mary gave birth to Jesus. He was born under the law, under the curse of sin, to redeem us from this curse. He was God's message of love to the world.

How many people heard God speak that morning? The shepherds did, Mary and Joseph did, and who else? I wonder? Today, when we celebrate the birth of our Savior, I hope we have ears to hear Him speak to us today, and we are reminded of the message of love that came to us on that first Christmas day.

Get alone, get quiet, and listen. You might hear the sound of a baby born long ago. A cry that tells the world of God's love and His sacrifice so we might become children of God. Oh, praise the name of Jesus!

Ponders of the Heart

During this Christmas season, have you taken the time to reflect on the wonder of God's love?

Have you voiced the wonder of Christmas to someone today?

Read John 1:1-14

Prayers of the Heart

Dear Father,

We bow before You on this day of celebration to worship You. You came to us to make us Your own. Give us ears to hear You, eyes to see You and a heart to worship and love You. Oh, Lord, You have already done that. You have given us Your Spirit; may we live by the power of Your life in us this day and worship You with all the fruit of Your presence! We praise You, our Lord. In Jesus 'name, amen.

December 26 ~ The Wind of Change

"Now the Lord is the Spirit, and where the Spirit of the Lord is, there is freedom. And we all, who with unveiled faces contemplate the Lord's glory, are being transformed into his image with ever-increasing glory, which comes from the Lord, who is the Spirit" (2 Corinthians 3:17-18).

Visiting a friend and looking at old pictures. I saw a picture of a beautiful young woman and asked my friend, "Who is that? " She smiled and said, "It is me." I could see the resemblance. What threw me was the color of her hair. She had always been a sandy, dark blond since I had known her, and this young woman had dark hair. I was shocked at the change.

I am reminded of the time I was shocked when I looked into the mirror after dying my hair. I tried a new brand of color in a lighter shade. When I washed it out, my hair was almost black. I called Bill and asked him if he ever wanted to be married to a dark-headed woman. He said he wanted to be married to me, and if I had dark hair, light, or bald, he'd take me anyway I came.

I thought that was a good answer, but I was waiting to see how true that was when he got home. He was a little surprised, but he handled it well. I was thankful he didn't pack his clothes and move out.

I hid out for a few days and washed my hair a lot, waiting for my hair appointment at the end of the week. During the wait, I told Chris, my son, about my mistake. He said, "Mom, your hair was dark, and over the years, you have changed it. I like it dark."

My mom said the same thing. So, I took out some old pictures, and sure enough, I had dark brown hair in my early years. I was the one who had made the change, and now the dark color looked odd.

Years have a way of other physical changes. I'm not crazy about my wrinkles, flab, or fading eyesight, but I hope my inner soul has changed over the years for the better.

If you knew me when I was 20 or 21, I wonder what changes you would see in me? Has there been a progression of grace and love, wisdom, and knowledge in my soul? Is there more light in my life and less darkness? Am I cooperating with His work and His call?

I know I have failed and fallen many times, but this doesn't mean I haven't grown. In fact, I tend to grow more in my failures than in my successes. How about You? God gives us promises in His word:

"For those God foreknew he also predestined to be conformed to the image of his Son, that he might be the firstborn among many brothers and sister" (Romans 8:29).

"You are of God, little children, and have overcome them, because He who is in you is greater than he who is in the world" (1 John 4:4 NKJV).

"Now may the God of peace Himself sanctify you completely; and may your whole spirit, soul, and body be preserved blameless at the coming of our Lord Jesus Christ. He who calls you is faithful, who also will do it" (1 Thessalonians 5:23-24 NKJV).

"Being confident of this very thing, that He who has begun a good work in you will complete it until the day of Jesus Christ" (Philippians 1:6 NKJV).

Ponders of the Heart

Who do you know whose life has been transformed by God's grace?

Do you pray and ask God for transformation?

Read Psalm 139: 1-24.

Prayers of the Heart

Dear Father,

You are the source and the power of our salvation and righteousness. We praise You. Lord, You have promised to change us from glory to glory. Only Your power can change a life, and You, precious Lord, are willing. We come offering our lives to You, for we want to live as Your children. In Jesus' name, amen.

December 27 ~ While We are Apart

"In My Father's house are many mansions; if it were not so, I would have told you. I go to prepare a place for you" (John 14:2 NKJV).

What season of life are you experiencing? Do you have a house full of children, a husband to care for, and a full-time job? Maybe you have raised your children, but they have come home for a while, and things are hectic. Or, like me, you are home alone most of the time. Every season has its challenges.

After all our children grew up and moved away, I wished to one day have all my family living in the same town and having Sunday dinner together each week.

For the most part, this has happened. All my children live in the same area, and every Sunday, we have Sunday dinner at my house. But two of my granddaughters live in Georgia with their mother, and my oldest grandson just got married and is living in Auburn, Alabama, with his bride. They are there while he finishes college.

Our family is close. In fact, we have two businesses, and my three children and daughter-in-law work with us. But we don't see or talk to each other every day. When I don't see them, I miss them and want to see their faces and hear their voices. The same is true for our grandchildren.

On Sundays, when the door opens, I get ready to see who is coming through. It is usually Elizabeth, our youngest. She comes bouncing in with a smile that lights up the room. Next, her brother, Clayton, comes around the corner. "Hey, Gi," he says and gives me a hug. The others are not that predictable, but each one is greeted with a hug and a welcome home smile.

When they are not around, the house is quiet and can feel empty even though there are pictures of their faces all around the house.

The grandchildren like to leave little reminders like socks and shoes they have left, or half-drunk water bottles. Occasionally, they leave other things like wet towels and wet bathing suits in the laundry room from the pool. They know I hate messes, and this is not a beach house, but my guess is they don't want me to forget them when they leave.

What about God's house? Does He have a hall of pictures kept in heaven so He can look at us? Is a new picture hung on the wall each time a new child is added to His family? Does He look forward to us stopping and talking with Him?

We don't live in the same town. His home is heaven, and so is ours, but for now, we are ambassadors for Him on this foreign soil. He is always available for us but does He long for us to come home as I long for my children and grandchildren to come visit me.

Hearing them over the phone is not the same as giving them a hug. My eyes want to see their expressions as we talk and visit, not just a picture on the wall. I wonder if our God is looking forward to the time when He will hug us and show us around, watching the wonder on our faces as we enter our heavenly home.

"Precious in the sight of the Lord is the death of his faithful saints" (Psalm 116:15).

Ponders of the Heart

Do you have special days set aside for family?

How can you make your time with God more exceptional?

Read 1 John 3:1-2.

Remember to smile as you think about your homecoming. Smile because God might just be framing your picture for His Hall of Fame.

Ponders of the Heart

Dear Father,

Do You long for us? Lord, as You prepare our new home, You are preparing us. We do look forward to the day that we will see you face to face and the day we will be free from our flesh. Lord, thank You for the promise of life everlasting in Your presence. Until then, keep our hearts faithful to You. In Jesus' name, amen.

December 28 ~ The Eyes

Your eye is the lamp of your body. When your eyes are healthy, your whole body also is full of light. But when they are unhealthy, your body also is full of darkness. See to it, then, that the light within you is not darkness" (Luke 11:34-35).

I have heard it said that eyes are the window to our souls. A child's eyes are full of the excitement of life. My youngest grandchild has not lost this joy; it shines through her beautiful blue eyes. The eyes of a puppy are brimming with life, and the eyes of a cat are mysterious. I have seen sad, weary, confused, and eyes of wonder. You can learn a lot about a person's heart through the window of their eyes.

In my lifetime, there have been some eyes that intrigue me. I have not seen these in many people, but they have a draw to me. These eyes are gentle, full of love, and always close to tears. They can look deep into you; somehow, they understand you, but you understand the depths of those eyes are beyond what you have experienced.

The eyes I am talking about belong to two women I have been friends with. Both have suffered great loss, but in their loss, they have embraced the Lord. They have endured great pain, and yet, somehow, they have come away with loving tenderness instead of bitterness.

The book *Shattered Dreams* by Larry Crabb says,

"Happy people do not love well, but broken people do."

As I contemplated this statement, these two ladies came to my mind. They have been broken, but their brokenness has served others with tender love. You see it in their eyes and experience it in their words.

No one would want to go through what they have endured. In fact, it scares me, but it also gives me hope. For if or when we go through a great trial or tragedy, we can embrace the Lord; He will carry us through.

God can take our broken hearts and give us eyes to see. Eyes that see and feel the pain people are experiencing and feeling around us.

I don't want pain or tragedy, but God can use all this fallen world throws at us and use it for our good and His glory.

Eyes are the window of the soul. The light of God's hope can shine with His grace, love, and His tenderness.

Ponders of the Heart

What trouble in your life is tossing you about?

What is causing you pain?

Read 2 Timothy 1:7-12, Romans 8:37-39, and Hebrews 4:14-16.

Let His Word give you hope, joy, and peace.

Prayers of the Heart

Dear Father,

Let us draw near to You with all our cares and sorrows. Let us allow You to work through our pain and our trials until our souls are full of Your light. Precious Father, we do not want pain and sorrow. We know You understand and feel our pain. But we also know that through our suffering, our hearts are broken of pride, and the sweetness of Your grace fills our souls. Father, it is true; nothing is too hard for You. In Jesus' name, amen.

December 29 ~ Mr.Bob

"But the fruit of the Spirit is love, joy, peace, forbearance, kindness, goodness, faithfulness, gentleness and self-control. Against such things there is no law. Those who belong to Christ Jesus have crucified the flesh with its passions and desires" (Galatians: 5:22-24).

My devotion today is written to honor all those who have gone before us and have lived in the power of the Holy Spirit.

Bob, my friend, was one of the first church members I worked with at First Baptist Church in Lagrange. We counted money together on Monday mornings for over six years. Bob was such an encouragement to me. He epitomized what a faithful servant of the Lord was like.

Bob encouraged me with words he spoke, but often with no words at all. He was a kind, soft-spoken man with a listening ear, which is a rare gift these days.

Even though you would characterize him as a quiet man, he was a man of vision. Bob was a rare person, gentle yet strong. People depended on him.

On a personal level, I loved the way Bob treated Sue, his wife. I can still see them walking together on Broad Street, sitting together at church surrounded by friends, and Bob teasing Sue about her trips to Mansour's, a dress store in Lagrange. They were friends and companions, and they gave marriage a good name.

In each of my praises of Bob, I could add the little phrase "in Christ." Bob was an encourager, a good listener, and a wonderful husband because he was "in Christ." He had a servant's heart because he had given his heart to Jesus. Bob was a friend and had friends because of his relationship with the Lord. And now Bob is with his Lord because he was in Christ.

Our church secretary wrote a note to Bob and attached it to his membership card. It read, "Bob, I am convinced that the best day of all is when a saint goes home to be with Jesus. " As I write this today, it is a reality for my friend Bob.

The day he arrived in heaven, I could see him walk into the throne room, roll up his sleeves, and say to his Lord, "What can I do?" And the Lord said, "Sit, my good and faithful servant. Sit with me for a while. I have prepared a place for you, a place with me, for you are mine, and I love you. " I think the note our secretary wrote is right. The best day of our lives will be the day we see the Lord face to face.

Ponders of the Heart

Who do you know has been a faithful servant of the Lord?

What was it about them that encouraged you in your walk with Jesus?

Read Psalm 116:1-17.

Ask the Lord to fill you with His Spirit so you might be a good and faithful servant in Christ.

Prayers of the Heart

Dear Father,

You call Your sons and daughters home. We grieve our loss but know they are rejoicing in You. Oh, to see Your face and to be free from the struggles of this life. Father, we all look forward to the day we will be with You and see all those we love again. Until then, Lord, we give ourselves to You. Use us for Your purposes and for Your glory. In Jesus' name, amen.

December 30 ~ Remember When

Alan Jackson's song, "Remember When," captures a person looking back over their life and remembering the journey. I am not sure we do this enough.

Each season of life is worth remembering and learning about who we are, where we came from, and what we have learned. It is especially important to see how God has been there every step of the way.

As I was remembering different things about this past year, I thought about how I react when I get sick. I become very emotional. I will cry at the drop of a hat. This is unusual for me because I am not a crier. But my little granddaughter, Elizabeth, when she gets sick, will not talk to her dad. Isn't that bizarre? We are all so different. I tell you this because these were my thoughts as I remember this past year.

Clayton, my youngest grandson, must have grown six to seven inches. He is going to be a big boy. This is huge in our family because most of us are short. I am only four feet and eleven inches. Another fact about Clayton is that he must have eaten 200 bags of chips this year.

We had our first cousin's sleepover this year and I even jumped in the pool with my clothes on. All these memories bring a smile to my face.

Our oldest grandchild, Collier, was married this past year, and the wedding was close to perfect. I might feel this way because Collier is close to perfect to me. We now have a new member in our family, Izzy. She is a beautiful, amazing person, and we all adore her.

After the wedding, we had a big family brunch with our family members who came to celebrate, and my small group fixed the food.

After Ryan, my son-in-law, cut down 15 to 20 trees, we now have beautiful grass in our backyard.

My husband's knees continue to give him a fit, and both of us are feeling our age at times. Bailey and Reagan will be seniors this year, and they are both beautiful girls. They are growing up so fast, but when they are together, they still giggle like they did when they were little girls.

Our Taylor is an exceptionally good pianist, but she tells me she doesn't like to be the center of attention. She is a tiny thing, and even though she has grown, she is still like a whisper.

All these things are in my memory book, with more to come as days go by. But One day, at the end of time, we will be ushered into our heavenly home and spend all eternity honoring our heavenly Father, who has given us life, love, and belonging. I wonder if there will be a slide show of all of us as we grow. A picture of our new birth, the day we were baptized, and every time we worshipped our Father.

If there is a slide show, forgive all the times I praised the Lord without makeup and in my pajamas.

I can't wait to see some of your hairdos and your choice of clothes during your life, but after all is said and done, and we've had a great time laughing at each other, we will spend the rest of eternity praising the One who calls us family.

Take time today to reflect on His presence and His love this past year and all the past years of your life. As you see His wonderful faithfulness, let's praise Him for the days, years, and eternity that are to come. Let's ask God to open our hearts wide to welcome those who are brought into His family as we all grow together in His grace.

Ponders of the Heart

What are some good things that happened in your life this past year?

What is something you are hoping for in the year ahead?

Read Psalm 19 and Psalm 103.

Let's end this year praising God for all the wonder of His love and provision.

Prayers of the Heart

Dear Father,

As we remember Your faithfulness, we tremble with gratitude. Our Lord and our God, we thank You and praise You for all Your benefits and blessings. Lord, from now until eternity, we praise You! Take our lives, past, future, and today and use them for Your glory. In Jesus' name, amen.

December 31 ~ Praising the Lord

"Praise the Lord, my soul; all my inmost being, praise his holy name. Praise the Lord, my soul, and forget not all his benefits—who forgives all your sins and heals all your diseases, who redeems your life from the pit and crowns you with love and compassion, who satisfies your desires with good things so that your youth is renewed like the eagle's" (Psalm 103:1-5).

Dear Father,

We do take this special time to praise You for all our benefits in Christ. Lord, how do we thank You? How can we bless You with all that is in us? Oh, Father, our love and thankfulness overflow as we look back over the past years and say, Lord, we made it by Your grace!

We also look ahead with praise and thankfulness, knowing You have been with us, and You will be with us forever! Father, truly, You are merciful and gracious to us, and we want to confess our love and thankfulness to You! You are our God and our hope.

"The Lord is compassionate and gracious, slow to anger, abounding in love" (Psalm 103:8).

Lord, You have protected us and provided for us through this past year and will be our protector and guide in the years to come. How wonderful it is to belong to You, our King and our redeemer.

"The Lord has established His throne in heaven, And His kingdom rules overall. Bless the Lord, you His angels, Who excel in strength, who do His word, Heeding the voice of His word. Bless the Lord, all you His hosts, You ministers of His, who do His pleasure. Bless the Lord, all His works, In all places of His dominion. Bless the Lord, O my soul" (Psalm 103: 19-22 NKJV).

In all this, we give You praise. In Jesus' name, amen!

Resourses

Alighieri, Dante. *The Divine Comedy*. 1321.

Anderson, Neil T. *The Bondage Breaker*. Eugene, OR: Harvest House Publishers, 1990.

Austin, Lynn. *Eve's Daughters*. Minneapolis, MN: Bethany House Publishers, 1999.

Barrett, Joanne. "Zeroes to Heroes." Kansas City, MO: Lillenas Publishing Company, 1990.

Brooks, Garth, Pat Alger, and Larry Bastian. "Unanswered Prayers." On *No Fences*. Nashville, TN: Capitol Nashville, 1990.

Carmichael, Ralph. "He Is Everything to Me." 1966.

Chambers, Oswald. *My Utmost for His Highest*. Grand Rapids, MI: Discovery House Publishers, 1992.

Chewning, Lawrence T. "The Anchor Holds." On *One Life*. 1993.

Chisholm, Thomas O., and William M. Runyan. "Great Is Thy Faithfulness." Chicago, IL: Hope Publishing Company, 1923.

Crabb, Larry. *Shattered Dreams*. Colorado Springs, CO: WaterBrook Press, 2001.

Crosby, Fanny, and Phoebe P. Knapp. "Blessed Assurance." 1873.

Dean Jr., Robert, and Herschel Hobbs. *Herschel Hobbs Commentary Sessions 1–4*. Nashville, TN: LifeWay Christian Resources, 2006–2012.

Dumas, Alexandre. *The Count of Monte Cristo*. 1844.

Eldredge, John. *Waking the Dead*. Nashville, TN: Thomas Nelson, 2003.

Foster, Richard J. *Celebration of Discipline: The Path to Spiritual Growth*. 20th Anniversary Edition. San Francisco: HarperSanFrancisco, 1998.

Frangipane, Francis. *Holiness, Truth, and the Presence of God*. Lake Mary, FL: Charisma House, 2011.

Giorgi, Raiza. "Mark Twain Wrote About April Fools' Day." *Santa Ynez Valley Star*, April 7, 2020.

"The Guardian." Created by David Hollander. CBS, 2001–2004.

Heber, Reginald. "Holy, Holy, Holy! Lord God Almighty." 1826.

Jackson, Alan. "Remember When." On *Greatest Hits Volume II*. Nashville, TN: Arista Nashville, 2003.

Jackson, Alan. "Where Were You (When the World Stopped Turning)." On *Drive*. Nashville, TN: Arista Nashville, 2002.

Jagger, Mick, and Keith Richards. "(I Can't Get No) Satisfaction." Performed by The Rolling Stones. London: Decca Records, 1965.

Jenkins, Jerry B., and Tim LaHaye. *Left Behind*. Wheaton, IL: Tyndale House Publishers, 1995.

Kingsbury, Karen. *One Tuesday Morning*. Grand Rapids, MI: Zondervan, 2003.

Kingsbury, Karen. *Where Yesterday Lives*. Sisters, OR: Multnomah Publishers, 1998.

Kipling, Rudyard. "If—." In *Rewards and Fairies*. London: Macmillan, 1910.

Lloyd-Jones, D. Martyn. *Spiritual Depression: Its Causes and Cure*. Grand Rapids, MI: Eerdmans Publishing Company, 1965.

Longfellow, Henry Wadsworth. "There Was a Little Girl." 1845.

Lowry, Robert. "Nothing but the Blood of Jesus." 1876.

Lucado, Max. *Grace for the Moment*. Nashville, TN: Thomas Nelson, 2000.

Lucado, Max. *No Wonder They Call Him the Savior*. Sisters, OR: Multnomah Publishers, 1986.

Manning, Brennan. *The Ragamuffin Gospel*. Sisters, OR: Multnomah Publishers, 1990.

Mansfield, Stephen. *The Faith of George W. Bush*. Lake Mary, FL: Charisma House, 2003.

McVey, Steve. *Grace Walk*. Eugene, OR: Harvest House Publishers, 1995.

Musser, Elizabeth. *The Swan House*. Minneapolis, MN: Bethany House Publishers, 2001.

Newton, John. "Amazing Grace." In *Olney Hymns*, Book 1, London: W. Oliver, 1779.

Piper, John. *The Passion of Jesus Christ*. Wheaton, IL: Crossway Books, 2004.

Powers, Margaret Fishback. "Footprints." 1964.

Rivers, Francine. *The Last Sin Eater*. Wheaton, IL: Tyndale House Publishers, 1998.

Shaara, Michael. *The Killer Angels*. New York: David McKay Company, 1974.

Stead, Louisa M. R., and William J. Kirkpatrick. "'Tis So Sweet to Trust in Jesus." 1882.

Tozer, A. W. *The Knowledge of the Holy*. New York: Harper & Brothers, 1961.

Warren, Rick. *The Purpose Driven Life*. Grand Rapids, MI: Zondervan, 2002.

"Westminster Shorter Catechism." Presented to the English Parliament, 1647.

"The Andy Griffith Show." Created by Sheldon Leonard. CBS, 1960–1968.

"Be Thou My Vision." Translated by Mary E. Byrne. 1905.

"Betty Crocker Cookbook." Minneapolis, MN: Washburn-Crosby Company, 1921.

"Coal Miner's Daughter." Directed by Michael Apted. Universal Pictures, 1980.

"The Count of Monte Cristo." Directed by Kevin Reynolds. Burbank, CA: Touchstone Pictures, 2002.

"Doc Hollywood." Directed by Michael Caton-Jones. Warner Bros., 1991.

"Family Man." Directed by Brett Ratner. Universal Pictures, 2000.

"Gettysburg." Directed by Ronald F. Maxwell. Turner Pictures, 1993.

"Let's Make a Deal." CBS, 2009–present.

"Mary Poppins." Directed by Robert Stevenson. Walt Disney Productions, 1964.

"Runaway Bride." Directed by Garry Marshall. Paramount Pictures, 1999.

"Twister." Directed by Jan de Bont. Universal Pictures, 1996.

"The West Wing." Created by Aaron Sorkin. NBC, 1999–2006.

"You've Got Mail." Directed by Nora Ephron. Warner Bros., 1998.

Hymns and Songs

Crosby, Fanny, and Phoebe P. Knapp. "Blessed Assurance." 1873.

Catesby Paget written in 1890, "Mind in Perfect Peace With God"

Gaither, William J. "He Touched Me." 1963.

Lowry, Robert. "Nothing but the Blood of Jesus." 1876.

Newton, John. "Amazing Grace." 1779.

Stead, Louisa M. R., and William J. Kirkpatrick. "'Tis So Sweet to Trust in Jesus." 1882

Additional Sources

Heber, Reginald. "Holy, Holy, Holy! Lord God Almighty." 1826.

"Westminster Shorter Catechism." 1647.

Unless otherwise indicated, all Scripture quotations are taken from the **Holy Bible, New International Version® (NIV®)**. Copyright © 1973, 1978, 1984, 2011 by **Biblica, Inc.®** Used by permission. All rights reserved worldwide.

Scripture quotations marked (NKJV) are taken from the **New King James Version®**. Copyright © 1982 by **Thomas Nelson**. Used by permission. All rights reserved.

Bibliography

Chambers, Oswald. *My Utmost for His Highest*. Discovery House, 1992.

Foster, Richard. *Celebration of Discipline*. HarperOne, 1978.

Walker, James. 'Human Touch: Jake Porter's Emotional Story.' *The Herald-Dispatch*, November 10, 2002.

Barrett, Joanne. *Zeroes to Heroes*. Pilot-Pont Music, Kansas City, MO, 1990.

Gillham, Bill. *Lifetime Guarantee*. Harvest House Publishers, 1993.

Peterson, Eugene. *A Long Obedience in the Same Direction*. InterVarsity Press, 2000.

Twain, Mark. 'The first of April is the day we remember what we are the other 364 days of the year.'

Newton, John. 'Amazing Grace.' Published 1779.

Kipling, Rudyard. 'If.' 1910.

Carmichael, Ralph. 'He Is Everything to Me.' 1966.

Chambers, Oswald. *My Utmost for His Highest*. Discovery House, 1992.

Sanders, Oswald. *Spiritual Leadership*. Moody Press, 1967.

Crocker, Betty. 'The best way to a man's heart is through his stomach.' Popular saying.

Peterson, Eugene. *The Message*. NavPress, 2002.

Westminster Assembly. *The Westminster Confession of Faith*. 1646.

CBS. *Let's Make a Deal* (television show). First aired in 1963.

BBC. *The Andy Griffith Show* (television series). First aired in 1960.

Newton, John. *Amazing Grace*. 1779.

www.ingramcontent.com/pod-product-compliance
Lightning Source LLC
Chambersburg PA
CBHW050254010526
44107CB00003B/318